## Copyright © 2003 by New Riders Publishing

## Trademarks

All terms mentioned in this book that are known to be trademarks or service marks have been appropriately capitalized. New Riders Publishing cannot attest to the accuracy of this information. Use of a term in this book should not be regarded as affecting the validity of any trademark or service mark.

Dreamweaver MX is a registered trademark of Macromedia.

## Warning and Disclaimer

This book is designed to provide information about Dreamweaver MX. Every effort has been made to make this book as complete and as accurate as possible, but no warranty of fitness is implied.

The information is provided on an as-is basis. The authors and New Riders Publishing shall have neither liability nor responsibility to any person or entity with respect to any loss or damages arising from the information contained in this book or from the use of the discs or programs that may accompany it.

**Publisher**
*David Dwyer*

**Associate Publisher**
*Stephanie Wall*

**Production Manager**
*Gina Kanouse*

**Managing Editor**
*Kristy Knoop*

**Acquisitions Editors**
*Elise Walter*
*Deborah Hittel-Shoaf*

**Senior Development Editor**
*Lisa Thibault*

**Senior Marketing Manager**
*Tammy Detrich*

**Publicity Manager**
*Susan Nixon*

**Project Editor**
*Stacia Mellinger*
*Julia Prosser*

**Copy Editor**
*Keith Cline*

**Indexer**
*Angie Bess*

**Manufacturing Coordinator**
*Jim Conway*

**Book & Cover Designer**
*Alan Clements*

**Composition**
*Amy Parker*

# dreamweaver MX
## web developmen

**New Riders**

201 West 103rd St. • Indianapolis, Indiana, 46290 USA

*To all those who have given their time and knowledge to answer my questions.*
*I owe you a debt of thanks.*

*To anyone who has a passion for web development and desire to learn*
*don't underestimate your own abilities.*

*To dear friends present and to friends who had to leave the party early: to Pat.*

# Overview

# Contents

# About the Author

**Drew McLellan** has been involved in web design and development since 1996. Starting originally as a hand coder, Drew quickly saw the great productivity benefits that could be brought by a visual editor with the arrival of Dreamweaver 1.2. Since then, Drew has been pushing the boundaries of Dreamweaver through its solid HTML-based methodology and powerful extensible architecture.

With literally tens of thousands of his Dreamweaver extensions in use around the globe, Drew has established a firm seating within the center of the online Dreamweaver community and can be found on a daily basis teaching and aiding fellow developers in Macromedia's news forums. Drew's online tutorials from his DreamweaverFever.com web site are recognized as one of the more valuable Dreamweaver resources available, due to their clear and "non-assuming" use of language.

Drew also helps out at the Web Standards Project (`http://www.webstandards.org/`) as a Dreamweaver expert, focusing on the issues surrounding web standards in Macromedia's flagship HTML editor.

As a Team Macromedia volunteer, Drew is a committed Dreamweaver user and enjoys nothing more than being able to share his knowledge and experience of the product with fellow developers. Drew has a wide knowledge of both web design and development, and is currently working for a design, marketing, and IT agency in London, UK.

# About the Technical Reviewers

These reviewers contributed their considerable hands-on expertise to the entire development process for *Dreamweaver MX Web Development*. As the book was being written, these dedicated professionals reviewed all the material for technical content, organization, and flow. Their feedback was critical to ensuring that *Dreamweaver MX Web Development* fits our readers' need for the highest-quality technical information.

**Massimo Foti** began using Dreamweaver on the very day the first beta was available, and he has used Dreamweaver ever since. Massimo has been a prolific extension developer since the pioneering days of Dreamweaver 1. He is the creator of www.massimocorner.com, and is a winner of the Macromedia Best Extension Developer award. His extensions are featured on the Macromedia Exchange for Dreamweaver and have been included in many books and magazines. Massimo works at www.amila.ch developing database-driven web sites using ColdFusion, PHP, and different kinds of databases.

**Nathan Pitman** has more than four years training in three-dimensional design, well equipping him for a career in new media. After diving in at the deep end with his first commercial project, the official Virgin Global Challenger web site, he's not looked back. Nathan is currently working as a "creative developer" for a UK-based agency, and wishing he would made the effort to look less cheesy when this photo was taken.

# Acknowledgments

Because so many people helped me write this book, it's impossible to thank them all. So first, sorry to those I've left out. If you've ever discussed web development with me, you've helped, and your name belongs here: Thank you!

Thanks to my technical editors, Massimo Foti and Nathan Pitman. These two have my utmost respect, and I couldn't have asked for better editors. When I first started to get under the hood with Dreamweaver, I emailed Massimo for some advice. He responded with his usual gentle words of wisdom, and we have been friends ever since. That was around the time of Dreamweaver 2. Ever since then, Massimo has been answering my questions and hasn't tired of me. He knows the technology, he always strives for improvement, and he has the friendly tact to be able to set me straight without destroying my confidence. Thanks Massimo.

Nathan and I met in 1999 as work colleagues. Nathan is a designer by trade, but has never been afraid to get dirty with the code to get the job done. Throughout the development of this book, I have relied on Nathan's real-life experience and attention to detail to catch my mistakes and sloppy explanations. I really can't thank and praise these two guys enough.

Many thanks to Rachel Andrew, without whom this project would have been abandoned mid-session—for bringing me food and beer and nagging me to sit down and write, for hugging me when I finished each chapter, and for making it all possible by acting as a contributing author when it all got tight and objects were threatening to hit fans. Thank you, Rachel.

Appreciation to those at New Riders for bringing this project to fruition. Thanks to Deb Hittel-Shoaf, to Linda Bump, to Lisa Thibault, to Stacia Mellinger, and to Elise Walter. You guys are the best.

Thanks to all those in the Dreamweaver community who have helped me out over the years and to fellow Team Macromedia members. Thanks to Al Sparber, Craig Foster, Jaro von Flocken, Joe Lowery, Joe Milicevic, James Shook, Eddie Traversa, Waldo and George, Paul Boon, Jules Roberts, Tim Payne, Rob Turnbull, Ray West, the marvelous Tom Muck, Gareth Downes-Powell, David Miles, Murray Summers, Dan Short, J.K. Bowman, and every single person on the Dreamweaver and UltraDev forums who has ever managed to find the time to answer a question.

For their active contributions during the writing of this book, thanks to Jim McNiven at Kerb; Matt Brown, JoAnn Peach, Billy Ray and Vernon Viehe at Macromedia; Jeffrey Zeldman and Dori Smith at the Web Standards Project; Karen Durham at Lateral; Tom Coates at Plasticbag.org; Christian Meyer; Eric Meyer; Peter Oakley, Craig Grannell, Mark Pierce, John Bragg, and the team at Designation; and to Andrew Hawken, Susanna Ratcliffe, and everyone at DKNI.

Thanks to the whole Dreamweaver product team at Macromedia; there's far too many of you to name, but you know who you are. It goes without saying that you are the guys who really make it happen. Thanks for such a great product and, most of all, for listening to the users.

On a personal level, I want to thank Mum and Dad for loving me whatever. Thanks to John and Katie for always being there for me, and to my little niece Hannah for making me smile. Thanks to Laurence and Alison for the unflagging support; it means so much to me. Thanks to Mike Smith for all the years of encouragement and education. Thanks to Mark, Ian, Neil, Chris, Eeeean, Pete, and all those around me who have been supportive and understanding.

# Tell Us What You Think

As the reader of this book, you are the most important critic and commentator. We value your opinion and want to know what we're doing right, what we could do better, what areas you'd like to see us publish in, and any other words of wisdom you're willing to pass our way.

As the Associate Publisher for New Riders Publishing, I welcome your comments. You can fax, email, or write me directly to let me know what you did or didn't like about this book—as well as what we can do to make our books stronger.

*Please note that I cannot help you with technical problems related to the topic of this book, and that due to the high volume of mail I receive, I might not be able to reply to every message.*

When you write, please be sure to include this book's title and author as well as your name and phone or fax number. I will carefully review your comments and share them with the author and editors who worked on the book.

Fax:        317-581-4663

Email:      stephanie.wall@newriders.com

Mail:       Stephanie Wall
            Associate Publisher
            New Riders Publishing
            201 West 103rd Street
            Indianapolis, IN 46290 USA

# Introduction

Today I have no Internet connection. No passage to the outside world. It's like someone has taken away my freedom, locked me up in a cell and thrown away the key. I'm still here, the same person as I was, but I have no contact with anyone else— I'm self-contained, isolated, no freedom to move.

It's strange to think that I used to sit at a computer all night for years on end without the Internet. I'm not sure what I did, but I must have enjoyed it; otherwise, I wouldn't have continued. I recall writing a few programs in BASIC—mainly around the one system function that I was familiar with, which took a bitmap and displayed it onscreen. I created a mini, hard-coded PowerPoint-type presentation system. I remember being staggered by my own excellence when I managed to make it interact with the mouse.

I'm not sure where the time went. I have nothing to show from it, other than years of bizarre knowledge and general computing experience that I can't explain, but call on every single day.

When I was about five years old, my father (a teacher by profession) started bringing home computers during school breaks. They were really simple computers— BBC Model B microcomputers with 32K of memory. The original ones had cassette recorders; the later ones had 5 1/4-inch floppy disks. Those disks were actually floppy, and I had to be ever so careful not to touch the exposed part of the disk through the window in the plastic envelope.

I played games such as PacMan, Chucky Egg, and Killer Gorilla. I used to get out of bed at six in the morning and just play with the simple word processor. I would write my name and print it. I would make it bold, italic, underlined. (Those were the options.) I couldn't manage much more than my name at that age.

When I was about eight years old, my father brought home a new computer that had been donated to the school. It was a 32-bit, RISC-based machine. It had a GUI and a mouse, and the keyboard was separate from the rest of the machine. It was a marvel. I sat and played on that thing for days upon days. The only applications we had were those supplied with the operating system—a simple text editor, a bitmap painting tool, a vector-drawing tool. I'm not talking Word, PhotoShop, and Freehand, either. These were primitive little free tools, but they were all I had.

When I started learning HTML, I found it to be a lot like that old word processing program. If I wanted to make some text bold, I had to place a marker at the starting point and another marker at the end of the section to be changed. It was pretty much the same as tag-based markup. Bold, italic, and underline were still more or less the available options. Now, not only could I type my name, but also I could put it on the web and bore other people with it.

Up until the release of Dreamweaver 1.2, I was more or less still running on very similar little tools. I wrote my web pages in Microsoft Notepad—it was easy to use and had a light footprint. Building a simple web site used to take an absolute age. Every single page update, design tweak, and contact form would take vast amounts of time to perform. I didn't mind, however, because I did it for love. I enjoyed every single moment of those boring, monotonous updates because creating web sites was my passion.

Today, creating web sites is still my passion, but is also my business. My time allocations are calculated on an hourly basis, and there's always more work than there are hours. Dreamweaver is a great tool. It enables me to express my passion for creating web sites (I always have full access to and control over the code), but it also enables me to make a living out of web development because it's fast.

No longer do I need to spend those hours on page updates, when a quick modification to a Template will run the change throughout the site. No longer do I need to worry about moving pages around or renaming them; after I have defined my site in Dreamweaver, the tool will managed the links for me.

Without Dreamweaver, most web shops would be still working in tools such as Notepad. Without Dreamweaver, a lot of those developers would be struggling to break even on a job and would be stressing out over every single sitewide modification. Without Dreamweaver, maintaining sites thousands of pages big would just be a nightmare. I like Dreamweaver—it's cool.

So, today I have no Internet connection, and it's made me stop and think about why I use Dreamweaver for web development. It's reminded me of how the web is no longer what it was, and how the sites we are building are not the sites we built five years ago. It's helped confirm to me that yes, Dreamweaver is a useful tool, and with all the new features and updates in the latest version, it looks like it's going to carry on being a useful tool. So we might as well learn some more about it.

## Who Should Read This Book

If, like me, you have a passion for creating web sites, or just an everyday need to create better sites, this book could be for you. You'll need a day-to-day knowledge of Dreamweaver MX. You need to know how to perform basic tasks such as creating pages with text, images, and links. You should know how to implement a basic Template, create a form, and maybe how to apply some CSS for text styling. You'll also need a good working knowledge of HTML, and any JavaScript know-how you have is a bonus.

If this doesn't sound like you, there are some other good New Riders titles that you might want to check out before starting into this book. If the preceding description matches you, welcome aboard, let's rock 'n' roll.

## Who This Book Is Not For

This book is not for complete web development beginners or for those who want to learn Dreamweaver from scratch. As highlighted earlier, this book is for those who already have a working knowledge of everyday Dreamweaver functions. If you're looking at starting out fresh with Dreamweaver, you can find better books than this with which to start.

## Overview

I've divided the book up into three different sections. The first section, "Advanced Design and Architecture in Dreamweaver MX," covers not only the topics of expert web design and site architecture, but also the issues surrounding designing for different browsers and platforms, working with HTML in Code view, and finally moving on to the broad topic of Dynamic HTML.

The second part of the book, "Workflow and Design Control," covers all the tools that exist to improve workflow, such as Templates, the Library, and the tools at a developer's disposal for controlling the design of a site. This includes information on tables, frames, browser windows, as well as a healthy chunk of Cascading Style Sheets.

The final part of the book, "Developing Projects Further," shows you how to customize your installation of Dreamweaver with your own preferences and extensions. This section also covers the big subject of web application development within Dreamweaver MX. Two chapters, "Building Web Applications" and "Tooling Up for Application Building" serve as a primer for anyone wanting to start to use Dreamweaver for developing applications in ASP, ColdFusion, PHP, or any of the server languages the software supports.

## Conventions

This book follows a few typographical conventions:

- A new term is set in *italics* the first time it is introduced.
- Program text, functions, variables, and other "computer language" are set in a fixed-pitch font. For example:

```
<a href="sample.html">An HTML sample</a>
```

# Part I

## Advanced Design and Architecture in Dreamweaver MX

# Chapter 1

# Expert Web Design

Objectives:

- Learn how to plan a new site and keep the project within its boundaries
- Discover how to prepare a site for growth and avoid creating sites that are difficult to expand on
- Identify methods of keeping your site interesting and encourage visitors to return

It may seem a little strange to open this book—a guide for Dreamweaver developers—with a chapter on web design. Let me explain my reasons. To the developer, the design of a site is not solely about where each element sits on a page and how the overall composition appears to the eye, although that is part of it. For the developer, web site design is as much about the way the site is constructed technically as it is about the overall look and feel. That is to say how each page is built within the development software (Dreamweaver), how the pages are related to each other, and how the user interacts with those pages are all primary concerns when designing a site. These elements pull the concept of expert web design right back to a Dreamweaver level.

From the very conception of a site, right through to delivery, or "going live," the experienced Dreamweaver developer has to consider the technical constraints and enabling technologies available. Luckily for us, Dreamweaver has been designed as a complete web-integrated development environment and enables us to follow the process from start to finish, from within the same authoring package.

# Planning a Site

Planning is everything. The Boy Scouts' motto is "Be Prepared," and look how far it got them. A well-planned site is going to be a pleasure to return to each time the client requests further changes, rather than the source of much confusion and wasted hours spent in unraveling the mess. What's more, you'll never get caught without a compass.

One of the most important tasks in planning a site is to understand the scope. It is vital to define the limits of a project early on and stay within them. With the Web being as naturally dynamic as it is, it has become all too easy for the scope to creep during the development of a site. Scope creep is a developer's worst enemy and should be avoided at all costs. It's almost as bad as being out after dark without a flashlight.

## Scope Creep

The insidious growth or change in a project, which happens while you are working on the project, is known as *scope creep*. It usually involves the modification or addition of extra functions and features as the project is in session. Scope creep occurs largely when the limits of a project—in our case a web site—are not laid down and clearly defined before a project commences. As the client (whether external, internal, or even yourself) begins to see the project evolve, he can turn to other ideas not originally considered when the project was first conceived. This typically leads to expensive rewrites and modifications, and nearly always significantly impacts the project's timeline or even the overall quality of the solution. The only way to manage scope creep is to define the limits of the project before work begins and to have an established procedure if vital changes must be made during the project's development cycle. (A good project manager helps too—but we all know how rare those are.)

## Define the Limits

Before starting work on a web site, it is important to sit down with the client and draw up a formal document defining the limits of the project. I use the word *formal* loosely. You don't usually need to have the document witnessed by independent parties or set your legal team on the case, but the client should sign it, and both parties should have a copy from which to work.

The document should include a blow-by-blow description of the main features of a site, the pages or templates to be produced, and the time frame for the project. It will also help to define the items that the client will supply to proceed, and similarly, any materials or guidelines the developer needs to supply to the client.

## Tip

**Be sure to name the person or group within the client's organization who will supply the textual content (or copy) for the site. This is classically a sticking point in the development of any site, so be sure to get names and set deadlines. It helps to formalize where the responsibility for each item lies.**

After this document has been signed off, you have a clear set of directions to work from, and there can be no debate when the final product is delivered.

Most of these points will actually be covered in the quote or estimate of costs for the project—because this is the initial document that lays out the scope, with an emphasis on what the client is getting for their money. It can sometimes be useful to tactfully refer back to the quote when the client is requesting more functionality, because the quote always lists what functionality comes at what price.

## Changes to the Scope

From time to time during a project, you will encounter changes that are not part of the original project definition, but are changes that must be made for the project to succeed.

I recall working on a web site once where the company, in their infinite wisdom, decided to spontaneously rebrand one of their key products. To continue to develop a site with an out-of-date brand would have been a waste of everybody's time, so it was necessary to define a change of scope.

You really need to cover your back when it comes to changes of scope. Having already drawn up a document defining the scope of the project, any change of scope must be equally well documented and acknowledged for you and your team to sleep easily at night.

It's not a bad idea to have a standard document dealing with changes in scope, and to get the client to agree when initiating the project that it will be used in case of changes. If needed, the document should include an exact definition of the new work and should indicate clearly which part of the original definition this new definition supersedes. The impact the change may have on the budget and on the project timeline should be detailed as well. This is normally known as a *change request form* and is the stuff that project managers' dreams are made of. Both you and the client should then sign the document, and a copy should be attached to your original project definitions.

Surely I can't be recommending all this paperwork for every new project and every single change of scope? In an ideal world, yes, and certainly for large-scale projects. For smaller projects with limited timescales and budgets, it is often enough to cover this process with a few emails. The important aspect is that the scope is laid down and agreed by both parties in such a way that it can be called up and referenced at a later date.

Defining a project from the outset lets everyone know where he stands. It keeps you, as the developer, on your toes, and prevents clients from taking advantage of your good will. The customer is always right, but that doesn't mean the customer is always logical. Many will change their minds with the wind given half a chance. Defining the scope provides protection for everybody, and it is as helpful to clients as it is to you.

After you have defined the scope of a project, the change-of-scope document lends a similar formality to any future changes. The main advantage of this, however, is that it discourages the client from making any changes at all unless they are absolutely necessary. Of course, you don't want to be seen as inflexible, but a bit of strategically placed red tape never hurt anybody—and often saves a few budgets from blowing. (A good Boy Scout carries tape at all times.)

### Allow for Change

Don't misunderstand—just because the scope of a project has been strictly defined does not mean that your work should not allow for growth. Scope creep applies only to the development time of one project. This isn't to say that the web site will not continue to grow to a different set of limits in the next project the client commissions from you. You want to protect against growth of features and functionality while the current level of functionality or features are being developed, but not after.

Throughout your development of a project, always consider the next step. This is how a developer prepares a site for growth and saves the client a lot of extra expense further down the line. (Remember that sites ready for growth are a huge advantage to the client, and so should be used as a selling point.)

# Preparing Your Site for Growth

Without an understanding of where the site might be in six months, it is unlikely that the delivered design will actually meet the requirements.

On many occasions, I've been asked to take on a project involving an existing web site. The client wants to push the site on to its next logical phase, involving the addition of new features, new sections, and even subsites. All too often, a brief look at the site's structure reveals the lack of careful planning put into the site at the initial stages. Of course, the client is never very impressed when he is told that the project will require 10 hours of work before it's even ready to start moving forward!

Very often, what might seem to be a simple web site project is just a seed for the client involved. A good rule of thumb when designing a site is to expect the best—expect the site to grow to twice its initial size in the following six months. If all goes to plan, it could grow to 10 times its size in the following couple of years. If you take an outlook that says the site could possibly get very big very soon, you are going to be able to cope when it does. If it doesn't, you've not lost anything. With this as a standpoint, you can rest easier knowing that if it's you the client comes back to for the updates in six months, you will be able to move the site forward without having to backtrack.

# Modular Design

It's not just the structure of the site that needs to grow, either; it's also any given feature or piece of functionality. How well will your Press Releases section hold up after the client decides he wants to integrate a live stream of industry-related news, for example?

It is usually the best practice to divide your web site into separate modules, which can be built and implemented individually. The aim of your modular approach is twofold:

- First, each module should be able to be changed or removed without affecting the rest of the site.

- Second, changes made to modules should seamlessly cascade through the site where appropriate.

Any logically minded person should be ranting and raving, pointing out that these two statements contradict each other immensely. In a logical world, this would be true, but this is the Web. To see why these points don't contradict themselves, let's look at them in more depth and with some examples.

- Each module should allow for modification or removal without affecting the rest of the site. An effectively designed module allows for its own deletion or modification without the remainder of the site falling over. For example, a poorly designed sequential site—moving from section A to B and then on to C—would fall to its knees were the developer to delete section B from the middle. Links would fail, and the remainder of the site would become inaccessible. A well-designed modular site allows for the removal of section B from the Navigation module, and the remainder of the site continues to function as intended.

- Modifications to a module should cascade through the site where appropriate. The beauty of modular design is that the modules are reusable. Any given module needs to be written only once, and then applied whenever that element is required again. This way, with only one copy of the module in existence, when it is modified, the changes are replicated throughout the site. A poorly designed, non-modular site might have several variations on its navigation system throughout its pages. Any changes to navigation would have to be considered for each variation and implemented many times.

A well-designed Navigation module would appear consistently on each page. Any changes to this module would cascade through the site—automatically or manually—with ease, due to this consistency.

## Being Consistent

Remember, if your site starts to do well and takes off as you hope it will, it is reasonably likely that over time you will not be the only developer working on it. What's more, you also might find that between working on the site and other projects, large gaps in time may occur when you are not directly involved in the development of the site; you might forget all its functional ins and outs.

For these reasons, it is vitally important to employ a consistent coding style throughout the site. This is obviously going to be easier if Dreamweaver is writing the HTML and JavaScript for you; but even if you are coding by hand, Dreamweaver provides some useful tools that will help you keep your code style uniform.

An excellent example is the Snippets panel. *Snippets* are small blocks of code stored for reuse time and time again. There's nothing particularly clever about them—they are not like Library items that can be updated from a central point—but they do help you to perform things in the same way over and over, and without having to look up what you last did. (If you're not already acquainted with the Snippets panel, you can open it from the Window menu. It's also part of the default Code panel group.)

Other techniques involve making use of the Clean Up HTML and Apply Source Formatting commands. Anything that will help to contribute to a consistent style will help other developers to pick up your code, and will do the same for you if you've not looked at it for two months.

# Making Your Site Sustainable

It may be one thing to build a site to be capable of scaling to huge proportions, but a site will never require that scaling unless it can prove itself popular. It must be possible to sustain a site at its existing scale to move forward and grow.

The ability to make a site popular and to allow it to grow stems from good, fresh content and ease of maintenance. As web developers, we don't need to worry about the content so much; it's likely that it will be coming from a different source. Our concern is ease of maintenance.

## Maintenance Time

When looking at ease of maintenance, we're really looking at time. Any web developer who has ever left responsibility for maintenance of a site to a client will tell you that unless the process is simple, the updates won't happen. In other words, if the system for updating the site is not totally straightforward and second nature to clients, they'll just give up and never update their site.

Realistically, most clients will take out a maintenance contract with the developer to look after the site for them, begging the question "why is it necessary to make the maintenance process simple?" The answer is simple: The less time it takes the developer to perform updates, the cheaper it is for clients to keep their site up-to-date (or the more money the developer can make—whichever way you look at it).

It all comes down to the old maxim that time is money—be that money for the developer or money for the client. A site designed to be quick to maintain not only allows for the site to sustain visit levels, but also frees development money, enabling it to grow.

By using Dreamweaver as a complete authoring and updating environment, the developer can get the most out of the powerful site-related features to make managing updates as simple as possible.

## Managing Updates

Dreamweaver MX has a number of excellent features the developer can harness to make updates both manageable and quick. We'll look at these in greater depth in later chapters, but for now here's a brief overview of the tools available:

- Templates
- Library items
- Server-Side Includes

- Find and Replace
- Respect for Application Code
- Site Reporting

## Templates

*Templates* prove to be an extremely powerful tool when it comes to updating content that appears on multiple pages. Of course, Templates are of limited use if the site hasn't been designed with them from the outset; but when all pages are based around a Template, they can save the developer hours of update time.

With your site correctly defined in Dreamweaver, you can make updates to a Template and Dreamweaver will run through your site replicating the changes on all your documents. For changes to items such as navigation or footers containing contact or legal information, again, Templates can save the developer hours of work.

In addition, because Template-based documents lock down all areas except those marked as editable, updates can easily be made by a different developer from the site's original developer or team. The editable regions enable less experienced or junior developers and nontechnical staff, such as content producers or copywriters, to make changes without the worry of altering code they didn't mean to. (Let's face it, some of our colleagues need all the help they can get.)

## Library Items

Another useful tool at our disposal is the Library. In a similar way to Templates, Library items can aid us when it comes to updating modules that are replicated across multiple pages. Like Templates, *Library items* are a Dreamweaver-specific technology that operates within Dreamweaver while you are working on the site.

Careful deployment of Library items can save the developer time by allowing a change to be made once, and then having Dreamweaver do the hard work by finding all other instances of the Library item and replacing them.

Retrofitting Library items is much simpler than with Templates, and can save time when working with a site not originally designed to use them.

## Server-Side Includes

*Server-side includes* (SSI) come in a number of different shapes and sizes. Found first in web servers such as Apache and later in technologies such as ASP, ColdFusion, JSP, and PHP, SSIs are a very practical way to keep your site well organized.

Just as images files are placed in an HTML document by the web browser as it displays the page, SSIs are additional files embedded inside a web page by the server. Because this process of including one file within another (and effectively making one page out of two component parts) is performed by the web server, specific browser support is required. This is the concept behind the term as *server-side include*, regardless of the particular flavor of server technology used.

Support of SSI in Dreamweaver is an invaluable tool for working with sites that already use SSI or for developers who prefer to use SSIs rather than Library items. Server-side includes enable the developer to compile a page from two or more source pages. They can be very useful for chunks of code common to many pages. The code chunk is kept in a separate file, which is then included in line with the rest of the page when the server delivers the page to the browser.

Dreamweaver will visually interpret any SSI in your document, enabling the developer to see how the final page will look when served. In addition to this, using the Preview in Browser function, the page can be viewed locally as it will appear when live. Dreamweaver parses the SSI for you, so you don't need a local server during the development process. This enables the developer to see exactly how a published page will look before it is uploaded to a live environment.

## *Note*

When using SSIs in a document, don't forget to check which file extension your server is expecting. Many UNIX servers require a file that uses SSI to have an .shtml extension, whereas Windows NT-based servers may require an extension such as .asp or .inc. Always check with your hosting company first if you're not sure.

## Find and Replace

A powerful tool that is often overlooked, the Dreamweaver *Find and Replace* feature enables the developer to use basic searches or even regular expressions to update specific items in the code. (*Regular expressions* are search terms written in a language developed specifically for searching. They initially look quite complex, but the searching syntax is easy to learn and is extremely powerful. We look at regular expressions further in Chapter 5, "Cleaning and Editing HTML Within Dreamweaver.")

The developer can search through one document at a time, a selection of documents, one folder at a time, or even the entire site. This can prove extremely helpful should you want to update specific items that could appear anywhere in the site.

A good example is telephone numbers. In the UK, the telephone company has made changes to dialing codes on numerous occasions in the past few years. Find and Replace has helped me immensely to locate telephone numbers in the pages of a site and replace them with the updated versions. To do this by hand could have taken literally days on a large site. Dreamweaver can handle the task in just a few seconds—faster than a speeding bullet, as someone once said.

## *Caution*

Find and Replace is an extremely powerful tool, but can be destructive if used incorrectly. Because it is not possible to undo any changes made across multiple files, always make a backup of your site before performing any major replaces.

### Respect for Application Code

Although able to create application code such as ASP or ColdFusion for you, Dreamweaver can also recognize server-side script and tags from other sources as being special and accordingly does not attempt to make any changes to them. This is a major advantage when working with an application server and a database, for example, because Dreamweaver has the intelligence to respect your code and not attempt to change it. Naturally, Dreamweaver identifies its own server-side application code and enables you to edit it freely.

Dreamweaver will enable the developer to edit the HTML surrounding application code on the page without destroying it. This opens the door to using technologies such as ASP to keep a site's content current.

### Site Reporting

Dreamweaver MX includes a handy site-reporting tool, first seen in version 4. This tool, which can be found as Reports under the Site menu, can help the developer spot any mistakes (such as documents without a title and images with missing `alt` attributes) quickly and easily.

The reporting tool should be viewed as an essential step before "going live" with any significant changes to the site.

## Making Your Content Appear Fresh—Even When It's Not

Keeping a site's content fresh is always a struggle. Visitors to a site like to see new content, they like to see things changing, and they like to see the site responding to their needs and requests. Without fresh content, a site's hit rate will soon drop off, and the site will become, at best, an online archive of information that was once useful. What's more, regularly changing content will encourage search engine bots to visit your site more frequently, thus giving your site a greater chance of a high search engine ranking.

Of course, you can make content appear fresh in many ways, some of which involve hard work, and others that involve a little bit of wizardry from the developer. (Okay, most of it still comes down to hard work, but we were never afraid of that, were we?)

## Keep It Fresh!

The obvious way to make content appear fresh is to actually keep it fresh! It may sound obvious, and I'm sure you don't need me to tell you this, but it really is the only way to sustain a site over a period of time. You can get fresh content for a site in a number of different ways. The main method is obviously to get the appropriate person to sit down and create it, but there are some cleverer ways too.

### Interaction

The Web is a dynamic and interactive medium. Many of the best and most interesting sites currently on the web are those that enable users to interact by contributing what is effectively their own content.

Amazon.com is a good example of an interactive site. Although primarily a commerce site, Amazon enables users to add a review against items such as books. This not only helps users to feel that they are contributing to the site (and thus gives them the confidence to spend more), but also provides Amazon with an almost endless supply of free book reviews. They don't need to employ professional reviewers to read every single title on sale and give their considered opinion when they can get free and constant reviews from the public.

Enabling the user to contribute content has many advantages. Primarily, it means that the site gets some free, fresh content, but it also encourages a sense of community around the site. This community feeling will not only keep users returning, but will also keep them submitting content. As more and more people submit content, the site changes more frequently, causing infrequent users to visit more often, and so it snowballs.

If the design and content of your site can allow for interaction in this way, try to harness it as much as possible. There is little point in paying for content to be produced when there could be people out there ready to contribute it for free—and usually content contributed by the visitors holds more weight with other visitors than something professionally produced.

### Content Feeds

Another popular way to find fresh content is to buy in to a content feed service. Such services, widely available and used on the Web, enable the developer to integrate outside information, such as news reports and stock market details, into their sites dynamically. (A good example of this is `http://www.moreover.com/`.)

Often using technologies such as Java applets or XML, you work with new and up-to-date data, which is fed into the page each time it is loaded. This sort of system is a good way to get fresh content onto the site, but it might not provide content quite as targeted to the site's needs.

## Keep It Moving!

It is widely known that many web site users will often only visit certain parts or favorite parts of the site each time they visit. By moving your content around, it can appear fresh to the user even if it's not brand new to the site.

Of course, I'm not suggesting that content be moved from section to section, but it is often worth considering the use of feature highlights, which put the spotlight on different content items as time goes on.

An example of this might be a corporate site with information on a number of the company's products. The site's home page might well include a Featured Product area that would draw the user's attention to a different product each week or each month. This way, visitors gain exposure to things that they wouldn't normally see.

## Randomize Content

Not as widely used as the methods already mentioned, randomized content is yet another way to keep the information on a site looking fresh.

It's a little bit like the old cup and ball magic trick. With randomized content, users never know what's going to turn up the next time they look under the cup. The developer knows exactly where all the balls are, but only reveals a little at any one time to keep users guessing. There's not usually organ-grinding monkeys involved, however. (Although, if you were able to introduce them….)

Each time users visit the site, they are likely to see something new. The main disadvantage to this is that users can never view all the content at one sitting; and if they return to the site expecting to see content in one place, it can be alarming to find that it's moved. (Change is not always welcome.)

## Case Study: Land Rover North America

The Land Rover North America web site handles the randomization of content very subtly. As you would naturally expect from a car manufacturer, their range of products is small and focused. A visitor may have come to the site after seeing a TV advertisement for the new Freelander but be more interested in the Discovery or Range Rover models. The Land Rover site (see Figure 1.1) handles this well by randomizing the main graphical element on its home page (`http://www.landrover.com/index_home.jsp`).

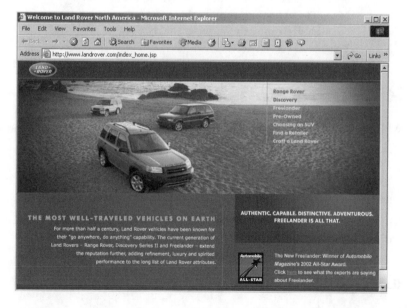

**Figure 1.1**

The Land Rover North America web site uses a randomizing script to highlight its products.

The picture is of the three cars (one from each model line) on a beach— one in the foreground, the other two in soft focus in the background. By randomizing three versions of the photograph, each with a different model in the foreground, users are exposed to the full range of cars. The Land Rover site uses some server-side JSP coding to choose a picture at random—this is a good choice because the rest of the site runs using JSP. Of course, the technique isn't limited to those using JSP; it can be implemented in ASP, ASP.NET, ColdFusion, PHP, or, maybe most commonly, in client-side JavaScript. In fact, a number of Dreamweaver extensions are available on the Macromedia Exchange for Dreamweaver to help you do this.

## Tip

**The Macromedia Exchange for Dreamweaver is a tremendous repository for all sorts of add-ons and extensions for Dreamweaver MX. If you've not visited it yet, go and take a look. You can access it at** `http://www.macromedia.com/exchange/`.

**On the Exchange, there is a command called Advanced Random Images by Paul Davis for doing exactly the job in hand. With careful use of this excellent (and free!) extension, you can re-create the same effect as Land Rover right from within Dreamweaver MX. (The extension won't enable you to drive through deep water or traverse muddy slopes, however.)**

# Handling Reusable Resources

With the web still operating as a low-band medium, it is essential for developers to handle their resources in a way that results in the smallest download possible to achieve the desired result.

One way to do this is to centralize objects such as code blocks so that they are downloaded only once. The developer can then take advantage of the browser's cache and thereafter refer to a locally stored version of the code.

## External Cascading Style Sheets

*Cascading Style Sheets* (CSS) are a vital part of the modern web developer's toolkit. Now that they can be comfortably used as a replacement for `<font>` tags for styling text, and increasingly as a replacement for code-heavy tables for creating page layouts, developers can centralize all their style definitions and have any changes to those styles cascade down through the site.

Although a basic principle of CSS is that all the style information is held in a single place, many developers have taken to using in-line styles embedded directly into each document. Although this offers the same level of formatting control, it does not offer the same flexibility in enabling site-wide changes to styles or in reducing download time for the user.

For this reason, it is often best practice to use an external CSS to hold the site's style information. This way, once the file is downloaded for the first page, it is held in the browser's cache and does not need to be downloaded a second time. What's more, containing your CSS within an external style sheet makes it much easier to provide different style sheets for different types of browsers. That may be as simple as creating a more basic style sheet for older browsers, right through to designing complex voice style sheets for audio devices.

## External JavaScript Files

In a similar way to the method used for CSS, JavaScript files should be looked at as another great way to reduce download times.

Nonprogrammers often overlook them, but pages using the same JavaScript functions work best sharing a central copy of the function and each linking to it. This is achieved by holding an external .js file on the server containing the shared functions. This can be particularly important for pages that use Dynamic HTML, because they can sometimes produce tens of kilobytes of code, which otherwise would need to be downloaded over and over by users.

By holding all the code in an external JavaScript file, once the file is downloaded for the first page, it is held in the browser's cache and does not need to be downloaded a second time.

Unfortunately, native Dreamweaver support for external JavaScript files is poor. This is one particular shortcoming of Dreamweaver as a modern coding environment, but it certainly doesn't spell disaster. The approach that needs to be taken is one of using Dreamweaver to create your JavaScript, and then cutting and pasting it out to an external file once the page is finished. Hopefully, this is one area where Dreamweaver will be able to improve in future versions.

## What to Take Away from This Chapter

- Planning is everything when it comes to site design. Be prepared—like the Boy Scouts (but without the penknife). Be aware that it's all to easy for the scope of a project to change; and without keeping proper tags on scope creep, it can throw your project into jeopardy.

- Define the limits of your development project carefully. This is important for both you and the client. You need to know what work is expected of you, and the client needs to know what they are getting for their hard-earned cash. Also define where responsibilities lie. If it's Bob's job to provide the content, make sure that Bob knows what to provide and when it's needed. If Janet has to get a copyright statement drawn up, make sure she knows too. (In fact, do that one first; you know how slow solicitors can be.)

- Write it up. After you've defined the scope of the project, what the deadlines are, and where the responsibilities lie, get it written up as a document for all parties to agree on. This helps to make everything crystal clear and gives a good starting point for resolving any problems that might crop up when memories start to fade. (Usually the client's memory fades the quickest.)

- Be flexible. If requirements have to change, they have to change. Use a change request form to record the new requirements, and state which parts of the original requirements document it supersedes. Again, get all parties affected to agree on it and make sure everyone knows his responsibilities and personal deadlines.

- Prepare your site for growth. Remember that if a site is a success, it usually makes sense to expand it and develop it further. Build for this right from the start and you won't find that you're having to tell the client that large sections of the site have to be thrown away and rewritten to move forward. (Only a couple things are more embarrassing than having to admit to your client that you've coded them into a corner—but we don't talk about those.)

- Be consistent in your coding style. You might not be the one developing the site in a few months; and even you are, you will have forgotten everything you once knew about the project. Clear, consistent coding will help you or your colleagues to quickly understand the structure of the page and hit the ground running.

- To keep a site sustainable, consider the maintenance process during the design and build. A site that is too expensive to maintain is going to fade away and die. Consider the methods that will be employed to keep the site up-to-date, and build to make maintenance as straightforward as possible.

- Take advantage of the tools at your disposal to make a site quick and easy to update and modify. Features such as Templates, Library Items, SSI, Find and Replace, Application Code, and site reporting can all help to make big site changes more digestible. (Frothed milk is the only thing that stands between an espresso and a latté, but look at the difference that makes.)

- Visitors usually won't return to a site if the content isn't updated. Help make the best of the content available, even if it's not practical to update it that often. Methods such as randomizing elements, pulling content out onto the home page, enabling users to contribute, and deploying content feeds from outside providers all help keep users coming back, even if you don't have a bottomless pit of fresh content to deploy. (And hey, if you do have a bottomless pit of fresh content, make sure you use it!)

- There's no point in making users hang around downloading things that they don't need. Use all the methods available to create reusable resources that take advantage of the browser's cache. Put your CSS into external CSS files, and your client side scripting into external JavaScript files; then the user only has to download that junk only once.

# Chapter 2

# Site Architecture

Objectives:

- Create a web site blueprint.
- Manage web site links with the Site Manager.
- Generate an automatic report on your web site with the site-reporting tool.

It is very easy, no matter how experienced the developer, to get into a mess if careful consideration is not given to the structure of a site. Even with the smallest of sites, if the structure is not defined from the outset, the files quickly become difficult to handle as the site starts to expand.

This chapter discusses the architecture of a site and good rules of practice when it comes to structuring a site. You will learn the best ways to organize files, how to handle assets and reusable resources, and how to make sure that the architecture can support the client's ambitions for a site.

In particular, this chapter covers the Dreamweaver MX Assets panel, the Site Manager, and the site-reporting tool.

## Structuring Your Site Logically

It has become more and more common for web design agencies to employ developers whose sole role is to plan and structure the flow of information through their web sites. So important is this structure that a web architect will spend a considerable amount of the overall project time drawing up a blueprint of how a site should fit together.

In building a large web site, the most logical way to structure your files is to mimic the structure of the information within the site. If a site has a Contact section with various pages of contact details, for example, it would be logical to group these files together in a folder called Contact under the site root. (This is assuming the Contact page is a primary link from the site's home page.)

For you and your coworkers to be able to understand and work with the information in a more complex site, this mimicking of information structure with file structure is a key method for easing workflow.

This planning process is becoming an absolutely vital part of site design, as the developer community begins to see the effect of poorly structured sites that grow beyond their limits. A little like building a house without strong foundations, your site might not stand firm when it comes to adding the first floor.

## Drawing Up a Blueprint

It is nearly always recommended that a blueprint of a site's architecture be drawn up before development commences. Even with a relatively simple site, it can prove very helpful to have a documented map of the site from which to work. The only exception to this would be for a very small, low-budget site whose aim is to turn out the goods quickly and inexpensively. For this type of project, a site architecture stage would likely be unnecessary and too costly.

Drawing up a blueprint should be considered as vital a part of site design as developing the look and feel or flowing in the copy. Especially in a multi-developer environment, the blueprint is an essential reference for any queries. Simply put, with a blueprint, every developer in the team will be working toward the same goal.

As far as how to draw up your blueprint, that's up to you. For me it's usually a collection of files in a particular folder structure, some being resource files and others being text files with descriptive instructions. Others I know like to draw up their blueprints on big sheets of paper or use tools such as Microsoft Visio. It's really up to you to find the way you like to work best.

The important thing is that the site is defined in a way that's easy to reference and to work with.

## What a Blueprint Should Contain

Many similarities exist between a traditional architect's blueprint for building a house and a web architect's blueprint for building a site. A traditional architect's blueprint contains the information detailing all the different rooms of the house, what size they are, and where they meet the neighboring rooms. In the same way, the web architect's blueprint should detail the different sections of the site, what size they are, what they contain, and where they meet (or link to) the other sections of the site.

The site blueprint should contain details of how each page should look, style guidelines and color swatches, and lists of any information or links that should be included on each page.

Descriptions of any Templates, Library items, CSS, or JavaScript files used should be included as well, alongside the details of the server on which the site resides.

Another great idea is to include any custom Dreamweaver extensions that may have been written for the site or used within the site. Site definition files should be included too, so that other developers could quickly add the site to their installation of Dreamweaver and hit the ground running.

### *Tip*

Dreamweaver MX enables you to export your site definition to a file that can be stored for later retrieval or shared with your development team. This is a new feature with Dreamweaver MX; and unlike previous versions of Dreamweaver, everything you need to import and export sites is built right in to the program.

It is possible to build any house from the details in its blueprint. In the same way, a web site's blueprint should tell everyone involved enough to build the site. The main difference is that a traditional architect's blueprint will roll up nicely into a cardboard tube, whereas yours is more likely to be a collection of electronic files living on a network server or even a CD. (You are well advised not to try and roll a CD up to fit into a poster tube.)

## What Should Not Be Included in a Blueprint

For every item included in the blueprint, there is an item that should *not* be included. Details such as copy or article images should not be included, because these form part of the content of the site, instead of telling how the site is constructed. You should not include news items or directions for visiting; it's enough to list the News page and the Contact section. However, details such as a common contact email address are useful to store because these might apply to many elements throughout the site.

The rule of thumb is if it describes the site, it should be included. If an item merely populates a site, that item should not be included.

## Making Changes to a Blueprint

The content of the blueprint should be such that it will not change frequently. Of course, a web site is a dynamic and living entity and will, by its very nature, change and grow. Modifications to the blueprint should need to happen only if major modifications to the site are required. These modifications should first be defined in the blueprint, and only after this has happened should they enter the production phase. It is important that the blueprint not be modified retrospectively to document changes occurring on the site.

# Case Study: Creating a Blueprint for Macromedia.com

To demonstrate the idea of building a blueprint for a web site, I have constructed a mini-blueprint for the home page of Macromedia.com. What I cannot include here is the electronic side of the blueprint—the graphics, templates, script files, and so on. The blueprint is obviously not exhaustive, but it's a good starting point (see Figure 2.1).

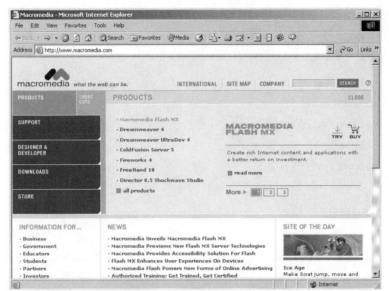

**Figure 2.1**

The home page of Macromedia.com.

## Styling

This section describes styling elements, such as the logo, navigation, and the different levels of text and headings used.

### *Logo*

Use Macromedia logo #1 with horizontal tagline. See `http://www.`
`macromedia.com/macromedia/style_guide/logos/macromedia/` for usage guidelines. Logo sits in upper-left corner of page, within the gray navigation bar. Whereas the logo on subpages acts as a home link, the logo on the home page should not.

### *Navigation*

Primary navigation is held within the top gray navigation bar. On the home page, this is limited to the following items:

* International
* Site map
* Company
* Search box, with a button labeled Search (not Go)
* Help button

Remaining primary navigation is held within the **home_main.swf** Flash movie. This movie is shared between product features and primary navigation. Navigation items included are as follows:

- Products
- Support
- Designer and Developer
- Downloads
- Store

### Headings

Headings are GIF files with transparent backgrounds. Text should be formatted uppercase (that is, ALL CAPS) with the following font settings:

- Face: Arial
- Size: 13pt
- Letter spacing: 7
- Letter width: 88%
- Color: #4583C0
- Strong Antialias
- Auto Kern

### Body Text

Body text is styled with CSS. Links are bold and blue (#333399). All nonlink text is black.

- Font size: 64%
- Line height: 127%
- Font family: Verdana, Arial, Sans-Serif

### Site Resource Files

This section describes how different resources such as Flash movies, style sheets, and JavaScript are used.

- Where Flash movies are used, the plug-in must first be detected. If the browser is not Flash-capable, an alternate static image is used.

- CSS is used for the styling of text only. Tables are used for positioning. A server-side detection script serves a different style sheet for each browser and platform to overcome browser-rendering differences.
- JavaScript is embedded inline within the page. JavaScript is used for the detection of the Flash plug-in and for opening pop-up windows.

## The Assets Panel

A valuable site-management feature in Dreamweaver MX is the *Assets panel*. It offers developers a single, simple tool to manage all of a site's resource files in one centralized location. It enables you to locate your Templates, Library items, images, colors, URLs, multimedia elements, and even scripts in one multitabbed panel.

Consolidating the functionality offered by the Templates panel and Library panel in early versions of Dreamweaver, and adding the new functionality to images and all those other useful resources, the Assets panel is the key to your Dreamweaver toolbox, as shown in Figure 2.2.

**Figure 2.2**

The Assets panel lists your site resources in a centralized location.

Just like the bookmark feature in a browser, the Assets panel enables you to keep an organized list of the items you need to access the most. In many ways similar to the Library in Macromedia Flash, the Assets panel gives you a certain amount of freedom in managing your own resources. To this end, the Assets panel is divided into two distinct sections:

- **Site assets.** All the assets of a particular type within the site are kept here.
- **Favorite assets.** Selected useful assets, such as logos and reusable script files, are located here. This type of asset follows a metaphor similar to that of favorites or bookmarks in a web browser.

Let's look at these two types of assets in greater detail.

## Site Assets

Every asset within the site is listed as a Site asset. Be they images, Templates, script files, or even colors, if they are resources within the defined site, they are Site assets. Inserting an asset into your document is easy and has been designed to be pinpoint accurate. Open the Assets panel from Window > Assets or by pressing F11. Unless your site has already been cached, you are first prompted to click the Refresh button to display your site's assets. Therefore, on first opening the Assets panel you need to click the Refresh button to load your resources into memory.

The Refresh operation just searches the site for assets and creates a cache for future reference. This cache file will help to speed up the referencing of assets as the development of your site progresses.

### Note

If you add an asset, such as a new image file, to the site after creating the cache, you need to click the Refresh icon again to make sure your new resource is listed in the Assets panel.

Very quickly, you can see the assets within your site listed under the appropriate sections of the Assets panel. Notice that as you click any given asset, detail such as a preview for an image or a view of the code for a script file displays in the upper region of the Assets panel. Selecting an image opens an image preview to aid your selection of the correct file. Note also that the Insert button becomes active and ready for use.

From this point, inserting an asset into your document couldn't be easier. You can do so in two ways:

- Select the asset and drag and drop it into the Document window.
- Select the asset and click the Insert or Apply button at the bottom of the Assets panel.

Either method produces the same result, although the latter offers a subtle advantage. Drag-and-drop techniques can be useful in the speed and visual approach they offer, but can sometimes lack accuracy. The added feature of the Insert button enables you to insert the asset at the absolute position of the cursor. This can prove extremely useful in situations where accuracy is paramount, such as inserting into narrow table columns.

### Caution

**Unlike the Insert Image object found in the Objects panel, the Assets panel will not warn you if inserting an asset causes an absolute local path link to be created. Dreamweaver creates these file:/// type links before your document is saved into your site so that Dreamweaver can locate such resources as images and CSS files. However, you don't want to leave these local paths in your pages, because they will fail once the page is on the Web. Get around this problem by always saving a document before carrying out any work on it. This way, Dreamweaver knows the context of your page within the defined site and can build more intelligent links.**

Inserting an asset really is as easy as that, which is why the Assets panel is so central to visual development with Dreamweaver MX. After an asset has been inserted into the document, you can treat it the same way you treat anything else in your document. There is no difference between a resource inserted manually and one inserted via the Assets panel.

## Favorite Assets

Site assets allow flexibility in working with resources; in a large site, however, it is not always easy to find your resources hidden among the masses. This is where Favorites come in.

In a very similar way that you can store links to web sites in your web browser as favorites or bookmarks for future reference, Favorite assets (or *Favorites* as referred to throughout this book) can be used to store assets that you need to access quickly and often. Two examples of this are a site's primary logo image and a transparent GIF (or shim) image used throughout the site.

In a large site, scrolling through the long lists of Site assets to find the one you're after can negate the advantages of the Assets panel altogether. Stored in a separate list, Favorites save you from searching down the list. Add an important asset to your Favorites and never have to search for it again!

### Accessing Favorites

Favorites are divided into the same sections as Site assets. To access a Favorites list, first select the appropriate tab of the Assets panel (Images, for example), and just click the radio button to switch the list to Favorites. Select the Favorites option to display a list of Favorites for the given category.

Notice that before any Favorites have been added, the list is blank, as you would expect.

### Adding Favorites

Having identified an asset you want to add to your Favorites list, adding it is a simple matter and will not affect any pages that already have that asset included within them.

1. Click the asset's name in the Assets panel to select it.

2. Click the Add to Favorites button at the bottom of the Assets panel. The Favorites icon resembles a real-world bookmark, and Add to Favorites has a plus sign.

A notice box will pop up to inform you that the selected assets have been added to the Favorites list.

Notice that the asset is not removed from the Site assets list, although it has been added to the Favorites. This is to avoid confusion later, and of course, a Site asset does not cease to be a Site asset even when it is a Favorite.

The asset you selected is now a Favorite and can be accessed any time from the Favorites list in the appropriate category of the Assets panel.

Inserting a Favorite into your document follows exactly the same process as inserting a Site asset, making Favorites very easy to implement and use.

## Note

The Templates and Library categories do not have the option to create a Favorite. Due to their nature, you would not find yourself needing large numbers of Templates or Library items under normal circumstances.

### Editing Favorites

Another useful feature of the Assets panel is the ability to quickly edit assets without having to locate them in your file system.

Selecting a Favorite and right-clicking offers you the choice to edit the asset in your default editor. This method works for Site assets too, but it is particularly useful for Favorites. Being so close at hand, editing your most frequently used files is now so easy that this little feature can really speed up your workflow.

### Removing Favorites

Should you find that you have a Favorite that you no longer use, or that you have added a Favorite by mistake, you will want to remove it from your Favorites list. Fortunately, Dreamweaver makes it easy to remove a Favorite.

Select the Favorite that you no longer want in your list, and click the Remove from Favorites button in the lower corner of the Assets panel.

## Organizing Favorites

Much like any web browser, Dreamweaver enables you to organize your Favorites into folders. This can be useful for identifying different types of assets and grouping them. For example, the folders in your Image Favorites might contain groups of logos, shims for spacing, article images, and navigation images. This organization would assist you in locating the asset as quickly as possible.

To add a new folder, just click the Folder button while in Favorites view. The Folder button can be found at the bottom of the Assets panel, and is styled to look like a box folder (or to my eye, a schoolchild's satchel). Adding a folder is an easy process and can help you organize your Favorites effectively.

After you've added your folder and given it a name, it's a simple case of dragging and dropping Favorites into a folder, just as you would with your standard Macintosh or Windows file-management tools. You also can move Favorites between folders by just dragging and dropping.

### *Tip*

You can harness the power of folders even more by creating subfolders, or folders within folders. Your Logos folder could contain two subfolders (Color, and Black and White, for example). Just create a new folder and drag it into any folder you like to make it a subfolder.

## Giving Favorites Nicknames

Try as we might to give our files descriptive names, the fact is that these names will rarely be easily recognizable English. The Assets panel enables you to give your Favorites nicknames.

Nicknames are a way to refer to an asset, without using its actual name. That is to say, giving an asset a nickname will not change the name of the file in your site; it just changes the way the file displays in your Favorites.

To nickname a Favorite, follow these steps:

1. Select the Favorite's name in the Assets panel.

2. Right-click (Command-click) to bring up the context menu.

3. Select Edit Nickname from the menu.

4. Type your chosen nickname for the Favorite.

As you can see, Favorites are a great way to organize your assets to reduce the time you have to spend searching among the files of a large site. Your Favorites profile is stored alongside the site files, so organizing assets into Favorites can benefit your whole development team, making Favorites a great productivity tool.

## Tip

> Being able to share Favorites is an excellent feature, best taken advantage of by the Colors section of the Assets panel. By adding new Favorite colors, your team can quickly pick colors from a defined color palette for the site—a great time-saver! Be careful to organize your Favorites carefully, however; the last thing you want to do is slow down your coworkers with badly named files!

## Assets in Detail

Dreamweaver defines nine different types of assets. It could be argued that a vastly greater number of media types are in use for web development, but Dreamweaver just focuses on the nine most common types.

- Images
- Colors
- Uniform resource locators
- Flash
- Shockwave
- Movies
- Scripts
- Templates
- Library items

## Images

Images are, without doubt, the most common media type for embellishing hypertext documents in use on the Web. Images of any recognized format (such as GIF, JPEG, or PNG) are listed in the Assets panel catalog. All images in the current site are listed, regardless of whether they are used in any documents.

Selecting a particular image opens a preview of that image in the preview area of the Assets panel. Images are initially listed in alphabetic order by filename, but they can be sorted on size, type or full path by clicking the corresponding column heading.

## Colors

Any color used within an HTML document in your site appears in the Assets catalog. Colors can then be reused to help maintain consistency throughout your site.

Remember that adding colors to your Favorites and giving them nicknames can be a great time-saver. Defining your color palette using Favorites before you start a project can speed up development and lessen the chance of accidentally picking the wrong color when formatting your page.

The preview area helpfully displays both hexadecimal and RGB values for colors when a Color asset is selected.

Colors can be easily applied to text, tables, or any other HTML element with a color property. Just select the item in the document and click the Apply button at the bottom of the Assets panel.

## Uniform Resource Locators

Any *uniform resource locators* (URLs) used within your site are listed in the URL section of the Assets panel. These URLs can be of any type, as long as they are external to the site. Internal links are not listed.

URLs of the following types are cataloged:

- **FTP (File Transfer Protocol).** An example is a link to a file to be downloaded from your site's FTP server.
- **Gopher.** A simple Internet protocol similar to HTTP. Gopher isn't really in use anymore but is supported here for old sites.
- **HTTP (Hypertext Transfer Protocol).** The regular protocol used for retrieving web pages. Most of your external links will use HTTP.
- **HTTPS (Hypertext Transfer Protocol Secure).** The secured version of HTTP.
- **JavaScript.** The scripting language supported by all modern browsers.
- **Email.** The standard for Internet messaging. Mailto links are listed as external URLs.

### Flash, Shockwave, and Movies

The Flash, Shockwave, and Movies categories catalog all the movies in your site. Be they Flash movies (created in Macromedia Flash), Shockwave movies (created in Macromedia Director), or standard movie files (such as MPEG or QuickTime), they are listed for easy insertion into your documents. The preview area enables you to see your movies in action, provided you have the correct plug-ins installed.

Movies can be treated very much like images in the way that they are inserted into your documents and otherwise dealt with from the Assets panel.

### Scripts

Scripts are JavaScript files. Any JavaScript files within your site are cataloged and can be inserted into your page. Clicking the Insert button will add a link to the file at the current cursor position in your document.

The preview area shows the contents of your JavaScript files. This can help identify whether a required function exists in a particular file.

### Templates and Library Items

The Templates and Library categories hold a catalog of all the Templates and Library items within your site. In Dreamweaver MX, the Assets panel becomes the hub for creating and managing these items. Unlike earlier versions of Dreamweaver and UltraDev, Templates and Library no longer have their own panels.

# Maintaining Your Site with the Site Manager

For the developer, the Site Manager is the key to keeping your site architecture under control. It is the central point where you can create, copy, and delete files, as well as launch documents for editing and run all sorts of sitewide tools.

The Site Manager has many powerful features to help you define your site architecture and keep it intact. To do so, however, you first need to define your site so that Dreamweaver knows what it's dealing with. In the Dreamweaver MX workspace, the Site Manager has been integrated into the panel structure, rather than its traditional separate window.

## Defining Your Site

For Dreamweaver to be able to keep track of your files, their links, and all of your assets, you must define the selection of files that form your site. This involves pointing Dreamweaver to the folder under which all your files reside.

Dreamweaver MX includes a new site setup wizard to help beginners configure their site. You can find this under the Basic tab when defining your site. If you want full control, however, you need to set up your site manually.

To begin, open the Site Manager by selecting Window > Site. The Site Manager panel opens and displays the files from the current site (see Figure 2.3).

**Figure 2.3**

The Site Manager shows a list of files contained within the current site.

Select Site > New Site from the panel itself to open a new site. A Site Definition dialog box opens.

## Local Information

The Local Info section in the Site Definition dialog box contains the name that will be given to the site and the site's location on your local computer (see Figure 2.4).

First, give your site a name. This will usually be the name of the project, and it might even be helpful to include a job number or other ID, if you have one. The site name can include numbers, letters, and spaces, but other special characters should be avoided.

Type or browse for the location of your local root folder. This is the folder that contains your site. Of course, when starting a new site, there is nothing to browse to, so make sure you have an empty folder ready to store your site files.

**Figure 2.4**

The Local Info
section.

The Refresh Local File List Automatically option can prove very useful. On opening the Site Manager, Dreamweaver can automatically refresh its file list, taking account of any changes. Without this selected, it is necessary to refresh the list manually.

### Tip

> If your site is very large, you may decide to turn off the Refresh Local File List Automatically option, because refreshing the file list unnecessarily could slow down your progress.

You have an option at this point to declare your site's default images directory, which can prove useful if you want Dreamweaver to help you manage your images and to place any new ones in a convenient place. It also means that browsing for images becomes a more streamlined process.

The next field is the HTTP address of the finished site. This enables the link-checking feature to identify links that are local and those that are external to the site. By knowing the address the site will reside at, Dreamweaver can determine which are links within the site and which link to external sites. This is important when running link checks, because you wouldn't want Dreamweaver to try and validate or update external links.

Finally, you are asked to choose whether to create a cache for the site. I strongly recommend that you do, because the Assets panel requires a cache to function, and the cache also speeds up a good deal of the other operations performed by the Site Manager across your site.

So, that's the Local Info setup. To continue, select the Remote Info option from the pane on the left.

## Remote Information

The Remote Info section enables you to specify the type of connection in place with the remote server (the web server). For a developer working alone on a small site, this could be an FTP connection to an external hosting company's server; for larger teams of developers, however, it is likely to be a network web server or a source control database system. The Remote Info section enables you to specify the remote server (see Figure 2.5).

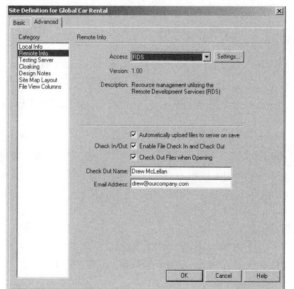

**Figure 2.5**

The Remote Info section.

If you are working purely locally and do not want to specify a remote server, the obvious choice is None from the list. This section contains no further options, and you can move on. Most people, however, will want to make a connection to a remote server. The remaining choices are as follows:

- **FTP.** Select this for connecting to a live server with a hosting company or elsewhere. If the server is the actual box connected to the Internet and serving the web site, you should always connect with FTP, even if it's on your own network.
- **Local/Network.** Select this to connect somewhere on your LAN. This is the circumstance in which most developers will find themselves, where their development web server is attached to their local area network.
- **RDS.** Select this to connect to a Remote Development Service resource-management source. This is a new feature in Dreamweaver MX.
- **SourceSafe Database.** Select this for connecting to a Microsoft Visual SourceSafe database.
- **WebDAV.** Select this for connecting to a WebDAV system for versioning and distributed authoring.

Defining an FTP connection should be a familiar process for anyone who has used any sort of FTP client before. The FTP options are familiar ground to web developers, but let's look at them briefly next.

The FTP Host field is the address of your FTP server. Enter the address of the server to which you would like to connect, and specify a host directory into which to connect, if any. You do not need to include the ftp:// at the beginning of the server address, because Dreamweaver assumes this anyway.

The Login and Password fields should contain the authentication details given to you by the administrators of the FTP server. Remember that many FTP servers are case-sensitive, so type the details exactly as they appear. You have the option to have Dreamweaver save your password for future use.

The Passive FTP and Firewall options are useful if you are trying to FTP to a server from behind a firewall. If your firewall requires you to use passive FTP, select this option too. The option to use Check In/Check Out is available as well for an FTP server.

Options for connecting to a local network server are much more straigh
forward. Choosing to use a server on your local network is simple. Specify
name or browse for the folder containing your site; this is all the informa
Dreamweaver needs. All that is left is the option to choose whether to a
matically refresh the remote file list. Unless your site is very big (and therefore would take a long time to scan), it's probably a good idea to select this.

The final three options available as the remote server are source or version
control systems, and the *Remote Development Service* (RDS).

## Application Server

When working with data-driven sites, it is necessary to define the application server. The *application server* is part of the system that takes your server-
side code and runs it to create a web page. This might be ASP or ASP.NET,
ColdFusion, PHP, or JSP. On the whole, the setup of your application server
settings are very similar to defining the remote site. One point of note is
the URL prefix box. This is the URL of the server that you would need
to type into a browser to be able to see your site. If you're working just on
your own machine, this might be as simple as `http://localhost/`.

### *Note*

> **Chapters 14, "Building Web Applications," and 15,
> "Tooling Up for Application Building," cover applica-
> tion servers in greater detail and explain how they fit
> into the bigger picture of creating dynamic, data-
> driven web sites.**

## Cloaking

*Cloaking* is a new feature in Dreamweaver MX. With cloaking enabled,
Dreamweaver doesn't show you files of certain types within your Site view.
A common use of this feature is to cloak files that need to be within your
site, but you don't need to select on a regular basis—such as downloads.

Alternatively, if you choose to store your source files within your site, you
can opt to have Dreamweaver hide all files with particular extensions, such
as PNG or FLA files.

Another particularly useful use of cloaking is for very large sites where the site structure might be too large and unwieldy for Dreamweaver to work with while still performing acceptably. By cloaking folders of resources that you just don't need to access that often, you can vastly increase Dreamweaver performance and make the site easier to work with.

## Design Notes

The next area to be defined in your site definition is *Design Notes*, which are data files, stored in your site, that carry extra information about files and your options. Attaching a Design Note to a file enables you to leave messages for other team members who may subsequently need to edit that file. They can consult the Design Notes and view any special requirements or comments that might exist.

If you are working in a team environment, it is desirable to choose Maintain Design Notes. Doing so will enable you to work more effectively with your team.

The remaining option is Upload Design Notes for Sharing. If the remote server is a development server rather than a live server, you will want to upload the Design Notes for your coworkers to access.

### Note

Dreamweaver also uses Design Notes to store preference options and all sorts of other bits of data. When you choose not to use Design Notes, you will still see a number of _notes folders within your site. This is because Dreamweaver is using them to support its internal functionality. There is no need to upload _notes folders to your live site.

## Site Map Layout

The Site Map Layout section of the Site Definition dialog box offers a number of different options for customizing the layout of the site map. The most important option is the Home Page field, which should be completed with the name of the file that is to be your home page. This can be typed in or browsed for. This file will be used as the root for the site map.

The other options are less important, but they enable you to tweak the map in different ways. The Icon Labels option enables you to choose between File Name and Page Title as the label for each item in the site map. You can choose whether to display Dependent files or any Hidden files that might be in your site.

### File View Columns

The File view lists all of the files in both the local and remote sites. This easy-to-understand interface offers a plethora of options as to the columns and sharing features available in the File view.

- Adding a column is just a case of clicking the plus (+) button at the top of the window. Similarly, a column may be removed by selecting it and clicking the minus (–) button. The up and down arrows in the upper-right corner allow for the reordering of columns, affecting how they display in the File view. Select a column and use the up or down arrows to change its relative position.
- If your development team uses Design Notes for collaborative working, a particularly useful feature enables you to create new columns based on the contents of a file's Notes. This enables the developer to see the status of a file at a glance.

## Managing Links

The Site Manager has a number of features that help when managing links. Working the traditional way, if you need to change the location of a file in your site, you have to check every document for a link to that file and update them all by hand. Thankfully, Dreamweaver can take all that hard work away.

### Moving Files

In the Site Files view of the Site Manager (Window > Site), you can move files just as you can in any other file-management tool—by dragging and dropping, as follows.

1. Click and hold on a file.

2. Drag it to a different folder within your site and release.

3. When Dreamweaver asks whether it should update links in the listed files, click Update to update the links.

Dreamweaver identifies all the files with references to the moved object. That's all there is to moving a file. There is no need to search the site for references; all the links have been updated for you.

## Caution

**Dreamweaver can work only with links it understands. This includes regular HTML links in anchor tags, but does not include links formulated by JavaScript or any server-side code, such as ColdFusion or ASP. If you have any file references within scripts in your site, you will either need to update these by hand or run a Find and Replace query to update them.**

### Updating Specific Links

Should you discover that a link in your site no longer points to the correct place, or that you want to change the location to which it points, the Change Link Sitewide feature can be a boon.

1. Open the Site window (Window > Site).

2. Choose the Change Link Sitewide option from the Site menu (Site > Change Link Sitewide).

3. In the dialog box that opens, enter the URL of the link to look for (or browse for the file if it is within the site).

4. Enter the URL that the link should be altered to point to (or browse for the file).

5. Click OK, and the link is updated.

### Checking Your Links

Before publishing or "making live" a site, it is always desirable to check your site for incorrect links. The Check Links Sitewide feature enables you to check for broken links, external links, and orphaned files within your site. Dreamweaver can check your links for you before uploading your site.

## Caution

As stated previously, Dreamweaver can only update links it understands. If you have any file references within scripts in your site, you will either need to update these by hand or run a Find and Replace query to update them.

1. Open the Site Manager (Window > Site).

2. Select the Check Links Sitewide option from the Site menu (Site > Check Links Sitewide).

The Results panel opens, searches through your site, and displays a list of problem links.

This feature, along with Change Link Sitewide and the ability to move files and have their links updated, make Dreamweaver an invaluable site-management tool. Fortunately, these helpful tools are only a hint of what the Site Manager can do.

## File Transfer

Dreamweaver works on the assumption that, at some point, you will want to transfer the files you've been working on to a web server. With this in mind, a useful little file transfer tool has been provided.

### Get and Put

Get and Put are the two main functions of any file transfer tool—Get, for retrieving (downloading) files, and Put, for sending (uploading) them. The Dreamweaver Get and Put tools are on the Site panel toolbar. Dreamweaver denotes the Get and Put buttons with down and up arrows.

Performing the Get and Put operations could not be easier:

1. Select a file in the local or remote site.

2. Click the Get or Put button as appropriate.

3. Decide whether to include dependent files, and the files are transferred.

Dependent files are any files downloaded by the browser when the page is requested, including image files, style sheets, and any JavaScript files linked to by the page.

### Caution

**Again, watch out for links within client-side and server-side scripts that Dreamweaver will not pick up and update.**

### Synchronizing Local and Remote Sites

After working on your site for a while, it is easy to lose track of which files have been changed. This is especially true if working in a collaborative environment, where you may not have been the only person working on a set of files. When it comes to uploading those files, you need to know which files have changed in order to upload the correct ones.

This is where the Synchronize feature comes into its own. Dreamweaver can compare the contents of your local and remote sites and perform one of three functions:

- Put newer files to remote
- Get newer files from remote
- Put and Get newer files

What's more, Dreamweaver gives you the opportunity to preview what it's going to do before the changes are actually carried out:

1. Open the Site Manager (Window > Site).
2. Choose Synchronize from the Site menu (Site > Synchronize).
3. Select whether to synchronize the Entire Site or Select Files Only.
4. Choose a Direction.
5. Click Preview.

The Delete Remote Files Not on Local Drive option is a useful feature, but should be used with caution. Without a level of forethought, it is entirely possible to accidentally delete files contrary to your intentions.

Clicking the Preview button brings up a dialog box like the one shown in Figure 2.6, showing all the files that are about to be transferred. Dreamweaver enables you to preview changes before they are made.

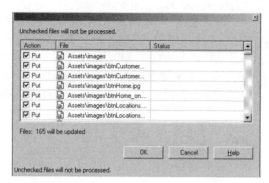

**Figure 2.6**

Previewing the files you are about to transfer.

By deselecting any of the checkboxes, you control which files are transferred. This is an extremely useful feature, and speaking from experience, it's well worth checking that you do actually want to transfer each of those files.

### Tip

> **Performing operations on your entire site can be dangerous. It is always best to make a backup of your site beforehand, to avoid problems if you make a mistake.**

# Site Reporting

Sometimes it really helps to know exactly what is going on with your site, especially when you think it's ready to be made live. Site reports might think otherwise, however, as they can reveal some interesting truths about your work.

Site reports are easily run, as follows:

1. Open the Site Manager (Window > Site).

2. Select Reports from the Site menu (Site > Reports).

3. Choose a type of report.

4. Enter any required settings.

5. Click the Run button.

The following sections discuss the different types of reports and their settings.

## Workflow Reports

The collection of Workflow reports center on the day-to-day issues that may crop up when developing a site. For example, you may need to know who has which files checked out, or which files have certain Design Notes. This is where Workflow reports really help out.

### Checked Out By

The Checked Out By report just lists all the files that are checked out and by whom. Optionally, you can choose to select only those reports checked out by a specific user.

### Design Notes

The Design Notes report enables you to search for files with an associated Design Note, or a Design Note with designated properties. Design Notes can be searched on name and value criteria.

The settings give options for entering name and value pairs of criteria to search on. For example, searching for "status contains draft" will return all the files denoted as being at the draft stage.

## HTML Reports

HTML reports concern the contents of the documents themselves. Anyone who has ever published a page with the title "Untitled Document" will appreciate the usefulness of the Untitled Documents report!

### Combinable Nested Font Tags

The Combinable Nested Font Tags report hunts through the HTML in your documents to find instances where `<font>` tags could be combined. For example, a pair of font tags like this

```
<font face="Arial, Helvetica, sans-serif"><font size="2">some
➥text</font></font>
```

could be combined to form this more efficient code:

```
<font face="Arial, Helvetica, sans-serif" size="2">some
➥text</font>
```

This report has no extra settings, but returns a useful list of all combinable `<font>` tags in the site.

## Missing Alt Text

The Missing Alt Text report searches through the site and catalogs all image tags that do not have an Alt attribute set. The Alt attribute is important for users browsing your site without images or with a speech browser, and should be included according to good practice.

This report has no extra settings, but returns a useful list of all images without Alt attributes set.

## Redundant Nested Tags

The Redundant Nested Tags report is similar to the Combinable Nested Font Tags report. Code such as

```
<b>this is <b>my</b> text</b>
```

would be detected for its redundant bold tags in the middle. This report has no extra settings, but helps to achieve efficiency in your code by listing all instances of redundant tags.

## Removable Empty Tags

The Removable Empty Tags report locates tags in your site that serve to mark up nothing. An example would be `<i> </i>`, where the italics tag marks up nothing but empty space.

The report has no extra settings, but will list all instances of removable empty tags in the site.

Untitled Documents

The Untitled Documents report searches through the site to locate any documents that have the default page title of "Untitled Document."

This report has no extra features, but highlights all documents without meaningful titles.

## Exporting the Results

Being XML-enabled as it is, Dreamweaver enables you to save the results of your report as an XML file. This file can then be imported into a program of your choice (such as a database, for example) or even into a Dreamweaver Template document. This technique is discussed later in the book when Templates are discussed further.

# What to Take Away from This Chapter

- To structure your site logically, and to make sure that structure is adhered to, it is beneficial to draw up a blueprint of your site.
- The Assets panel is a great tool for managing the resources within your site.
- Favorite assets can help speed up development time by enabling you to quickly locate files that might otherwise be difficult to find.
- The Site Manager can help you maintain and update links in a few easy steps. Dreamweaver will keep track of your links for you.
- The built-in file transfer tool can help when you want to upload files to live servers.
- Keeping the local and remote versions of your site up-to-date is made easier with the Synchronize tool.
- Site reports can help you keep track of your site structure and goings-on within it, by generating clear and exportable reports.

# Chapter 3

# Advanced Forms

Objectives:

- Gain an understanding of the form elements available in the web developer's toolkit.
- Build a complex, multipage form with input validation.
- Use cookies to store and retrieve data from the user's computer.

In a day and age when interaction in web sites is becoming a key practice, forms are the crux of many sites. Be it using a simple search facility, gathering data from users, or sending an email, forms are central to the whole information-gathering process.

Forms are the principal method for capturing user input, because they are the one element offered by standard HTML that enables us to do things, not just display them.

In this chapter, we will be looking closely at forms and methods of processing their output. We will be looking at the design considerations involved and seeing how the arising issues are best dealt with. To this end, we will examine the process involved in creating forms across multiple pages, how to store and retrieve form data with cookies, and how to perform routine tasks such as sending an email.

# The Form Elements

HTML has a whole selection of components at the developer's disposal when it comes to constructing forms. Each of these components serves a different purpose and, in turn, must be treated differently itself.

Dreamweaver has all the standard form elements available in the Forms tab of the Insert panel. Figure 3.1 shows how the form elements are presented for easy insertion into your pages.

**Figure 3.1**

Dreamweaver lists the common form elements.

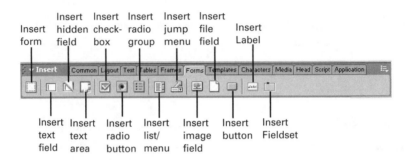

The guide that follows does not attempt to be a comprehensive catalog of the form elements and each of their attributes, but rather offers a brief summary of the items we shall be dealing with throughout this chapter.

## Form Tag

The form tag, `<form>`, is the basis of all web forms. It is the parent tag that houses all the other form elements. The key attributes are as follows:

- **Name.** A name for your form. This is useful if you need to address the form or objects within it from another object (such as a JavaScript function) within the page. Although a name is not essential, when building advanced forms it is often desirable.

- **Method.** The method used to submit the form; can be Get or Post. The differences between Get and Post are highlighted later in this chapter.

- **Action.** The URL of the object to which the form should be submitted. This could be another page, a script, or even a JavaScript function within the same page. This attribute is required if the form is to perform any task at all.

- **Enctype.** The encryption type used to format the results from the form. This is not encryption in the sense of data security, but in terms of formatting the data to be appropriate for its contents. A form that is used to send files needs an enctype of multipart/form-data so that the files are sent correctly, for example.

- **Target.** Just like the target attribute in a regular HTML link, the form tag's target attribute specifies the window or frame that the instructions or data should be sent to.

A point to be wary of with form tags is the small amount of whitespace they create. This can sometimes cause problems if you're not expecting the slight margin on either side of the tags, but you can often work around this. Consider wrapping your form tags around a larger section of the page, or even around the entire page. The form elements must be within your form tag, but there's nothing to say you can't include other things as well. You also can use CSS to reduce the default margins produced around your form tag.

## *Caution*

It can sometimes be tempting not to include form tags around basic forms, such as jump menus, that submit via JavaScript. Although the menu will display and function correctly in Internet Explorer, it will not work with other browsers, such as Netscape Navigator, without the form tags. It's important to note that all current HTML standards require that form tags be explicitly included when you place form fields on a page—to leave them out will invalidate your page. The visual space that form tags take up can be removed with CSS for most modern browsers.

### Input Tag

The input tag is a little like the roll of duct tape you keep in your under-stairs cupboard—you can fix anything with it, and it will get you out of any trouble fairly easily. The input tag has 10 main types, as discussed in the following sections.

### Button

The button input has no specific defined use. It does, however, offer a standard interface object to which you can attach an event. Such events as `onClick` offer the power of JavaScript to be unleashed when the button is clicked.

Standard buttons such as Submit and Reset actually have their own input types and are not covered by the scope of the button input. All three button types, however, are collected together as a single configurable object in the Dreamweaver Insert panel. A standard gray button is easily inserted with the `Insert Button` object.

### Checkbox

The checkbox input is for inserting a standard checkbox into your form. A checkbox has two states: checked and unchecked. Dreamweaver enables you to assign a value for the checkbox to return when checked. The checkbox returns nothing if left unchecked. When used in groups, the checkbox will return a comma-separated string. A group of checkboxes will allow any number and combination of selections within the choices available in that group. You can create a checkbox group by giving a number of checkboxes the same name. All boxes in the group must exist within the same form, naturally.

### Hidden

The hidden input type is a particularly useful type for advanced form trickery. Allowing a value to be submitted with the form, but without displaying a physical element on the page, the hidden input can prove to be a useful tool for passing extra information to your server scripts or other form-processing object. Dreamweaver uses a special icon to denote the placement of hidden fields within a form. The hidden input icon looks like a small yellow shield (see Figure 3.1)—one of the many uses Dreamweaver makes of these yellow shield style icons.

### File

The file input type displays a field that enables the user to browse for a file to upload to a server. The server has to support this upload, of course; in many situations, however, the file input type can be extremely useful.

The user is presented with a text box for entering a URL directly, but also with a Browse button for locating the file on the local system. The user can browse for a file to upload.

### Image

The image input type is similar to the button type in that it offers developers an input device to which they can attach actions.

Image is useful as a Submit button, if your site design requires something a bit more interesting than the standard gray box.

### Password

The password input type is exactly like the text input type except that it echoes its contents to the screen as asterisks.

It shares a Dreamweaver object with the text type and the textarea type, because all three are very similar in function, allowing free-form entry and returning only their contents.

### Radio

Radio buttons are nearly always used in groups. They allow a single selection per group; and when any selection is made, previous selections are lost.

Giving a number of radio buttons the same name is all that is needed to form a group, and the value of the selected button is returned when the form is submitted. A group of radio buttons allows only one selection.

### Reset

The Reset button just reloads the form into its initial state. This button is used mostly with more traditional forms for gathering large amounts of data, and not so much with smaller forms used by many web applications today. The Reset button has potential for usability problems, because it can be easy to click the wrong button and clear your data rather than submit the form.

The Reset button shares the Dreamweaver `Button` object with the Submit button and the regular button input types.

### Submit

The Submit button is the final step in any form. It's the trigger that says that the form is complete and should be sent for processing. It shares the Dreamweaver `Button` object with the Reset and regular button input types. The Submit button is pivotal to your form.

### Text

The final input type is the good old text field. The text field is the mainstay of your forms and allows free text to be entered on a single line. Text fields just return the data input by the user.

The text input type shares the Dreamweaver `Insert Text` object with the password and textarea input types. Text fields have many different uses, from the usual to the not so usual.

## Select Tag

The select tag is useful in situations where you need to confine the user's options to just one or a number of predefined selections, but do not want to devote valuable screen space to radio buttons or checkboxes. A Select box will always take up the same amount of vertical space on a page, no matter how many options there are to choose from, because the number of options to display at any one time is configurable. However, the longest item within your Select box will dictate the width of the box on the page.

### Single Selections

A single selection Select box is the most common. It is often used for devices such as jump menus and in larger forms for selecting from a long list, such as a list of countries.

The options in the list are entered via the List Values button in the Property inspector. The list is populated in name/value pairs, or more specifically, label/value pairs. The label is displayed to the user in the list, and the value is submitted with the form. Dreamweaver refers to this type of select box as a *menu*.

### Multiple Selections

The multiple-selection Select box predictably allows the user to make one or more selections, using the Shift and Ctrl keys with the mouse. The selection is submitted as a comma-separated values list. Dreamweaver refers to this type of select box as a *list*.

## Textarea Tag

A *text area* is just a multiline text box. It is especially useful when you want to allow the user to enter a lot of information, such as in a Comments box.

The textarea tag shares the `Insert Text Field` object. Just insert a regular text field, and then select the Multi Line option. A multiline text area enables the user to insert lines of text freely.

# Submission Methods

There are two ways to send a form's contents: Get and Post. Get appends the data to the end of the URL that the form is being submitted to. There are disadvantages to this method. Browsers and proxy servers can store Get data along with the URL in their cache, which might not be ideal for some purposes. In addition, data appended to the URL is free for users to read and change if they want to do so.

The second method, Post, sends the data embedded in the HTTP stream and is invisible to the user, making it more difficult to alter. There is also no limit on the amount of data that can be sent by Post, whereas Get can run into some problems with the browsers limiting very large amounts of data being placed on the URL.

Both methods have their uses, and it is important to be aware of which you are using for any particular form, because processing methods have to take account of this too.

## Note

Dreamweaver lists a "default" method in the form Property inspector. This setting omits the method attribute from the form tag, leaving it up to the browser to use its default setting. I would advise against using a default setting; it's best to make a choice so that you are always sure of the format the data will arrive in. This is particularly important when building web applications, because it vastly increases the efficiency of your code.

# Processing a Form

After you have decided on the content of your form and the method you're going to use to send it, you need to decide what you're sending it to. There are a great many ways to process forms, and in the next few sections we'll look at some of the most common.

If it isn't obvious why you need a processing device, let me explain. I see a great many questions asked in the Dreamweaver community about how to "make a form do this" or "make a form do that." Of course, it's not the form that does things at all; it's the device that processes the form that makes all the powerful stuff happen.

An HTML form is just a device for gathering information. The different field types enable you to gather the information in an organized way, but it is still just gathering information. This information is then output as a text string to whatever object is named in the `Action` attribute of the form tag. It is then up to that object to accept the data and deal with it appropriately.

There's a whole host of different ways to process forms, from CGI scripts to ASP, ColdFusion, PHP, and JSP pages, and from client-side JavaScript and VBScript to custom COM objects and programs running on the user's computer. All of these different methods have their own uses and advantages.

Let's look at some common uses for forms and methods for processing the data.

## Sending an Email

A good number of web sites use forms purely for sending emails. This simple task can be performed in a number of ways, some of which are examined here.

### *mailto* Method

Although the `mailto` method is not recommended as a final solution for sending emails from a form, it can be a handy fix to get things working quickly.

By setting the form's action to `mailto:email@somedomain.com`, you can have the browser send the contents of the form using the user's default email client. This relies on the fact that users have an email client set up on their computer, and that they agree to the security warning that will flash up when they click the Submit button. Follow these steps to set up a form that can be sent using the `mailto` method:

1. Build your form, including all the different fields you need to collect the information you want.

2. Select the `<form>` tag using the tag selector in the lower-left corner of the Document window.

In the Action box, enter **mailto:** followed by the email address to which you want the form sent.

## CGI Script

The most common way to send form results by email is still a CGI script. There are a great many CGI scripts for sending emails, but the most popular is FormMail by Matt Wright. FormMail is written in Perl and will work on most UNIX servers. Similar CGI scripts can be found for Windows NT servers, but FormMail can be downloaded from Matt's Script Archive (`http://www.worldwidemart.com/scripts/`).

FormMail and other similar CGI scripts work by passing a set of predefined hidden fields to the script along with the form output. This is how the script knows who to send the email to, how the email should be formatted, and which page the user should be redirected to after the email has been sent.

Often, ISPs and hosting companies will have a CGI script such as FormMail preinstalled on their server, enabling you to start sending forms to email without too much setting up. You might like to ask them which they use and where you can find the instructions to get going with it. Follow these steps to use a CGI script:

1. Build your form, including all the different fields you need to collect the information you want.

2. Create hidden fields with any information the CGI script requires to process your form. These might include the recipient's email address and the page to redirect to, to confirm the email has been sent.

3. Select the `<form>` tag using the tag selector in the lower-left corner of the Document window.

4. In the Action box, enter the URL of the CGI script (for example, **http://www.mydomain.com/cgi-bin/formmail.pl**), and set the method to POST.

## Application Servers

If your site uses Active Server Pages, ColdFusion, PHP, or maybe even Java Server Pages, you might find that you can send email via the same system. For example, ASP servers often have a component called CDONTS installed, which enable you to send email using ASP. Other application servers have similar systems, and again, it's best to speak to your system administrator to find out what methods are available to you on the server. There are also a whole host of server behaviors available on the Macromedia Exchange for Dreamweaver that enable you to take advantage of these features.

## Sending Data to Another Page

In many circumstances, it is desirable to send the results of a form to another page. This page will then have some script in it to accept and interpret the data. The page could use ASP, ColdFusion, or some other scripting language to read in the data; but a script is needed, because this is beyond the capabilities of HTML. (It's even possible to do some basic processing with client-side JavaScript.)

Very often in web applications, the action of the form might be the URL of the same page, so that the form is submitting to itself in a way. The page will have a script in it to detect whether data has been sent to it, and will perform different actions accordingly.

Seldom will a page within a standard flat HTML site submit to itself or to another page. This behavior would be more common in a web application. You can read all about web applications in Chapters 16, "Controlling Your Environment," and 17, "Installing Extensions."

## Storing Results in a Cookie

A common use for forms is to store data in a cookie. This data can then be retrieved at a later date and used within your pages. A simple example of this would be storing the user's name in a cookie on his machine, and then welcoming him back to the site by name the next time he visits.

A number of cookie behaviors are available for Dreamweaver, the best-known of which are the Webmonkey behaviors. This group of behaviors includes Set Cookie, Read Cookie, and Kill Cookie, and is available for download from `http://www.hotwired.com/webmonkey/javascript/code_library/ed_ext`. These behaviors were written for Dreamweaver 1.2 and so are fairly old. You can find a version of the behaviors fixed up and packaged for Dreamweaver MX on the site that supports this book: `www.dreamweaverfever.com`.

The principle behind using a cookie to store data is simple. On submitting the form, the data is written to a cookie on the user's machine. When your web site needs that information back, it just retrieves the cookie by name and immediately has the data available. When you are sure you have finished with the data, you can kill the cookie and clean up behind yourself.

When you want to store data in a cookie, you can use the Webmonkey Set Cookie behavior to set a cookie holding any data from your form.

# Preprocessing Forms

Often it is necessary to perform processing actions on a form even before the user has had a chance to fill in any data. It is an important usability issue to ensure that the correct field has focus and fields that are prefilled with data where appropriate.

## Initializing a Form

Web developers often overlook that on being presented with a form; the user will want to be able to type into the first field without having to select it first. Giving a form element *focus* is a relatively easy task and will be more than appreciated by the users of your site.

One line of JavaScript enables you to give a form element focus:

```
document.theForm.textField.focus();
```

This assumes that your form has the name `theForm` and the field to which you would like to assign focus is called `textField`. The code is, obviously, very easy to change to meet your particular needs. This code could be called from the `<body>` tag `onLoad`:

```
<body onLoad="document.theForm.textField.focus();">
```

Another possibility to consider is the default text or state you assign for each form field. If users are likely to check a box, precheck it for them and save them the trouble. Similarly, if a text field has a common value, set that value as the default. Users can always delete it and set it to something else if they want.

## Reading Values from Cookies

Forms can often be prefilled with data that the web site already possesses. A prime example of this is when you already have certain data pertaining to the user in a cookie. Filling out a form field with a user's name, for example, can save users a lot of time and increase their confidence in your site's ability to perform.

Having already set the cookie, you have done the hard work. Reading a cookie back is a relatively simple task. The Webmonkey Read Cookie behavior enables you to read a cookie by name and assign the results to a form field of your choice. Performing this task onLoad will populate the form before the user is even aware of it.

## Reading Values from a Query String

Reading in values from a *query string* (variables attached to the end of the URL) is not quite as simple as reading from a cookie. No behaviors are available to do this at the present time; but because it is perfectly possible to create one, keep an eye on the Macromedia Exchange for Dreamweaver.

# Multipage Forms

When very long forms are required, it is desirable not to overwhelm users with too many questions at once. Although the basic HTML model for a form deals only with a form on one page (HTML is only ever concerned with one page at a time), you can use various tricks to split forms into manageable chunks. Of course, it's always best to keep a form on one page if at all possible, but there are going to be times when it's not.

The following sections discuss three different methods for splitting forms into digestible pieces. Of course, more methods are available, but these three should help you get started.

## Layers

A good trick can be to give the illusion of a multipage form by splitting your questions across multiple DHTML layers in a page. Start by having all but the first layer hidden, and use a button input at the bottom of each layer to hide the current layer and display the next. In the final layer, replace the button input with a Submit button.

### Caution

It is not enough to just change the Z–index (stacking order) of a layer to hide it from view. Because form elements are part of the group classed as "active" elements, they will always come to the top, and therefore show through the layers above them. For this reason, it is necessary to turn off the visibility of each layer when it does not need to be displayed.

As long as all the *anchor points* for your layers are within the form tag, the contents of the inputs on each layer will be submitted to the form, but the user sees only a small subset of the questions at any one time.

The anchor point of a layer is the point at which the `<div>` tag appears within the source code. Although a layer can be positioned anywhere on (or even off) the page, the tag that contains its description always remains static within the code. The position of this tag is the anchor point.

Figure 3.2 shows a form split into multiple layers, with the anchor point for each layer residing within the form tags.

**Figure 3.2**

Layers can be used to split up a form.

## Cookies

Another method for splitting up a form is to place your questions over a number of pages. The obvious problem that then arises is how to keep track of all the data until the final question has been completed and the user clicks the Submit button. A way to maintain data across pages that we are already familiar with is the use of cookies.

Despite the fact that all the questions make up a logical form, to split the questions across pages, you actually need to use a new form on each page. After you've submitted the results to a cookie for each page, the final page can then read back the results from the previous pages and place them in hidden fields. The final page, now holding all the data, performs the submit to the final location. When the form is submitted, the results from the previous pages are then submitted too.

## Staged Processing

The next best thing to keeping a form all on one page is to process your questions in multiple chunks. If your processing method is a server script or something similar, it is likely that you will be writing this yourself or having it written specifically for the task. With this as a basis, it is a good opportunity to have the script written to accept the data in a number of smaller stages. Ultimately, combining the data at the processing stage is the most reliable way to split forms across multiple pages.

# Confirmation and Acknowledgment Pages

An important part of any form-based system is confirming with users that their data has been sent and received correctly. Many users are still nervous about giving information online, however basic or straightforward the questions they are asked.

It is important to keep this in mind; and whenever you ask users to submit a form, redirect them to a page with a confirmation message, acknowledging that the process has gone smoothly and that everything is under control. This will help to build the users' confidence in your web site, and will give them the assurance that their data is safe in your hands.

In addition to thanking users for their input, it is courteous to offer a link back to a logical page on your web site. It is common to see form confirmation pages that just thank users and then leave them stranded, with no clear direction as to where they should go. Avoid this by offering a simple link to an appropriate place.

When acknowledging the receipt of a form, be specific. It's not enough just to present users with a page reading "Thank you"; let them know what they've just done and what the next step is. If they have submitted a form requesting that the web site owners contact them, thank them for entering their contact details and let them know that they will be contacted shortly.

Figure 3.3 shows a good example of a confirmation page thanking users for submitting a "contact" form. Not only does it thank them, it also tells users what the next step is (that they will be contacted), and then goes further to offer an alternative method of contact if the user's needs are urgent.

**Figure 3.3**

A comprehensive confirmation page.

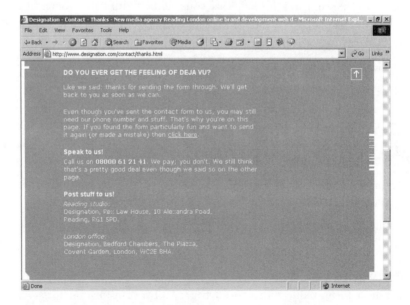

# Manipulating Form Elements with JavaScript

From simple or complex form validation right through to altering the contents of a form element on-the-fly, JavaScript has most of the answers. To go through all the possibilities would be a book in itself, and one focused more on JavaScript than Dreamweaver, so we'll look at the built-in facilities Dreamweaver has for manipulating form elements.

## Form Validation

Dreamweaver has a behavior that enables you to validate the contents of your form with relative ease. The Validate Form behavior offers a number of features to help monitor and influence the quality of data being entered into a form. Figure 3.4 shows the basic options available.

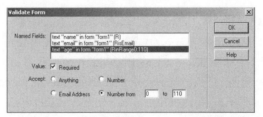

**Figure 3.4**

The Dreamweaver Validate Form behavior.

The Validate Form behavior enables you to specify whether a field is mandatory, whether it should be a number or a number range, or whether the input data should be an email address. If the data input does not meet the criteria you specify, the user is presented with an error message, and the form is not sent.

### Applying Standard Form Validation

To apply the Validate Form behavior to your page, make sure you have a form (obviously) and that it includes all the text fields you want to validate. It also pays to make sure all your fields have logical names.

1. Select the `<form>` tag to ensure that the entire form is selected. You want to apply this behavior `onSubmit` so that the `<form>` tag is the logical one.

2. Select Validate Form from the Behaviors panel to evoke the behavior.

3. Figure 3.4 shows the dialog box with which you are presented. Select the first form element you want to validate.

4. Choose whether the text field is required with the checkbox.

5. Choose which sort of value to accept with the radio buttons. The choices are as follows:

   - Anything

   - Number

   - Email Address

   - Number range

6. If choosing a number range, enter the range (for example, 1 to 10).

7. Click OK to apply the behavior.

### Advanced Form Validation

A number of more advanced JavaScript validation behaviors are available for download from the Macromedia Exchange for Dreamweaver (`http://www.macromedia.com/exchange/dreamweaver/`). Among them is a range of validation behaviors for specific purposes, including behaviors to compare the contents of two fields (such as Massimo Foti's Compare Fields) and even for filtering out inappropriate language (WebAssist.com's Swearing Validation). There are also some great alternatives to the standard Macromedia validation behavior, such as Jaro von Flocken's Check Form. One particular advantage many of these third-party extensions have over the default ones is that they enable you to specify your own error message. This is an important step for helping users to solve the problems with their input, instead of just suggesting that a mistake has occurred.

In particular, Macromedia's own JavaScript Integration Kit for Macromedia Flash extension offers an enormous range of high-quality form validation behaviors that you can use with regular HTML forms as well as Flash forms. Originally developed to enable Flash developers to offer standard, intuitive validation to their forms, 18 different advanced form validation behaviors in the JavaScript Integration Kit cover a variety of validation tasks. All of them enable you to enter your own error message, which means you can phrase the errors in words appropriate for your audience and the task at hand.

The kit uses a master behavior called Advanced Validate Form to use as a controller for any number of additional, specific, field validation behaviors applied to tackle special circumstances. To make use of the specialized behaviors, you also must apply Advanced Validate Form to act as a foundation.

## Tip

Try to include examples in your error messages of the sort of input required. If users got it wrong once, it is likely that they don't understand the format in which the data should be entered. An example at this point will help to keep users happy.

Descriptions and examples of the 18 validation tasks follow:

- **Alphanumeric validation.** Allows only letters and numbers to be input; special characters are disallowed.

- **Credit card validation.** Checks that the number entered is of the valid format to be a credit card number. If not, a customizable error message displays.

- **Date validation.** Offers a wide range of options for checking that the input value is a date. It can allow dates from the past, from the future, or from a range, and enables the developer to specify the format in which the date should be returned.

- **Email validation.** Checks for the presence of @ and a period. As these two items are common to all email addresses, this offers reasonable validation of the format of the address.

## Note

It's not generally possible to check the validity of an email address without sending mail to that address and asking the user to respond. Performing an address lookup and querying to see whether there's a mail server willing to accept the email is a good starting point, but really the best you can do is to check that the format of the address is correct to begin with. After all, it's at the input stage that the error is most likely to occur.

- **Entry length validation.** Checks the number of characters input. This can be a range between any two numbers. If you check the option to strip out spaces, only actual characters and not spaces will be included in that count.

- **Floating-point validation.** Enables you to check for any number, or a number within a range.

- **Integer validation.** This is similar to the floating-point validation, except that it requires the input number to be an integer.

- **International phone validation.** Checks for the format of the input data to make sure it matches the international phone number format. To prevent users being unnecessarily stopped by this type of validation, it's often helpful to give an example of the sort of required input next to the box on the page. It's rare for a user to realize that an international phone number format is required, for example.

- **Like entry validation.** This is extremely helpful for checking that a user has entered, for example, the same password twice. The behavior enables the developer to require that two fields in the form hold the same value. If the match fails, there is the option to clean the field, because the entry will need to be retyped. The option to make the validation case-sensitive is also available.

- **Mask validation.** Checks the input against a format mask. If the input needed to be three letters followed by three numbers (for example, ABC123), the mask would be AAA###. Letters are represented by A, numbers are represented by #, and ? indicates either.

- **Nonblank validation.** Makes the field a required, or mandatory, field. If the input is blank, the error message displays. This is a very simple but useful behavior.

- **Radio button validation.** Checks that one of the radio buttons in the defined button group is selected. If all radio buttons in that group are left deselected, the error message is evoked.

- **Selection made in list validation.** Checks that an item has been selected from the chosen list box. This forces users to make a selection before they can proceed.

- **Social security validation.** Checks that the input is formatted in the correct way to be a U.S. social security number. Be careful using this sort of validation. If your users are international, they might have valid data to input, but the format could be different.

- **Time validation.** Checks the input for a valid time value. Any valid time value can be accepted, or you can specify a time range. This is useful for preventing people from requesting appointments outside of business hours, for example.

- **URL validation.** Checks that the input is the valid format to be a URL. This includes checking for a commencing http://.

- **U.S. phone validation.** Checks for a valid format for a U.S. phone number. Be aware that this could make life difficult for international users; so if you don't actually require only a U.S. phone number, don't use this behavior.

- **U.S. zip code validation.** Checks for a valid format for a U.S. postal code. Again, be cautious about using this if there's any chance of an international user filling out your form.

## Manual Manipulations

JavaScript's interaction with forms does not stop at validation. Many other procedures can be performed using behaviors available for download from the Macromedia Exchange for Dreamweaver.

However, you also might need to perform manipulations for which there are no convenient ready-made solutions. Many of these will be easily carried out with JavaScript, on the simple premise that all form values can be read and set with ease.

## Case Study: Microsoft.com

I'm sure most people are familiar with the techniques used by Microsoft with forms and various other page elements, where based on user interaction segments of the page or form can be hidden and revealed. The idea is to make the information easier to digest by focusing the user's attention on only the relevant data. The technique is implemented using JavaScript and CSS, and can be re-created in Dreamweaver using the Change Property behavior.

A good example is of an online order form that enables users to specify whether they want to enter a different address for shipping to that which they have specified for billing. Selecting to use a different shipping address would reveal an additional set of text boxes for the shipping address. Let's look at how that might be done.

1.  On a new page, construct your form with all the required fields. I suggest that you start with a set of fields for Billing Address.

2.  Add a pair of radio buttons. The first should be titled Use Billing Address for Shipping, and the second Use Different Address for Shipping.

3.  Add a set of fields for Shipping Address. Select the fields that make up your shipping address. Click the Quick Tag Editor, and wrap the selection in a `<div>`. Give the `<div>` an ID attribute of **shipping**.

4.  Select the `<body>` tag from the tag selector in the lower left of the Application window, and use the Behaviors panel to apply a Change Property behavior.

5.  In the Change Property dialog box, set the Type of Object to `div`. The shipping `div` should appear in the list of named objects. Select it.

6.  Enter your own property. We want to hide this DIV when the page loads, so enter **style.display** with a new value of **none**.

7.  Okay the behavior. It should be applied to the `<body>` tag `onLoad`.

8.  Repeat this process on your first radio button—the option to Use Billing Address for Shipping. When the user clicks this radio button, we want the shipping address to remain hidden, so a display setting of none is appropriate here also. This behavior should be applied `onClick`. Set the default state of this radio button to checked.

9.  Apply a Change Property behavior again to the second radio button. This is the button that we want to reveal the extra shipping fields. Set an entered property of **style.display** again, but set the new value to **block**. Again, this should be applied `onClick`.

10. Save and preview your page. You should find that the shipping fields are hidden by default, but toggling the radio buttons will show and hide the fields as needed.

In this example, we are using JavaScript and the DOM to set a CSS property of an HTML element. It's Dynamic HTML in one of its purest forms in that we are making use of every aspect of DHTML. As such, support is required by the browser. Old browsers such as Netscape 4 don't cope too well with showing and hiding elements. However, they default to showing all, so that the form fields in the preceding example would remain useable. You can read more about DHTML and CSS in Chapters 6, "Dynamic HTML," 7, "Cascading Style Sheets," and 8, "Advanced CSS Design."

## Tip

> **You can find an example of this technique on the web site that supports this book,** http://www.dreamweaverfever.com/.

# What to Take Away from This Chapter

- Having a good grasp of the available form elements and an understanding of their use will enable you to build effective forms.

- Knowing the pros and cons of each of the possible form submission methods will enable you to make an informed choice as to which is best to use for any given circumstance.

- You can choose from many different ways to process a form, ranging from simple JavaScript solutions to complex server-side CGI scripts.

- By performing some preprocessing of a form, you can provide some timesaving aids for your web site's users.

- Long forms can be split up over a number of pages using a range of different techniques.

- A well-written confirmation page not only helps build user confidence in your web site, but also looks professional.

- Form elements can be manipulated with JavaScript and a range of behaviors built into Dreamweaver are available for free download from the Macromedia Exchange for Dreamweaver.

# Chapter 4

# Advanced Browser and Platform Compatibility

Objectives:

- Understand that different browsers exist and each has its own way of rendering a page.

- Understand that different computer platforms render web pages differently, even with the same browser.

- Build a web page that will happily work across all the major browsers and platforms.

Designing for the World Wide Web brings with it a cartload of problems that were not associated with traditional media. The simple fact that a web developer cannot be sure exactly how a page will display on the end user's computer screen (or television, or PDA, or mobile phone, or Braille reader) is a serious consideration. What you can do, however, is use code known to work across different platforms and test with the most common hardware and software configurations.

Such problems do not exist with traditional media, although they have problems of their own. In the world of print, after you've seen what's coming off the printing press, you can be 100-percent sure that is exactly how your audience will be viewing your work. Of course, it can be a tricky job to get the finished article to come out right, but that's another matter—you always have the chance to see your work in the same way your audience will see it.

When a web developer launches a site, there is always the chance that a user somewhere will be viewing the site with a hardware and software configuration that was not tested for. With the wild differences in the way pages look under different circumstances, this quickly becomes very complicated. What's more, you may never know that there is a problem unless someone is kind enough to report it. Most users will just leave the site if it doesn't work properly for them.

## Available Browsers

A great number of browsers are available on the Internet. Some are excellent groundbreaking products, whereas others are just small hobby projects. Table 4.1 lists a number of the most commonly used browsers available at the time of writing and a usage percentage from three different sources. Note that many browsers are available, most of which are used by very few people, and some of which do not report their identity properly, making them impossible to detect or log.

| Table 4.1    Browsers Currently in Common Use and Their Market Share | | | |
|---|---|---|---|
| | Source 1 | Source 2 | Source 3 |
| Internet Explorer 6 | 29% | 27% | 36% |
| Internet Explorer 5 | 59% | 62% | 40% |
| Internet Explorer 4 | 4.0% | 3.1% | 2.3% |
| Internet Explorer 3 | 0.1% | 0.05% | 0.5% |
| Internet Explorer 2 | 0.05% | 0 | 0.1% |
| Netscape Navigator 6 / Mozilla | 1.0% | 1.0% | 5.9% |
| Netscape Navigator 4 | 5.0% | 5.1% | 5.8% |
| Netscape Navigator 3 | 0.1% | 1.4% | 0.25% |
| Opera versions | 0.5% | 0.15% | 0.5% |
| (Other) | 1.5% | 0.15% | 8.0% |

Source: Browser News (`http://www.upsdell.com/browserNews/`), March 10, 2002.

The statistics in Table 4.1 were gathered from three different sources, as detailed here:

- **Source 1.** Statistics are from sites that use a hit counter, which excludes many popular, professionally made sites.

- **Source 2.** Statistics are from Proteus the Internet Consultancy (`http://www.proteus.co.uk`), and are primarily from UK sites, with a somewhat regional audience. Note the anomalously high Netscape Navigator 3 percentage. This may include browsers that mimic Netscape, which other sources classify as "other" browsers.

- **Source 3.** Statistics are from `www.upsdell.com`. Because of its special audience, its statistics apply to a narrow segment of the population.

As you can see, Internet Explorer has the dominant market share, and the nearest competitor (Netscape Navigator) is a long way behind. With Internet Explorer being shipped with every copy of Microsoft Windows, we can only expect that lead to grow.

*Tip*

> **You can keep up-to-date with the latest statistics at the Browser News web site (`http://www.upsdell.com/browserNews/`).**

Even though you can estimate that approaching 90 percent of your site's visitors will be using a modern version of Internet Explorer, that doesn't mean you can totally ignore the rest. Roughly 10 percent of visitors still use a browser other than Internet Explorer 5 or 6, and that's a percentage that needs considering before it is ignored out of hand. This is one reason why it is still important to create cross-browser web sites and not lose a potential 10 percent of your customers.

## Support for Technologies

With so many different technologies out there on the web, and with so many different browsers supporting a selection of each, designing a widely compatible web site becomes a nearly impossible task for any Web developer.

Table 4.2 offers a guide to which technologies are supported by which browsers. Of course, all have their idiosyncrasies in the way they support these technologies; so the information needs to be taken with a pinch of salt and should not be considered a substitute for thorough testing.

| Table 4.2 Browsers and Their Supported Technologies | | | | | | | | | | |
|---|---|---|---|---|---|---|---|---|---|---|
| | HTML 3.2 | HTML 4.0 | Java | Java Script | CSS 1 | CSS 2 | XML | DOM 1 | DOM 2 | I-frames | Plug-ins |
| **Windows** | | | | | | | | | | | |
| Explorer 5.5 | Y | Y | Y | Y | P | P | P | P | P | Y | Y |
| Explorer 5.0 | Y | Y | Y | Y | P | P | P | | | Y | Y |
| Explorer 4.0 | Y | | Y | Y | | | | | | Y | Y |
| Netscape 6 | Y | Y | Y | Y | Y | P | Y | Y | P | Y | Y |
| Navigator 4.7 | Y | Y | Y | Y | Y | P | | P | | | Y |
| Navigator 3.0 | Y | | Y | Y | | | | | | | Y |
| Opera 5 | Y | Y | Y | Y | Y | P | Y | P | P | Y | Y |
| Opera 3 | Y | Y | Y | Y | Y | P | | | | | |
| **Macintosh** | | | | | | | | | | | |
| Explorer 5.0 | Y | Y | Y | Y | Y | P | Y | P | | P | Y |
| Explorer 4.5 | Y | | Y | Y | P | | | | | Y | Y |
| Netscape 6 | Y | Y | Y | Y | Y | P | Y | Y | P | Y | Y |
| Navigator 4.72 | Y | | Y | Y | Y | P | | | | | Y |
| Opera 5pre | Y | Y | Y | Y | Y | Y | Y | P | P | Y | Y |
| Opera 3 | Y | Y | Y | Y | Y | Y | P | | | Y | Y |
| Icab 2.4pre | Y | Y | Y | Y | | | | | | Y | Y |
| **Linux** | | | | | | | | | | | |
| Netscape 6 | Y | Y | Y | Y | Y | P | Y | Y | P | Y | Y |
| Mozilla | Y | Y | Y | Y | Y | P | Y | Y | P | Y | Y |
| Navigator 4.74 | Y | Y | Y | Y | Y | P | P | P | | | Y |
| Amaya | Y | Y | Y | | Y | Y | | | | | |
| Opera 5 | Y | Y | Y | Y | Y | P | Y | P | P | Y | Y |
| Opera 3 | Y | Y | Y | Y | Y | | | | | | Y |

| | HTML 3.2 | HTML 4.0 | Java | Java Script | CSS 1 | CSS 2 | XML | DOM 1 | DOM 2 | I-frames | Plug-ins |
|---|---|---|---|---|---|---|---|---|---|---|---|
| **UNIX** | | | | | | | | | | | |
| Explorer 5.0 | Y | Y | Y | Y | P | P | P | P | | Y | P |
| Navigator 6 | Y | Y | Y | Y | Y | P | Y | Y | P | Y | Y |
| Navigator 4.7 | Y | Y | Y | Y | Y | P | | P | | | Y |

**Key:** Support for a technology is denoted by a letter Y. Partial support is denoted by a letter P.

Source: `http://www.qodox.com/browser/`, March 10, 2002.

# HTML Rendering Differences

It is well known that different web browsers display (or *render*) HTML documents slightly differently. Each browser has its own way of interpreting HTML tags and drawing them on the screen. This is, of course, what makes browsers different, because their entire purpose is to interpret and display HTML.

When HTML was designed, it was supposed to be a system for marking up text (a markup language) and for providing links between documents (hypertext). Originally, the markup only generically described the way a particular tag should be rendered and left the rest to the browser. For example, HTML specification states that the H1 tag should indicate the top level of structure within the document, with H2 forming the second level. There was nothing to say that H1 should be Times New Roman, 48 pixels, and bold—that was left to the browser to decide.

The idea behind this methodology was to allow a browser to display hypertext documents in a way best suited to the device and the user's preferences. If the user is viewing a document on a PC with a large screen, a 48-point heading is no problem; if the viewer is using a Personal Digital Assistant with a 3-inch screen, however, a 48-pixel heading might take up the whole display. This is why the flexibility in displaying text is left with the browser.

For today's World Wide Web, the reality is different. Although most people view web pages with Microsoft Internet Explorer 5 or 6 and a reasonably sized desktop screen, developers must work to strict design templates and be sure that the page will look good in whichever browser it is viewed. Whether this is the best state for the web to be in or not, it is the situation we have and the one we need to accommodate.

## HTML in Dreamweaver

Dreamweaver MX creates standard HTML or XHTML, depending on your preference. The default operations you can perform on your document in Dreamweaver will output HTML that should be understood by most browsers. As a web developer, you would be hard-pressed to find differences between the basic HTML that Dreamweaver outputs and what you might produce yourself, except for the fact that the Dreamweaver code might be presented better and contain fewer mistakes! This very important fact means that you can rely on the HTML that Dreamweaver outputs and don't need to be concerned that working in a visual environment might produce substandard code.

Another vital point is that Dreamweaver does not modify any hand-written HTML by itself. If you dip into the code and make some changes, Dreamweaver will not overwrite them unless it is told to do so. This feature, known as Roundtrip HTML, means that you can rest easy, knowing that whether you choose to develop in the Dreamweaver visual environment, or within the Dreamweaver HTML editor, your code will not be messed with as you switch between the two.

The only circumstance in which Dreamweaver will make any changes at all to your document is when it comes to code formatting. Depending on your code formatting preferences, Dreamweaver will reformat your code into a more logical and understandable form when making changes in Design view or when running a command specifically to format the source—such as Apply Source Formatting. However, Dreamweaver doesn't change the code itself, just how it is formatted within the Code view.

The same holds true if you decide to use another, external program, such as HomeSite, to edit your source code. Moving between the Dreamweaver visual environment and an external editor does not result in the loss of any code integrity, no matter how many times you flip between them.

These factors result in the code that Dreamweaver outputs, being very reliable and compatible with most browsers. As already noted, however, all browsers are different and render code differently. No two available browsers render code in the same way. For this reason, sometimes Dreamweaver HTML is not rendered correctly by some browsers. The fault, in these circumstances, lies with the browser in 9 out of 10 cases.

### XHTML (a.k.a. The Acronym Section)

New with Dreamweaver MX, you can now author your pages in XHTML. *XHTML* is a new version of HTML based on XML (*eXtensible Markup Language*). In fact, an XHTML document is actually just an implementation of XML, with a DTD (*document type definition*)—so similar to HTML 4 that primitive browsers need not be concerned with the difference.

There won't be any new versions of HTML after version 4. XHTML is here to take its place for the moment, and eventually XHTML itself will be replaced by a more pure form of XML, totally removed from anything we're used to currently. What this does mean, however, is that the sooner we start to author pages in XHTML, the better. Because XHTML is really just XML with an HTML-style DTD, future browsers will always be able to display our XHTML pages by applying the correct DTD.

*Tip*

> **XHTML is an interesting subject, and is worthy of more detailed research—probably more detailed than I am able to document in this book. You might like to check out the New Riders book *XHTML*, by Chris Minnick and Chelsea Valentine (ISBN: 0735710341), or the section on the W3C web site dedicated to markup (`http://www.w3.org/MarkUp/`).**

# Overcoming Rendering Differences

When coding a web page, you may find that the effect you are trying to achieve does not render properly in a particular browser. You can address this problem in a number of different ways, most of which work as viable solutions.

## Belt and Braces

Fortunately for the developer, HTML is a fault-tolerant language. If a browser comes across some markup that it doesn't know how to display, it just ignores it and moves on to the next piece of code it does recognize. The user isn't presented with any errors or warnings; the browser just quietly ignores code that it doesn't understand.

This helpful feature of HTML enables you to include both the valid code for displaying your pages in compliant browsers and the nonstandard code for the awkward browsers, without the user seeing any errors.

In many cases, this approach enables you to enter different sets of code and attributes where you would otherwise use only one. This "belt-and-braces" approach enables you to compensate for the differences between browsers.

For example, the two major browsers (Microsoft Internet Explorer and Netscape Navigator) use different methods to display zero page borders. Both browsers use attributes added to the body tag for this option, but those attributes differ. Figure 4.1 shows the Dreamweaver Page Properties dialog box with its four margin dimension options.

**Figure 4.1**

Dreamweaver offers four margin size options.

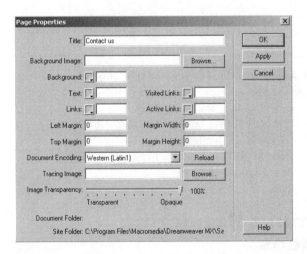

The first two, Left Margin and Top Margin, cater to the margin options for Internet Explorer. The second two, Margin Width and Margin Height, cater to Navigator. Each browser interprets those it understands and ignores the others.

This method is widely used when different browsers support different attributes for a given tag; but what about when it's not just a different attribute you're dealing with, but a whole different tag?

Fortunately, these circumstances are fewer and farther between than attribute differences, but they can be treated in more or less the same way. Following the same principle that tags that are not recognized are ignored, just include both tags, and both browsers will cope.

## Multiple Versions

Under some circumstances, you may find that complex pages become nearly impossible to render the same way in all browsers. Making the design work in one browser requires a totally different methodology than getting it to display in another. Under these circumstances, it may be necessary to produce different versions of the page for different browsers.

### Caution

> **Think very carefully before deciding to build multiple copies of a page; maintaining those pages takes a lot longer than just updating one copy.**

Using the Dreamweaver Check Browser behavior, you can detect which browser and version users are viewing your page with, and then redirect them to the appropriate version of the page for their browser. This enables you to design a separate page for any awkward browsers you may need to consider.

Figure 4.2 shows the Check Browser dialog box. It takes three different URLs into consideration: the URL to redirect to, an alternate URL to redirect to, and the same page the behavior is being applied to.

Check Browser enables you to choose a page for Internet Explorer (IE) viewers from a version of your choosing, for Navigator (NN) viewers from a version of your choosing, and finally, for all the rest. The defaults that Dreamweaver starts with are good choices. In most cases, you will find that you might want a page for IE 4 users and above, NN 4.0 and above, and then all the minority browsers and older versions of the primary ones. Note, however, that unless your web site caters to a specialist technology market (a site about the Linux operating system, for example), 9 out of 10 of your visitors will be using Internet Explorer.

**Figure 4.2**

You can redirect users with specific browsers.

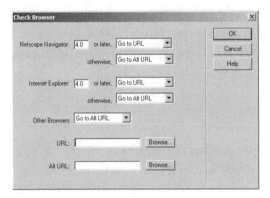

# Scripting Languages Differences

Although various browsers support different scripting languages, JavaScript is far and away the most supported language for putting executable content into web pages. Now with an international standard, called ECMAScript (the name JavaScript is owned by Netscape), different browser companies have taken to JavaScript as the language of choice for integrating into their browsers.

Just as different browsers use slightly different implementations of HTML, so do they use different versions of JavaScript. From the latest browsers using JavaScript 1.2 through older browsers using version 1.1, 1.0, or sometimes not at all, support for JavaScript varies from product to product.

Not only do different browsers use different versions of JavaScript, but they also chip in with their own interpretations of those versions. Just as browser programmers decided to invent their own tags, they also use their own twist on JavaScript properties and functions. Hardly anything is sacred.

## JavaScript in Dreamweaver

The JavaScript used by Dreamweaver is carefully written to work with as many browsers as possible. Where code is too complex for a particular version of a browser to understand, the code fails without error. Although this is fantastic for developers in that they can be comfortable using JavaScript in Dreamweaver, safe in the knowledge that if a user visits their page with an older browser the user will not be presented with an error, it can have its downside as well.

To work in as many browsers as possible, Dreamweaver JavaScript uses a careful belt-and-braces approach to cater to different circumstances. For example, Internet Explorer and Netscape Navigator often need totally separate versions of a function to perform the same task. The downside is that, as a result, Dreamweaver outputs more code than you would have to if you knew all your visitors had the same browser.

For this reason, users of other software often criticize Dreamweaver JavaScript, saying that it is "bloated." The reality is, of course, that you actually have very tight cross-browser-compatible code that is going to cope with every eventuality.

JavaScript is applied to Dreamweaver pages primarily through the use of behaviors, but also by some commands. Behaviors consist of two distinct elements: an action and an event. The action is a JavaScript function that performs some task. It is inserted into the head of a page and is dormant until it is called. The event calls an action. Events describe the circumstance whereby the action is called. (You can spot them easily; most start with `on`). Examples of events are `onClick`, `onMouseOver`, `onLoad`, and `onSubmit`.

Commands in Dreamweaver can insert JavaScript (as well as other things) anywhere in your document. Commands are often used for more complex pieces of coding that don't just fall into the event and action model.

Although Dreamweaver built-in behaviors are very well written to cope with cross-browser compatibility, keep in mind that any extra behaviors that you might download and install from the Macromedia Exchange for Dreamweaver (`http://www.macromedia.com/exchange/dreamweaver/`) might not exhibit this attribute. As thorough and accurate as the code within them might be, there is no guarantee that the behaviors have been thoroughly checked for cross-browser compatibility unless they specifically state so. The way to get around this—as with any aspect of web development—is to test at every stage. Nearly every web browser available is free to download, and so competent web developers have no excuse for not testing their work in every browser in which they expect their site to be viewed.

### *Tip*

**Although browsers are free to download, testing on other hardware platforms is a different matter. Many Internet cafes have a range of hardware that may differ from your own. Renting some time in one might save you an awful lot of redevelopment time later on.**

## Overcoming Scripting Differences

When it comes to overcoming potential script differences, Dreamweaver really does all the hard work for you by providing a good foundation of behaviors with strong and cross-browser-compatible code. There will come a time, however, when you will need to write or copy some custom JavaScript.

In most cases, basic JavaScript will work happily in most major browsers, but there are obviously some things that won't. Whether there are two different versions of the code needed, or whether you require the code to be used only for one particular browser (for example, to be used in Internet Explorer but not Navigator), eventually you will need to detect which browser is being used to view the page. What's more, browsers change from version to version, so what works in IE 5 might not work in IE 5.5.

Unfortunately, Dreamweaver provides no simple solution for selecting script to execute depending on the browser. Based on the code that the Check Browser behavior uses, however, the logical solution is this:

```
<script language="JavaScript" type="Text/JavaScript">
<!--
var app=navigator.appName, verStr=navigator.appVersion,
➡version = parseFloat(verStr);
```

```
if (app.indexOf('Netscape') != -1) {
     alert("netscape " + version); // script for Navigator
     }
if (app.indexOf('Microsoft') != -1) {
     alert("ie " + version); // script for Internet Explorer
     }
// -->
</script>
```

This code example uses a simple `alert()` function to display the name and version of the browser being used. This is just to show that the script is detecting the browser correctly, and that the `alert()` functions should be replaced with the browser-specific code to be implemented.

Of course, if you have already gone to the trouble of detecting browsers and redirecting to browser-specific pages, the use of browser-dependent JavaScript is not a problem. Just be careful to thoroughly test any script in the target browsers.

Remember, as well, that not every user will access your site via the home page. Search engines will index different lots of pages from your site, and visitors may follow external links to the site; so you can't guarantee that every user will hit your browser-detection code unless it is included in every page.

This is an important factor, and you may want to address the problem by including the code in an external JavaScript file, which is then linked to every page.

An alternative way to deal with this sort of code is to check whether the browser supports the code you are trying to use before you use it—for instance, if you are attempting to perform an image rollover effect, but need to know whether the browser supports it. This code would address the issue:

```
if (document.images) {
     alert("This browser supports rollovers")
}
```

This code checks to see whether the browser can return `document.images` as true and, if so, executes the code. This is the property that a browser must support to perform a rollover; so if the property doesn't exist (causing the value to return as false), the code is skipped. This is sometimes a better way to address browser-compatibility problems when it comes to JavaScript.

# Making Web Sites Accessible to All

If there's one thing that makes the practice of getting a page to look good in Internet Explorer and Netscape Navigator trivial, it's the whole concept of designing pages that can be read on any device, by any person. Accessibility is a big issue—but need not be a big nightmare. The concept of web accessibility is just to construct pages that can be understood by a visitor using any sort of web-enabled device and any sort of web browser.

Dreamweaver MX has introduced a whole load of new features to help you accomplish this goal without too much trouble. Unfortunately, they hid them away a bit, so the first thing to do is go and switch all the accessibility features on.

Open the preferences (Edit > Preferences) and you'll find a new Accessibility tab. On the Accessibility tab, you can find a selection of checkboxes labeled Show Attributes When Inserting. It is here that you select the elements for which you want to be prompted to enter details to aid the accessibility of your page. I usually check all of these boxes so that I can make a conscious decision to ignore them when appropriate. I find it's safer to do it that way, because by default I should usually be making pages accessible whenever possible.

Section 508 (`http://www.section508.gov/`) is a piece of U.S. legislation that dictates (among other things) that all federally funded web sites should be fully accessible to all, including those with disabilities. At the time of writing, the U.S. government does not fund most of us, and so we have no legal requirement to make our sites accessible. However, I don't think it'll be too long before this is stepped up to cover a wider range of people, and aside from the legal requirements, surely we have moral requirements to make our sites accessible to everyone? Ask any company that has received bad press for not having wheelchair access to their facilities, and they will tell you of the implications of not fully catering for those who equally deserve to be catered for.

## Case Study: Sydney Olympics

Legislation against organizations for not providing accessible web sites is known. The highest profile case was against the Sydney Olympics.

"In Australia in June 1999, Bruce Maguire lodged a complaint with the Human Rights & Equal Opportunity Commission (HREOC) under a law called the Disability Discrimination Act. His complaint concerned the Web site of the Sydney Organizing Committee for the Olympic Games (SOCOG), which Maguire alleged was inaccessible to him as a blind person.

"According to the complaint, Maguire, unlike most blind people online, does not use a screen reader to read aloud the elements of a Web page. Instead, he uses a refreshable Braille display. But neither technology can understand and turn into voice an image that lacks a text equivalent. Nearly all Web pages online have some kind of graphics, including high-profile sites like those associated with major sporting events.

"Maguire contended that significant parts of the SOCOG Web site, Olympics.com, were inaccessible to him.

"On 24 August 2000, the HREOC released its decision and supported Maguire's complaint, ordering certain access provisions to be in place on the Olympics.com site by 15 September 2000. SOCOG ignored the ruling and was subsequently fined A$20,000." (Source: Reader's Guide to Sydney Olympics Accessibility Complaint, `http://www.contenu.nu/socog.html`)

The implications of this case are tremendous. The precedent has now been set, thus making it easier for disabled web site visitors such as Bruce Maguire to take legal action to get the access to the web that they rightfully deserve.

# What to Take Away from This Chapter

- Many different browsers are available and are in use.

- Each different browser renders HTML slightly differently, and these differences need to be compensated for in your code.

- It is possible to include information in a page for all browsers and their different ways of working, because a browser will ignore any code it doesn't understand.

- With complex page designs, it is sometimes necessary to build different versions of a page for different browsers, although this has a maintenance overhead.

- JavaScript is the language of choice for scripting within web pages.

- Different browsers support different versions and interpretations of JavaScript.

- Where different code is needed for different types of browsers, you can use some simple JavaScript to detect the browser and thus choose which piece of code to implement.

- Of all the many different browsers available and in use, Internet Explorer has the largest market share, and this is expected to increase.

- It is important to turn on the accessibility features in Dreamweaver MX and make a conscious decision not to use them if there is an exception, instead of having to remember all the extra steps needed to make a site accessible to all.

# Chapter 5

# Cleaning and Editing HTML Within Dreamweaver

Objectives:

- Clean up a Microsoft Word HTML file.
- Clean up a messy HTML file by hand.
- Use the Find and Replace feature to detect and remove unwanted code.

Sometimes during the development of a web site, you may be given Word documents to convert to web pages, or even older versions of pages that need incorporating. More often than not, these can be very large documents that would take hours to re-create, and so you must work with what is provided.

Although Dreamweaver outputs very clean, well-formatted, and compliant code, other HTML editors aren't always as helpful. In particular, the HTML generators inside Microsoft Office products can produce rather bloated code that needs to be processed before it can be used on the Web.

It's not just HTML editors that are responsible for messy code too. Sometimes is can be that you need to deal with old pages containing outdated coding methods, or even perhaps it's just that the code you have to work with was sloppily written.

Fortunately for the developer, Dreamweaver MX includes many powerful functions for cleaning HTML. These are the functions discussed in this chapter.

# Cleaning HTML Generated by Microsoft Office

Microsoft Office is used worldwide for its supremacy and ease of use compared to other products on the market. So many companies use the Microsoft Office suite as the basis for their word processing, spreadsheet, database, presentation, and electronic communication needs that without a doubt, at some point a web developer will be given a Microsoft Office file to turn into a web page.

As good as Office products are for their designed purpose, they don't tend to be great at outputting HTML. Although most have a Save as Web Page option, the code that is produced tends to be bloated and doesn't often work well on the multiplatform web.

These problems aside, if you were presented with a complex document in, for example, Microsoft Word, you would have to spend hours converting it to HTML by hand. By taking advantage of the Save as Web Page function in Word, you can convert the document to HTML in a matter of seconds. All that is then left to do is strip the bad code out of the file and resave the document, and it's ready to go up on the web.

The following example is HTML output by Word's Save as Web Page feature:

```
<p class=ProductionDirective style='margin-left:36.0pt;
text-indent:-18.0pt;mso-list:l1 level1 lfo2;tab-stops:list
➥36.0pt'>
<![if !supportLists]><span lang=EN-US style='font-
➥family:Symbol'>·
<span style='font:7.0pt "Times New Roman"'>
       </span></span>
<![endif]>
<span lang=EN-US>Clean up a Microsoft Word HTML
➥file</span></p>
<p class=ProductionDirective style='margin-left:36.0pt;
text-indent:-18.0pt;mso-list:l1 level1 lfo2;tab-stops:list
➥36.0pt'>
<![if !supportLists]><span lang=EN-US style='font-
➥family:Symbol'>·
<span style='font:7.0pt "Times New Roman"'>
```

```
       </span></span>
<![endif]><span lang=EN-US>Clean a messy HTML file by
➥hand</span></p>
<p class=ProductionDirective style='margin-left:36.0pt;
text-indent:-18.0pt;mso-list:l1 level1 lfo2;tab-stops:list
➥36.0pt'>
<![if !supportLists]><span lang=EN-US style=
➥'font-family:Symbol'>·
<span style='font:7.0pt "Times New Roman"'>
       </span></span>
<![endif]><span lang=EN-US>Use the Find and Replace feature to
➥detect and remove unwanted code </span></p>
```

Now compare it to the standard HTML version to produce the same output:

```
<ul style="line-height:36pt">
  <li>Clean up a Microsoft Word HTML file </li>
  <li>Clean a messy HTML file by hand </li>
  <li>Use the Find and Replace feature to detect and remove
  ➥unwanted code</li>
</ul>
```

It soon becomes apparent that Word is storing much more information than is generally useful for a web page. This information adds to the size and therefore download time of a page, and might even confuse the browser. What's more, because a lot of the code is for Word's own internal use, it just doesn't make sense to have it in a web page. It is therefore desirable to be able to detect and remove this extra code, and to replace any abnormalities with standard HTML tags.

## The Clean Up Word HTML Command

Thankfully, Dreamweaver comes to the rescue when it comes to cleaning up files output from Word. The Clean Up Word HTML command has been designed to remove a lot of the extra data added to the HTML Word outputs. (Commands > Clean Up Word HTML).

Of course, you must treat a fine line when deciding how much of this data should be left in and how much should be stripped out. The Clean Up Word HTML command gives you many options as to which elements to strip out, although you will invariably want to leave all the options selected. Dreamweaver does tend to leave in a large amount of the formatting data. If it stripped this out too, the formatting of the document could be lost completely, and so any further cleaning is left to your expert eye. You'll learn some ways to clean documents by hand later in this chapter; for now, however, the discussion focuses on the Clean Up Word HTML command.

Figure 5.1 shows the Basic tab of the Clean Up Word HTML dialog box. Options are available for the version of Word used (although this should autodetect the version), for specifying what to clean up, and even for setting a background color for the document.

**Figure 5.1**

The Clean Up Word HTML dialog box.

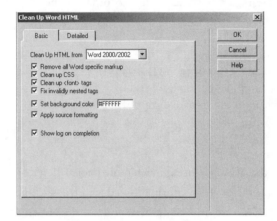

In addition to these options, the Detailed tab offers a host of advanced options. Figure 5.2 shows the Detailed tab and the options available. The Detailed tab gives some further choices for the Remove All Word Specific Markup and Clean Up CSS options from the Basic tab.

Having run our code sample through the Clean Up Word HTML command, let's see how it's done:

```
<p class=ProductionDirective style=''>
<span lang=EN-US style='font-family:Symbol'>·
<span style='font:7.0pt "Times New Roman"'>
        </span></span>
<span lang=EN-US>Clean up a Microsoft Word HTML
➥file</span></p>
<p class=ProductionDirective style=''> <span lang=EN-US
style='font-family:Symbol'>
```

```
·<span style='font:7.0pt "Times New Roman"'>
            </span></span>
<span lang=EN-US>Clean a messy HTML file by hand</span></p>
<p class=ProductionDirective style=''> <span lang=EN-US
style='font-family:Symbol'>·<span style='font:7.0pt
➥"Times New Roman"'>
        </span></span>
<span lang=EN-US>Use the Find and Replace feature to detect
➥and remove unwanted code </span></p>
```

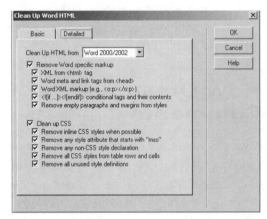

**Figure 5.2**

The Detailed tab offers a host of options.

As you can see, there's been a vast improvement in the code straightaway, but consider this: The code example comes from the first line of our Word document. Before running the Clean Up Word HTML command, the example I gave began on line 381 of my original page. After cleaning up, the same code starts on line 27 of the page. That's 354 lines of unnecessary code stripped out. For a document that renders the same way in a browser, that's a phenomenal improvement. The Clean Up Word HTML command managed to shave off 10K from our page, bringing the total file size down to 5K. For a simple text-based document such as this, that 10K is a fantastic saving.

You will be able to see, however, that the code we're left with is still far from perfect. The Clean Up Word HTML command does all it can before human intervention is needed to discern which code should be removed and which code should stay.

Later in this chapter you will learn how to clean up a page using Find and Replace and also by hand.

*Tip*

Microsoft has released a new version of the HTML filter for Word and Excel 2000. The new version claims
to export HTML that is more compact and has fewer
proprietary tags. Although it's still not perfect and
needs to be cleaned using the methods outlined in this
chapter, the new version is an improvement on the
standard version, and once installed, adds a new
Export to Compact HTML icon to your main Word
toolbar. The new filter can be downloaded for free
from `http://office.microsoft.com/
downloads/2000/Msohtmf2.aspx`.

# How Dreamweaver Uses HTML Comments

A vast amount of the software's usefulness is due to the fact that it works
directly on HTML documents. A number of the HTML editors that
were available when Dreamweaver was first released worked in their own
proprietary file format and only exported HTML as a final process. This
methodology results in distancing such editors from the actual HTML that
should be underlying the document and preventing such features as
Roundtrip HTML.

Along with all the advantages that working directly on an HTML document brings, there are always slight disadvantages. When it comes to
storing information required by the file that is not a standard part of
HTML, Dreamweaver needs to find a place to store it. This problem is partly
overcome by the use of HTML comments. (The rest of this problem is
addressed with Dreamweaver Design Notes.)

To keep track of Templates, Library items, and information related to
Fireworks and your graphics, Dreamweaver needs to store a small amount
of information about each document affected by these elements. Instead
of creating extra files containing lots of information or using a proprietary
file format, Dreamweaver uses HTML comments to store this information.

The result of this use of comments is a very small overhead in file size. Usually this will be less than 1K per document, but could be more depending on the requirements. When file size is critically important (to the extent that every last 1K saving needs to be made on each file), it can be desirable to remove these Dreamweaver comments. However, doing so could hamper your ability to update the Templates or Library items in the files, and generally limit much of the timesaving functionality available in Dreamweaver.

Should you decide that you need to remove the HTML comments used by Dreamweaver, a couple of handy features enable you to do it: The first is the Export Without Markup feature; the second is the Clean Up HTML command.

*Tip*

> **Because removing Dreamweaver HTML comments disables so much functionality, it's a good idea to back up your files first. This way, if you need some of that functionality back at a later date, you will be able to reinstate it.**

## The Export Without Markup Feature

Recognizing the need for developers to output as clean a version of their code as possible, new with Dreamweaver MX is an option to export the site without Dreamweaver markup. This includes all of the comments used by the Templates system for denoting editable and noneditable regions.

The feature is hidden under the Modify > Templates menu, and offers a small number of options. Figure 5.3 shows the dialog box that displays when the command is run.

The command will export your site to a new folder, and of course without the Dreamweaver-specific markup. This feature is an absolute gem. It means that you can maintain a development site will all the Dreamweaver HTML comments, and just do an export before you upload. The best of both worlds.

**Figure 5.3**

The Export
Without Markup
command strips
out unwanted
comment tags.

## The Clean Up HTML Command

Figure 5.4 shows the Clean Up HTML command. As you can see, many more features are available than just removing Dreamweaver HTML comments.

**Figure 5.4**

The Clean Up
HTML
command.

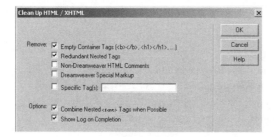

### Removing Empty Tags

One of the primary features of the Clean Up HTML command is to allow the removal of empty tags. Tags are considered to be empty if there is nothing between the opening of a tag and its closing. The following code is an example of what Dreamweaver considers to be empty tags:

```
<font color="#006633"></font>
```

In contrast, the following code would not be considered empty:

```
<font color="#006633">I was green with envy</font>
```

### Combining Nested Font Tags

Another very useful feature of the Clean Up HTML command is the ability to combine nested font tags. Nested font tags commonly occur when the developer has not been careful and accurate in making selections to which to apply font changes. The resulting code can look something like the following example:

```
<font face="Arial, Helvetica, sans-serif">
    <font size="4">
        <font color="#006633">
            I was green with envy
        </font>
    </font>
</font>
```

The Clean Up HTML command can rationalize this code and make it more efficient by combining it into the following:

```
<font face="Arial, Helvetica, sans-serif"
size="4" color="#006633">
    I was green with envy
</font>
```

As you can see, this code is much more efficient because the three font tags have been combined into one. This not only makes rendering easier for the browser, but also cuts out code, reducing the overall file size of the page.

## Removing HTML Comments

Dreamweaver provides two options that enable you to remove two different sorts of comments: Non-Dreamweaver HTML Comments and Dreamweaver Special Markup. *Non-Dreamweaver HTML comments* are any comments within the page that Dreamweaver did not place there itself. Selecting this option will remove any HTML comments that you may have typed into the code yourself.

The second option is to remove Dreamweaver special markup. *Special markup* refers to the HTML comments discussed earlier that hold a lot of information about Templates, Library items, and so on. You should think carefully before removing these comments, and it is advisable to make a backup first.

### Removing Specific Tags

The Clean Up HTML command also has a facility to remove specific HTML tags from your page. With the ability to remove multiple tags simultaneously, the Remove Specific Tag feature can prove extremely useful.

If you were trying to revamp an old page by removing the font tags to implement a CSS solution, for instance, you could enter **font** as the tag to remove, and all instances of `<font>` throughout the document would be removed. So the original line of code

```
<font color="#006633">I was <em>green</em> with envy</font>
```

would look like this:

```
I was <em>green</em> with envy
```

By separating tag names with commas, multiple tags can be dealt with. Entering a value of **font, em** would return just the following:

```
I was green with envy
```

All the features available within the Clean Up HTML command combine to make it a very useful tool when it comes to cleaning and editing HTML within Dreamweaver.

## Cleaning Fireworks HTML

*Macromedia Fireworks MX* is a feature-rich and elegant web graphics program. Its close integration with Dreamweaver MX allows for some very swift round-trip editing and conveniences for the user. Many people use Dreamweaver and Fireworks together; because the integration between them is so good, it can literally shave hours off the development time of a project. What's more, Fireworks is the leading web graphics program available, and many users own a copy solely on that basis.

Choosing to edit a Fireworks image from the Property inspector in Dreamweaver will launch Fireworks with your original master file for editing. Without this integration, the most Dreamweaver would be able to do is launch a graphics program with the current web-optimized version of the graphic, and not the master source file.

To offer this brilliant time-saver, Dreamweaver has to store some extra code in HTML comments within your document. Although this data doesn't take up much space, after your graphical content has been finalized, you may want to delete it.

The Clean Up HTML command unfortunately doesn't remove Fireworks HTML comments. You can strip such items out in other ways, however, with little effort.

By using the Dreamweaver Find and Replace feature, you can define a simple rule that strips out any Fireworks HTML comments. Figure 5.5 shows the Find and Replace dialog box. By using regular expressions, you can track down any Fireworks HTML comments and remove them.

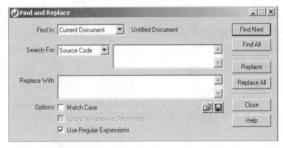

**Figure 5.5**

The Find and Replace feature.

The next section covers the Dreamweaver Find and Replace feature in greater detail. For now, however, this section discusses how a simple Find and Replace can help remove unwanted Fireworks HTML comments.

Regular expressions allow the use of various wildcards to match specific chunks of code. Because you know that Fireworks comments begin with `<!-- fwtable` and end with a `-->`, you can use a simple regular expression to find all those comments. By searching for anything starting with `<!-- fwtable` and ending with `-->`, you can then replace those with nothing. This is a regular expression that will perform the search:

```
<!-- fwtable [^>]*-->
```

By placing this regular expression into the Find field of the Find and Replace dialog box, and by leaving the Replace box empty, you can seek and destroy most Fireworks HTML comments.

## Note

Remember to check the Use Regular Expressions box so that Dreamweaver knows to interpret the Find string, instead of just taking it as is.

# Editing with the Find and Replace Feature

The preceding section briefly discussed how to use the Find and Replace feature to remove Fireworks HTML comments. This section takes a further look at how you can use the Find and Replace feature to do some powerful things to pages.

You are probably familiar with the basic Find and Replace options available in Dreamweaver. These enable you to search on source code, body text, and even specific tags. The real power, however, comes through the use of regular expressions.

## Using Regular Expressions

*Regular expressions* are a powerful tool for finding and replacing strings within your document. Any search that needs to be performed where an unknown factor is concerned can be achieved with regular expressions. Although they are not covered in full here, we will look at a few specific examples of how regular expressions can be used to perform efficient searches.

In the preceding section, you saw how a regular expression can be used to locate HTML comments beginning with `fwtable`. Let's look at that regular expression again:

```
<!-- fwtable [^>]*-->
```

This regular expression says to match anything beginning with `<!-- fwtable` and then any characters except `>` until it hits `-->`. This will find Fireworks HTML comments beginning with `<!-- fwtable`; but Fireworks comments sometimes begin with `<!-- Fireworks`. For these, you need a more complex regular expression:

```
<!-- (fwtable|fireworks)[^>]*-->
```

This regular expression is very similar to the preceding one, but contains an extra factor. This regular expression says to find any HTML comments beginning with `fwtable` *or* `fireworks` and then any characters except > until it hits `-->`.

The important thing about regular expressions in Dreamweaver Find and Replace is knowing that the capability is there. They are a great fix for those frantic moments when you're trying to clean up some impossible code, or even replace some hard-to-identify element on an entire web site. You may not find yourself using them on a day-to-day basis (although it's feasible that you could), but remembering that the facility is there can be a lifesaver.

### Note

**If you plan to make heavy use of regular expressions, I recommend that you read a book on the subject. The mere fact that they are so powerful means that they become a huge topic in themselves—much more than I can cover here. If you're interested in improving your JavaScript or server-side scripting skills, regular expressions are also a great tool to have under your belt.**

O'Reilly & Associates has a good book by author Jeffrey E. Friedl. *Mastering Regular Expressions* (ISBN: 1565922573) can be found in good computer books shops.

## Saving and Retrieving Searches

After you've written your complex regular expression, and pieced together which tags with which attributes you are trying to locate and what to replace them with, it would be a waste to run that search once and have to rebuild it again the next time you need to perform the same search.

This is where Dreamweaver comes to the rescue by enabling you to save and retrieve your Find and Replace settings. The familiar Save and Retrieve buttons sit below the Replace With box on the Find and Replace dialog box.

After you have defined a search, saving it is simple. When you click the Save button, a prompt asks you to enter a name, and your query is saved as an XML file (with a .dwr extension) into the Configuration/Queries folder. These files can then be shared with your development team or anyone else using the same version of Dreamweaver.

Of course, retrieving a search is easy too. Click the Retrieve button and select the DWR file that contains your query. The query is then loaded back into the Find and Replace dialog box.

# Making Edits by Hand

Sometimes you will need to clean a document that has no discernible repeating patterns for which you can search. Under these circumstances, there is little option but to clean up the code by hand.

Dreamweaver has a very accomplished HTML editor. Complete with live syntax coloring, useful formatting tools, and auto-indenting, the Dreamweaver Code view is a versatile editor for adjusting or coding by hand.

The Dreamweaver Code view has many useful facilities for the hand coder. Live syntax coloring means that both HTML and JavaScript are easier to interpret with the eye and more intuitive to work with. The auto-indenting feature results in code that is well laid out, with an easy-to-understand structure.

When it comes to making edits by hand, it is important that the working environment aids you as much as possible in the understanding and clarity of the code. The Dreamweaver Code view enables the developer to quickly and simply make edits to the code from within one program. Figure 5.6 shows the Code view with its indenting and line numbering.

By clicking in the left margin of the Code view, you can select an entire line or multiple lines simultaneously. This can prove very useful for deleting lines of code when cleaning up, or for selecting code to drag and drop to reorder the execution of items in a page.

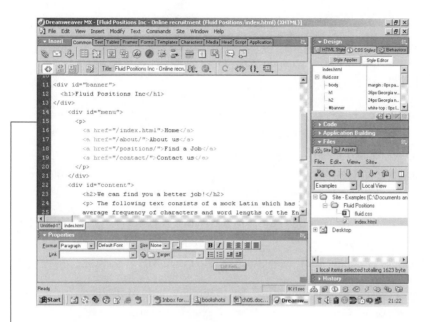

**Figure 5.6**

The Dream-
weaver Code
view offers
many useful
features.

Click here to select multiple lines at once.

When you highlight an element in the code and click the Reference button on the Code view toolbar, Dreamweaver opens the Reference panel and automatically goes to the reference page related to your current selection.

# Roundtrip HTML

Dreamweaver is famous for its introduction of Roundtrip HTML. Many visual editors on the market presume that they know better than the developer, and give developers no option but to have the editor "correct" their code. Dreamweaver broke this trend by introducing Roundtrip HTML.

Roundtrip HTML describes the process whereby you can move from your visual editor (Dreamweaver) to a code editor (such as the Dreamweaver Code view or Macromedia HomeSite) and back again without your code losing any integrity. Roundtrip HTML ensures that wherever external editors or internal aspects of Dreamweaver alter any of your code, they can't do it without your say-so.

This factor is invaluable for the professional developer. It can be infuriating to have a piece of software change your valid, or even deliberately invalid, code without your permission or even a choice as to whether it should do so.

Fortunately, Dreamweaver offers the developer 100-percent choice when it comes to code rewriting. If Dreamweaver does locate any genuinely invalid HTML syntax, it highlights the invalid tags in yellow to draw them to your attention. When you click a yellow tag, a suggested solution displays for correcting any mistakes, should you choose to do so.

The options available in the Code Rewriting preferences give you full control over your code. The Editors preferences enable you to choose an external code editor for use with Roundtrip HTML.

After an external code editor has been defined, swapping between Dreamweaver and your external editor couldn't be simpler. Press Ctrl+E to launch your defined external code editor and load the current document into it. On saving your page in the external editor and returning to Dreamweaver, you will be informed that the page has changed and be prompted to reload it, which of course you'll want to do.

Throughout this whole process, your code stays intact—only the edits you want to be in there will be added. Roundtrip HTML puts the developer back in control.

# HTML Cleaning Dos and Don'ts

A thorough understanding of HTML is required for cleaning code at any level. Without an understanding of what the code is doing, you cannot possibly hope to clean it effectively. Here are some simple guidelines when it comes to cleaning and editing HTML:

- *Do* have a good understanding of the code you are dealing with. Without knowing exactly what each tag does, you will soon become lost as to which parts of the code are necessary and which parts can be deleted.

- *Don't* just delete stuff you're not familiar with. If you come across code you don't recognize, take the time to research it on the Web and find out what effect it's having before removing it.

- *Do* use regular expressions to search and replace elements that may crop up more than once in a document. Spend some time learning the basics, and you'll soon find that you can do some very powerful things and save yourself a whole lot of time.

- *Don't* just rely on the output of any HTML editor. Even when it comes to Dreamweaver, check that the HTML that is being output is clean and to your own personal satisfaction. Ultimately, you are responsible for the code you produce, whatever tool you have used.

- *Do* test each page thoroughly in all your target browsers. You may have accidentally cleaned something out that you thought wasn't important that may have been there for the benefit of a specific browser.

- *Don't* just rely on Dreamweaver to clean up bad code for you. Because so many things still require the judgment of the human eye, Dreamweaver cannot do this all on its own. As you saw with the Fireworks comments, sometimes you need to remove things by hand.

- *Do* make a backup of any pages before cleaning them up. Accidentally removing too much can wreck the design and layout of a page, as well as possibly damage its integrity. Make sure you have a backup of files so that if things do go wrong, it won't take you long to restore the file.

## What to Take Away from This Chapter

- Microsoft Office is good for the tasks it was designed for, but doesn't produce very web-friendly HTML.

- The Clean Up Word HTML command can help strip out a lot of the extra code Word puts into its HTML files.

- Dreamweaver uses HTML comments to store useful information in your document. Removing them before publishing a page can save a few kilobytes, but will disable a lot of the useful functionality of Dreamweaver for that file.

- The Clean Up HTML command can help remove Dreamweaver comments and other HTML comments, combine nested tags, and even strip out specific tags.

- Macromedia Fireworks also uses HTML comments to store useful information. There is no automatic way to strip these out of a page; with careful use of the Find and Replace function, however, you can remove them.

- Regular expressions are very powerful and can help in queries where an unknown factor is involved.

- Queries can be saved as an XML file and retrieved later to perform the same search again and again.

- Dreamweaver has a sophisticated Code view for editing HTML and JavaScript by hand.

- Roundtrip HTML puts the developer back in control of the code by not rewriting any code without the developer choosing to do so.

# Chapter 6

# Dynamic HTML

Objectives:

- Understand Dynamic HTML enough to use the Timeline comfortably.
- Create a scrolling slide show presentation.
- Build a drop-down menu using a timeline.

*Dynamic HTML* (DHTML) was introduced as a technology into what are commonly termed "version 4 browsers." Both Netscape Navigator and Microsoft Internet Explorer included DHTML support in their version 4 releases, signaling a major change in the way web pages would be constructed from that point forward.

Up until this point, there hadn't been much of a change in the way web pages were created. New versions of HTML were offering new tags and attributes, as well as stabilizing the way pages should be constructed; in essence, however, all that these improvements did was offer more of the same—tags that enabled you to display things on a page.

Of course, there was nothing wrong with this; in fact there was everything *right* about this, because HTML is a markup language, and this is what the new tags were enhancing. However, the web was changing, and HTML was starting to grow and become more than a basic markup language.

The time had come for a powerful supplement to HTML. It was no longer good enough to be able to display things in a certain way; developers were demanding the ability to control those elements via a standard scripting and Document Object Model. This is exactly what they were given, and this new set of technologies—this innovation that took that defining step beyond the simple markup of elements within a page—was called Dynamic HTML.

# What Is Dynamic HTML?

DHTML is a term describing four major new technologies: the *Document Object Model* (DOM), *Cascading Style Sheets* (CSS), and JavaScript, along with the ability to manipulate elements on the page.

Although all four of these are important parts of DHTML, it is absolute positioning of objects with CSS, combined with some JavaScript manipulation of those elements via the DOM, that is commonly thought of when we use the term DHTML. The DOM enables the developer to address and script nearly every object within a page. Combine this with CSS positioning, and you have a way to animate plain HTML.

However, a lot more powerful features are available than just making things move. The real power is in the fact that everything on a page is *scriptable*—that is to say, the developer can write some code to control almost anything within the document. Underpinning this is the DOM.

## The Document Object Model

The DOM is an interface into your document. It enables you to describe and address all the elements on your page. It describes the structure of a page, free from the hang-ups of dealing with content, and enables you to perform all sorts of useful tasks.

Think of it like a tree. The tree is an HTML file, planted in the ground (which is the web). Your tree has an `<html>` trunk, with `<head>` and `<body>` branches coming off it. Coming off the `<head>` branch is a `<title>` branch, a `<script>` branch, and a healthy selection of `<meta>` twigs. On each of these twigs is some fruit—your content.

In just the same way, your `<body>` branch might split off into a `<form>` branch, a `<table>` branch (with many `<td>` twigs on it) and a number of `<div>` branches.

If you need to know, for instance, how many `<div>` tags a document contains, or which radio buttons are checked, the DOM can access these elements through the logical branches and report back. By using the DOM, you can even change the values of elements, such as the position of a layer, or the contents of a text field. You can even pinpoint a pair of tags and pick up the content that lies between them.

The DOM enables you to address any given item on the page, and without being able to refer to items on the page, there is no way to control them. If the human race hadn't worked out how to give each family a name, and each individual within a family a name, how would we be able to direct information at any particular person? So it is with the DOM—it provides a methodology for addressing items in a page (and some other items as well).

However, the DOM goes further than this. In the dark and distant past when version 3 browsers ruled the roost, the DOM existed only in an extremely limited form. Any references to page elements were often limited in availability, and much of the hard work was left to whichever scripting language you were using at the time. The modern DOM (as defined by the W3C) is vastly superior. The DOM is now housed totally within the browser, meaning that whatever scripting language you choose to implement, the DOM is central and can be accessed by that language. What's more, every element in the page can be accessed, not just those under the banner of the scripting language being used.

For the day-to-day use of Dreamweaver, the DOM doesn't come into play all that much, but the developer has bigger fish to fry. Dreamweaver is like a browser in a lot of ways. It takes advantage of the DOM to address its own elements within HTML documents at design time. This means that when it comes to extending Dreamweaver, the DOM is used extensively.

## Cascading Style Sheets

CSS is probably the most commonly used aspect of DHTML at the moment. CSS enables the developer to describe all sorts of aspects of a page's appearance by attaching an appropriate style sheet to it. This could range from just stating the size, font, and color of some text, right through to where an item should be placed on the screen.

At a very basic level, CSS can be seen as a replacement for HTML's `<font>` tag. At a more complex level, CSS is a powerful tool for dictating the design and layout of information within an HTML document.

A lot of the day-to-day usefulness behind CSS comes from the fact that a style sheet is a reusable resource. Fundamentally, a single style sheet can be linked to all the web pages that make up a site. The style sheet defines how every element of the site looks and where it is placed on a page. By changing a style definition in the central style sheet, the changes filter down through the site without having to change any other files.

Theoretically, redesigning a web site could be just a case of swapping in a different style sheet; unfortunately, however, for some audiences we're a little ways from that. Inconsistent support in old browsers, disregard for the outlined standards, and the fact that some people are still using version 4 or earlier browsers mean that sites fully designed in CSS have to be very aware of the types of browsers the audience is using. It's a challenge to have a fully CSS-designed site working in all your visitors' browsers, but it's a challenge that can be met with a little care.

On top of this, CSS has the added benefit of enabling the web developer to separate styling information from the content. By keeping the style definitions in one document, the content in another, and allowing the browser to combine the two, a great amount of flexibility is gained. For example, this makes it very easy to provide different styling for a page under different circumstances, without having to produce and maintain multiple versions of the same document.

At the current time, most web sites, personal and professional, are using CSS for the formatting of their textual elements. Until more people upgrade their browsers to versions that support web standards (including CSS-1 and CSS-2), we are going to have to tread carefully with CSS layouts. When the support is there, we will begin to see more and more sites taking advantage of the positioning aspects of style sheets.

*Note*

CSS is covered in greater depth in the next two chap-
ters. If you are interested to read more still about CSS,
New Riders has published an excellent book by CSS
guru Eric Meyer on *CSS: Mastering the Language of Web
Design* is available from the same outlets as this book
(ISBN: 073571245X).

## Scripting Events

Even after a web page has loaded, the browser keeps an eye out for any
activity on the page. Every mouse movement and click, every press of a key
on the keyboard, and any other bits of information sent to the browser by
the operating system are monitored. If an element on the page is clicked,
or if a certain key is pressed, the browser knows about it. These are called
*events*, and alongside a scripting language such as JavaScript, they are the
technologies that enable the developer to make interactive web pages.

By assigning an action (*do this* or *do that*) to an event, the developer can
control the environment and how it behaves in response to the user. A basic
example of this is a graphical *rollover* effect, widely used in navigation to aid
feedback to the user. When the user passes the mouse pointer over a
menu graphic, the image is swapped for another. When the pointer moves
off the image, it is swapped back to the original.

You deal with two mouse events to make a rollover effect. The first is moving
the mouse over the image (`onMouseOver`), which triggers the code to
swap the image to the new one. The second is moving the mouse off the
image (`onMouseOut`), which triggers the code to swap the image back.

There are, of course, a great many more events than these. To make use of
every physical or electronically generated event (such as pressing a key or
printing a page), the browser must support it with an *event handler*
(`onKeyPress` or `onPrint`). Event handlers usually begin with *on* followed
by one or more words to describe what the event is. Microsoft Internet
Explorer 6 boasts an enormous array of event handlers, much more than
any other browser to date. Unless you're coding for an audience who all
use IE6, however, your choice is going to be limited to the more common
events.

Table 6.1 lists common event handlers, along with a description. As you can see, event handlers cover a wide range of different inputs and happenings that enable you to build more interactive web pages. Becoming familiar with the features that are at your disposal will enable you to build sites that engage the user.

| Table 6.1   Commonly Available Event Handlers | |
| --- | --- |
| Event Handler | Description |
| onBlur | An element, such as a form field, has lost focus. This could be the result of clicking away from the element, or even switching to another window. |
| onChange | The content of an object, such as a form field, has changed. |
| onClick | The mouse button has been completely pressed and released on the object. |
| onFocus | An element, such as a form field, has been given focus. This could be a result of clicking on it or moving to it with the Tab key. |
| onKeyDown | A keyboard key has been pressed to the down position. |
| onKeyPress | A keyboard key has been pressed down and released. |
| onKeyUp | A keyboard key has been released from being pressed. |
| onLoad | An element has finished loading into the browser. This is used most commonly in the <body> tag, and is called when the document has finished loading, but is equally useful on elements such as images. |
| onMouseDown | The mouse button has been pressed to the down position. |
| onMouseMove | The mouse pointer has been moved from its previous position. |
| onMouseOut | The mouse pointer has been moved from on top of an object. |
| onMouseOver | The mouse pointer has been moved on top of an object. |
| onMouseUp | The mouse button has been released from the down position. |
| onMove | The browser window is moved. |
| onReset | A Reset form button has been operated, or a form has been reset by a scripting language. |

| Event Handler | Description |
|---|---|
| onResize | The window or another object has been resized. |
| onSubmit | A form is being submitted. |
| onUnload | The document is about to be unloaded from the browser, either by closing the window or moving to a new page. |

## Absolute Positioning

In the early days of the web, HTML was always intended for structuring information, not visually styling a page. Because of this, plain vanilla HTML is not well equipped for laying out a page in the same way you might in a desktop publishing package. Although HTML allows some positioning of elements relative to each other, this has to be done by forcing things into place with tables and transparent GIFs and all sorts of jiggery-pokery.

DHTML brings with it the positioning ability of CSS. As the name suggests, absolute positioning enables the designer to place items on the page in a specific place—accurate to the pixel. At last, web designers have total control over the layout of a page.

The web developer, on the other hand, also has cause for celebration, because absolute positioning also results in dynamic positioning. Dynamic positioning enables the developer to move elements around the page at will, creating animations and other effects. The ability to move elements around the page brings with it some distinct advantages over static HTML:

- Advanced interaction can be created, changing the environment to react to the user's movements.

- Better use of screen real estate can be introduced, through the use of the Z-index (stacking order).

- Animation can add value to information and convey a high level of detail a lot more quickly than the written word can.

In DHTML, positioning is usually performed by using coordinates from the upper-left of an object's container. That is, if item A is on an otherwise empty page, its coordinates are taken from the upper-left corner of the page.

If item B is then placed inside item A, item B's coordinates will be taken from the upper-left corner of item A. This is because item A is a container for item B.

# Uses for Dynamic HTML

DHTML is not a technology with a specific purpose as such, but more of an enabling technology. You cannot really send people to your web site to show them the marvels of a page that you have made by taking advantage of the DOM, for example—or even absolute positioning, unless you've created some wild and wacky effect as a result of it. However, the use of DHTML does provide some real advantages, from more efficient formatting to improved usability.

## Efficient Formatting with CSS

As previously discussed, not only does CSS give you greater control over the appearance of your text, it also makes managing that text easier and takes up less code than using plain HTML formatting. Especially when it comes to items such as large tables, using CSS to format the content of a table can save literally tens of kilobytes on page size. Let's look at that in detail.

With HTML and the `<font>` tag, formatting needs to be applied to each table cell. The formatting does not persist across cells. As a simple example, suppose that you want the contents of each cell to be formatted with a basic Arial font group. Without CSS this is the amount of code you would need to add to each and every table cell:

```
<font face="Arial, Helvetica, sans-serif"></font>
```

This font tag and its appropriate closing tag are 49 bytes in size. Not very big, I'm sure you'll agree, but then consider what happens for a ten-by-ten table. Multiplying that code by 100 cells results in approximately 5KB of font tags alone.

Take a look at how you can format the table the same way using CSS:

```
<style type="text/css">
td {  font-family: Arial, Helvetica, sans-serif}
</style>
```

By adding this CSS code to the <head> tag of the page, you are adding about 1KB to the size of the file. However, no further formatting needs to be done. Regardless of the size of the table, no extra code needs to be added. Therefore for a table that is one-by-one, you need 1KB of code; and for a table that is ten-by-ten, you still need only 1KB of code.

## Animation

One of the primary features associated with the phrase *DHTML* is animation. Up until the advent of DHTML, there was no way to provide any sort of scripted animation (rather than sequential frame animation like a GIF can provide) on a web page without requiring that the users have a plug-in installed (such as Macromedia Flash). Because DHTML is part of the actual browser, no plug-in is required to make use of the animation possibilities created through dynamic positioning.

Recognizing how useful the possibility of animation can be, Dreamweaver has a built-in timeline tool. Similar to the principles involved in creating animations in Macromedia Director or Flash, the timeline enables the user to create animations simply. By defining *keyframes* as start and endpoints, Dreamweaver JavaScript functions can calculate the animation in between.

Animation on a web page can help bring your page to life. It can make diagrams and demonstrations more meaningful; it can enable you to create slick, attractive techniques for navigating around a site; or it can just make a page more entertaining and fun.

## Interactivity

Interactivity is a key part of web sites in the current climate. Static pages are seen to be the territory of books, and web pages should enable users to interact with the site. DHTML offers a host of choices when it comes to interactivity. The scripting events enable you to write code that reacts to user movements and selections.

This is the basis of web interactivity—displaying something that prompts a reaction from the user, which then the page can itself react to.

## Usability

DHTML gives you much more control over web pages. This control can then be exerted to advance a page in terms of usability. The ability to position elements more precisely and to modify their location in reaction to user movements means that sites can be designed to be much more user-friendly.

The same factors have implications in terms of accessibility. The greater control over design and interactivity enables developers to accommodate the needs of users who are partially sighted or have other special needs.

# The Dreamweaver Timeline

When it comes to scripted animation, the *Dreamweaver timeline* is your first port of call. The timeline works in a very similar way to the timelines of Macromedia Flash or Director. Figure 6.1 shows the Dreamweaver MX timeline. If you are used to working in Flash MX, it will look familiar.

**Figure 6.1**

The Dream-
weaver timeline
is similar to that
of Flash.

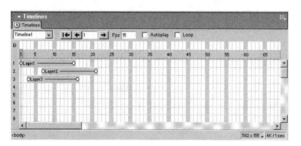

Offering the ability to animate the position, size, visibility, and stacking order of elements such as layers and to change the source (filename) of images, the timeline creates all sorts of possibilities for animation.

## What Can the Timeline Control?

The timeline controls three basic elements:

- Layers

- Images

- Behaviors

Although a list of only three controllable elements might not look that impressive, looking more closely at these reveals just how powerful the time-line can be.

## Controlling Layers

A Dreamweaver layer can house any HTML element. The timeline can control the $X$, $Y$, and $Z$ values of a layer, as well as its width, height, and visibility. Through this manipulation of layers, the doors are opened to the animation of all sorts of objects that can be placed in those layers.

Just about any HTML object you can name can be placed in a layer, and then that layer can be controlled by the timeline. This facility makes layers the tool of choice when it comes to building DHTML animations.

## Controlling Images

You also can control images by the timeline. Although you won't have as many options as a layer provides, it is possible to change the source (file-name) of an image on a timeline event. This allows for animated swapping of images, which can be very useful indeed.

### *Tip*

**If you need to animate an image in other ways than just changing its source, you can place the image inside a layer and control it that way.**

## Controlling Behaviors

Dreamweaver behaviors can be triggered by the timeline too. By adding a behavior to a point on the Behaviors channel of the timeline, that behavior will be triggered when the appropriate frame is reached.

The ability to control behaviors proves very useful when creating special effects (such as drop-down menus) and takes you beyond the level of the simple animation offered by moving layers around.

## Adding an Object to the Timeline

Adding objects to the timeline is very simple indeed. With the Timelines panel open (Window > Others > Timelines), just drag an image or layer onto the timeline in the desired place. Adding behaviors to the timeline is also easy (refer back to Figure 6.1); notice how the top line of the grid is labeled "B" for "behaviors." Click in the desired frame of that Behaviors channel, and then add a behavior to it as if it were any normal object. The behavior will be triggered when the timeline hits that frame.

## Controlling the Timeline with Behaviors

Before long, you'll want to use elements within your page to control the timeline, making it play, stop, and go to frames in reaction to events on the page.

Dreamweaver provides a useful set of controlling behaviors (in the Timelines section of the Behaviors panel) for doing most things. Play, Stop, and Go To Frame are included, covering most day-to-day needs. Other behaviors also are available for controlling the timeline from the Macromedia Exchange for Dreamweaver (http://www.macromedia.com/exchange/dreamweaver/), including my own Remote Timeline suite for controlling timelines across framesets, and Jaro von Flocken's Timeline Extensions suite for doing nifty things such as playing a timeline backward.

After you have created your timeline, adding controllers to your page isn't a complex task. Figure 6.2 shows a simple timeline controlling a layer, and a simple text Play button to start the timeline on the user's command.

Timeline behaviors can be attached to any normal HTML object. In Figure 6.2 I used a simple form button, but it's more likely that you would want to use an image as a more substantial button to trigger the behavior.

Figure 6.3 shows the Play Timeline behavior dialog box. As you can see, it's just a matter of selecting the name of the timeline. I strongly recommend that you give your timelines meaningful names, instead of sticking with the default Timeline1, Timeline2 pattern. After you have several timelines in place, you will find it easier to work with them if they have meaningful names attached to them.

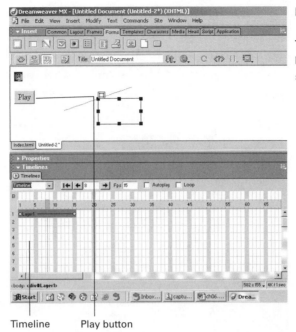

**Figure 6.2**

Timeline behaviors are simple to use.

Timeline          Play button

## Note

Dreamweaver allows multiple timelines to be used on one page. This can be very useful, because all the timelines run independently of each other. This enables you to create some more interesting effects, such as the drop-down menus we will look at later in this chapter.

**Figure 6.3**

The Play Timeline behavior dialog box.

# Building a Slide Show Presentation

At times, you may want to build a slide show or PowerPoint-style presentation on a web page. We're going to build a simple one here as a good example of using the Play and Stop Timeline behaviors.

The aim is to have a selection of layers containing the content, and to have them scroll in and out when you click a button (see Figure 6.4)—it's a very simple idea, but a helpful demonstration of attaching behaviors to both an object in a page (the Play button) and the timeline itself (the stop commands).

**Figure 6.4**

A simple slide show system using layers.

First, let's set up the layers. I'm going to use just three content layers, which is enough for our purposes (see Figure 6.5).

**Figure 6.5**

The layers are set up, ready for animating.

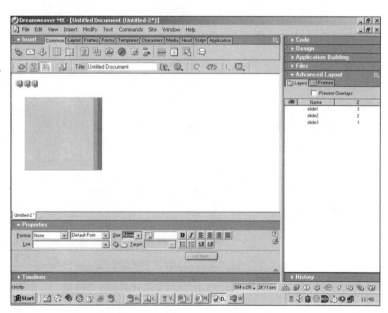

Each layer needs to be animated in two steps. First you need to move it into the center of the page (the viewing area) and make it stop there. Second, you need it to move back out again, off to the right. On your timeline, the animation should look like Figure 6.6.

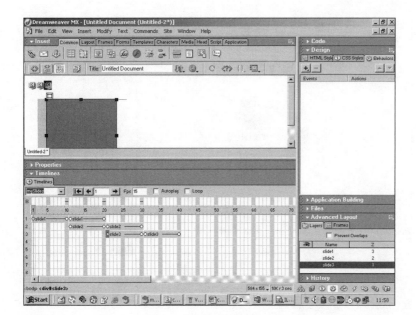

**Figure 6.6**

Animate each layer in turn.

Notice how one movement takes the layer to the viewing area, and the second moves it out. All you need to do now is add a Stop Timeline behavior to the middle frame, so that the timeline stops and waits for user input before moving on to the next slide. Click in the Behavior plane of the timeline at frame 10 and apply a Stop Timeline behavior, against All Timelines.

After you have done this, it's a case of performing the same process with the other layers on the same timeline. The effect you want to achieve is of one slide scrolling off and another coming on. To do this, you need to stagger the animation accordingly. Your first layer starts to scroll off on frame 11, so this is where you'll have your second layer scrolling on.

Repeat this process with all your layers until your timeline is complete. The timeline should visually indicate the effect it is achieving, and by clicking the forward and back timeline frame buttons in the Timelines panel, you can see your animation in action.

Next you use two more layers to cover up the starting and stopping positions of the content layers, so that the content layers can be seen only in your viewing area (see Figure 6.7). By giving these masking layers the same background color as the page background, they make an effective cover.

**Figure 6.7**

Only the "current" slide is visible.

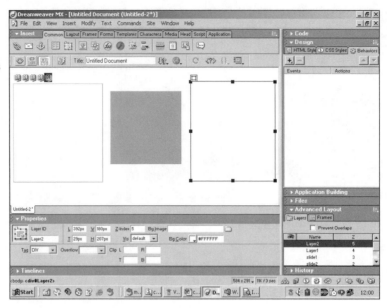

All that is left to do now is to add a button to control the timeline (see Figure 6.8). I'm going to create a text link and label it "Next." By attaching the Play Timeline behavior `onClick`, I can get the timeline to advance to the next slide each time I click the Next button.

**Figure 6.8**

The Play Timeline behavior sets the timeline running.

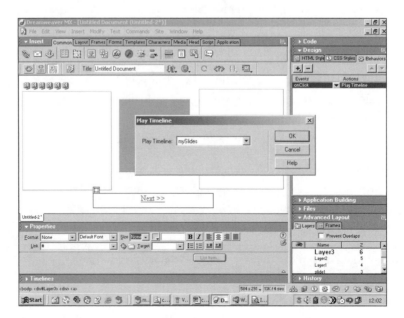

Our scrolling slide show presentation is complete. Press F12 to preview your work in your default browser. Remember that clicking the Next button will progress the animation through the different slides.

A finishing touch to the presentation would be to add the ability to return to the beginning after all the slides have been shown. For this, you can use the Go To Timeline Frame behavior. This behavior enables you to make the timeline jump to any given frame.

I'm going to add a simple "Back to the start" link and attach the Go To Timeline Frame behavior, sending the timeline back to frame 1 (see Figure 6.9).

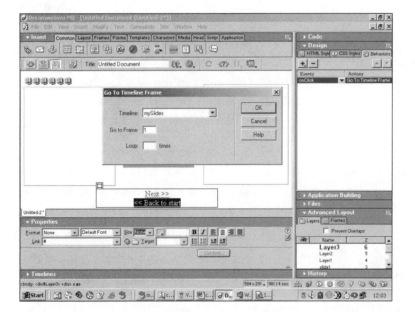

**Figure 6.9**

The Go To Timeline Frame behavior is used to send the animation back to the start.

That just adds a little finishing touch to the presentation, and now it really is complete. Later in this chapter, we'll look at taking what we've learned about the timeline and build a more complex system—a DHTML drop-down menu.

## *Note*

You can download the files used for all the examples in this chapter from www.dreamweaverfever.com.

# Overcoming Code Overhead

So, you've mastered the timeline and built some great little animations. However, have you stopped to look at the code that's being produced? If you have, then, like me, you're probably in the process of nursing your jaw, having retrieved it from the floor.

Performing DHTML animations with the timeline produces an awful lot of JavaScript. When you think about it, it's quite reasonable that such complex mathematics should produce this enormous amount of code, but it naturally goes against everything a web developer stands for in terms of file size.

This amount of JavaScript shouldn't really be a problem; it's all text and so will compress and download fairly quickly. (After all, 10KB of text will download quicker than 10KB of graphics due to the compression methods used by modems.) However, you should think carefully about what you're using DHTML animation for and whether it's really worth the overhead.

If you have timelines operating reusable elements, such as site navigation or other important elements, the code overhead is probably worth the wait. What you'll want to avoid is using timelines for nonessential items. Making a "Welcome to Our Web Site" message fly across the screen probably isn't a good use of resources when it comes to DHTML animation.

## Designing Reusable Timeline Code

When your timeline code is going to be used on multiple pages (or at least more than one page), it's worth taking the code out of the page and putting it into an external JavaScript file. It may be timeline code, but really it's no different from any other JavaScript and should be treated in the same way when it comes to saving download time.

After the code has been cut out and put into an external file, you can just set up a link to it:

```
<script src="timeline.js" type="text/javascript"></script>
```

Dreamweaver will happily read the timeline code from the linked file, and you will still be able to see your timeline when editing your pages. It is best to finalize your timeline before moving it out to its own file, however, because Dreamweaver cannot write to a timeline in an external file.

### Caution

**If you try to edit a timeline having already moved it out into a different JavaScript file, Dreamweaver will reenter the code into your page, causing scripting conflicts.**

## Browser Compatibility

With web technologies moving so fast, in the scheme of things DHTML is still quite a new technology. Whereas other web technologies take advantage of browser plug-ins, DHTML is so fundamental to the browser that it requires direct browser support. This results in its penetration to the market being a much slower process, because users must upgrade their browsers.

In addition to this, because support is coded into the browser directly by the manufacturers of the browser (and not by the company responsible for the innovation of the technology, as happens with plug-ins), the programmers can create their own interpretation of the technology. The result is that each browser uses DHTML in a different way.

For the developer, this is disastrous. When creating a DHTML page, you are severely limited in options. You can either design a specific version of each page for each browser you want to support, or you are restricted to the few aspects of DHTML that work in most browsers.

Because developing multiple pages is very expensive in terms of time, the people at Macromedia have chosen to concentrate on support for those elements common between the major browsers. This results in Dreamweaver generating DHTML code that, with careful implementation, will work across all major browsers with DHTML support. Where there are differences that are easily compensated for, the Dreamweaver code addresses those differences. This is also the reason why the Dreamweaver code can appear to be over-verbose and unwieldy. Addressing all the differences in so many browsers can involve many lines of code that wouldn't be needed if the code had to work only in one particular browser.

# Building a Drop-Down Menu

A question I see asked a great deal in the Dreamweaver community is this: "How do I build a drop-down menu like those on Microsoft.com?" The answer, surprisingly enough, involves the use of timelines.

Of course, with Dreamweaver MX comes the new Show Pop-up Menu behavior, which to a basic level will enable you to accomplish this task. As soon as you need to take this concept further, however—refining the functionality and customizing the design—you need to be able to build drop-down menus yourself.

Those of you with any experience in using layers in Dreamweaver will have worked out that the main principle behind drop-down menus is the Show-Hide Layer behavior. However, the Show-Hide Layer behavior is not enough on its own to achieve this effect. Figure 6.10 shows a typical example of a drop-down menu, as used on Microsoft.com.

**Figure 6.10**

Drop-down menu on Microsoft.com.

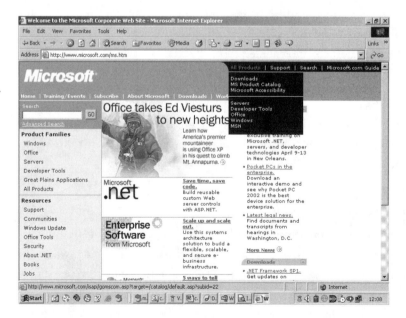

If we examine just one drop-down menu (you would probably have several in a row on a web site), we can identify several key elements:

- The trigger image, which opens the menu

- The menu layer itself

- The images making up the menu items

If you were to place a Show-Hide Layer behavior to display the menu onMouseOver of the trigger image, and another to close the menu onMouseOut, the result would be that the menu would close before the user is able to get the mouse pointer onto any of the menu items. This is because the menu would close as soon as the mouse pointer leaves the trigger image, and there would then be no menu options to sustain the menu being open.

You can overcome this by using the timeline to delay the closure of the menu. So, instead of having a Show-Hide Layer behavior closing the menu onMouseOut, you trigger a timeline onMouseOut, which then closes the menu after a delay.

First things first, you need to create your base elements before you can think about timelines and behaviors. The trigger image is the menu's opener. When the user moves the mouse pointer atop this image, the menu will open (see Figure 6.11).

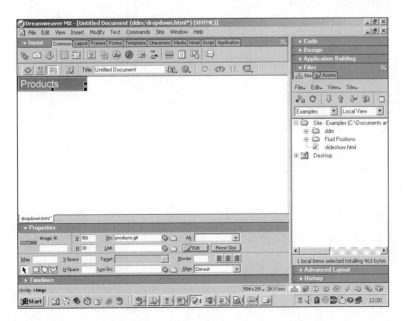

**Figure 6.11**

Opening the menu with your mouse pointer.

Next you need to create a layer to house your menu items. Give your layer a meaningful name. If you're building, for example, a Products menu, it might be sensible to name your layer productsMenu.

Make sure the layer is a good size to house the images. It pays to work out the dimensions of the layer by taking the width of your images, and by adding together the heights of all the menu items. After the layer has been completely set up, you can insert the menu items.

Now for that timeline we were talking about. We need to create a time-line with only one behavior in it—no moving layers, no changing images, just a single behavior. This will be a Show-Hide Layer behavior to hide the productsMenu layer after a number of seconds (see Figure 6.12).

**Figure 6.12**

Create a timeline with only one behavior.

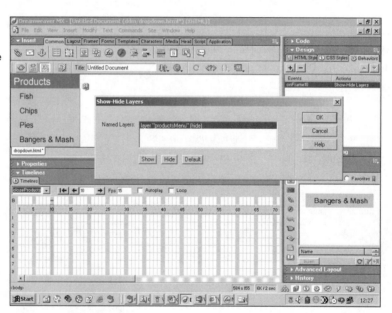

I've found that usually about 10 frames feels right with the timeline running at its default speed of 15 frames per second. This equates to roughly two thirds of a second. Depending on the look and feel of your site, you might want to experiment with this to find a setting that feels right.

This timeline will then close your menu when it hits frame 10. This should give the user time to move between menu items. It's then a case of playing your timeline onMouseOut instead of just hiding the layer straightaway.

A number of behaviors must be applied to both the trigger image and all
the menu items. Let's take a close look at those:

| | | |
|---|---|---|
| OnMouseOver | Go To Timeline Frame | Force the timeline back to the start. |
| OnMouseOut | Play Timeline | Initiate the closing of the menu. |
| OnMouseOver | Stop Timeline | Make sure the menu isn't closed if the timeline has already been started. |

And on the trigger image only:

| | | |
|---|---|---|
| OnMouseOver | Show-Hide Layer | Open the productsMenu layer. |

These four behaviors, added to the trigger image, and the first three,
added to the menu items, should ensure that the menu opens and closes
at the appropriate times (see Figure 6.13).

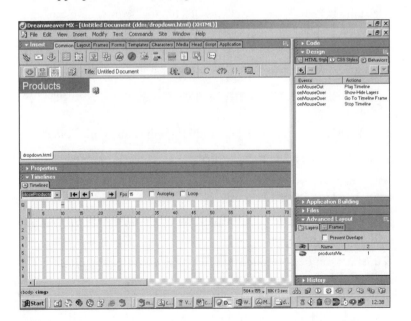

**Figure 6.13**

Viewing all four
behaviors.

### Tip

When applying behaviors to the Behaviors channel of the timeline, the cursor can sometimes get stuck and not want to leave that channel. This makes it impossible to add any behaviors to any other objects. The way to release the cursor is to click elsewhere in the timeline, and the cursor will be freed up.

Finally, you need to use the Layers panel to set the visibility of the menu layer to Hidden so that the menu isn't displayed by default.

The timeline can be tweaked to change the delay before the menu closes. Depending on the number of menus you have and the desired feel of your web site, you might like to play with this setting.

## What to Take Away from This Chapter

- Dynamic HTML is a relatively new technology comprising the Document Object Model, Cascading Style Sheets, scripting events, and absolute positioning.

- Uses for DHTML range from the traditional to the more radical.

- CSS can save both development and download time by its frugal use of code.

- Simple animation can be achieved through dynamic positioning.

- DHTML can be a key to web interactivity.

- Many usability issues are raised by the use of DHTML and its capability to add to the user experience.

- The Dreamweaver timeline enables you to control layers, images, and behaviors across a time scale.

- Timelines can be controlled by behaviors—starting, stopping, and making them jump to specific frames.

- A large amount of JavaScript is needed to produce a DHTML animation, but this can be pooled into an external file to save download time.

- Because it's a new technology, browser support for DHTML is far from perfect.

- You can create drop-down menu effects using DHTML layers and the Dreamweaver timeline.

# Part II

## Workflow and Design Control

# Chapter 7

# Cascading Style Sheets

Objectives:

- Understand Cascading Style Sheets and their place in web development.
- Gain a thorough understanding of the technology underpinning CSS.
- Build style sheets with greater confidence and skill.

The first part of this book briefly covered *Cascading Style Sheets* (CSS) and their importance in the context of DHTML. This chapter focuses on CSS in greater detail, and you will learn how Dreamweaver enables you to create complex style sheets quickly and with relative ease.

This chapter also discusses the support that various browsers have for CSS and the standards set out for this technology by the World Wide Web Consortium (W3C).

As a Dreamweaver user, you should come to this chapter with an understanding of how CSS works within Dreamweaver on a day-to-day basis. As I said in the introduction to this book, I cannot try to teach you the basics if we are going to progress to the really meaty stuff. If you're not already comfortable with using style sheets and the Dreamweaver CSS panel, maybe it's time to put the book down for half an hour or so and play with Dreamweaver. That's probably all it takes—in just half an hour, you should have all the knowledge you need to progress through this chapter. Now, on with the show.

Cascading Style Sheets are a vital part of a modern developer's toolkit, and must be studied in detail to gain the fullest benefit from them. Web developers who don't know CSS like the back of their hand are not equipped to develop for today's web. It's as simple as that. The days of using standard HTML for text formatting, for example, are way behind us. Everything must focus on the future, and that future is standards-shaped. Particularly with the advent of XML, CSS becomes of ever-increasing importance and should not be pushed to the sidelines. What's more, with CSS degrading so gracefully in older browsers, there's no reason not to push forward with confidence that you are not causing your visitors problems.

## Browser Support

At present, browser support for Cascading Style Sheets is pretty good, but not 100% there. Basically, there are plenty of browsers with good strong support for CSS, but it's taking a little while for the great-unwashed public to upgrade. At the very least, the browsers in use tend to have acceptable support for CSS for text formatting, and a good number go beyond that too.

The most up-to-date browsers (for instance, Internet Explorer 6) support advanced features, such as positioning, very well, and most CSS effects can be reliably used. However, older browsers (such as the version 4 releases of Internet Explorer and Netscape Navigator) are a bit shakier when it comes to CSS positioning. They do fairly well when it comes to the formatting of text, however.

What this means to the developer is that you're constantly coming up against problems when it comes to browser support. It's the same old story but with newer technology—what works in one browser may not work in another. The main difference, however, is that CSS is at last a technology designed specifically for the job. Right from the outset, CSS was developed to help the developer lay out pages and create visual style, not just provide an information structure. This means that when the standards work their way through to the major browsers (they're nearly there), you will be able to deliver stronger, better-designed pages.

# Cascading Style Sheets and the W3C

The World Wide Web Consortium was founded in October 1994, with an aim to "lead the World Wide Web to its full potential by developing common protocols that promote its evolution and ensure its interoperability." As a body, it is responsible for laying out specifications and guidelines for web technologies and is generally accepted as the group to listen to when it comes to the web. The W3C (`http://www.w3.org`) recommended the first level of Cascading Style Sheets (CSS1) to be adopted by web developers.

Further levels of CSS are also in existence. The current level, CSS2, was made a recommendation by the W3C in May 1998, and CSS3 is not too far around the corner now. CSS1 is currently the best-supported level of CSS, because it has been around the longest. Working in CSS1, web developers can be fairly sure that the code will work in most of their viewers' browsers, because it's been around long enough to settle and become stable.

The W3C web site holds all the latest specs and documentation for all versions of CSS, as well as the many other technologies they support (such as XML). It is worthwhile spending a few minutes every month or so browsing around the W3C web site, keeping an eye on the latest developments. Technology moves very quickly in web development, and it pays to keep your finger on the pulse.

The bulk of the chapter covers CSS in detail. Because CSS1 is the more widely supported of the CSS levels, I have focused on that. Any further information you require can be found in the following chapter, or in the CSS section of the W3C web site.

# Style Sheets in Detail

In the same way that it is important to know HTML when using a visual editor such as Dreamweaver to understand the way the tool is working, it is equally important to know how CSS works. Although Dreamweaver can make life so much easier by enabling you to write new style sheets within its visual environment, unless you have an understanding of the technology that lies underneath, you are likely to get into a mess sooner or later.

In this chapter, you will learn the basic syntax for creating styles. After you learn the code that Dreamweaver is writing for you, you will be able to use the CSS editor with much greater effect and with greater precision and confidence.

## Style Sheet Syntax Primer

The syntax for constructing a style sheet rule is very simple. Suppose, for instance, that I want to make sure that all the horizontal rules on a page are blue. I would create a rule like this:

```
hr {
    color : Blue;
    background-color : Transparent;
}
```

If I want to style all my paragraphs in black, 12px Arial, this again would be a simple task:

```
p {
    font-family : Arial, Helvetica, sans-serif;
    font-size : 12px;
    color : #000;
    background-color : transparent;
}
```

This example shows a case where an HTML tag has been redefined. The instruction being given to the browser is something like this: "Don't use your own definition of what a paragraph tag should look like; *this* is how a paragraph should look!" This technique proves very useful, because it requires no extra markup in the page. Just redefining existing tags offers a thorough and simple way to style a page.

If I want to apply a different style to all paragraphs marked with `class="errorMessage"`, however, I could do so as follows:

```
.errorMessage{
    font-family: Arial, Helvetica, sans-serif;
    font-size : 14px;
    color : #fff;
    background-color : #f00;
    font-weight : bold;
}
```

This is an example of a class definition. You can apply a class to any number of tags, which then take on the styling of that class. It's useful for common styles that you want to apply to a number of different objects, but it isn't as clean and simple as redefining an existing HTML tag.

## Units of Measure

Cascading Style Sheets are far more flexible than HTML when it comes to units of measure. Whereas HTML enables you to declare values only in pixels or percentages, color names or hexadecimal equivalents, CSS offers a host of different units, which means superior control and convenience.

Like HTML, you can declare property values in CSS in two ways: absolute and relative.

### Absolute Values

Absolute values have a specific and fixed value. They are not dependent on any runtime factors or influences. An absolute value is a static unit of measure defined against a scale. An example of an absolute value is the point:

```
{font-size: 12 pt}
```

Table 7.1 gives examples of absolute values.

| Table 7.1 | Absolute Value Examples | |
| --- | --- | --- |
| Unit | Abbreviation | Example |
| Point | pt | `{ text-indent: 48pt }` |
| Pixel | px | `{ text-indent: 14px }` |
| Pica | pc | `{ text-indent: 1pc }` |
| Centimeter | cm | `{ text-indent: 2cm }` |
| Inch | in | `{ text-indent: 1in }` |
| Millimeter | mm | `{ text-indent: 36mm }` |

In this world of different viewing platforms and browsers, however, almost nothing is absolute (as physics would define it). Macintosh computers might display 12 pixels in a different size from a PC, for example. Fortunately, you can be sure that 6 pixels is always half the size of 12 pixels, because the mathematics will always hold true, no matter how the system chooses to display things.

## Relative Values

Relative values are dependent on, or interconnected with, another value and have no fixed value of their own. They cannot be strictly defined because the way they are rendered depends on a runtime factor. Examples of relative values are bolder, lighter, or even 60%.

```
{font-weight: bolder}
```

Relative values are great for making pages that display in a way that depends on, for example, the size of the browser window. Relative values often provide a better viewing experience for your audience, because the sizes will adjust to their circumstances. Table 7.2 lists examples of relative values. (An em is the size of an uppercase *M* in the current font size.)

| Table 7.2 | Relative Value Examples | |
| --- | --- | --- |
| Unit | Abbreviation | Example |
| Em | em | `{ text-indent: 6em }` |
| X | ex | `{ line-height: 3ex }` |
| Percent | % | `{ line-height: 60% }` |

## Colors

Color is a crucial element in both the communication of information and in aesthetic design and style. CSS offers fantastic control over color and, as always, offers much more control and color options than HTML.

### Color Values

Whereas HTML offers only two ways to specify a color, CSS offers the developer four different ways:

- By color name
- By hexadecimal RGB value
- By decimal RGB value
- By RGB percentage

This range of options offers superior control over color and enables the developer to work with as precise color as delivered by a graphic designer. The primary colors of light are red, green, and blue. Computer screens therefore use a mixture of these three colors to create the correct color onscreen. For this reason, most colors on computers are expressed in *red*, *green*, and *blue* (RGB) values.

CSS enables you to specify RGB values in a number of ways. The first of these is hexadecimal RGB. Any Dreamweaver developer will be familiar with notation such as #FFFFFF for expressing a color. This is a hexadecimal value, which is denoted with a hash. The six numbers are actually three pairs, the first pair giving a value for red, the second for green, and the third for blue. The colors are mixed over a scale of 256 degrees, with FF (or 255 in decimal) being the highest. In CSS a color would be expressed in hexadecimal like this:

```
{ color: #996699 }
```

CSS also enables you to express colors in their more familiar decimal RGB vales:

```
{ color: rgb(153, 102, 153) }
```

As shown in the preceding example, decimal RGB values must be preceded by the letters *rgb*, and then the numbers must be separated with commas and enclosed in brackets.

The final way to express color is using RGB percentages. With this system, 100% equates to 255 and 0% to 0.

```
{ color: rgb(60%, 40%, 60%) }
```

Although less commonly seen, this method of specifying colors can prove useful if you are working with a graphics package that also uses percentages to define its color palette.

## The Color Table

If you are familiar with basic HTML, you will be familiar with the way that names can be used to specify a particular color. This can make life a bit easier, because color names can be more readily memorized than numbers. Also the color names are far more descriptive, in case you need to worry about anyone studying your code.

Usually, you will find that specifying absolute hexadecimal or decimal RGB values will offer a greater degree of control, however. Table 7.3 lists the reserved color names and a conversion of their values.

| Table 7.3 | HTML Color Name Translations | | |
| --- | --- | --- | --- |
| Color Name | Hexadecimal | Decimal | Percentage |
| Aliceblue | F0F8FF | 240, 248, 255 | 94%, 97%, 100% |
| Antiquewhite | FAEBD7 | 250, 235, 215 | 98%, 92%, 84% |
| Aqua | 00FFFF | 0, 255, 255 | 0%, 100%, 100% |
| Aquamarine | 7FFFD4 | 127, 255, 212 | 50%, 100%, 83% |
| Azure | F0FFFF | 240, 255, 255 | 94%, 100%, 100% |
| Beige | F5F5DC | 245, 245, 220 | 96%, 96%, 86% |
| Bisque | FFE4C4 | 255, 228, 196 | 100%, 89%, 77% |
| Black | 000000 | 0, 0, 0 | 0%, 0%, 0% |
| Blanchedalmond | FFEBCD | 255, 235, 205 | 100%, 92%, 80% |
| Blue | 0000FF | 0, 0, 255 | 0%, 0%, 100% |

| Color Name | Hexadecimal | Decimal | Percentage |
|---|---|---|---|
| Blueviolet | 8A2BE2 | 138, 43, 226 | 54%, 17%, 89% |
| Brown | A52A2A | 165, 42, 42 | 65%, 16%, 16% |
| Burlywood | DEB887 | 222, 184, 135 | 87%, 72%, 53% |
| Cadetblue | 5F9EA0 | 95, 158, 160 | 37%, 62%, 63% |
| Chartreuse | 7FFF00 | 127, 255, 0 | 50%, 100%, 0% |
| Chocolate | D2691E | 210, 105, 30 | 82%, 41%, 12% |
| Coral | FF7F50 | 255, 127, 80 | 100%, 50%, 31% |
| Cornflowerblue | 6495ED | 100, 149, 237 | 39%, 58%, 93% |
| Cornsilk | FFF8DC | 255, 248, 220 | 100%, 97%, 86% |
| Crimson | DC143C | 220, 20, 60 | 86%, 8%, 24% |
| Cyan | 00FFFF | 0, 255, 255 | 0%, 100%, 100% |
| Darkblue | 00008B | 0, 0, 139 | 0%, 0%, 55% |
| Darkcyan | 008B8B | 0, 139, 139 | 0%, 55%, 55% |
| Darkgoldenrod | B8860B | 184, 134, 11 | 72%, 53%, 4% |
| Darkgray | A9A9A9 | 169, 169, 169 | 66%, 66%, 66% |
| Darkgreen | 006400 | 0, 100, 0 | 0%, 39%, 0% |
| Darkkhaki | BDB76B | 189, 183, 107 | 74%, 72%, 42% |
| Darkmagenta | 8B008B | 139, 0, 139 | 55%, 0%, 55% |
| Darkolivegreen | 556B2F | 85, 107, 47 | 33%, 42%, 18% |
| Darkorange | FF8C00 | 255, 140, 0 | 100%, 55%, 0% |
| Darkorchid | 9932CC | 153, 50, 204 | 60%, 20%, 80% |
| Darkred | 8B0000 | 139, 0, 0 | 55%, 0%, 0% |
| Darksalmon | E9967A | 233, 150, 122 | 91%, 59%, 48% |
| Darkseagreen | 8FBC8F | 143, 188, 143 | 56%, 74%, 56% |
| Darkslateblue | 483D8B | 72, 61, 139 | 28%, 24%, 55% |
| Darkslategray | 2F4F4F | 47, 79, 79 | 18%, 31%, 31% |
| Darkturquoise | 00CED1 | 0, 206, 209 | 0%, 81%, 82% |
| Darkviolet | 9400D3 | 148, 0, 211 | 58%, 0%, 83% |
| Deeppink | FF1493 | 255, 20, 147 | 100%, 8%, 58% |
| Deepskyblue | 00BFFF | 0, 191, 255 | 0%, 75%, 100% |
| Dimgray | 696969 | 105, 105, 105 | 41%, 41%, 41% |
| Dodgerblue | 1E90FF | 30, 144, 255 | 12%, 56%, 100% |
| Firebrick | B22222 | 178, 34, 34 | 70%, 13%, 13% |

*Continues*

| Table 7.3 | Continued | | |
|-----------|-----------|--|--|
| Color Name | Hexadecimal | Decimal | Percentage |
| Floralwhite | FFFAF0 | 255, 250, 240 | 100%, 98%, 94% |
| Forestgreen | 228B22 | 34, 139, 34 | 13%, 55%, 13% |
| Fuchsia | FF00FF | 255, 0, 255 | 100%, 0%, 100% |
| Gainsboro | DCDCDC | 220, 220, 220 | 86%, 86%, 86% |
| Ghostwhite | F8F8FF | 248, 248, 255 | 97%, 97%, 100% |
| Gold | FFD700 | 255, 215, 0 | 100%, 84%, 0% |
| Goldenrod | DAA520 | 218, 165, 32 | 85%, 65%, 13% |
| Gray | 808080 | 128, 128, 128 | 50%, 50%, 50% |
| Green | 008000 | 0, 128, 0 | 0%, 50%, 0% |
| Greenyellow | ADFF2F | 173, 255, 47 | 68%, 100%, 18% |
| Honeydew | F0FFF0 | 240, 255, 240 | 94%, 100%, 94% |
| Hotpink | FF69B4 | 255, 105, 180 | 100%, 41%, 71% |
| Indianred | CD5C5C | 205, 92, 92 | 80%, 36%, 36% |
| Indigo | 4B0082 | 75, 0, 130 | 29%, 0%, 51% |
| Ivory | FFFFF0 | 255, 255, 240 | 100%, 100%, 94% |
| Khaki | F0E68C | 240, 230, 140 | 94%, 90%, 55% |
| Lavender | E6E6FA | 230, 230, 250 | 90%, 90%, 98% |
| Lavenderblush | FFF0F5 | 255, 240, 245 | 100%, 94%, 96% |
| Lawngreen | 7CFC00 | 124, 252, 0 | 49%, 99%, 0% |
| Lemonchiffon | FFFACD | 255, 250, 205 | 100%, 98%, 80% |
| Lightblue | ADD8E6 | 173, 216, 230 | 68%, 85%, 90% |
| Lightcoral | F08080 | 240, 128, 128 | 94%, 50%, 50% |
| Lightcyan | E0FFFF | 224, 255, 255 | 88%, 100%, 100% |
| Lightgolden rodyellow | FAFAD2 | 250, 250, 210 | 98%, 98%, 82% |
| Lightgreen | 90EE90 | 144, 238, 144 | 56%, 93%, 56% |
| Lightgrey | D3D3D3 | 211, 211, 211 | 83%, 83%, 83% |
| Lightpink | FFB6C1 | 255, 182, 193 | 100%, 71%, 76% |
| Lightsalmon | FFA07A | 255, 160, 122 | 100%, 63%, 48% |
| Lightseagreen | 20B2AA | 32, 178, 170 | 13%, 70%, 67% |
| Lightskyblue | 87CEFA | 135, 206, 250 | 53%, 81%, 98% |
| Lightslategray | 778899 | 119, 136, 153 | 47%, 53%, 60% |

| Color Name | Hexadecimal | Decimal | Percentage |
| --- | --- | --- | --- |
| Lightsteelblue | B0C4DE | 176, 196, 222 | 69%, 77%, 87% |
| Lightyellow | FFFFE0 | 255, 255, 224 | 100%, 100%, 88% |
| Lime | 00FF00 | 0, 255, 0 | 0%, 100%, 0% |
| Limegreen | 32CD32 | 50, 205, 50 | 20%, 80%, 20% |
| Linen | FAF0E6 | 250, 240, 230 | 98%, 94%, 90% |
| Magenta | FF00FF | 255, 0, 255 | 100%, 0%, 100% |
| Maroon | 800000 | 128, 0, 0 | 50%, 0%, 0% |
| Mediumaquamarine | 66CDAA | 102, 205, 170 | 40%, 80%, 67% |
| Mediumblue | 0000CD | 0, 0, 205 | 0%, 0%, 80% |
| Mediumorchid | BA55D3 | 186, 85, 211 | 73%, 33%, 83% |
| Mediumpurple | 9370DB | 147, 112, 219 | 58%, 44%, 86% |
| Mediumseagreen | 3CB371 | 60, 179, 113 | 24%, 70%, 44% |
| Mediumslateblue | 7B68EE | 123, 104, 238 | 48%, 41%, 93% |
| Mediumspringgreen | 00FA9A | 0, 250, 154 | 0%, 98%, 60% |
| Mediumturquoise | 48D1CC | 72, 209, 204 | 28%, 82%, 80% |
| Mediumvioletred | C71585 | 199, 21, 133 | 78%, 8%, 52% |
| Midnightblue | 191970 | 25, 25, 112 | 10%, 10%, 44% |
| Mintcream | F5FFFA | 245, 255, 250 | 96%, 100%, 98% |
| Mistyrose | FFE4E1 | 255, 228, 225 | 100%, 89%, 88% |
| Moccasin | FFE4B5 | 255, 228, 181 | 100%, 89%, 71% |
| Navajowhite | FFDEAD | 255, 222, 173 | 100%, 87%, 68% |
| Navy | 000080 | 0, 0, 128 | 0%, 0%, 50% |
| Oldlace | FDF5E6 | 253, 245, 230 | 99%, 96%, 90% |
| Olive | 808000 | 128, 128, 0 | 50%, 50%, 0% |
| Olivedrab | 6B8E23 | 107, 142, 35 | 42%, 56%, 14% |
| Orange | FFA500 | 255, 165, 0 | 100%, 65%, 0% |
| Orangered | FF4500 | 255, 69, 0 | 100%, 27%, 0% |
| Orchid | DA70D6 | 218, 112, 214 | 85%, 44%, 84% |
| Palegoldenrod | EEE8AA | 238, 232, 170 | 93%, 91%, 67% |
| Palegreen | 98FB98 | 152, 251, 152 | 60%, 98%, 60% |
| Paleturquoise | AFEEEE | 175, 238, 238 | 69%, 93%, 93% |
| Palevioletred | DB7093 | 219, 112, 147 | 86%, 44%, 58% |
| Papayawhip | FFEFD5 | 255, 239, 213 | 100%, 94%, 84% |

*Continues*

| Table 7.3 | Continued | | |
|-----------|-----------|---|---|
| Color Name | Hexadecimal | Decimal | Percentage |
| Peachpuff | FFDAB9 | 255, 218, 185 | 100%, 85%, 73% |
| Peru | CD853F | 205, 133, 63 | 80%, 52%, 25% |
| Pink | FFC0CD | 255, 192, 205 | 100%, 75%, 80% |
| Plum | DDA0DD | 221, 160, 221 | 87%, 63%, 87% |
| Powderblue | B0E0E6 | 176, 224, 230 | 69%, 88%, 90% |
| Purple | 800080 | 128, 0, 128 | 50%, 0%, 50% |
| Red | FF0000 | 255, 0, 0 | 100%, 0%, 0% |
| Rosybrown | BC8F8F | 188, 143, 143 | 74%, 56%, 56% |
| Royalblue | 4169E1 | 65, 105, 225 | 25%, 41%, 88% |
| Saddlebrown | 8B4513 | 139, 69, 19 | 55%, 27%, 7% |
| Salmon | FA8072 | 250, 128, 114 | 98%, 50%, 45% |
| Sandybrown | F4A460 | 244, 164, 96 | 96%, 64%, 38% |
| Seagreen | 2E8B57 | 46, 139, 87 | 18%, 55%, 34% |
| Seashell | FFF5EE | 255, 245, 238 | 100%, 96%, 93% |
| Sienna | A0522D | 160, 82, 45 | 63%, 32%, 18% |
| Silver | C0C0C0 | 192, 192, 192 | 75%, 75%, 75% |
| Skyblue | 87CEED | 135, 206, 237 | 53%, 81%, 93% |
| Slateblue | 6A5ACD | 106, 90, 205 | 42%, 35%, 80% |
| Slategray | 708090 | 112, 128, 144 | 44%, 50%, 56% |
| Snow | FFFAFA | 255, 250, 250 | 100%, 98%, 98% |
| Springgreen | 00FF7F | 0, 255, 127 | 0%, 100%, 50% |
| Steelblue | 4682B4 | 70, 130, 180 | 27%, 51%, 71% |
| Tan | D2B48C | 210, 180, 140 | 82%, 71%, 55% |
| Teal | 008080 | 0, 128, 128 | 0%, 50%, 50% |
| Thistle | D8BFD8 | 216, 191, 216 | 85%, 75%, 85% |
| Tomato | FF6347 | 255, 99, 71 | 100%, 39%, 28% |
| Turquoise | 40E0D0 | 64, 224, 208 | 25%, 88%, 82% |
| Violet | EE82EE | 238, 130, 238 | 93%, 51%, 93% |
| Wheat | F5DEB3 | 245, 222, 179 | 96%, 87%, 70% |
| White | FFFFFF | 255, 255, 255 | 100%, 100%, 100% |
| Whitesmoke | F5F5F5 | 245, 245, 245 | 96%, 96%, 96% |
| Yellow | FFFF00 | 255, 255, 0 | 100%, 100%, 0% |
| Yellowgreen | A9CD32 | 169, 205, 50 | 66%, 80%, 20% |

## The *Color* Property

The syntax for setting the `color` property is as follows:

```
{ color: colorname | #hex | rgb(R, G, B) | rgb(R%, G%, B%) }
```

The `color` property sets a foreground color such as the color of text or a horizontal rule. The text within a paragraph could have a color assigned in any of these ways:

```
P { color: #708090 }
```

```
P { color: rgb(112, 128, 144) }
```

```
P { color: rgb(44%, 50%, 56%) }
```

```
P { color: slategray }
```

Each of the preceding snippets of HTML performs the same task: setting the foreground color of a paragraph to a specific color. For a paragraph, the foreground element is obviously the text. However, CSS always takes us further than HTML, so it's even possible to specify a background color for an element such as a paragraph.

### *Note*

In a style sheet, a color setting should always be paired with a background-color setting. Otherwise you could end up setting your foreground color to the same value as the user's own defined background color—rendering your object invisible.

## Backgrounds

CSS enables you to manipulate backgrounds in a number of ways. From background colors, through background images and the way they display, CSS strives to offer the greatest amount of control.

## Background Colors

The syntax for setting the background color is as follows:

```
{ background-color: colorname | #hex | rgb(R, G, B) |
↪rgb(R%, G%, B%) }
```

The `background-color` property, as you would expect, offers control over the background color of an HTML element. When assigned to the `<body>` tag, this would be the page background, and it could even be assigned to a paragraph or table cell.

The background color will fill the entire assigned background space for any object. For example, an `<h1>` tag takes control of the entire line of text, so its background color would also.

The CSS for this effect looks like this:

```
h1 { background-color: #AAAACC }
```

## Background Images

The syntax for setting a background image is as follows:

```
{ background-image: url(file path) }
```

Just like HTML, a CSS background image runs behind any content within that element and reveals the background only in the gaps. A background image is addressed with a URL, and a relative or absolute path to the image should be entered.

### Tip

If you plan to use a central style sheet instead of including CSS information in each individual page, you may want to consider using an absolute (site-relative) path to your image, to help to ensure that the path is correct each time the style is applied, regardless of circumstance.

For example, a background image could be applied to the entire page by attaching a style to the `<body>` tag:

```
body { background-image: url(/assets/sandstone.gif) }
```

### Caution

> If you try to use an image that has brackets in its name as a background, this will cause problems with the way CSS uses brackets to encase URLs. Do not use characters such as brackets in filenames—stick to letters and numbers. This is the only way to ensure you do not come across such problems on the different systems on which your site is required to work.

### Tiling Backgrounds

The syntax for setting the tiling properties of a background image is as follows:

```
{ background-repeat: repeat | repeat-x | repeat-y | no-repeat }
```

The background-repeat option enables you to control how a background image should tile. Four options are available:

- Repeat in both X and Y directions.
- Repeat only in the X direction.
- Repeat only in the Y direction.
- Don't repeat at all.

```
body { background-image: url(/assets/sandstone.gif);
       background-repeat: no-repeat }
```

### Scrolling and Static Backgrounds

The syntax for setting the background attachment property is as follows:

```
{ background-attachment: scroll | fixed }
```

CSS allows for a background image to be "attached" to the page and scroll as the page scrolls, or for it to be fixed in the same position on the screen regardless of how the page is scrolled.

```
body { background-image: url(/assets/sandstone.gif);
       background-attachment: fixed }
```

The ability to fix the position of a background can alleviate the need to create a very large or tiled background image for pages, because users won't ever see the edge of the image (so long as they aren't viewing the page in an enormous browser window, of course).

## Background Positions

The syntax for setting the position of the background image is as follows:

```
{ background-position: vertical horizontal | vertical%
→horizontal% | top/center/bottom left/center/right }
```

CSS background images can be positioned more so than HTML backgrounds. With HTML, a background will always start at the upper-left corner of the object, but CSS enables you to change this value. Even negative positions are allowed; so an image can be positioned precisely to match with the contents of an object, for example.

Values can be given in absolute measurements (such as cm), percentages of the available area, or with a value of top, center, or bottom, and left, center, or right. Examples of each of these methods are listed here:

```
body { background-image: url(/assets/sandstone.gif);
       background-position: 4cm 4cm }
```

```
body { background-image: url(/assets/sandstone.gif);
       background-position: 0% 20% }
```

```
body { background-image: url(/assets/sandstone.gif);
       background-position: top left }
```

## Treatment of Text

The most common use for CSS at the present time is for manipulation and formatting of text elements. The ability to use a central style sheet to hold text definitions for an entire site is often an opportunity too good to pass up for many web developers. The following sections discuss the different methods CSS offers for the treatment of text.

### Font Sizes

The syntax for setting the `font-size` property is as follows:

```
{ font-size: absolute keyword | relative keyword |
➥unit value | percentage }
```

You can specify font size in four different ways. Each has a different application.

- **Absolute keyword.** Possible values are `xx-small`, `x-small`, `small`, `medium`, `large`, `x-large`, `xx-large`. These display according to the browser's internal table of sizes. Each keyword is mapped to a font size defined by the browser.

- **Relative keyword.** Possible values are `larger` and `smaller`. These sizes are relative to the context in which they are used.

- **Unit value.** This can be specified in points, picas, or even em.

- **Percentage.** This is relative to the size settings on any parent elements.

Examples of each of these methods are as follows:

```
P { font-size: large }
P { font-size: smaller }
P { font-size: 12px }
P { font-size: 150% }
```

### Font Faces

The syntax for setting the font face (`font-family`) property is as follows:

```
{ font-family: name, generic family }
```

Like HTML, CSS recommends providing a list of fonts rather than a specific one. The list is scanned until a matching font is found on the viewer's system. It is advisable to use a generic font family name (such as `serif` or `monospace`) at the end of your list, because the browser will recognize this and pick the most appropriate available font. This way, even if users don't have any of the specified fonts on their system, they will still see the page in the same generic type of font that was intended (see Table 7.4).

| Table 7.4   Generic Font Family Names | |
| --- | --- |
| Name | Example Display |
| Serif | Times New Roman |
| Sans-serif | Helvetica |
| Cursive | Zapf-Chancery |
| Fantasy | Western |
| Monospace | Courier |

### Font Styles

The syntax for setting the font style is as follows:

```
{ font-style: normal | italic | oblique }
```

The CSS alternative to HTML's `<i>` tag is font-style. Taking things one step further than HTML does, CSS enables you to specify an oblique version of the face if one is available.

If a parent element is dictating an italic or oblique style, this can be reset for the element in question by using the normal option, as follows:

```
P { font-style: italic }
```

## Variations on a Font

The syntax for setting the font-variant property is as follows:

```
{ font-variant: normal | small-caps }
```

If there is a small-caps version of the selected face available, it can be selected using the font-variant property, as follows:

```
P { font-variant: small-caps }
```

## Font Weights

The syntax for setting the font-weight property is as follows:

```
{ font-weight: normal | bold | bolder | lighter |
➥100 | 200 | 300 | 400 | 500 | 600 | 700 | 800 | 900 }
```

The CSS alternative to HTML's <b> tag is font-weight. By allowing the use of numeric values, CSS offers more precise control over the weight of the font.

With a value of 400 equating to normal and 700 to bold, the higher the number chosen, the bolder the text. Each number is at least as bold as the one it follows. These two examples are equivalent, both displaying a paragraph in the same weight:

```
P { font-weight: 700 }
P { font-weight: bold }
```

## Line Spacing

The syntax for setting the line-height property is as follows:

```
{ line-height: number | unit value | percentage }
```

Line spacing can be controlled with the line-height style. You can specify the height in three different ways:

- **Number.** If a number with no units is given, it is multiplied by the current font size to give a height. So, for example, if a value of 1.5 is given, and the text is 12pt, the line height will be 18pt.

- **Unit value.** Units such as 12pt or 20em can be specified.
- **Percentage.** A percentage of the current height also can be given. With the example of 12pt text, a percentage of 150% gives a line height of 18pt.

With a given text size of 12pt, the following examples are, again, all equivalent:

```
P { line-height: 1.5 }
P { line-height: 18pt }
P { line-height: 150% }
```

## Indenting Text

The syntax for setting the `text-indent` property is as follows:

```
{ text-indent: unit value | percentage }
```

This particularly useful CSS feature enables you to indent text. Values can be given as a percentage or as a unit value, such as 20pt.

```
P { text-indent: 20pt }
```

## Text Alignment

The syntax for setting the text alignment is as follows:

```
{ text-align: left | right | center | justify }
```

The `text-align` property enables you to align text. Whereas HTML uses a number of different tags for aligning text, CSS offers a single property with four different options. The addition of justified text pleases typographers, but can make pages difficult to read if not used wisely.

```
P { text-align: center }
```

## Decorating Text

The syntax for setting the `text-decoration` property is as follows:

```
{ text-decoration: none || underline || overline ||
➥line-through || blink }
```

Although web developers steer away from underlining text to prevent confusion with links, the options are all here in the `text-decoration` property. A particularly useful way to use this property is to prevent links from being underlined.

If style dictates that your links should not be underlined (maybe setting a link color is enough to indicate their status), you can set the value of this property to **none** and remove that dreaded underline. You also can use more than one value for this attribute.

```
A { text-decoration: none }
```

## Manipulating Text

The syntax for setting the `text-transform` property is as follows:

```
{ text-transform: capitalize | uppercase | lowercase | none }
```

The `text-transform` property offers a number of different text–manipulation options. `Capitalize` makes the first letter of each word uppercase. `Uppercase` and `lowercase` convert all text to their own property, whereas none will clear any property inherited from a parent element.

```
P { text-transform: uppercase }
```

## Letter Spacing

The syntax for setting the letter spacing is as follows:

```
{ letter-spacing: normal | unit value }
```

A value for the space between characters can be set with this property. Entering a value such as **6pt** will increase the space between characters by 6 points.

```
P { letter-spacing: 0.2em }
```

## Word Spacing

The syntax for setting the word spacing is as follows:

```
{ word-spacing: normal | unit value }
```

A value for the space between words can be set with this property. Entering a value such as `12pt` will increase the space between words by 12 points.

```
P { word-spacing: 1.8em }
```

## Positioning Elements

One of the great advantages of CSS is that it enables you to control the positioning of elements. The next few sections examine the CSS properties that provide this control and explain why using this control might benefit the task at hand.

### Note

Chapter 8, "Advanced CSS Design," examines the benefits of using CSS for positioning elements within a page, compared to the relative merits of using HTML elements such as tables.

### Positioning

The syntax for setting the `position` property is as follows:

```
{ position: normal | relative | absolute }
```

This property defines an element's position in the page. By default (`normal`), the element's position is calculated according to other elements on the page. The relative value is calculated from the element's default position, and a setting of `absolute` defines the element's position precisely, according to the position of any parent elements.

```
P { position: normal }
```

### Positioning from the Left

The syntax for setting the `left` positioning property is as follows:

```
{ left: unit value | percentage }
```

This property enables you to position a block a set distance from the left of its containing block.

```
IMG { left: 3cm }
```

## Positioning from the Top

The syntax for setting the `top` positioning property is as follows:

```
{ top: unit value | percentage }
```

This property enables you to position a block a set distance from the top of its containing block.

```
IMG { top: 1in }
```

## Element Visibility

CSS brings a new concept to web development: the idea that elements can be hidden from view, be made visible, and can overlap with a set stacking order.

The following sections look at the visibility options available in CSS and how to apply them to some everyday elements.

## Displaying an Item

The syntax for setting the `display` property is as follows:

```
{ display: none | "" | block | inline | list-item }
```

Different from the `visibility` property (discussed in the following section), the `display` property can hide an element from view and remove it from the page's layout. In a similar way to commenting out a chunk in the code, if `display` is set to `none`, the code is treated as if it never existed. Set the option to `""` to reset the property, and the element displays.

You can, of course, control this with JavaScript and create interesting DHTML effects.

The block, inline, and list-item properties are used to specify what kind of element the object is.

```
P { display: none }
```

## Visibility of an Item

The syntax for setting the visibility property is as follows:

```
{ visibility: visible | hidden }
```

The visibility property sets whether an element is to be visible or hidden. In contrast to the display property, the element still remains within the page and affects its layout, but it just cannot be seen.

```
P { visibility: hidden }
```

## Setting the Stacking Order

The syntax for setting the z-index property is as follows:

```
{ z-index: number }
```

You can set the stacking order of elements with this property, so that when elements overlap, the desired objects can be on top. The number is literally the order in which objects are stacked, with zero being the lowest level.

```
P { position:absolute; z-index:4 }
```

## Spacing

With good old HTML, the developer can't do much in terms of spacing. HTML pages across the web are riddled with all sorts of transparent GIFs and hidden tables of all sorts, just to get the correct spacing in and around objects.

Cascading Style Sheets help to make these sorts of practices a thing of the past with some advanced spacing properties. The following sections identify those properties and how to best use them.

## Clearing

The syntax for setting the `clear` property is as follows:

```
{ clear: none | left | right | both }
```

This property specifies whether an element will have floating elements next to it. It offers the opportunity to specify on which sides floating objects are *not* allowed. Set to `left`, an element will be moved below any floating element on the left side. Set to `none`, floating elements are allowed on all sides.

```
P { clear: both }
```

## Floating Objects

The syntax for setting the `float` property is as follows:

```
{ float: left | right | none }
```

The `float` property enables you to place an element, such as an image, to the left or right of the object in which it resides, and allows elements such as text to flow around it. It is similar to the `align` attribute of the `<img>` tag in HTML, but the `float` property works with all sorts of elements, not just images.

```
IMG { float: left }
```

## Setting the Height of an Object

The syntax for setting the `height` property is as follows:

```
{ height: unit value | auto }
```

Although this property can be used to set the height of objects such as text, you will find it most useful for defining the height of images and the like.

When a specific height is given, and if no width is specified (or if the width is set to `auto`), the object will be scaled to keep proportion. Similarly, if the `height` property is set to `auto`, the object will take on its default size unless the `width` property is specified, and thus scale to keep proportion.

```
IMG { height: 4cm }
```

## Setting the Width of an Object

The syntax for setting the `width` property is as follows:

```
{ width: unit value | percentage | auto }
```

Again, this property is most useful for defining the height of images and the like.

When a specific width is given, and if no height is specified (or if the `height` property is set to `auto`), the object will be scaled to keep proportion. Similarly, if the `width` property is set to `auto`, the object will take on its default size unless the height is specified, and thus scale to keep proportion.

```
IMG { width: 50% }
```

## Borders

Although standard HTML styling offered some examples of borders (with tables, for instance), there was no standard way to apply borders to any object. This is exactly what CSS brings to the table with its different border properties.

## Declaring a Border Color

The syntax for setting the `border-color` property is as follows:

```
{ border-color: colorname | #hex | rgb(R, G, B) | rgb(R%, G%, B%) }
```

This property just declares a color for the object's border. The color can be expressed using any of the four common color formats.

A noteworthy point is that `border-color` must be used in conjunction with `border-width` and `border-style` to ensure that it renders correctly in the user's browser.

```
IMG { border-color: rgb(200, 183, 32) }
```

## Declaring a Border Style

The syntax for setting the `border-style` property is as follows:

```
{ border-style: none | dotted | dashed | solid |
⮑double | groove | ridge | inset | outset }
```

CSS offers a great many different border styles, as you can see. An element can be assigned up to four values, one for each side. If only one style is assigned, it is used as the style for all four borders. If two styles are assigned, they are taken to be horizontal and vertical, respectively. Multiple styles may be used within this attribute, in the example following the table. Table 7.5 describes the appearance of the styles.

| Table 7.5 | Border Styles |
|---|---|
| Style | Description |
| None | No border is drawn. |
| Dotted | The border is a dotted line drawn on top of the background of the element. |
| Dashed | The border is a dashed line drawn on top of the background of the element. |
| Solid | The border is a solid line. |
| Double | The border is a double line drawn on top of the background of the element. |
| Groove | A 3D groove is drawn in colors based on the `color` value. |
| Ridge | A 3D ridge is drawn in colors based on the `color` value. |
| Inset | A 3D inset is drawn in colors based on the `color` value. |
| Outset | A 3D outset is drawn in colors based on the `color` value. |

The following example shows one way to set the `border-style` property:

```
P { border-style: solid dotted }
```

## Setting the Width of a Border

The syntax for setting the `border-width` property is as follows:

```
{ border-width: unit value | thin | medium | thick }
```

This property sets the width of an object's border. There can be from one to four values, with the following interpretation:

- **One value.** All four border widths are set to that value.

- **Two values.** Top and bottom border widths are set to the first value, right and left are set to the second.

- **Three values.** Top is set to the first, right and left are set to the second, and bottom is set to the third.

- **Four values.** Top, right, bottom, and left, respectively.

The following example shows one way to set this property:

```
P { border-width: thin medium thick thin }
```

## Setting a Top Border

The syntax for setting the `border-top` property is as follows:

```
{ border-top: width style color }
```

This property enables you to set the top border's width, style, and color all at once.

```
P { border-top: thin solid blue }
```

## Changing the Width of a Top Border

The syntax for setting the `width` property of the top border is as follows:

```
{ border-top-width: unit value | thin | medium | thick }
```

This property enables you to set the width of the top border. It is identical to the `border-width` property, except that it controls exclusively the top border.

```
P { border-top-width: thick }
```

## Setting a Bottom Border

The syntax for setting the `bottom-border` property is as follows:

```
{ border-bottom: width style color }
```

This property enables you to set the bottom border's width, style, and color all at once.

```
P { border-bottom: thick dashed #885533 }
```

## Changing the Width of a Bottom Border

The syntax for setting the width property of the bottom border is as follows:

```
{ border-bottom-width: unit value | thin | medium | thick }
```

This property enables you to set the width of the bottom border. It is identical to the border-width property, except that it controls exclusively the bottom border.

```
P { border-bottom-width: 2cm }
```

## Setting a Right Border

The syntax for setting the border-right property is as follows:

```
{ border-right: width style color }
```

This property enables you to set the right border's width, style, and color all at once.

```
P { border-right: 12px dotted rgb(72, 255, 255) }
```

## Changing the Width of a Right Border

The syntax for setting the width property of the right border is as follows:

```
{ border-right-width: unit value | thin | medium | thick }
```

This property enables you to set the width of the right border. It is identical to the border-width property, except that it controls exclusively the right border.

```
P { border-right-width: 18px }
```

## Setting a Left Border

The syntax for setting the `border-left` property is as follows:

```
{ border-left: width style color }
```

This property enables you to set the left border's width, style, and color all at once.

```
P { border-left: thin none rgb(5%, 4%, 2%) }
```

## Changing the Width of a Left Border

The syntax for setting the `width` property of the left border is as follows:

```
{ border-left-width: unit value | thin | medium | thick }
```

This property enables you to set the width of the left border. It is identical to the `border-width` property, except that it controls exclusively the left border.

```
P { border-left-width: medium }
```

## Setting Multiple Borders Simultaneously

The syntax for setting the `border` properties is as follows:

```
{ border: width style color }
```

This property enables you to set all the values for all four borders in one hit. The limitation is that all four borders must have the same formatting, but that's probably a common situation.

```
P { border: medium solid black }
```

# Margins

Another topic that was brushed on with HTML, but never continued through to a useful extent, was margins. A margin is space outside of the object's container (in contrast to padding, which occurs within the container).

### Declaring a Top Margin

The syntax for setting the `margin-top` property is as follows:

```
{ margin-top: unit value | percentage | auto }
```

The margin is the space outside or around the object. This is in contrast to padding, which falls inside the object. This property enables you to specify a top margin in the usual measurements. A setting of **auto** leaves the choice to the browser.

```
P { margin-top: 30% }
```

### Declaring a Bottom Margin

The syntax for setting the `margin-bottom` property is as follows:

```
{ margin-bottom: unit value | percentage | auto }
```

The bottom margin—the space underneath the object—can be set using this property.

```
P { margin-bottom: 4cm }
```

### Declaring a Right Margin

The syntax for setting the `margin-right` property is as follows:

```
{ margin-right: unit value | percentage | auto }
```

The margin is the space outside or around the object. This is in contrast to padding, which falls inside the object. This property enables you to specify a rightmost margin in the usual measurements. A setting of **auto** leaves the choice to the browser.

```
P { margin-right: auto }
```

### Declaring a Left Margin

The syntax for setting the `margin-left` property is as follows:

```
{ margin-left: unit value | percentage | auto }
```

The left margin—the space before the object—can be set using this property.

```
P { margin-left: 10% }
```

### Setting Multiple Margins Simultaneously

The syntax for setting the margin properties is as follows:

```
{ margin: unit value | percentage | auto }
```

This property can be used to set all four margins around an object simultaneously. There can be from one to four values, with the following interpretation:

- **One value.** All four border widths are set to that value.
- **Two values.** Top and bottom border widths are set to the first value; right and left are set to the second.
- **Three values.** Top is set to the first, right and left are set to the second, and bottom is set to the third.
- **Four values.** top, right, bottom, and left, respectively.

The following example shows one way to set this property:

```
P { margin: 1cm }
```

## Padding

Unlike margins, which set aside space outside of an object's container, padding creates space within the container. This is very much like the effect achieved in table cells by setting a degree of padding.

### Setting Top Padding

The syntax for setting the padding-top property is as follows:

```
{ padding-top: unit value | percentage | auto }
```

Padding is the space within the object. It creates an area of invisible space between the contents of an object and that object's border. This property enables you to set the top padding for an object. Relative padding values are based on the dimensions of the object itself.

```
P { padding-top: 10% }
```

## Setting Bottom Padding

The syntax for setting the `padding-bottom` property is as follows:

```
{ padding-bottom: unit value | percentage | auto }
```

This property enables you to set the bottom padding for an object. A setting of `auto` leaves the choice to the browser.

```
P { padding-bottom: auto }
```

## Setting Right Padding

The syntax for setting the `padding-right` property is as follows:

```
{ padding-right: unit value | percentage | auto }
```

This property enables you to set the right padding for an object. Values can be given as a percentage, or as a precise value in the usual CSS units.

```
P { padding-right: 2.1cm }
```

## Setting Left Padding

The syntax for setting the `padding-left` property is as follows:

```
{ padding-left: unit value | percentage | auto }
```

This property enables you to set the left padding for an object. It creates an area of whitespace between the contents of an object and that object's left border.

```
P { padding-left: 30% }
```

### Setting Multiple Padding Options Simultaneously

The syntax for setting the `padding` properties is as follows:

```
{ padding: unit value | percentage | auto }
```

This property can be used to set all four padding settings within an object simultaneously. There can be from one to four values, with the following interpretation:

- **One value.** All four padding widths are set to that value.

- **Two values.** Top and bottom padding widths are set to the first value; right and left are set to the second.

- **Three values.** Top is set to the first, right and left are set to the second, and bottom is set to the third.

- **Four values.** Top, right, bottom and left, respectively.

The following example shows one way to set this property:

```
P { padding: 20% 10px 10px 25% }
```

# Implementing a Basic Style Sheet

Dreamweaver makes the creation of style sheets very easy. Using its simple CSS editor, you can visually select fonts, colors, and so on, without the need to type a massive amount of code. For this to be of real benefit, however, you must understand the code being written for you. I have known less experienced developers to get in a mess, however, because they do not have the basic CSS understanding required to use the tool effectively.

There are four main elements to the Dreamweaver CSS interface. The first is the CSS panel. As a Dreamweaver user, you will already be familiar with applying a style by highlighting an element in your document and then selecting a style from the CSS panel, but are you aware of the full implications of that style and which precise element it's being applied to?

I once had enormous trouble with a site I was producing for a client. It was a business-to-business extranet, and I was using HTML tables to hold the structure of the page together. Fairly late in the design process (I'm a fool for not testing earlier!), I found a strange problem cropping up in Netscape Navigator. There seemed to be extra space surrounding some of my table cells, and I couldn't get my graphics to align properly. Had I been more aware of the effect a particular style would have on my table cells, I could have saved myself a lot of time. The problem occurred because I specified the line height for all text within a `<td>` to be 140 percent. I now know that Navigator will add that 140 percent to my graphics too!

The solution was to remove the `line-height` value from my `<td>` definition and create a new `.copy` class to apply to all the cells that contained copy. Fortunately, I had created the site using Dreamweaver Templates, making the solution much, much quicker to implement across all my pages.

When applying a style to an object on your page, make sure you have the correct object selected. I know that sounds obvious; if you don't have the correct selection, however, you may find Dreamweaver adding lots of `<span>` tags to your page when they really aren't necessary. Try to use the tag selector in the lower left of the Design view to select an object before applying the style.

### *Tip*

> You can right-click the tag selector and choose a CSS class to apply to that particular tag. This is a very precise way to apply styles, ensuring that you don't end up with wasted `<span>` tags all over your document.

Another great way to apply styles to objects in your page is using the new CSS view of the default Property inspector. Selecting CSS mode (click the yellow A icon) enables you to apply styles to the current object with just a few clicks.

The CSS panel has four small icons in the lower-right corner. From left to right, these are as follows:

- **Attach style sheet.** If you already have an external style sheet defined, this button enables you to attach it to the current document.

- **New style sheet.** Choose this option to create a new internal or external style sheet.

- **Edit style sheet.** If a style sheet is currently in place, the Edit button will open the Edit Style Sheet window, enabling you to modify, add, remove, duplicate, and link style sheets and their styles.

- **Delete style.** Choose this option to remove the currently selected style from the style sheet.

The second of the four main CSS elements in Dreamweaver is the New Style window (see Figure 7.1). As you can see, the New Style window enables you to make a choice regarding the type of style that is to be created and also where it is to be created.

**Figure 7.1**

The New CSS Style window in Dreamweaver.

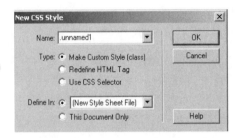

Nine times out of ten, you'll want to create a style within an external style sheet. It is very rare these days to include styles in the page itself, although your circumstances could, of course, dictate this.

The third CSS element is the most important. Figure 7.2 shows the Style Definition window that you use to define a particular style to meet exact requirements.

**Figure 7.2**

The Style Definition window is the hub of CSS activity.

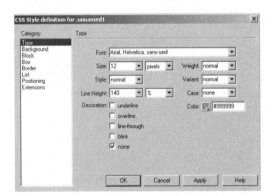

Within this window, you'll find all the CSS1 elements discussed previously in this chapter, along with a few little extras thrown in for good measure. This window is pretty much self-explanatory to anyone who has a grasp of the code that goes into CSS (as you now have).

After you have defined your style, click OK, and you'll see it added to the CSS panel.

Figure 7.3 shows the Edit Style Sheet window, which is the fourth element of the Dreamweaver CSS interface. This window is the key to modifying a style sheet after it has been created. Just about everything can be accessed from here, and a familiarity with this window will make things a lot easier when it comes to editing your CSS.

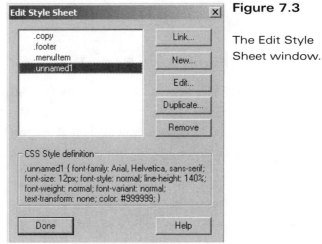

**Figure 7.3**

The Edit Style Sheet window.

With these four elements defined, you have all the tools you need to build a simple style sheet in Dreamweaver.

# Tips and Tricks

This section identifies a few tips and tricks that help when creating and applying CSS. These range from great time savers for the developer, to enabling a page to degrade gracefully in bad browsers.

## Redefine HTML Tags

Many devices, such as search engine spiders, text-based web browsers, speech browsers, and the like, use HTML's information-structuring features to process your pages. For example, a search engine spider might take any text in a <h1> tag as a heading and give it higher importance when it comes to placing a page in the search engine's database.

For this reason, it is good practice to redefine headings and other tags to fit your own visual styling, instead of creating custom classes from scratch.

This also has the huge advantage of preserving the structure of the text in your page, even if the user doesn't have a CSS-enabled browser. In version 3 web browsers, CSS is ignored; if your page uses the <h1> through <h6> tags for heading levels, however, these will keep the page in a logical structure for those using browsers with no awareness of the style sheet.

## Formatting Body Text

It may seem like an obvious step to redefine the <body> tag with the style of text you want to use for your site. As soon as you put any content into a table, however, you might find that this text formatting is lost. This loss occurs because in some browsers the table does not inherit the body's text style.

A good way to sidestep this problem is to duplicate your body definition as a <td> definition. This way, any text within a table cell will be formatted the same as text in the body of the document.

## Using a Design Time Style Sheet

If you find that Dreamweaver doesn't render your style sheet quite as well as the browsers do, you may want to consider using a different style sheet while you work with your pages visually. By right-clicking in the CSS Styles panel, you can choose a list of style sheets to include and hide at design time.

# What to Take Away from This Chapter

- Cascading Style Sheets have a specific role to play in defining how elements of a page are formatted and placed.

- Newer browsers support CSS, but full support of all of its features by all browsers is still in the future.

- Within the browsers that support CSS, the implementation of that standard can differ.

- The World Wide Web Consortium recommends CSS1 and now CSS2 for building web pages. However, CSS1 is the most widely supported.

- Style sheets are built from of a huge number of possible properties, designed to help you control the way pages look.

- Dreamweaver has an excellent interface for building CSS, but it's important to know CSS quite well to get the most out of it.

- There are a few good tips and tricks to remember when building a style sheet, such as redefining HTML tags instead of creating fresh classes.

# Chapter 8

# Advanced CSS Design

Objectives:

- To learn the differences between CSS layouts and table-based layouts, and to understand the implications of each.
- To discover the differences in the way that different browsers can render a page.
- To build a simple page using CSS layout techniques and try to address any problems that may occur.

Dreamweaver was the first visual design tool to bring the power of DHTML into the visual environment. This chapter discusses what CSS positioning is, its relative merits, and how it compares to other technologies. This chapter also covers the support available for CSS positioning in browsers, and what the various authorities on web technology have to say about them.

Toward the end of this chapter, we will build a page using CSS for layout where traditionally we might have used tables. Through this, you should gain an understanding of the way that CSS works, its advantages, and any limitations.

## What Is a CSS-P?

*CSS positioning* (CSS-P) is the application of the layout capabilities of *Cascading Style Sheets* (CSS). In basic terms, this can involve positioning a page element with what Dreamweaver calls a layer.

Layers are strange objects, and in fact are not objects at all. The layer analogy Dreamweaver uses is very helpful for understanding their use, but is actually a bit confusing when it comes to understanding what the technology behind them is.

Suppose that you have a block of text in your page like this:

```
Hello, I am a block of text with no real properties of my own.
```

HTML contains elements known as *block elements*. These are any element that defines a region in the code. An example is the `<body>` tag and the `<head>` tag, but also things such as paragraphs (`<p>`) and even tables (`<table>`). The text might look like this if treated as a block:

```
<p>Hello, I am a block of text with no real properties of my
➥own.</p>
```

By using CSS, you can give each block element an ID within the page and then apply definitions to them and dictate their attributes.

```
<p id="greeting">Hello, I am a block of text with no real
➥properties of my own.</p>
```

This is extremely useful; but what if you want to use CSS on a selection of objects and treat them as one? HTML provides an answer in the form of the *division*. A division is a block marked out by `<div>` `</div>` tags and can be given an ID and addressed like any other block element. Its purpose is to indicate a logical block or group.

```
<div id="greeting">Hello, I am a block of text with no real
➥properties of my own.</div>
```

All of a sudden, you can take any chunk of code and make it a unit or division that can be addressed and manipulated independently from other items on the page. The block could even look like this:

```
<div id="greeting">
<table width="100" border="0" cellspacing="0" cellpadding="0">
    <tr>
      <td>Hello,</td>
      <td>I am a block of text</td>
```

```
      <td>with no real properties</td>
    </tr>
    <tr>
      <td>of my own.</td>
      <td>None at all.</td>
      <td>It's quite sad.</td>
    </tr>
  </table>
  <hr>\
</div>
```

Layers in Dreamweaver are just divisions with CSS positioning applied. However, Dreamweaver applies the style definition inline with the <div> tag, whereas you would normally want to define your styles in a linked style sheet.

Consider the code for a basic, empty layer.

```
<div id="Layer1" style="position:absolute; left:42px;
➡top:42px; width:326px; height:188px; z-index:1"></div>
```

This then enables the developer to position units of code anywhere on the page and to set their dimensions and stacking order and all sorts of other attributes. This is essentially what a layer is: a unit of code surrounded with <div> tags and positioned with CSS. Equally, this code could (and usually should) be implemented in a linked style sheet. Now take a look at how you would do that.

First, you would want to reduce the tag in the document down to something more like this:

```
<div id="Layer1"></div>
```

Better still, give it a logical name. No point taxing your brain any more than necessary.

```
<div id="greeting"></div>
```

In the corresponding style sheet, you would need to create a definition for the object called `greeting`. In CSS, a specific object (rather than a class or a tag) is picked out using a hash or pound (#) sign. The style sheet rule would look like this:

```
#greeting{
    position : absolute;
    left : 42px;
    top : 42px;
    width : 326px;
    height : 118px;
    z-index : 1;
}
```

The obvious benefit of this approach is that it not only makes it easy to change the style across all pages in your site, but it also streamlines your HTML pages.

The positioning of the preceding division is fairly basic. The style specifies that it is 326 × 118 pixels, and that it is 42 pixels from both the left and the top. This position is rightly termed *absolute*, because come what may, the box will always be 42 pixels from the top and from the left. As you already know, the top left of the browser window is a constant as far as an HTML page is concerned.

The other common method of positioning is *relative*. This dictates an object's position from another object on the page. This is usually the direct containing block. With relative positioning, a top or left setting is taken from the containing element rather than from the top-left corner of the browser window.

Dreamweaver layers use only absolute positioning and always apply the styles inline, so they're not so great. If you create your CSS positioning in a linked style sheet as demonstrated earlier, however, Dreamweaver will happily display the page using the defined rendering style.

# CSS-P Versus Tables

It is widely accepted in the web development community that tables are the best way to lay out a page and have it work in as many browsers as possible. Any new users who stumble into a forum for help are quickly informed that tables are the path to HTML heaven, and any developer who hasn't mastered full control of his tables is going straight to the depths of markup hell.

Until not so long ago, I held this opinion myself. In fact, it is for the main part still true. If your customers are demanding web sites that are going to work in the browsers that most people are using, tables are a reasonable solution for layout. However, tables were never designed for the visual layout of pages of text, navigation, graphics, and so on. In fact, tables were put into the HTML specification for the purpose of organizing tables of data for presentation on a web page. Tables are really no more of a visual layout tool than Excel is. Can you imagine trying to lay out a magazine in Excel? Ouch.

Visually, of course, tables do a reasonable job of laying out a page. Granted, we have to pack hidden rows full of transparent GIFs, chop up graphics into rectangular slices to fit around the shape of the cells, and have to trick the browsers with conflicting cell heights and widths; for the most part, however, the pages we output look pretty reasonable in most browsers— most browsers, but not all browsers, however. And the fact is that table-based pages don't work well on anything other than a standard browser on a desktop computer. What's more, the code needed to generate all these tables is reasonably substantial and cannot be reused from page to page.

So why do we continue to lay out our pages with tables? Surely we need some new technology designed specifically for the visual control of web pages, right? The good news is that we have such a technology, and its name is Cascading Style Sheets. The not-so-good news is that although support in browsers for basic CSS features, such as text formatting, has been around since 1997, it is only in the most recent browser versions that full, standards-compliant CSS support is available for the more advanced features such as positioning (CSS-P).

So, how does CSS help solve our problems? Well, first it enables us to lay out pages with far more control than tables ever did. CSS (in conjunction with standards-compliant browsers) brings us much closer to being able to offer pixel-accurate web page layouts, for those users with standard desktop browsers. More about this later.

The second real advantage to using CSS for layout is that it enables us to separate style from content. The way we currently build sites, all the formatting and layout (the page's style) is coded into the page along with the content. This makes things very inflexible and means that an awful lot of page reworking has to be done when it comes to changing the style of the site. When using CSS, we can separate the elements that define how the page is styled from those that define the content. By marking up the content in terms of page structure (this is a heading, this is the navigation, and this chunk here is a footer), we can then use a style sheet to define how those elements are styled and where on the page they are placed.

The result is that instead of one file with the content and styling all jumbled together, we now have our pages of content and then a style sheet controlling the styling of those pages. When it comes to redesigning the site, only the style sheet needs be changed for the entire site to reflect the new style.

This methodology has another significant implication. We can now specify different style sheets for different purposes without having to maintain multiple copies of our content pages. This enables us to offer, for example, a stripped down version of our design for those browsing with a PDA and another for those using WebTV. We can offer a high-contrast or even speech-only version for those with impaired vision. We can even present the page differently when it is printed.

This is the real crux of the matter. Not only does CSS make life easier for the web developer, it also makes pages more accessible for users. It makes our pages comparatively quicker to download (the style sheet needs to be downloaded only once per site) and makes the content more portable for future use.

So why aren't we using CSS already? The answer is that many of us are—but to greater and lesser extents. A good many of us are used to using CSS for styling our text instead of using font tags. However, this is as far as most people go due to the support available for CSS in 1997 browsers (such as IE4 and NN4).

The latest browsers on the market (IE6, NN6, Opera 6, Konqueror, and so on) all support a standard set of web technologies, including CSS. This really opens up the possibilities for designing sites with CSS and abandoning the bad markup we've all got so used to. You can read more about web standards from the site of the Web Standards Project (`http://www.webstandards.org/`).

So what about older browsers? What happens when someone hits a bright new CSS-driven site with an old browser that doesn't support CSS properly? In the first instance, they could see a total mess, but we have ways around that.

Just as it is possible to deliver a style sheet for a PDA or a speech browser, we also can deliver a watered-down style sheet for those with limited browsers. Rachel Andrew's Old Style New Style Dreamweaver command enables you to specify a style sheet for browsers that support web standards and one for those that don't. You can find it at `http://www.edgeof myseat.com/developers/dreamweaver_ext.asp`.

A different approach is to redirect users of noncompliant browsers to a page telling them to upgrade to a better browser. This cheeky approach is great for raising awareness of web standards and the need for a compliant browser. Whether you can get away with this approach depends on the site's audience. If you think you can, Rachel Andrew's Go Away Old Browsers command will help you do it. You can find it at the same URL.

So should we start to use CSS? You've probably guessed my opinion on this by now. Whether you like the idea or not, this is the direction the web is going, and it's your responsibility as a web developer to make sure you are up-to-speed with the latest developments. If you don't, you could find yourself left behind with unmarketable skills. Of course, on some projects you just won't be able to go with such new technologies. Our clients are the ones who put food on our tables; and if they want a site that will work perfectly in all the current "desktop" browsers, that's what we deliver. At the moment, that obviously means tables for layout.

However, I urge you to start fully using CSS wherever you can. If you run any personal sites, consider using CSS if you can. When you're happy with the new technology and methods, start recommending it to your clients as a preferred solution. Show them the benefits. Tell them about accessibility legislation. Let them know they could be pushing the boundaries. See what they say. It's worth a try.

The longer we delay moving to these new technologies, the longer we have to put up with bad browsers and bad working methods. Currently, every site built using CSS is helping the movement toward good browsers. You really can make a difference to the direction of the web and at the same time teach yourself new skills that will keep you in work for a while to come.

## Advantages of CSS-P

There are a great many advantages to using style sheets to lay out your pages. Each of these is covered throughout this chapter, but they all boil down to the same central point. CSS-P was specifically designed for the laying out of web pages. Tables were never meant to be used in this way. As a result, CSS-P is a much more comprehensive way to lay out a page, albeit a bit of a tricky process to begin with.

## Advantages of Tables

There are a good number of advantages to using tables rather than CSS-P for laying out a web page. The most obvious is the fact that nearly every browser in use knows how to render a table and can manages to do so without too much trouble. This is an advantage over CSS-P because it's really only the latest generation of browsers that render CSS according to the rules. The previous generation made a good attempt, and much of CSS-P is usable in version 4 browsers; for anything earlier, however, it's a no-go. This leaves tables with a marginal upper hand for browser compatibility, because nearly every visual browser in use can render tables accurately. This topic is covered in more depth in the next section.

# Browser Support for CSS-P

As touched on earlier, browser support must be carefully considered when using CSS for layout. The most important aspect of this is knowing which browsers your audience is using so that you can make sure you cater for their needs. Chapter 4, "Advanced Browser and Platform Compatibility," covered some browser-usage figures from various sources on the Internet. These sorts of statistics coupled with the information from your own site's server logs will help you to make an informed decision as to whether you can reliably use CSS-P for laying out your site.

So what are you looking for? Which browsers actually support this stuff? The answer is probably more than you think. For instance, Netscape Navigator 4 is a pretty old and basic browser, but it will still display some of the more basic CSS-P designs to one extent or another. Internet Explorer 4 achieves a similar level, but isn't in wide use any more. Anything newer than these old browsers (such as Internet Explorer 5 and up, Navigator 6, Opera 5 and 6, and the Linux browser Konqueror) have pretty capable support. So realistically, the browsers actually in use on the web today have support for CSS-P.

What is meant by *support*? As with anything, different browsers have different levels of support. Navigator 4 and IE4 will render basic layouts that use absolute positioning (which doesn't mean nonliquid, as discussed later). Internet Explorer 5 does pretty well, and IE5.5 and 6 do a marvelous job. Navigator 6, Opera 5 and 6, and Konqueror on Linux are also very much up to the task.

For a really detailed look at which CSS properties the various browsers support, Westciv Webware have compiled a fantastic online resource. The compatibility charts can be found at `http://www.westciv.com/ style_master/academy/browser_support/`.

## Known Issues

There are, of course, a handful of known issues—where browser support lacks. Developers should always be on the lookout for these. Most of these are fairly trivial and turn up only under certain circumstances. As always, the rule is to test everything you implement in the browsers that your audience will be using.

## Tip

**Nearly all browsers report their name and version to the web server when a request is made for a page. This information is stored in your web server log files and can be easily extracted with a log-analysis tool. This can prove to be vital information when it comes to testing. If your logs report that 100 percent of your visitors are using IE6, you can forget about coding for Netscape!**

## The Default Width

When using CSS-P to position an object, if you don't specify a width, the browser will guess a width for you. In Internet Explorer, objects have their width default to the width of the view port (the visible area). In Navigator 4, the width defaults to the width of the contents of that block.

To compensate for this, you need to always make sure that a width is specified, unless the difference doesn't affect your design. When creating a layer in Dreamweaver, the dimensions will always be specified for you; should you remove these, however, things could go slightly wrong for your viewers.

## Clipping Versus Sizing

Unlike Internet Explorer, Navigator 4 does not let the developer make property or attribute changes with JavaScript that will change the flow of the document's existing content. Basically, Netscape cannot dynamically redraw the page; the document has to be reloaded for that to happen. You can, of course, force the page to refresh by dragging the size of the window, but this cannot be done programmatically without totally reloading the page.

What this means is that you cannot change the width and height of a positioned element to cause the contents to be redrawn. Instead, when you change the width and height in Netscape, you are only clipping the contents so that some of the contents are no longer visible. In CSS terms, you are changing the CSS clip property, not the CSS width or height. In Netscape, if the contents don't fit, they are always clipped.

Internet Explorer, on the other hand, enables you to change both the clip property and the width and height. Changing the width of an element causes the contents to rewrap to the new size. Changing the height of an element may or may not affect the element, depending on the CSS overflow attribute, which defines the object's behavior if the contents don't fit to the specified size.

### Netscape Resize Issue

There is an extremely well documented bug with Netscape 4 that causes the contents of a page not to be redrawn when the window is resized. This causes all sorts of layout oddities, and often renders the page almost unreadable.

Dreamweaver has a useful tool to overcome this problem. The Add/Remove Netscape Resize Fix command adds a useful bit of JavaScript to the page that causes Netscape browsers to reload the page if the window is resized.

Just applying this command is all that is required to add the code to your page. You can even have Dreamweaver insert this fix for you whenever you add a layer (although it will add it only once per page, as you would expect). By checking the option in the Layer section of the Preferences, you won't have to remember to do it manually each time you use a layer, if that is the approach you choose to take.

### Setting the Stacking Order

According to the CSS definitions, when no Z-index is specified, positioned objects should default to a stacking order above the level of body text. However, this is not always the case. It has been noted that Internet Explorer for the Macintosh tends to put objects behind the text. It is recommended that you always specify a Z-index property to avoid browsers misinterpreting your positioned elements and getting the order wrong (like a bad waitress).

## Standards-Compliant Browsers

In this day and age when the web is proving more popular than ever and is being seen as a viable way to run a business, more and more people are realizing the need that exists for standards.

The *World Wide Web Consortium* (W3C) recommends technologies and the way in which they should be used. It is those browsers, which make use of these technologies and implement them correctly, that are considered to be standards-compliant.

The Web Standards Project campaigns for the implementation and support of standards on the web—both in browsers and tools such as Dreamweaver. On their site, they state this:

> "The World Wide Web Consortium (W3C) has established standards for interpreting web-based content.
>
> By releasing browsers that do not uniformly support those standards, browser makers are injuring web developers, businesses and users alike.
>
> Lack of uniform support for W3C standards makes using and developing web-based technologies unnecessarily difficult and expensive.
>
> We recognize the necessity of innovation in a fast-paced market. However, basic support of existing W3C standards has been sacrificed in the name of such innovation, needlessly fragmenting the web and helping no one.
>
> Our goal is to support these core standards and encourage browser makers to do the same, thereby ensuring simple, affordable access to web technologies for all."

(`http://www.webstandards.org/mission.html`, March 20, 2002)

The site goes on to list the technologies that they consider to make up a standards-compliant browser. These are as follows:

- **Structural languages**

  HTML 4.0

  XML 1.0

- **Presentation languages**

  Cascading Style Sheets 1

  Cascading Style Sheets 2

  XSL (under development)

- **Object models**

  Document Object Model 1 Core HTML/XML

- **Scripting**

  ECMAScript (the "official" version of JavaScript)

This support and correct implementation of this collection of technologies are brought together to form a standards-compliant browser.

The Web Standards Project continued with the following:

> "These standards were created by W3C (with the exception of ECMAScript) with the intention of balancing the needs of designers for a sophisticated set of presentation and interactive features against the desire to make the web accessible to the largest possible number of browsers (and other client devices) and environments.

> Each layer of a web document was designed as part of a whole framework to achieve this balance. This is why the separation of structural HTML or XML from the presentation of a document is so important or why having a generic and predictable object model is critical. And it is also why full support of these core standards should be the first priority of browser makers before they attempt to add their product-specific innovations."

## Tip

It is well worth visiting the Web Standards Project web site (http://www.webstandards.org/). It has a host of useful information and developer resources for making sure you are able to build a standards-compliant web site. It is essential reading even if you think that the issues won't effect you until further down the line.

## Version 4 Browsers

Both Netscape Navigator 4 and Microsoft Internet Explorer 4 have support for CSS-P. Unfortunately, both support them in different ways, and neither is "correct" as far as the W3C is concerned. Most importantly for us, both have poor implementations of the CSS box model (discussed later in this chapter).

## Version 3 Browsers and Earlier

Anything earlier than a version 4 browser basically doesn't support CSS-P in any way at all. According to current web usage statistics, those who are using browsers that predate version 4 technologies are so few in numbers that they are hardly worth considering any more.

Take a look at those statistics again:

| Table 8.1   Browsers Currently in Common Use and Their Market Share | | | |
|---|---|---|---|
| | Source 1 | Source 2 | Source 3 |
| Internet Explorer 6 | 29% | 27% | 36% |
| Internet Explorer 5 | 59% | 62% | 40% |
| Internet Explorer 4 | 4.0% | 3.1% | 2.3% |
| Internet Explorer 3 | 0.1% | 0.05% | 0.5% |
| Internet Explorer 2 | 0.05% | 0 | 0.1% |
| Netscape Navigator 6 / Mozilla | 1.0% | 1.0% | 5.9% |
| Netscape Navigator 4 | 5.0% | 5.1% | 5.8% |
| Netscape Navigator 3 | 0.1% | 1.4% | 0.25% |
| Opera | 0.5% | 0.15% | 0.5% |
| (Other) | 1.5% | 0.15% | 8.0% |

Source: Browser News (http://www.upsdell.com/browserNews/), 10 March 2002.

These statistics were gathered from three different sources, as follows:

- **Source 1.** These statistics are from sites that use a hit counter, which excludes many popular, professionally made sites.

- **Source 2.** These statistics, from Proteus the Internet Consultancy (`http://www.proteus.co.uk`), are primarily from UK sites, with a somewhat regional audience. Note the unusually high Netscape Navigator 3 percentage. This may include browsers that mimic Netscape, which other sources classify as "other" browsers.

- **Source 3.** These statistics are from `www.upsdell.com`. Because of its special audience, its statistics apply to a narrow segment of the population.

As you can see from this data, only about 1 percent of users works with less than a version 3 browser; and because all the major browsers are free of charge, it's probably about time they upgrade.

# What the W3C Says About CSS-P

The W3C was founded in October 1994, with an aim to "lead the World Wide Web to its full potential by developing common protocols that promote its evolution and ensure its interoperability."

As a body, it is responsible for laying out specifications and guidelines for web technologies, and is generally accepted as the group to listen to when it comes to the web. The W3C (`www.w3.org`) was responsible for recommending the first level of Cascading Style Sheets (CSS1) to be adopted by web developers.

As you would expect from a body such as the W3C, its line is to always push for what is "correct" rather than what just "works." In the original specification for HTML, tables were designated devices for the laying out of tabular data. Tables were never intended to be used for alignment of page elements, and certainly not in the way they are used today.

For this reason, the W3C recommends against using tables for layout and pushes for the sole use of CSS-P for the layout of pages.

This could be seen as a rather radical statement when you look at how the world's web pages are constructed at the moment. Virtually all web sites make use of tables for the layout of their pages. For a body such as the W3C to step in and say that this is bad practice is quite a significant move. However, it isn't like this is a radical new proposal—the case is that CSS-P hasn't been a viable alternative to tables until recently.

## Accessibility

One of the main points that the W3C brings up about the use of CSS-P in preference to tables is that of accessibility. One of the key points to consider when developing a web site for high levels of accessibility is the use of unusual user agents (browsers), such as text-to-speech browsers.

With such browsers, the page is not rendered in the usual way, but read through (minus the markup) from top to bottom. This causes interesting results when it comes to tables. Take a look at a regular table and how it might look in a standard browser (see Figure 8.1). (I'm not much of a story-teller).

**Figure 8.1**

How the table might look in a standard browser.

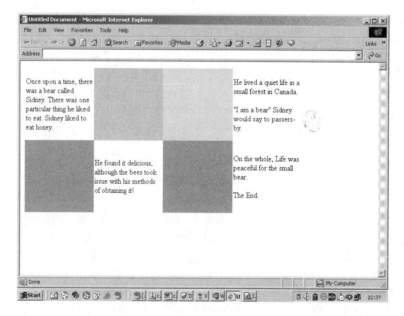

Obviously, a user would read the text blocks in a certain order with a regular browser. However, that's not how the text appears in the code.

```
<table width="600" border="0" cellspacing="0" cellpadding="2">
  <tr>
    <td width="150" height="150">
      <p>Once upon a time, there was a bear called Sidney.
      ➥There was one particular
        thing he liked to eat. Sidney liked to eat honey.</p>
      </td>
    <td width="150" height="150" bgcolor="#CCCCCC"> </td>
    <td width="150" height="150" bgcolor="#E1E1E1">
      <p> </p>
      </td>
    <td width="150" height="150">
      <p> He lived a quiet life in a small forest in Canada.</p>
      <p>&quot;I am a bear&quot; Sidney would say to
      ➥passers-by.</p>
      </td>
  </tr>
  <tr>
    <td width="150" height="150" bgcolor="#999999"> </td>
    <td width="150" height="150" bgcolor="#FFFFFF">He found it
    ➥delicious, although
      the bees took issue with his methods of obtaining
      ➥it!</td>
    <td width="150" height="150" bgcolor="#999999"> </td>
    <td width="150" height="150" bgcolor="#FFFFFF">
      <p>On the whole, Life was peaceful for the small
      ➥bear.</p>
      <p>The End.</p>
      </td>
  </tr>
</table>
```

Consider the order in which the text blocks would be read in by a text-to-speech browser. As you can imagine, things would soon become very confusing for the user, because all the text would be delivered in the wrong order. This is how a user with a text-to-speech browser would hear the story:

```
Once upon a time, there was a bear called Sidney. There was one
➥particular thing he liked to eat. Sidney liked to eat honey.

He lived a quiet life in a small forest in Canada.
"I am a bear" Sidney would say to passers-by.

He found it delicious, although the bees took issue with
➥his methods of obtaining it!

On the whole, Life was peaceful for the small bear.
The End.
```

As you can see, the story no longer makes much sense. The process this browser has been through is known as *linearization* of a table. The W3C Accessibility Check List specifies that a table must make sense when linearized; otherwise, an alternative must be provided. This basically rules out the use of tables for the laying out of a web page; because when the table is linearized, it will make little to no sense at all.

For this reason, the W3C specifies the use of CSS-P for accessibility. When elements are positioned using CSS, the literal position of the code in the page makes no difference to the final layout. For this reason, pages that use CSS-P can be structured to cope with linearization of the page.

Take a look at the same page built with Dreamweaver layers (an implementation of CSS-P). The code for this page looks far more complicated at first glance, but remember that text-to-speech browsers ignore markup and concentrate only on text.

```
<div id="Layer1" style="position:absolute; left:5px; top:5px;
➥width:150px; height:150px; z-index:1">Once
   upon a time, there was a bear called Sidney. There was one
   ➥particular thing
   he liked to eat. Sidney liked to eat honey.</div>
<div id="Layer6" style="position:absolute; left:155px;
➥top:155px; width:150px; height:150px; z-index:6">He
   found it delicious, although the bees took issue with his
   ➥methods of obtaining
   it!</div>
<div id="Layer4" style="position:absolute; left:455px;
➥top:5px; width:150px; height:150px; z-index:4">
```

```
  <p>He lived a quiet life in a small forest in Canada.</p>
  <p>&quot;I am a bear&quot; Sidney would say to
➥passers-by.</p>
    </div>
<div id="Layer8" style="position:absolute; left:455px;
➥top:155px; width:150px; height:150px; z-index:8">
  <p>On the whole, Life was peaceful for the small bear.</p>
  <p>The End.</p>
    </div>
<div id="Layer2" style="position:absolute; left:155px;
➥top:5px; width:150px; height:150px; z-index:2; background-
➥color: #CCCCCC; layer-background-color: #CCCCCC; border: 1px
➥none #000000"></div>
<div id="Layer3" style="position:absolute; left:305px;
➥top:5px; width:150px; height:150px; z-index:3; background-
➥color: #E1E1E1; layer-background-color: #E1E1E1; border: 1px
➥none #000000"></div>
<div id="Layer5" style="position:absolute; left:5px;
➥top:155px; width:150px; height:150px; z-index:5; background-
➥color: #999999; layer-background-color: #999999; border: 1px
➥none #000000"></div>
<div id="Layer7" style="position:absolute; left:305px;
➥top:155px; width:150px; height:150px; z-index:7; background-
➥color: #999999; layer-background-color: #999999; border: 1px
➥none #000000"></div>
```

Of course, you can place the layers in any order in the code, because they each have a absolute positioning style that will dictate their final resting place when the page is rendered in a browser. Because of this, a text-to-speech browser would now read the page like this:

```
Once upon a time, there was a bear called Sidney. There was
➥one particular thing he liked to eat. Sidney liked to eat
➥honey.

He found it delicious, although the bees took issue with his
➥methods of obtaining it!

He lived a quiet life in a small forest in Canada.
"I am a bear" Sidney would say to passers-by.

On the whole, Life was peaceful for the small bear.
The End.
```

As you can see, the story now makes much more sense when it is linearized. The W3C web site holds all of the latest specs and documentation for web site accessibility, as well as the many technologies they are behind (such as CSS and XML). It is worthwhile spending a few minutes every month or so browsing around the W3C web site, keeping an eye on the latest developments. Technology moves very quickly in web development, and it pays to keep your finger on the pulse.

# Controlling Your Page with CSS-P

A web developer of worth will be used to designing pages using tables. He will be familiar with the way in which tables operate, how they stretch, how they compress, and how they generally behave under various circumstances. The idea that all web sites should be laid out using CSS-P may seem a little daunting.

That fear is perfectly natural and understandable. After working in one way for so long, web developers naturally don't want to have to retrain to be able to create web layouts using CSS-P rather than tables.

Developers must learn many new things when transitioning between tables and CSS-P. To then discover that your layout did not work as you had expected can come as a bit of a blow.

Basically, working with style sheets is a whole different ballgame to working with tables for layout. Discard everything you know and make space for some highly confusing new rules.

Creating liquid web sites (sites that stretch and reflow to fit the browser window) with tables was a simple task. Things may not seem to be so easy with CSS-P if you are used to the way that Dreamweaver implements layers. After you manage to clear your mind of preconceptions, you'll find that liquid layouts are actually more of a natural state than fixed ones.

By default, Dreamweaver gives all layers absolute widths and heights. This often leads to the assumption that CSS-based layouts can be only of a fixed size and cannot be stretched. This is not so, and even a Dreamweaver layer can easily be given a width of 100 percent, for example.

The real differences come with the way in which CSS treats boxes. Take a look at the simple, one-cell table in Figure 8.2.

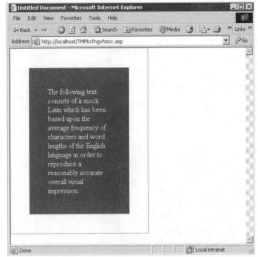

**Figure 8.2**

A look at a simple, one-cell table as displayed by Internet Explorer.

Nothing special, I'm sure you'll agree. It is 300-pixels wide and has 40-pixel cell padding and 40-pixel cell spacing. The code looks like this:

```
<table width="300" border="0" cellspacing="40" cell-
padding="40">
  <tr>
    <td bgcolor="#333333">
      <p> The following text consists of a mock Latin which
      ➥has been based upon
        the average frequency of characters and word lengths
        ➥of the English language
        in order to reproduce a reasonably accurate overall
        ➥visual impression.
      </p>
    </td>
  </tr>
</table>
```

As you would expect, the table has kept its width of 300 pixels by absorbing the spacing and padding into the overall width calculation.

Now take a look at a layer with the same settings—300 pixels wide, with 40-pixel padding and 40-pixel margin (what HTML calls *spacing*). (See Figure 8.3.)

**Figure 8.3**

A layer with the same width and padding values—but a different visual width.

As you can see, it's somewhat wider. The code looks like this:

```
<div
 id="Layer1"
 style="position:absolute;
 left:0px;
 top:0px;
 width:300px;
 z-index:1;
 background-color: #333333;
 layer-background-color: #333333;
 padding: 40px;
 margin: 40px;">
 The following text consists of a mock Latin which has been
➥based upon the average frequency of characters and word
➥lengths of the English language in order to reproduce a
➥reasonably accurate overall visual impression.
</div>
```

You can clearly see that the padding and margin values are set to `40px`, but the layer displays differently. The reason for this is to do with the CSS box model. Figure 8.4 shows how the box model works.

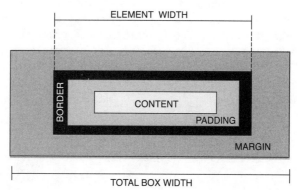

**Figure 8.4**

The CSS box model.

When you set a layer width in Dreamweaver, you are setting the element width. As you can see from Figure 8.4, any padding, borders, or margins are added on to the element width to create the overall box width. This means that, according to this example, the layer is the equivalent of a 420-pixel table. This is because padding and margin from each side is added on to the total width. Because we have 40-pixel padding on each side (80 pixels in total) and 40-pixel margin on each side (80 pixels), this leaves our original calculation quite a bit off. As strange as it may seem, here's how it works:

```
300px + (40px + 40px) padding + (40px + 40px) margin = 420px
```

This means that our layer is actually rendering at 420 pixels when we need it to render at 300 pixels. To do that, we need to subtract the surplus 160 pixels to give us a layer width of 140 pixels in Dreamweaver. After we have modified the code of our layer to take account of this, the code looks like this:

```
<div
 id="Layer1"
 style="position:absolute;
 left:0px;
 top:0px;
 width:140px;
 z-index:1;
```

```
background-color: #333333;
layer-background-color: #333333;
padding: 40px;
margin: 40px;">
The following text consists of a mock Latin which has been
➥based upon the average frequency of characters and word
➥lengths of the English language in order to reproduce a
➥reasonably accurate overall visual impression.
</div>
```

When placed in the same page as the table, the new adjusted width shows to be correct (see Figure 8.5).

**Figure 8.5**

Side by side, the to content areas are now the same width.

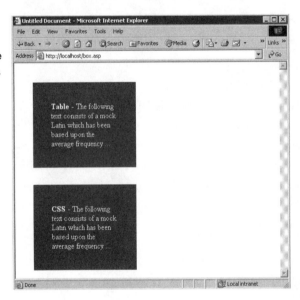

## Caution

Internet Explorer 5 gets this calculation wrong. IE5 counts the padding margin only once, instead of once from each side. This results in the developer needing to specify a width of 220 pixels in IE to achieve an equivalent width of 300 pixels.

An understanding of the CSS box model is critical for designing pages effectively with CSS-P. Without this, all of your calculations will fail, and the page will not display as you intended.

When it comes to designing liquid pages, a thorough understanding of CSS-P and the box model is crucial. In addition to this, further challenges are presented by the fact that one of the more common browsers in use today (Internet Explorer 5) does not render the box model correctly. For this reason, controlling a page layout with style sheets can be particularly challenging for even the most seasoned developer.

It soon becomes clear why Dreamweaver layers are given fixed sizes by default. If you are developing a page using solely layers of a fixed width for layout, these problems seem less of an issue; if one calculation is wrong, all the others are wrong too, and the page still holds together.

However, it's not considered particularly good design to create a page that does not adjust to the user's settings or browser window. However, it is still possible to create a liquid design with CSS-P. In the next section, we will be doing just that.

## Building a Page with CSS-P

As you learned in the preceding section, designing a page with CSS-P can at first present a bit of a challenge because of the following reasons:

- Not all browsers support the CSS box model correctly.
- Some common effects that can be created with tables are not always straightforward.
- The best support for CSS-P is when fixed, absolute dimension and positioning values are used.

To build an effective, liquid page design, start really simple until you get the hang of it.

Figure 8.6 shows a diagram of the sort of simple page we are going to build. It has a top banner and two columns—a Menu column and a Content column.

This is the sort of page we all built when we were trying to learn HTML in the first place. A good, basic design like this will help you get to grips with the techniques.

**Figure 8.6**

The Plan: a really simple starting project.

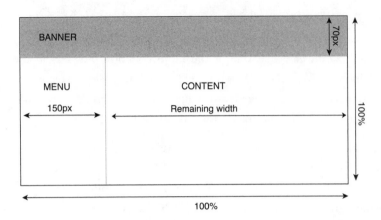

## Step 1: The Page

It may be tempting to jump right in and start doing things with CSS, but the first thing you need to set up is a basic page. Our page is going to contain three main blocks: a top banner, a menu for navigation, and our main content. We'll create each of these in a division so that they can be easily addressed as separate block elements.

### Top Banner

The first item to place in the page is our top banner. We'll place this in its own division with an ID of `banner`.

```
<div id="banner">
    <h1>Fluid Positions Inc</h1>
</div>
```

Things don't get much simpler than that. The name of the imaginary online recruitment company this site is for has been placed inside <h1> tags, because it's the highest level of heading on the page.

## Navigation Menu

Next up is the division into which we will place a series of navigational links. The important thing to note is that I haven't separated the links with line breaks, even though I want each link to live on its own line. I'll put the breaks in later in the CSS. The important thing here is to keep the structure, so I have to consider how the page will display with no style sheet attached. This also makes the page more flexible if I decide to change the layout in the future.

We'll call this one menu. Here's how the menu division looks:

```
<div id="menu">
    <p>
        <a href="/index.html">Home</a>
        <a href="/about/">About us</a>
        <a href="/positions/">Find a Job</a>
        <a href="/contact/">Contact us</a>
    </p>
</div>
```

I've wrapped the whole lot in a paragraph tag to give it the structure of a paragraph.

## Content Area

The third and final block is the main content area. The heading within this area is a level-two heading; it's the next most important thing after the company name. I have also included a couple of paragraphs of text to pad out the design and make it easy to work with. We'll call this division just content.

```
<div id="content">
    <h2>We can find you a better job!</h2>
    <p> The following text consists of a mock Latin which has
    ➥been based upon the average frequency of characters and
    ➥word lengths of the English language in order to
    ➥reproduce a
    <a href="javascript:;">reasonably accurate</a> overall
    ➥visual impression. Lorem ipsum dolor sit amet,
    ➥consectetur adipscing elit,
    sed diam nonnumy eiusmod tempor incidunt ut labore et
    ➥dolore magna aliquam erat volupat. </p>
```

```
<p> Et harumd dereud facilis est er expedit distinct. Nam
➥liber a tempor cum soluta nobis eligend optio comque
➥nihil quod a impedit anim id quod maxim placeat facer
➥<a href="javascript:;">possim omnis</a> es voluptas
➥assumenda est, omnis dolor repellend. Temporem autem
➥quinsud et aur office debit aut tum rerum necesit
➥atib saepe
veniet ut er repudiand sint et molestia non este recusand.
</p>
</div>
```

## Attaching a Style Sheet

The only thing left to do before we're ready to write some CSS is to create and attach a new blank style sheet to the page. There are lots of different ways to create your style sheets. Dreamweaver has its own editor—although it is something of a token gesture. Many developers code their CSS by hand, often in a dedicated CSS editor such as Bradbury Software's TopStyle (`http://www.bradsoft.com/`). Nick Bradbury, creator of TopStyle, was the developer behind HomeSite before (and while) it was bought by Allaire and then later Macromedia. TopStyle is generally considered the best CSS editor for the Windows platform, and it integrates with Dreamweaver extremely well.

For Macintosh users, Westciv Webware (`http://www.westciv.com/`) have a number of extremely capable CSS tools, as well as a wealth of useful CSS information on their web site.

To get the style sheet going, you can start by defining a few quick rules. The first makes sure the `<body>` tag doesn't have any default margins or padding set. The following two are just a bit of text formatting for the two levels of heading used.

```
body{
    margin : 0px;
    padding : 0px;
}

h1{
    font-family: Georgia, "Times New Roman", Times, serif;
    font-size: 36px;
    white-space : nowrap;
    padding : 10px 0px 0px 10px;
    margin : 0px;
}

h2{
    font-family: Georgia, "Times New Roman", Times, serif;
    font-size: 24px;
    font-weight : normal;
}
```

## Step 2: Positioning the Banner

The first thing to do in this nice clean style sheet is to position the top banner. As you have seen, the banner is just a division with a top-level heading inside of it. I want the banner to stretch right across the window, and be about 70 pixels high. I am going to give it a gray background and back that up with white as my foreground color to ensure anything within it can be clearly read.

Because this is a named element being positioned, the CSS selector should start with a hash or pound (#) sign.

```
#banner{
    top : 0px;
    left : 0px;
    width : 100%;
    height : 70px;
    color : white;
    background-color : gray;
    z-index : 100;
}
```

As you can see, I have also given the banner a Z-index (stacking order) of 100 to make sure it is always on the top of the pile. Previewing your page at this point might come as a bit of a surprise, because all sorts of items will have started overlapping. Don't worry; it's going to look a bit strange until all the elements are properly positioned.

## Step 3: Positioning the Menu

Up next is the menu. This is going to sit on the left side of the window, just under the banner. It will be 150 pixels wide.

```
#menu{
    position : absolute;
    top : 70px;
    left : 0px;
    width : 150px;
    color : black;
    background-color : transparent;
    padding-left : 30px;
    padding-top : 74px;
    z-index: 10;
}
```

Note that I have used absolute positioning to place the menu. That is because it shouldn't be reliant on any other elements in the page. I always want it to start 70 pixels from the top, and tight against the left edge. The padding is to move the content of the menu away from the top and the left.

Previewing the page again at this point, note that everything still looks a mess. Most notable, however, is that the navigational links are not wrapping onto their own lines. Also the links could really do with a little formatting to make them look smarter. To do this, we need to redefine the <a> tag. However, we want this rule to affect links only within the menu and not the rest of the page. The easiest way to accomplish this is to create a selector that says "any link within the item with an ID of menu." This is how we do it:

```
#menu a{
    font-family: verdana, Geneva, Arial, Helvetica, sans-serif;
```

```
    font-size : 11px;
    color : maroon;
    background-color : transparent;
    text-decoration : none;
    display : block;
}
```

The last two properties set are the most interesting. Text-decoration refers to the browser's method for visually indicating a link—obviously an underline by default. There are other options—overline is one—but I have opted to have no text-decoration because it should be obvious that these are links.

The final property is pure magic. Display : block; tells the browser to treat the element as if it were a block element. As you are aware, block-level elements (such as tables and forms) always break onto a new line when displayed, so the effect this has is to push each link onto its own line, giving the arrangement we were after.

All that's left to do on the menu is to make the links react on hover, and to add a little line spacing.

```
#menu a:hover{
    color : navy;
    background-color : transparent;
    text-decoration : underline;
}
#menu p{
    line-height : 140%;
}
```

## Step 4: Positioning the Content Area

The last item to deal with is the content area. It is essential that we manage to keep the content area flexible so that the text gently reflows with the browser window. I usually find it best not to position the main content division itself, but instead mold its dimensions using margins and otherwise let it sit in its natural position in the page. This approach tends to avoid strange problems with setting the width of an object to a certain dimension and running the risk of forcing unnecessary scrollbars.

I have also added a left border to the content area, to provide a small dividing line between the menu and the content.

```
#content{
    margin-top : 0px;
    margin-left : 180px;
    margin-right : 30px;
    padding-top : 10px;
    padding-left : 20px;
    border-left : dashed 1px silver;
    z-index: 50;
}
```

Most of the padding and margin settings are just to place the content away from the edges. The important one to note is the left margin. This is set to 180 pixels to allow space for the menu (which is 150 pixels) to sit. The menu is actually set inside the margin of the main content, and both items have their left extreme on the far left of the browser window. This approach proves very useful to circumvent the otherwise tricky 100 percent minus 150-pixel problems with making the content area flexible.

All that's left to do is add some formatting to the text itself, and to give the links within the content some styling of their own.

```
#content p{
    line-height : 140%;
    font-family : verdana, Geneva, Arial, Helvetica, sans-serif;
    font-size : 12px;
}
```

```
#content a{
    text-decoration : underline;
    color : maroon;
    background-color : transparent;
}
```

```
#content a:hover{
    color : maroon;
    background-color: #eee;
    text-decoration : underline overline;
}
```

A quick preview in your browser should now reveal a basic but tidy page with a flexible layout.

### Step 5: Browser Testing

A crucial part of working with CSS-P—just like any other aspect of web development—is to check your work in as many browsers as possible.

To be sure that our page will work correctly for all those viewing our site, we must open the page in different browsers and perform a number of tests. In the case of the page we have been working on, I think that these are reasonable tests:

1. Is the content displayed?
2. Do the columns take up the correct width without overlapping?
3. When resizing the window, does the page adjust correctly?
4. Do scrollbars appear in the correct places?
5. Do any scrollbars work as expected?
6. Are any other abnormalities apparent?

With the page in question, these six simple tests should reveal most abnormalities. After all, this is quite a simple page, and we shouldn't really encounter too many problems.

# Affecting Positioning with JavaScript

Because CSS is fundamentally a DHTML technology, you can access and manipulate it in a great number of ways with JavaScript.

With anything from just centering a division to making it follow the mouse pointer around the screen, JavaScript is a very powerful way to manipulate positioned elements and enhance the user experience on your web site.

As covered earlier in this chapter, the principal way to deploy CSS-P from within Dreamweaver itself is layers, and so the most support in this area can be found when treating CSS-P under that same metaphor.

The Macromedia Exchange for Dreamweaver is host to a huge number of extensions for manipulating layers; in fact, a whole category of the Exchange is dedicated to just that. I suggest that you pop along to the Exchange and take a look (`http://www.macromedia.com/ exchange/dreamweaver/`).

As well as the vast numbers of third-party extensions available, Dreamweaver has a few layer-specific behaviors already built in.

## Set Text of Layer

This handy behavior enables the developer to specify the HTML contents of a layer. Triggered by an event (such as `onMouseOver` or `onClick`), this can be useful for creating some more dynamic effects without having to rely on image swapping. Figure 8.7 shows the Set Text of Layer dialog box. Any HTML can be added at this point.

**Figure 8.7**

The Set Text of Layer dialog box.

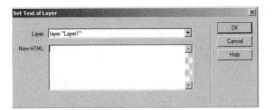

## Drag Layer

By adding the Drag Layer behavior to a layer itself (using the `onDragStart` event), you can specify that the user is able to drag a layer around the page and position it. You can even set an area that, if the layer is released over it, will snap the layer to fixed coordinates.

Figure 8.8 shows the Drag Layer dialog box.

**Figure 8.8**

The Drag Layer
dialog box.

### Show-Hide Layers

As the name suggests, this behavior enables the developer to either show
or hide a named layer. This is toggling the CSS `visible` element, and so
an option for default visibility is available as well.

Figure 8.9 shows the Show-Hide Layers dialog box.

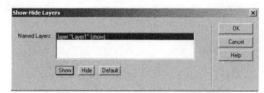

**Figure 8.9**

The Show-Hide
Layers dialog
box.

# What to Take Away from This Chapter

* Layers in Dreamweaver are actually just HTML divisions with CSS-P
  applied to position the layer precisely.

* CSS-P has an advantage over tables in that it has been designed for
  the job of web page layout, whereas tables have not.

* Tables have an advantage over CSS-P in that they are supported in
  virtually all browsers in use today.

* It is important to specify a default width for objects; otherwise, the
  browser might try to guess and make a mistake.

* There are differences between Internet Explorer and Netscape
  Navigator when it comes to the way clipping and sizing of positioned elements are handled—especially as far as JavaScript is concerned.

* Netscape Navigator cannot redraw the page if the window is resized;
  a special fix is needed to do this.

- It is always important to specify a Z-index (or stacking order) for any positioned elements; otherwise, the browser could get its positioning wrong.

- The W3C recommends the use of CSS-P for web page layout over the choice of tables. It is recommending tables be used only for the presentation of tabular data.

- Many accessibility issues relate to web sites and, in particular, those that use tables that fail to linearize.

- It is possible to gain a good degree of control over the design of a page using CSS-P, but there are also a number of associated challenges.

- Internet Explorer 5 doesn't calculate the CSS box model correctly, which can cause all sorts of problems if you don't plan for it.

- Dreamweaver includes a host of built-in behaviors for working with layers, but there are also many third-party ones available on the Macromedia Exchange for Dreamweaver.

# Chapter 9

# Advanced Template Design

Objectives:

- Identify the best uses for Templates.
- Learn when to use a Template appropriately.
- Learn to work with Templates in a collaborative environment.

Back in the "good old days" of web development, we would sit through long nights of coding raw HTML into our favorite text editors, previewing it in a browser, scratching our heads, making changes, and reviewing them again. It was a long, laborious process, devoid of any joy or daylight. At the end, however, we would present our masterpiece to the client—having lovingly slaved over this collection of beautifully hand-coded documents for dozens of hours—and the client would say, "Hey, it's great, but could we have the navigation bar on the right rather than the left?"

That was it—doomed. The budget for the project would be out the window. Each page of the site would have to be modified by hand and each table restructured to move the navigation from the left to the right. Complex tables that made perfect sense at the time would need to be reinterpreted and coded back-to-front, and everyone would grumble and reach for more coffee.

Thankfully, we don't make web sites like that anymore. It just doesn't make economical sense, and besides, we would rather all be out snowboarding than worrying about hundreds of lines of code that need to be rewritten. Hey, we're web developers, not monkeys, after all.

Introduced back in Dreamweaver 2.0, Templates have fast become the de facto standard for producing quick, easily maintained web sites for the majority of the web development community. By enabling the developer to set out one document on which to base the others, and to specify which regions can be changed and which cannot, Templates have become the basis for a very powerful system indeed.

These are not templates in the standard sense of the word. In a real-world template, like a dressmaker's template, the dress that is made from the template resembles it perfectly at the time of cutting, but that tends to be the end of the story. The sorts of templates we're dealing with here not only enable the creation of identical pages, but also automatically update all pages if the template changes.

Imagine if you bought a dress one season (this may take more imagination for some of us than others!)—a nice, pretty pink dress with frills. Cut perfectly from the designer's template, the dress fits like a glove and is currently all the rage in the New York fashion houses. Come the following season, however, that pretty pink dress is no longer the fashionable item it once was. Imagine if you will, that the designer is able to recut the dress template to take account of the new season's fashions, thus updating every single pretty pink dress already made. What joy—a dress for all seasons!

Granted, that example may be a little over the top; but nevertheless, it is relevant. Dreamweaver Templates enable you to go back and make changes to the Template and then have the changes cascade through the existing pages, updating them to reflect the changes made to the Template.

The sheer simplicity of the Template concept is its great strength. Requiring no additional support or features from the web server, the functionality behind Templates is held totally with the application itself. What's more, because the Template information is basically held in HTML files, Dreamweaver Templates become cross-platform-compatible, making collaboration with those on different systems easy and straightforward.

With Dreamweaver holding such a huge market share, its Templates have become commonplace across the web. Many developers find them indispensable for the creation of consistent, easily maintainable web sites.

This chapter covers Dreamweaver Templates in detail. As a Dreamweaver user, you should already be familiar with how a basic Template is constructed and applied, so this chapter looks at the reasoning and uses behind Templates to help you refine your Template skills a little further.

# The Many Uses of Templates

As with just about any tool, different people find different uses for Templates. Of course, there is a lot of common ground, but Templates are so flexible that you can use them pretty much any way you like.

This part of the chapter looks at some of the more common "textbook" ways of using Templates. Don't let the list constrain you, however—if you have an idea for a way to use Templates, go for it and see whether it works. Templates are a major building block or keystone to your solution; they are not the solution themselves.

## Maintaining Consistency

A great way to use Templates is to maintain a consistent look and feel across your entire site. If you build a single Template for the whole site (or even a small number of Templates) and lock down everything but the content areas, you're going to have a pretty solid site that feels professional as you navigate around it.

A major problem with coding things the old way was maintaining consistency. It can be really difficult to keep the positioning of elements consistent when coding by hand. The beauty of Templates is that anything you don't need to change is locked down and cannot be changed. This is good news, because it means that no matter how unforgiving the content, the structure of a page should always remain the same.

Most people are still using tables to build their web sites due to good browser support and their relative flexibility. Tables and Templates work well together, because it's possible to lock the dimensions of your table and its rows and columns, and only make the areas within certain cells editable.

This means that as content is entered, the table will adjust to the content in the way that it was designed to, but it's not possible to widen a column, for example, because the Template locks this. The net result is that all elements positioned using the table remain static, and a consistent look and feel is maintained.

Without the ability to lock items such as table rows and columns, it would be possible for the person entering the content into the page, either accidentally or deliberately, to drag the table around to make it fit the content more appropriately. However, the developer ultimately knows best when it comes to this sort of thing, and the locked regions will prevent such changes.

## Reducing Development Time

Templates really come into their own during the development of a web site. Having agreed with the client on a look and feel for the site, you can then set about making a Template, or group of Templates, for the site.

Web sites these days seem to be more complex than they ever were, and building up the design of a page can take a huge amount of time compared to entering the content and creating the navigation system. This is where Templates save development time. After you have created one page, you can save it as a Template and then use it as the basis for all the other pages of the same design. Whereas in the old days, the developer needed to build up the design again for every new page, with Templates it's just a case of selecting File > New and choosing the appropriate Template from which to work.

You no longer need to regenerate the page over and over. Dreamweaver will give you a perfect copy of the page, ready to be filled with content. This approach can literally shed hours off development time, and generally makes things less painful for the developer too. Not only do you save time by not having to build new pages, but you also don't have to be the one creating new pages for every single piece of content. A content author can happily go about creating new pages without any further input from the developer. Content authors and web developers can get along once again.

## Reducing Maintenance Time

Another benefit of Templates is that they enable you to save hours and hours when it comes to updating and maintaining a web site. Traditionally, if a site comes back to the development team for some changes to this or that, the process involves defining the changes and then going through every single page on the site to implement the changes. Huge numbers of man-hours would be required should a table need to be rejigged, for example, and every single page in the site would need to be reengineered. What's more, there's no saying that the pages would then hold their design tightly enough, and several more hours might be required to put them right.

It's more than likely that discrepancies will creep into the site as large numbers of pages are reworked to take account of a change in design. The hours it takes to get it right could be better spent. With Templates, this enormous headache is lifted. Should a change in design be required, it only needs to be made to one page—the Template—and that will then update the rest of the site for you, no matter how many pages.

The really great thing is that these pages will all have identical changes made to them, meaning that the design will keep the same integrity it always held. What's more, updating a Template doesn't introduce any more steps into your workflow. It really is as simple as making the changes on the Template (a more-or-less regular HTML page) and then agreeing to let Dreamweaver stomp through your site, updating pages as it goes.

The simplicity of this process makes it a real time-saver. If you had to perform all sorts of complex procedures to update a Template, it might end up being quicker just to change every page by hand. Because editing a Template is the same as editing a regular HTML document, however, performing an update becomes a breeze, and what would have taken hours of work can be performed in a few minutes.

## Protecting Content Authors from Themselves

As you are aware, Templates use a system of locked and editable regions. Whether you designate an area locked or editable when creating a Template requires much more than just an arbitrary decision. This section examines the other factors you need to consider before making such designations.

In any serious security system, you start by closing all the gaps and locking everything down, and then release only the items you need—so it is with Templates. By default, the whole of a Template is a locked region, and then you go through and make editable regions of only the items you want to make available to change. This approach ensures that your Template structure will hold true, that each page maintains its consistency, and that you keep maximum control over the pages.

After a region has been made editable, you lose control over its contents. Imagine a scenario in which the entire Template is editable. The web developer then has no option to make any changes, because only the contents of locked regions are replaced during an update. If this weren't so, you would lose all the content from editable regions every time you made a change to the Template.

Templates help developers and content authors work together by locking down everything except the items authors need to be able to work on. The last thing that should concern content authors when working with your Template is the layout or HTML of the page. They should just be able to get on with their job without worrying about what they might accidentally do to the page's structure.

More than this, you also get the occasional content author who thinks he is a web designer. I think we probably all know one. I'm talking about the sort of person who will always try to spot a "problem" with the page so that he can "fix" it and prove his superior knowledge and status. Well, locked regions are for him, too. Locking down everything possible will save your pages from those who like to tinker, and as a result, save you many hours of fixing the problems.

## Templates Versus Library Items

Both Templates and Library items are indispensable tools for a Dreamweaver web developer. They both help you manage your site in a more orderly and economical way. However, there seems to be confusion among some groups of Dreamweaver developers as to which should be used for which situation.

I am often asked whether a Template or a Library item should be used for a specific situation, and why one should be chosen over the other. These questions usually come from developers familiar with only one of the two technologies. It really takes an understanding of both systems, Templates and Library items, to see which is best suited to any particular job. When you are familiar with both, you will find that the choice becomes obvious.

### Note

Chapter 10, "Advanced Library Item Design," looks at Library items in greater detail and considers different ways of working with the Library.

Next we are going to be looking at some common situations and considering the most appropriate technology to use—Library items or Templates.

## Whole Pages Versus Page Elements

In very general terms, the choice between a Template and a Library item often comes down to whether you want to control an element within a page or the whole page itself. Of course, there are exceptions to this, as there always will be with such a flexible program as Dreamweaver; for the most part, however, this rule of thumb holds true.

If you want to control the entire layout and code of a page, making only certain elements available to change, use a Template. On the other hand, if you just need particular items (navigation, footers, and so on) to remain consistent and updateable through your site, but not the whole page, use a Library item.

To be more specific, when you want all the pages on your web site to follow the same look and feel, yet want to make certain areas of a page editable with different content, you're looking for a Template solution. When you want a consistent navigation bar, page footer, or similar page element to appear on every page, or a number of pages, within your site, you're looking for a Library item solution.

The latter situation is where Library items really come into their own—not for controlling large areas of a page or even a whole page, but for making up parts of a page. They're the sort of elements that might appear as part of a Template, but not be the Template itself.

## Sitewide Items

Elements that span the entire site could fall into either category. The decision, yet again, comes down to whether you want to control the entire page or just a subset of that page. For sitewide work, Templates are often ideal. Basing each page of your site on one Template offers maximum control and stability for your site's design and structure. However, you do not want to create a Template for some items.

If you need total freedom across your web site, and don't want to have to comply with a Template throughout, it is pointless to create a Template just to have a common copyright notice across the bottom of your page. A Template should normally have more locked areas than editable regions. In this example, all but the copyright notice would need to be an editable region, so Templates are clearly not the right solution for this job. Adding a Library item to the page containing the copyright information is a much better solution, offering the convenience of being able to update the message at any point, but also giving the freedom to manage the page as you desire.

## Section-Specific Items

A section-specific item, such as subnavigation that changes depending on the area of the site in which it is contained, is a prime example of a good place to combine the use of Templates and Library items. A well-designed Template could contain an editable region into which you would be able to place a Library item. Then, by carefully constructing a group of navigational Library items, you could insert the appropriate Library item into each page, depending on the content.

The advantage of this approach is flexibility. The Template provides the stability and consistency of design, while maintaining the ability to update easily; and the Library items offer the freedom of providing a structured, maintainable solution for applying only in specified areas.

# Template Advantages

Of course, you gain many advantages when using Templates; otherwise, we wouldn't be here in the first place. Templates are a great time-saving tool, a tool for protecting your pages and the consistency of your design, as well as a tool that offers tremendous possibilities when it comes to working as part of a development team.

## Fast Updates

The primary advantage to Templates is the ability to update all the pages in your web site in a single action. Just modifying the Template sends the changes cascading through your web site, without your having to address the changes on each page individually. This saves endless hours of development time, and makes updates much speedier in the process. In real terms, this means that every time a client comes back to you to make changes to common elements on her site, the work can now take only minutes, rather than the hours it would have taken if you had not used Templates in the design of your site.

Of course, you could pass these savings on to your clients, or—because your clients are actually receiving the same value as before—you could count your wise choice of Template implementation as profit, and pocket the money yourself. This is business, after all!

## Code Protection

With Templates being constructed of a system of editable and noneditable regions, using a Template offers a degree of protection for your code. The mere fact that Dreamweaver will not allow modification of the code on a Template-based page brings with it all sorts of benefits when it comes to security and protection of page integrity.

The ability to protect code in this way is pretty much unique in web development; any similar solutions require much more cumbersome and expensive technologies behind them to perform the same task. Dreamweaver excels by having Templates built in to its very core and therefore, by having such an affinity with the code, can lock and unlock regions at will.

Note, however, that nothing stops someone from opening your page in an editor outside of Dreamweaver to change the code; but as long as users stay within the Dreamweaver environment, the code receives a good deal of protection.

You've already learned how content authors can benefit from having most of the document locked down, so that they don't get themselves into a mess either accidentally or deliberately by making modifications to the page layout. This applies to the code as well and is an enormous asset to web developers, who won't need to spend time patching up messed-up code after the event has occurred.

## Design Consistency

The next great thing about Templates is that they help to hold your design together and give your site a consistent look and feel across all the pages. Because you can base all the pages in one site on a single Template, or on a small number of similar Templates, all the pages in your site can be styled in a consistent way.

Whereas with traditional web development methods each page is created by hand, Dreamweaver electronically bases each page on a master Template, making sure that no discrepancies creep in, as they are likely to do if an entire site is coded by hand.

People may be much better at design than computers, but when it comes to keeping elements pixel-perfect throughout a web site, this task is best left to the expert. In this case, the expert is Dreamweaver, dictating the rules to all the pages in the site based on the Template you initially created for it.

No longer do you need to worry about making sure your header doesn't jump around as you click from one page to the next. The Template will take care of this hassle for you, making it much easier to create a web site with a consistent and seamless look and feel.

## No Need for Server-Side Includes

Traditionally, a great deal of the work that Dreamweaver developers carried out with Templates had been performed with *server-side includes* (SSIs). For those not familiar with SSI, it is a system whereby a web page can reference another file to be inserted at a given point on the page. The web server carries out this process before the page is passed to the user agent via HTTP, so there are no extra requirements on the browser.

The advantage of SSI is that a page can be constructed of elements pulled from central resources on the server. For example, your standard navigation bar could be kept in a separate file, which is "included" in each page at the appropriate point by the server. When used like this, SSI is like Library items in Dreamweaver—useful for including common items across a number of pages. Used the other way around, however, where the basis of your page is hard-coded, pulling in the content as and when it is needed, you have a system similar to Templates in Dreamweaver.

The really useful thing about SSIs is that to update an element, it's often just a case of updating one include file on the server, and the whole site updates from that moment on, as each page is constructed on-the-fly. A slight disadvantage, however, is that building the pages at runtime puts a small amount of load on the web server, which could possibly impact performance on very busy sites.

Templates take a slightly different approach from that of SSIs. With Templates, all the work is done at design time rather than runtime. The obvious advantage to this is that you are not putting that extra load on the server, nor does the server need to support SSI.

When you create Template pages you are literally outputting finished, complete HTML pages; therefore, the process is very clean and simple. There are no major considerations if you decide to move your web site to a different server, or even to a different type of server, because the Templates themselves require no specific server support or special extensions. Of course, you might have other elements on your page that require server support, but the Templates are just good, clean HTML.

Templates also make it easier to develop the site if you do not have access to a local web server. You still need to have a server running to browse the complete site in your browser to work with SSI, although Dreamweaver does a great job of displaying SSI in the Design view to aid the design process.

### Tip

Dreamweaver displays SSI for you as you are designing. This feature enables you to visualize the entire page, and not have to deal with the individual fragments of a page as you traditionally would. A really neat thing is that if you use the Preview in Browser feature (F12) on a page with SSI, Dreamweaver will build the page along with the includes on-the-fly, enabling you to see how that one page will look when it is delivered by the server.

Keep in mind that not all web sites are delivered from the web. It's becoming more common to use HTML to create all sorts of information presentation systems in all sorts of places. I use HTML for creating presentation "slides" that most people still use PowerPoint to produce. The great thing about HTML in this circumstance is that it doesn't have to be linear like PowerPoint; you can hop about at will, and an HTML browser is less resource-intensive to run!

Many software companies are using HTML to provide the interactive help systems that ship with their software. Like a mini web site, the collection of HTML pages enables users to jump to whichever related page takes their interest. This job used to be performed by heavy custom hypertext systems, so HTML is the obvious replacement.

Many information kiosks are starting to use HTML-based systems to provide appropriate information to their users; and as with the web, kiosk users are finding these systems and their familiar interface much easier to use than the nonstandard, multimedia, information-defending devices of the past.

With such alternative presentation systems as these, you wouldn't normally have a web server running in the background and keeping the site alive. In these situations, the pages would normally be called straight from the machine's hard disk, just like the good old days of web design. Templates can find an enormous number of uses here. Just imagine the convenience of being able to set up the look and feel for your product's help system in one document, and then making it into a Template and being able to just go through populating it with content. All of a sudden, you've taken the headache out of building the help system. You have to construct the page only one time, and then you can concentrate on the important bit—the information that is going to empower your customers to use your software more effectively. Templates enable you to create any such system with the greatest of ease, because you can rely on their simple, flat HTML approach, without having to be concerned about the need for a web server to make use of SSIs.

## Collaboration

In the early days of the web, a majority of the sites were developed by hobbyists or by lone developers who worked freelance, producing web sites for whoever approached them in need of one. In the past five years or so, as the web has really taken off, web agencies have begun to spring up, and large companies have started to employ web development teams to look after their web presence.

Even more recently, with the advent of dotcoms, large teams of developers all work on a single site. These teams need some method of collaboration. Thankfully, Dreamweaver is there with a solution, and Templates cope with teamwork admirably.

Presuming that all the members of your development team are working from a central copy of the web site (as is the norm), Dreamweaver can pick up all the Templates for the site and make them immediately available for each developer to work with. Later in this chapter, you will learn how Templates can be used in a team environment and how they are best implemented. In the "Templates and Third-Party Management" section of this chapter, you'll see how Templates can be used in-house when working with a development team and with content authors. The section also covers how Templates can be shared with clients, and the problems that this both causes and solves.

# Template Limitations

Templates, like any technology that brings enormous benefits, bring with them a handful of limitations as well. With any technological approach, there are going to be a number of things that the solution cannot cover or achieve. Templates are no exception to this; and although they provide enormous benefits to Dreamweaver web developers, they also have their limitations.

## Changes to Every Page

Earlier in this chapter, you learned that Templates offer an alternative to SSIs and how a Templates solution does not require any specific server support because all the work is being done at design time. Dreamweaver outputs standard, flat HTML pages that require no more processing.

The advantage of SSI, however, is that should something change in your site and you've got that element in an include file, it's just a matter of updating that one include file and uploading it to the server. Because the server then generates all the pages on-the-fly at runtime, this updated include file is pulled in as each page is requested. The result is very fast updating of a site by changing only one file.

Because Dreamweaver performs its processing of pages at design time, however, should an element need to change, you make that change to the Template and let Dreamweaver go through and re-create all the pages. You then are in the situation of needing to upload the entire site again, to make those changes go live.

Now suppose that you are working on a number of new features for your web site—all of which are at different stages of development and implementation. If you need to make a simple change, such as updating a footer with a new copyright notice, making this update with Templates introduces a number of problems. With the SSI method, you would just update the footer include and upload it to the server—job done. With Templates, you need to re-upload every single page, but some of those pages are now in different states of development and are not fit for going live.

This leaves you between a rock and a hard place because you need to make some crucial updates, but are unable to do so without uploading pages not yet ready to be uploaded. This is really a version-control problem—one which you'll no doubt be familiar with if you work in any sort of team development environment.

In addition to this, if the Template needs to be modified while other team members are working on pages created from that Template, they risk their work being overwritten, or the page just not receiving the update, depending on where they are in their editing process. This again is a serious problem, especially with larger teams.

### Tip

**Version control is a huge issue, and is way beyond the scope of what you would expect Dreamweaver to deal with. However, Dreamweaver does integrate with some of the major version-control systems—Microsoft Visual SourceSafe and WebDAV, for example— enabling you to tackle version-control problems in an integrated, managed way.**

## Extra Code

Although not normally a major issue, those of you who are fanatical about trimming every single last bit of unnecessary code from your pages should be aware of how Templates work. As with a number of other features, Dreamweaver uses standard HTML comments to hold information within the page, telling it which Template to use and marking the editable regions.

This code actually adds only a tiny amount to the size of your page (and it's text, which compresses well), but even so, if your aim is to produce trim code, you might want to strip these comments out. Be warned, however, that as soon as you do so, Dreamweaver can no longer update your page from the Template. Removing the HTML comments effectively detaches the page from the Template, because Dreamweaver no longer has a record of that page belonging to any particular Template. If you want to remove the comments when you are ready for uploading your page, you will probably want to make a backup of the site first, giving you the option to go back and start using the Template again.

### Note

Chapter 5, "Cleaning and Editing HTML Within Dreamweaver," examines the way Dreamweaver uses HTML comments to store several bits of information that allow it to make some useful features available to you. Chapter 5 also discusses the methodology behind stripping any unwanted HTML comments from Templates to save on file size.

## Powerful, Yet Dangerous

Templates are a powerful tool for any web developer. Like any other powerful tool, however, if treated carelessly, they can be dangerous too. On several occasions, I have made serious mistakes when updating my Templates and managed to overwrite large sites full of content. Of course, it was my own fault for not watching what I was doing, but it is very easily done if you are performing major restructuring with Templates.

Aside from being careful in the first place and not making obvious mistakes, the best advice is to make an additional backup of your site before doing any major Template work. I just make a Zip file of the web site using WinZip (`http://www.winzip.com/`) before making changes that are going to replicate through the site. If there are any mistakes that aren't easy to fix, you can resort to your basic backup Zip file. It goes without saying that you should be backing up your web site regularly anyway; more often than not, however, your network administrator backs up sites onto DAT. Although the data can be retrieved, it usually takes an awfully long time to do that. By making a backup to a quick Zip file, you can be sure that you can easily and quickly restore your site should anything go wrong.

You should look out for a number of things when updating Templates, particularly when changing the structure of the regions, including the following:

- Avoid changing the names of editable regions.

- When adjusting the position of editable regions, be aware that any loss of area could result in loss of page data.

- Try to determine the final structure of your Template before basing too many pages on it. Large structural changes to the Template are possible, but require a greater deal of precision than smaller updates.

# Editable and Locked Regions

A number of factors should influence your choice of what to make an editable region and what to make a locked region. When it comes to protecting your pages and keeping them solid to work with, you'll want to lock down everything that isn't content. This, of course, restricts users from changing the structure of the page at all. If they are allowed to change only the content, and not the element bounding the content, you are more or less safe from the pages being destroyed accidentally.

Another factor to consider in locking regions is what happens if you want to totally redesign the site. If you have used editable regions that describe the content and the content alone, you can move this content around your page, placing it wherever you please. If the editable regions contain fragments of table cells, for example, not only do you run the risk of those cells being changed, you also immediately lose the flexibility when it comes to redesigning.

My general advice is to keep all structural elements, such as tables and layer information, locked, and only make editable regions out of the content areas. If your editable regions contain only raw content, you achieve maximum flexibility for redesigning and a good level of protection for your layout and code.

# Working with Templates and Scripting Elements

A number of issues surrounds the subject of scripting elements—by which I mean JavaScript and possibly any VBScript in your pages—and Templates. With the nature of scripts being different from that of HTML, any given script might not fall into a convenient pattern with the HTML that might be needed to insert it into a Template-based page.

The next few sections discuss the different sorts of scripts that can be implemented with Dreamweaver and how these do or do not work when used in conjunction with a Template-based page.

## Templates and Behaviors

Anyone familiar with previous versions of Dreamweaver knows how Template-based documents caused problems when it came to using behaviors. With behaviors, some code is attached to the object to which the behavior is being applied, and a JavaScript function is placed in the head of the document.

Until Dreamweaver 4, in which a special condition was created, the head of the document was always a locked region. This resulted in the behavior failing to apply properly, because it could not insert the code it needed into the head.

In Dreamweaver 4, an exception was created for JavaScript functions inserted by behaviors. Templates no longer deny access to the head to behaviors, and a behavior can insert any code it needs into that locked region. This holds true in Dreamweaver MX. What's more, when a Template is updated, the JavaScript functions are preserved and not overwritten, even though they are not in an editable region.

## Templates and Commands

Dreamweaver commands are a somewhat different beast from behaviors. Whereas behaviors fall into a nice pattern of a piece of trigger code and a JavaScript function in the head, commands have the power to insert any code anywhere in the document.

Building a rule to define how commands should affect a Template then becomes very difficult. Because a command can manipulate the document in an almost infinite number of ways, it is impossible to enable command support in Dreamweaver without jeopardizing the core functionality that makes Templates so useful.

This is not to say, however, that commands can never be used in Template-based documents. Because commands are all different and can insert code more or less where they like, perhaps certain commands may be inserted into editable regions or the document head where they can be treated like behaviors. On the whole, however, most commands that insert code tend to place it in areas that might cause problems with Templates.

A prime example is where a command might try to insert an attribute to the <body> tag. This tag cannot be an editable region, because there is just no way to specify it as such without making the whole of your document editable. If a command tries to insert code here, it will fail and Dreamweaver will create an audible "ding" to indicate the fact.

A possible way to get around this problem is to insert the code into the Template itself, but of course this will work only in some circumstances. Most of the time, you won't want that extra code in your page when it's not needed.

To summarize, many commands will fail when used on a Template-based document. In some circumstances, a command will work, but it is more likely that the insert will fail.

## Importing and Exporting XML

As I'm sure you are aware by now, XML is a very useful technology for moving data in a structured way between systems that have little or no knowledge of each other. This standard, yet extensible format for exchanging data opens the door to a great many things.

Dreamweaver has internal support for XML and uses it to control most of its own menu system and other configuration details. Now, in Dreamweaver MX, you also have the opportunity to use XML in conjunction with Templates.

## Exporting as XML

If you have already created a site based on Templates, you may be interested to know that you can export the editable regions of each page as an XML file. Dreamweaver offers no all-around solution of which this is a part, but the feature is there should it meet the user's needs.

XML is a common format for the transport of data. Being able to output your data in XML format enables you to then take that data and process it with any other software package on any other system where XML support is also available.

With a Template-based page open, selecting File > Export > Template Data as XML enables you to save the page as an XML file, which you can then use for any purpose you see fit.

## Importing XML

To accompany its Export as XML feature, Dreamweaver also offers the opportunity to import an XML file into the editable regions of a specified Template. Importing XML is a simple concept, but may prove trickier in practice. Opening a new document and choosing File > Import > XML into Template enables you to perform the import.

By selecting this option, a new document is created based on the Template specified in the XML file. Dreamweaver then fills in the contents of each editable region in that document using the data in the XML file. If the specified Template is not found, Dreamweaver prompts you to select a Template to use.

If your XML file isn't set up exactly the way Dreamweaver expects, you may not be able to import your data. Dreamweaver cannot second-guess what you were trying to achieve, and needs XML only in the format it specifies.

### *Tip*

Export a dummy XML file from Dreamweaver so that you'll have an XML file with exactly the right structure. Then copy the data from your original XML file into the exported XML file. The result is an XML file with the correct structure that contains the appropriate data, all ready to be imported.

# Advanced Template Features

New with Dreamweaver MX came a host of useful Template additions. Taking the feature set on from just Templates with editable regions, Macromedia has introduced some powerful new features, such as nested Templates, optional and repeating regions, as well as editable tag attributes—which was previously impossible from within Dreamweaver.

You may already be familiar with how to implement these new features; but how should you be using them? What are they actually for, and how can they benefit your workflow? This section answers these questions.

## Nested Templates

Suppose that you are building a corporate web site using Dreamweaver Templates. The site exists to support the company's brand, but also to offer product information, downloads, and technical articles and help sheets.

Working in the traditional way with Templates, you would probably end up with something like four different Templates for the site—each sharing a lot of the same information. You would have a general page Template, one for the Products section for displaying product information, one for the Downloads pages (probably taking on a list-style layout), and a Template for technical articles and help sheets.

Some items within these Templates would be based in the Library. It's likely that the navigation would be made into a library item to keep it central. However, the fact remains that you will have a number of Templates that are largely the same, just with small changes to the main content area. The page structure and common elements would be held in each Template, making it a pain to keep them all updated and synchronized.

What's happened is that the problem of keeping your web pages in step and easily maintainable has just moved up a level into your Templates. Now Templates are difficult to manage and to keep together and looking professional. The solution to this is to create a Template for your Templates. (It makes my head spin, too!)

This is essentially what a nested Template is: It's one Template (such as your Products section) based on another master Template (which would contain the navigation, site logo, page structure, and so on). You create your product pages from the Products Template, which in turn has been created from the master Template.

After you have your Products section sorted out, you use the same master Template to create your Downloads Template. You would then create your Downloads pages from the Downloads Template.

So, you still end up with an awful lot of Templates, but the advantage is that you have removed the duplicate information. Each Template holds only the bits unique to it; the rest is inherited from your master Template (or even Templates) from above. Of course, as soon as a change is made to the master Template, this change cascades to the section Templates, and to all documents based on the section Templates as well.

## Repeating Regions

A *repeating region* is a region of a Template page that can optionally be repeated over and over in a page based on that Template. Although a repeating region isn't an editable region in itself, the chances are you will want to use them in conjunction with editable regions. Repeating regions are used most commonly on tables. Consider the example of a Downloads section.

In a site's Downloads section, you might have a page of product trials, a page for updates, a page for white papers, and maybe a page for product add-ons and extensions. It's likely that these would be laid out in a table, and that there would be a different number of items listed on each page.

For layout purposes, it would be good to have each download listed in an editable region so that the page is kept tight and consistent. This is where repeating regions come in. In your Template, you would create just one table row for listing one single download. Editable regions would be created for the download name, its file size and the download link, and then the whole row would be made a repeating region.

When you then create a page based on that Template, you can add as many lines to the table as you need. The code within the repeating region is just copied by Dreamweaver along with the editable regions. For every download you need to list on the page, it's just a case of adding an extra row from the repeating region.

## About Template Parameters

If you've ever done any programming or even written your own JavaScript, you are familiar with the concept of variables. *Variables* are little containers into which you place a chunk of data to use again later. Dreamweaver Template parameters are just variables that you can define in your page. These tell the Template how to behave when applied to a new page.

Template parameters just support the option regions and editable tag attributes; they have no functionality in themselves, but they are important to recognize before trying to understand some of the more advanced Template features.

Taking the format of HTML comments, Template parameters consist of a parameter name, a data type, and a default value. These are saved at the top of your document and can be edited via the Modify > Template Properties command.

For example, the following Template parameter might be defined in the head of your document:

```
<!-- #TemplateParam name="boxshot"
 type="boolean" value="true" -->
```

This parameter would tell an optional region called boxshot to display. The type of Boolean means that the value can either be true or false.

## Optional Regions

Like repeating regions, optional regions are not editable by default, but can be used in conjunction with editable regions.

In a Template, any region of the document can be marked up as optional. This means that it will either be included or be left out of a page based on that Template, depending on which Template parameters are set. Consider the preceding example, which contains a parameter for an optional region called boxshot.

Here's how the Template parameter in the head of the document reads:

```
<!-- #TemplateParam name="boxshot"
 type="boolean" value="true" -->
```

This parameter tells an optional region called boxshot to display. The type of Boolean means that the value can either be true or false. Here's how the optional region might look:

```
<!-- #TemplateBeginIf cond="boxshot" -->
<p><img src="/images/product.gif" width="30" height="80" /></p>
<!-- #TemplateEndIf -->
```

Based on the preceding parameter, this option region is included in the instance page. If the parameter were set to false, the region would be omitted. This can prove useful in a number of circumstances.

Consider a Products section, for example. You could have a bunch of links that apply to one product family but not another. You won't really want these links to change from page to page, but you would want them to appear only for certain products. This is where the optional region comes in handy. Apply an optional region to your links in the Template, and then set a Template parameter in each of the instance pages (pages based on that Template), stating whether the links should be shown.

This enables you to keep your pages uniform, but does not restrict you to keeping each page identical. The most important thing is to keep information on the page relevant to the subject matter.

## Editable Tag Attributes

One of the limitations of Dreamweaver Templates has always been the inability to edit tag attributes. Because Templates have traditionally relied solely on HTML comment tags to mark out editable regions, no HTML tag could be "broken" to insert Template markup.

New to Dreamweaver MX, you can edit specified tag attributes. By setting a Template parameter in the head of the document, and a special marker within the tag attribute, you can allow each instance page to set the value of a specific tag attribute. Suppose, for instance, that you want each page to be able to specify a different class for the <body> tag. Your Template parameter would look something like this:

```
<!-- #TemplateParam name="bodyclass"
type="text" value="standard" -->
```

As you can see, I've set a parameter called "bodyclass", and here it is given a value of "standard". Take a look at how this works in the <body> tag:

```
<body class="@@_document['bodyclass']@@">
```

Dreamweaver uses special @@ delimiters for the editable attribute markers. As you can see, this one is calling on a Template parameter called "body-class"; that's the one we've just set up.

So how can this be used? Suppose you have some pages in your Products section that have special offers or promotions on them. You could change the class of the body tag to give you different styling effects to make the page more interesting. This also could work for meta tags. It's obvious that you want different keywords, depending on the page content, so making the right attributes editable in your Template meta tags would enable you to enter different keywords for each instance page.

This new addition to the Template family really opens up the possibilities for designers and developers alike. Don't forget: You also can use it with JavaScript events such as onload or onclick.

## Checking Template Syntax

If you have made any manual changes to the Template code, or are working with a particularly complex Template, you may want to check the syntax of your Template code every so often. This will prevent unwanted errors creeping in that might hamper Dreamweaver capability to update your Template instance pages correctly.

To check the syntax of your Template, chose the Modify > Templates > Check Template Syntax command. If your Template contains any errors, this command should identify the line number on which it (or they) occurs. If everything's good, it will tell you that as well.

# Templates and Third-Party Management

Templates are a great resource that sometimes needs to be shared. Whether you share Templates with other developers, designers, copywriters, or even your clients, it pays to be prepared for Template sharing and to make sure you have all your bases covered.

These final sections discuss how to share Templates with those both within your organization and out; they also cover the advantages as well as the pitfalls of doing so.

## In-House Use

The most common situation in which a web developer will be sharing Templates is when working in a team environment. Team members may be other web developers, they may be content authors, or they may even be designers; but they all need to work from the same Template.

This section discusses helpful tips to remember when sharing Template files with those in your building.

### Sharing Templates with Your Development Team

Assuming that you and your team are working from the same development server (and have the same site defined in Dreamweaver), Dreamweaver will recognize the Templates folder within your site, and all the Templates will immediately be available to anyone on the team.

Creating pages from a Template is then a matter of course, requiring no special treatment. The difficulties come when you need to start making modifications to a Template. As you are aware, when you make changes to the *Dreamweaver Template* (DWT) file and save, Dreamweaver prompts you to allow it to update all the pages based on that document. You want to do this, of course, because that's the point of using the Template in the first place.

Now consider this. In a multiuser environment, several developers might be working on different pages within the site. If they have pages open when you try to update them via the Template, something has to happen.

Basically, Dreamweaver rips through the site and updates all the copies of the files saved to disk. If any members of your team have any of these files open, they will be prompted with a message saying that the file they are working on has been updated, and would they like to reload the file.

If they were to reload the page at this point, any changes they made since first opening the page would be lost. If they answer no to the prompt, that page remains the same and doesn't reflect the changes in the Template. The developer then has three choices: sacrifice the changes to the Template god, run the risk of having an out-of-date page, or save the changes as another file and try to stick the page back together by hand. None of these are good solutions to the problem, and the only way to solve the problem is to avoid the scenario in the first place.

Thinking about it logically, if a project is large enough to warrant a team of developers, it's probably going to need clearly defined stages that have to be signed-off by the client. Because most changes to Templates reflect changes to look and feel, you want to finalize your Templates before letting the developers loose on them anyway. It doesn't work like that in real life, however; and Templates are a tool for real-life situations.

The best thing to do is to make sure that no other developers have a Template-based page open at the time you need to make the updates. With really large teams (possibly not all in the same work area), this can be tricky. Because the Template updates all pages, however, not a lot prevents you from leaving your update until the end of the workday, or at least until a lunch break. Otherwise, it's a case of making sure that nobody is working in any Template-based pages, and clicking the Update button.

Although it depends on how many pages your site has, updating from a Template doesn't usually take very long; so you shouldn't have too many problems asking all members of the team to exit their documents. By doing so, you totally avoid the problem. When team members reopen their documents to resume work, they immediately see the effect the Template update has had on the page.

This is all well and good if you are the one controlling the update. Remember, however, that any other developers in the team who are authorized to update the Template need to be aware of this limitation. Without everyone's cooperation, updating Templates on sites that are being actively developed can be a real pain.

Another thing to watch out for when updating Templates in this sort of environment is file locking. If you are developing on a web server (as is normal), and developers in the team are browsing the site to check it, the web server can sometimes place a lock on the file. These locks are no problem if you are uploading files to the site via FTP, because this is an exception and can usually overwrite the locked files; but because Dreamweaver works directly through the file system, it can come across these files, which are locked by the web server.

If you try to update a Template and some of the files in the site that use that Template are locked, those pages will not be updated. Dreamweaver gets to them in the list, tries to update them, and finds that they are locked, and so moves on to the next.

The solution to this is to wait 30 seconds or so after browsing pages on the site to allow the locks to clear. This delay should enable you to avoid the problem totally. Dreamweaver is very helpful in that it gives a report after updating the site. Take note of this report; it often provides useful information that would be lost were you to dismiss it totally. The crucial fact it reports is the number of pages it successfully managed to update, alongside the total number of pages. If it has failed to update any, it's probably because they are locked or damaged, and you should pay attention to those pages before proceeding with any further updates to the Template.

## Caution

When working with Templates in a team environment, you often will be using the Dreamweaver Check In and Check Out facilities. If you plan to run an update of the Template, you *must* confirm that all files in the site are checked in, so that Dreamweaver can modify them. If files are still checked out, they are not updated.

## Sharing Templates with Content Authors

It is common in large web production houses for a group of content authors to work with Dreamweaver Templates to add content to a web site. The development team has created the Templates and the site, and now the content authors come along, create new pages based on the Template, and enter all the content.

Normally, this would be no problem, although the same rules about updating Templates within a development team apply to content authors. The thing to watch out for is that everything that can be locked down is locked down.

Content authors are employed because they are good at authoring content. This by no means dictates that they should be computer-literate or even responsible for their own actions! They should be treated with the same caution as clients when it comes to protecting your precious pages. This works both ways, of course. If you have locked down your pages properly, the content authors have less opportunity to change what they should not be changing, thus making your Template easier for them to work with. Locking everything down is good for the developers and good for the content authors.

Another thing to watch out for is an overenthusiastic colleague. A content author who thinks he's a web developer is a very dangerous thing indeed. I recommend using operating system–level security to protect your Templates folder from modification by anyone other than yourself and your development team. The last thing you want is for a content developer to try to "fix" something without warning. (This may sound extreme, but it is not unknown!)

Of course, authors need read access to the Templates folder to create new pages based on the Template; if possible, however, you should restrict their access to prevent them from making deliberate or accidental changes to the Template.

## Giving Templates to Clients

There comes a time in every web developer's life when the thing most dreaded comes to fruition. A nontechnical client has managed to get hold of a copy of Dreamweaver and is determined to maintain his site himself. More often than not, this is a bad thing. As the creator of the site, you are the expert. You know the site well, and you are skilled in all the right techniques to maintain it. The client, on the other hand, is skilled in what he does best. This tends not to be web development, or he would never have hired you in the first place.

This is not to say that this scenario cannot work. Sometimes the client is knowledgeable enough to make changes to his site himself, and even to keep Dreamweaver on a tight reign. The key to managing this situation is to plan for it from the outset.

Working for a design agency, I was once approached to construct an extranet for a dotcom startup. Although they had an in-house web team, they either didn't have the time or (I suspect) the skills to build this site from scratch themselves. They did, however, have copies of Dreamweaver in-house, so the decision was reached that I would develop the site using Dreamweaver Templates and Library items.

With the knowledge that my Templates would have to be used by someone else, I was able to build on this and create a good solution. Thinking about it, if I took this approach with every Template-based site, 9 out of 10 would take a lot less time to get up to speed every time an update is needed.

For this project, I made sure that not only were my editable regions clearly named, but that they also had meaningful default content within them. If there was an editable region for a banner advertisement, I gave that region the default content of "Ad banner goes here," for example. Not only that, but where a Library item was to be inserted, I opted for "Insert Library item here," just to make things doubly clear.

Another approach I took was to lock down as much as humanly possible. If I knew a certain table cell always needed a particular style applied, I locked that style into the locked region just to make sure it couldn't be forgotten or changed. If I were creating a Template for my own use, I would normally not be so strict about these things, thinking that any changes to the style could be made in the CSS file.

Ultimately, it's about making the client's life as easy as possible while making sure you're not going to have to waste many hours just cleaning up the mess after them. If you keep things locked down, the client can't get confused, and you don't get left with a mess. It's more or less as simple as that.

# What to Take Away from This Chapter

- Templates have many different uses, including maintaining consistency, reducing development and maintenance time, and protecting pages from unskilled users.

- Templates and Library items are quite different, and each has its own uses. There are times when each is the best choice, but they don't tend to overlap.

- There are many advantages to using Templates for web development. These include increasing the speed of updates, protecting your code, maintaining consistency in design, team working benefits, and the ability to do away with server-side includes.

- Like any technology, Templates have their limitations as well.

- You must consider a number of factors when working with Template-based documents and scripting elements, including behaviors and commands.

- Dreamweaver can import and export XML documents to and from Templates, which can then be used in a number of different ways.

- You must consider a number of factors when working in a team environment with Templates, including working with those in-house, such as developers and content authors, and also with those outside of the organization, such as clients.

# Chapter 10

# Advanced Library Item Design

Objectives:

- To recognize the situations in which the use of a Library item can enhance your workflow.

- To gain an understanding of the different ways in which the Library can be used.

- To build a complex, multistate navigation Library item.

Of the many tools and features Dreamweaver offers, I have come to believe that the Library is one of the most underused and misunderstood. However, those who manage to get their heads around the situations in which Library items can help out will be the first to tell you just how useful they can be.

The natural partner to Templates, Library items offer a methodology for including common elements across a number of pages on your site. Whereas Templates offer total consistency across the site by dictating the page layout and regions, Library items are closer to code snippets that are optionally included in a page, or equally left out if the circumstance permits. What's more, once inserted, those code snippets can be updated throughout the site by editing the master.

Both Templates and Library items are indispensable tools for a Dreamweaver web developer. They both help you manage your site in a more ordered and economical way.

*Note*

A great many similarities exist between Templates and the Library. Both offer enormous timesaving functions that enable the developer to increase the speed at which sites can be developed. As a result, some of this chapter applies equally to both. If you are reading the chapters sequentially, feel free to skip things you think you've already covered. Also refer back to Chapter 9, "Advanced Template Design," for a more in-depth discussion of some of the topics glossed over here.

# What Are Library Items Used For?

You can use a Library item in a great number of ways. Such is their flexibility, Library items can adapt to a huge number of tasks. These can range from page footers to navigational elements and beyond. This section covers some practical uses for Library items, explaining their purpose and how they may be used.

## Navigation

Putting common sets of links into Library items is a great way to keep consistency across your site and also to make your navigation easily maintainable. Traditionally, if a link within the site changed, the developer had to go through each page and look for all instances of that link to update them. With navigational items held in a Library item, maintaining links becomes a breeze. By just updating the Library item, Dreamweaver will then go through the site for you, updating all instances.

Used in conjunction with Templates, Library items make a great solution for subnavigation. Quite often when I build a Template, my main navigation is a structured part of the Template, because this will not change from page to page—it remains constant throughout the site to help visitors to find their way around. With subnavigation, however, I like to leave an editable region in the Template into which I can insert a Library item containing the links for that particular page or section.

It's just a case of creating a number of Library items with the appropriate links for each subsection and inserting them into the Template's editable regions in the correct place. Figure 10.1 shows the Template-based page with an editable region housing a navigational Library item.

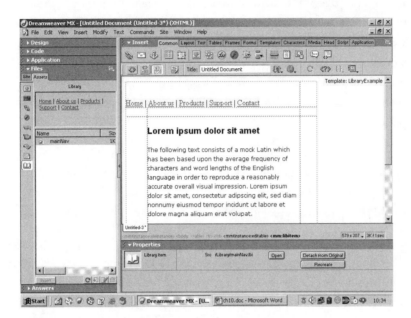

**Figure 10.1**

Templates and Library items work hand in hand.

## Footers and Copyright Notices

When it comes to adding common elements such as footers or copyright notices to the bottom of your web site's pages, Library items offer a great solution that enables the developer to keep those items up-to-date across all the pages with minimum fuss and effort. The convenience of being able to perform an update of a whole site by just modifying the code in one place is more than often an opportunity too good to pass up. Especially in sites where an entire Template solution would be overkill or even just too restricting, the Library can offer a great solution for updating small items such as footers.

## Complicated Objects

I once worked on a project where the company's logo was being used in conjunction with a product logo, to form a strange co-branded affair. This would normally be all well and good, but because of the nature of the logos, some parts compressed better as GIFs and other parts as JPEGs. The result was that each time we used the logo on the site, a small table holding the mixture of slices together had to be used.

Because the logo was to be used over and over again on the site, I decided to make it into a Library item. This enabled me to insert the logo as if it were a single, unified object rather than fragments of different images that would need aligning each time. By inserting the logo as a Library item, I was able to control it very easily and was in no danger of the table falling apart or being damaged by other items in the page, because Dreamweaver protects against this.

As it happens, it was a really great choice to use the Library, because three months later the client came back because the company had rebranded and the logo needed to be changed. Thanks to the Library, a process that would have proved an absolute nightmare was very easily dealt with by just making the changes once in the Library.

By making a complicated, volatile object into a Library item, I gained not only the convenience of working with the complex item as a solid unbreakable block, but also gained the ability to update all instances by making the changes only once and letting Dreamweaver handle the difficult stuff for me.

## Library Items as Assets

Dreamweaver treats the Library just like any other category of assets. The difference being, of course, that they are native to Dreamweaver and edited within it. In all other respects, however, they can be treated as any other sort of asset.

The Assets panel is the central hub for working with the Library. It enables you to created, edit, view, insert, and delete Library items with a few simple controls. The ease of accessibility of Library items from the Assets panel means that Library items are easier than ever to work with. From this one central point from which you are inserting your images, picking your colors, and linking in scripts, you can insert Library items and Templates as well.

# Library Item Advantages

Library items are a useful technology to add to your Dreamweaver toolkit. They provide many advantages over the use of traditional methods. Traditionally, when a common item needed to be updated, the web developer had to either manually search through the site or use a search and replace tool to go through the site and make the changes to the code to reflect the changes in all the pages. This could be a highly time-consuming task, regardless of the size of the update, which is effectively irrelevant once a Library-based solution has been implemented. This section examines some of the many advantages to using Library items to construct your web site.

## Fast, Cascading Updates

Traditionally, as you are aware, updating small elements across a web site can be an enormously time-consuming task. Not only does the developer need to locate all the pages that contain a particular item, they then have to locate that item within the page and make the appropriate changes to each instance individually. This repetitive work is not only lengthy and therefore costly on your time, it also is extremely boring.

I have yet to meet a web developer who claims to enjoy performing small, monotonous updates to multiple web pages when he could be getting his hands dirty with some innovative coding or more creative problem solving. This is where Dreamweaver steps in to save the day again. One way to get rid of these tedious and time-consuming updates is to use the Library to control common elements within your web site.

One of the great advantages to the Library is the ability to update all the pages in your web site in one single action. Just modifying the Library item sends the changes cascading through your web site, without you having to address the changes on each page individually. Library items share many of these time-saving advantages with Templates. When used together, you gain massive potential to save tremendous amounts of both your own and your clients' time.

## Centralizing Code

Many people fall into the trap of thinking that Library items are purely for one particular use. True, they are particularly good at a few things and are the only tool for the job, but there are also some less obvious but equally useful ways to implement Library items.

If you have a common JavaScript function used in a number of pages, the obvious thing to do is to put it into an external file and link it in to the appropriate pages. However, consider the case in which that JavaScript needs to be included inline rather than as a function. The solution for this is to paste it into each individual page by hand. A better solution, in fact, is to put that code into a Library item and to insert the Library item whenever appropriate. The great advantage of this is that the code is now centralized. If any further modifications, bug fixes, or tweaks are carried out on the code, the change replicates across all the pages without any further manual updating required.

Centralization of code is a fundamental programming principal, and Dreamweaver offers a way to achieve that for inline JavaScript. Of course, it needn't end with JavaScript. If you use a server page technology—such as ASP, JSP, ColdFusion or PHP—Library items can equally well contain chunks of server-side code. This offers the facility of centralized code without having to process server-side includes (SSIs).

So, we are happy with using the Library for our chunks of HTML, and we have now seen how a Library item can hold JavaScript or server-side code, too. More or less anything that can be inserted into a web page can be made into a Library item.

### *Caution*

Dreamweaver uses HTML comment tags to keep a track of Library items within a page. These comment tags can present a potential issue if you plan to put a fragment of code into a Library item and continue it in the main page. For example, you cannot have two lines of JavaScript in a Library item and then insert that inside some other lines of JavaScript, because the resulting comment tags will not be interpreted correctly.

### Design Consistency

Of course, the great thing about Library items is that they help to hold your design together and give your site a consistent look and feel across all the pages. This is another feature that Library items share with Templates, making it easier to gain massive advantages without having to break out of comfortable working methods.

### No Need for Server-Side Includes

Traditionally, a great deal of the work that Dreamweaver developers carried out with the Library was performed with SSIs. SSIs are a lot like Library items in Dreamweaver—useful for including common items across a number of pages. However, Library items take a slightly different approach to SSIs. With the Library, all of the work is done at design time rather than runtime. The obvious advantage to this is that the server need not even support SSI.

## Library Item Limitations

As useful as they are, Library items have their limitations just like any other enabling technology. This section discusses some of the limitations of Library items to enable you to make a balanced decision as to when Library items are a good solution for a particular task and when the job might be better suited to a different technology.

### Changes to Every Page

Earlier in this chapter, you read how Library items offered a great alternative to SSIs and how the Library does not require any specific server support, because all the work is being done at design time. Dreamweaver outputs standard flat HTML pages that require no more processing.

Because Dreamweaver performs its processing of pages at design time, should a page element need to change, you make that change to the Library item and let Dreamweaver go through and re-create all the pages. You then must re-upload the entire site again for those changes to become live.

This potential source-control problem is shared with Templates, and although version-control software, such as Microsoft Visual SourceSafe, can take a step toward helping with this sort of issue, there really is no complete solution.

## Extra Code

Although not normally a major issue, those of you fanatical about trimming out every single last bit of unnecessary code from your pages should be aware of how Library items work. Like a number of other Dreamweaver features (including Templates), Dreamweaver uses standard HTML comments to hold information within the page telling it when to use a Library item, and where it starts and finishes.

This code actually adds only a tiny amount to the size of your page (and it is text, which compresses well); but even so, if your aim is to produce trim code, you might want to strip these out. Be warned, however, that as soon as you do so, Dreamweaver can no longer update your page from the Library. Removing the HTML comments effectively detaches the Library item, because Dreamweaver no longer has a record of that code belonging to any particular Library item. If you want to remove the comments ready for uploading your page you will probably want to make a backup of the site first, giving you the option to go back and start using the Library again.

### *Note*

Chapter 5, "Cleaning and Editing HTML Within Dreamweaver," examines the way in which Dreamweaver uses HTML comments to store several bits of information that enable it to make some great features available to you. In the same chapter, you read how the Library and Templates work, and the methodology behind stripping out any unwanted HTML comments to save on file size.

# Library Items Within a Template

By far the most powerful use for Library items is including them within the editable regions of a Template. The basic premise of a Template is that you have certain items that remain fixed and then you have those items that are different for every page (editable regions). However, what happens when you have items that are the same across a number of pages, such as a site section?

One answer can come in the form of Library items. By inserting a Library item into a Template's editable region, you can then maintain consistency and update ability across a number of pages, such as a site section, without having to use a new Template for each section. This approach offers extraordinary flexibility, and the combination of Templates and Library items makes an extremely powerful solution for maintaining and updating your web site.

# Working with the Library and Scripting Elements

Library items consist of a small chunk of HTML code that falls within the body of a document. Because Dreamweaver Behaviors place their code in the head of the document, it becomes difficult to add behaviors to Library items, because a Library item has no head region. Dreamweaver addresses this problem by inserting the JavaScript code inline into the Library item. What this means is that instead of putting the code in the head of the document, the code is inserted with `<script>` tags in among the HTML.

This is a good solution to the problem, but it does come with its drawbacks. If you are using the same behavior in other Library items used in the page or even within the page itself, the code will duplicate unnecessarily. There is no need for a behavior to be in a page more than once; any items within that page can access the same copy. This means that if a behavior is used more than once, it is using up unnecessary file space, and could even cause problems, because strictly there should not be more than one JavaScript function with the same name in each page.

Because your Library item is going to be inserted into a number of pages, it makes good sense to put the JavaScript functions into their own file and to attach them to each page. This way, the code will be downloaded only once, and the user saves the wait time. I suggest that it is best to attach the JavaScript file to the Template because this will offer the assurance that the code is available in every single page; and because the code is downloaded only once, it makes no difference whether the code is used in a page.

The remaining job is to remove the inline code for the Library items, and then update each page that relies on that Library item so that the changes are reflected.

## Creating a Navigation Library Item

This section steps you through the process involved in creating a Library item to be used as navigation for a web site. Our navigation bar is going to use images as the links and include some simple rollover effects to make the navigation easy to use and to give it a more professional look and feel.

First, you need to create a new Library item for your navigation bar. To add a new Library item, click the plus (+) button in the lower-right side of this window. At this point, a prompt asks you to name your new Library item. (I will call mine mainNav to remind me that it will be the main navigation component for my site.) See Figure 10.2.

### Tip

If you have decided to make a Library item out of something that already exists on the page, Dreamweaver makes this very easy for you. Just select the element (do this in the Code view if you need to) and then click the plus (+) button. Dreamweaver converts the code chunk into a Library item; all you have to do is name it.

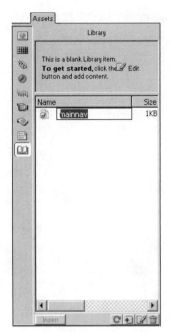

**Figure 10.2**

The Assets
panel.

After you have named your Library item, you need to open it to begin editing it. Double-click the newly created Library item to open it. A blank Dreamweaver document displays. You need to start creating your navigation item. I'm going to create a very simple navigation bar with basic image links (see Figure 10.3). I need to add the links to the images, but I also need to give each image a distinct name. It is easy to perform both tasks using the Property inspector.

## *Caution*

Be careful when specifying links. These should be relative to the Library folder or to the site root. It is best to use the browse facility to select the files to link to instead of entering the links by hand. This should ensure the integrity of your links when the Library item is inserted into your pages.

**Figure 10.3**

A simple
navigation bar is
created using
images.

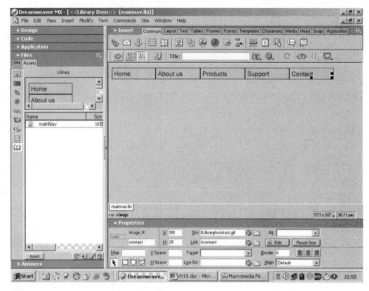

After you have inserted the links and given all the images unique names,
it's a good time to add the rollover images. For this it's best to use the Swap
Image behavior. Add the Swap Image behavior for each image, choosing
to preload and to restore the images onMouseOut (see Figure 10.4). You now
have a navigation bar that is almost ready to go. All that is left to do is to
remove the inline JavaScript code and move it to your global JavaScript file
so that it can be included for all pages.

**Figure 10.4**

The Swap Image
behavior makes
rollovers simple.

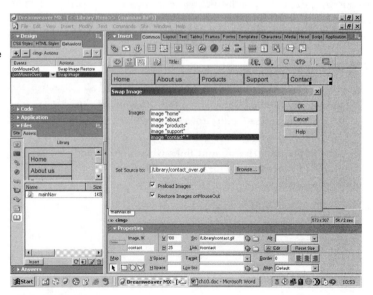

The Library item should now be ready to insert into your documents. It's best to insert it into an editable region of a Template-based page; however, it will work equally well inserted into a non–Template-based page of your choice.

### Note

**Make sure that your external JavaScript file is linked into the Template. Without this, the rollovers will not work (see Figure 10.5).**

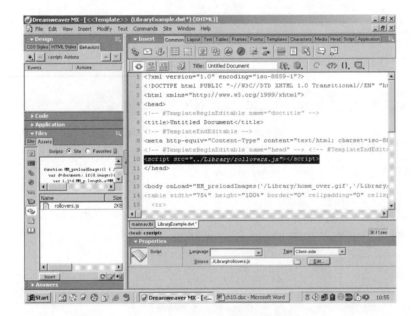

**Figure 10.5**

Make sure that your external JavaScript file is linked into the Template.

# Creating a Multistate Navigation Library Item

You have already created a basic navigation bar using a Library item and some simple rollover images. This works well, but the icing on the cake is to be able to have the current section highlighted in the bar without having to create a different Library item for each site section. Figure 10.6 shows my navigation bar in the Contact section, with the Contact image permanently in the rollover state to show the current section.

**Figure 10.6**

The current section is shown with a rollover state.

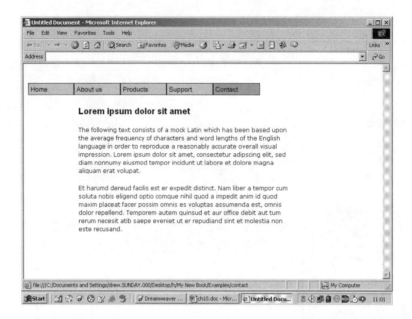

## The Solution

The answer comes from a bit of clever JavaScript. By using JavaScript, it is possible to tell each page which section it belongs to, and then use this information to change the appropriate image to its "over" state. The code you need is very simple indeed. It's an extremely watered-down version of what the Dreamweaver Swap Image behavior does, and in principal is the same. Take a look at the code:

```
document[thisPage].src = thisPage + "_over.gif"
```

This code presumes a number of things. First of all, you need to have set a value for the variable called `thisPage`. If my page were from the Contact section of the web site, this value would be set to `contact`. The code also presumes that my "over" state images all end in `_over.gif`. In this instance, my Contact "over" state image would be called `contact_over.gif`.

The third thing that the code presumes is that my images all have been given the name of their section—that is, that my Contact section link is called `contact`. Next you need to put this code into a useful form whereby it can be happily executed within your page. The obvious answer is to make it into a function, and to add it `onLoad` from the `<body>` tag, as follows:

```
<html>
<head>
<script language="javascript" type="text/javascript"
➥src="/common.js">
</script>
<script language="javascript" type="text/javascript">
<!—
function selectNavigation(thisPage){
if (document[thisPage].src){
document[thisPage].src = thisPage + "_over.gif";
}
}
//—>
</script>
</head>
<body onload="selectNavigation('contact');">
<!— Our Library Item and page content here. —>
</body>
</html>
```

As you can see, I'm passing a parameter, called thisPage, to the function. By changing this value (perhaps to about or products), you can change which menu item is initially selected for that particular page.

## Why Not Use Swap Image?

Of course, you could achieve a similar effect using the built-in Swap Image behavior. The advantage of this watered-down version is that it is extremely quick to modify. You need to change only the name of the section in the <body> tag, and the page will then show itself as being part of that section. The crucial factor is development time, and so being able to keep the edits to a minimum enables you to speed up production time immensely.

Swap Image is very capable and extremely comprehensive, but the preceding code will offer a more specific, tailored solution for this particular problem.

The great thing is that you now have to maintain only a single Library item for all your navigation—you don't need to create duplicate Library items with different highlighted states. This makes updating the Library item much less of a task.

*Tip*

> The more capable coders among us might like to think about the next step in this problem. How do we get a page to automatically detect which section it's in? The solution could lie in looking for folder names within document.location and setting the variable that way. Consider it a challenge if you are looking to streamline production time even more!

# What to Take Away from This Chapter

- Library items have a great number of uses, ranging from navigation, to page footers, through to complicated repeated objects.

- The Library is part of the Dreamweaver Assets panel, and Library items can be treated like most other assets.

- The use of Library items provides a number of advantages over traditional methods of updating a site. Library items offer fast, cascading updates, centralization of code, design consistency, and almost eliminate the need for SSIs.

- Library items also have their limitations, including needing to upload each page when a change is made to the Library.

- Combining Templates and the Library provides an extremely powerful solution for rapid site design and maintenance.

- A handful of issues surround the use of JavaScript and Library items, but these are easily addressed if you are prepared for them.

- Combined with the use of some JavaScript, a multistate navigation item can be built using the Library, which can save hours off your production time.

# Chapter 11

# Advanced Table Design

Objectives:

- Implement an effective table, using the best possible markup for the highest level of clarity.

- Design a table with a high level of accessibility by as many users as possible, including those with nongraphical browsers.

- Build a simple page using tables as a flexible and compatible layout tool.

Tables saw their first introduction into a web browser with Netscape Navigator 1.1. Since then, it's fair to say they haven't really changed all that much. The same rules apply as they always did, because in truth, there's nothing much that *can* change about tables; otherwise, they would no longer *be* tables.

This chapter on tables covers how tables are used in modern web development, focusing particularly on tables as a layout tool. Tables have become the de facto method for laying out web pages, although that looks set to change in the not too distant future. However, tables are still a tool in use for page layout, and like it or not, there are times when they must be used.

## What Is a Table?

What exactly is a table? We know it's a means of laying out a page in HTML, but is that it? Here's what the dictionary (`http://www.dictionary.com/`) thinks a table is:

"An orderly arrangement of data, especially one in which the data are arranged in columns and rows in an essentially rectangular form."

This tells us quite a lot about tables, even in the context of HTML. We are told that tables have a rectangular form. We know this to be true, because an HTML table cannot be L-shaped or round.

We also are told that the data is arranged in columns and rows, which again we know is true of HTML tables. As far as orderly goes, that depends entirely on the individual web developer doing the work! Simply put, an HTML table is a method of presenting data in rows and columns that, all together, make up a rectangular area, or grid.

## Back to Basics

I am aware that this is basic stuff, but stick with me because I'm leading somewhere. A basic table is made up of three different tags.

| Start Tag | Purpose | End Tag | Closure |
|-----------|---------|---------|---------|
| `<table>` | Start a new table | `</table>` | Required |
| `<tr>` | Table row | `</tr>` | Optional |
| `<td>` | Table data (cell) | `</td>` | Optional |

Ipso facto, a basic table like the one in the preceding table might look like this in HTML:

```
<table>
  <tr>
    <td>Start tag</td>
    <td>Purpose</td>
    <td>End tag</td>
    <td>Closure</td>
  </tr>
  <tr>
    <td>&lt;table&gt;</td>
    <td>Start a new table</td>
    <td>&lt;/table&gt;</td>
    <td>Required</td>
  </tr>
  <tr>
```

```
    <td>&lt;tr&gt;</td>
    <td>Table row</td>
    <td>&lt;/tr&gt;</td>
    <td>Optional</td>
  </tr>
  <tr>
    <td>&lt;td&gt;</td>
    <td>Table data (cell)</td>
    <td>&lt;/td&gt;</td>
    <td>Optional</td>
  </tr>
</table>
```

Figure 11.1 shows this table as it looks in Dreamweaver. As you can see, Dreamweaver inserts closing `<tr>` and `<td>` tags, even though the HTML specification allows them to be left empty. Dreamweaver does this to ensure maximum browser compatibility, because some browsers can't cope with tags left unclosed even when the specification allows for it. In addition, the XHTML specification requires that all tags be closed, so this is definitely a good practice.

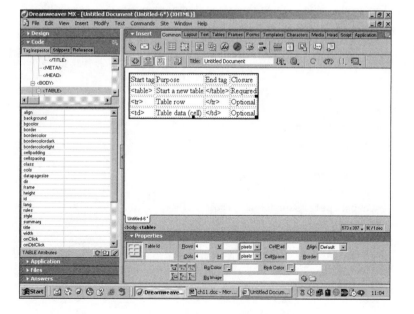

**Figure 11.1**

Our HTML table in Dreamweaver.

## Data Markup

The purpose of HTML has always been to label text in a way that identifies its structure. For example, an `<h1>` tag says that the data within it is a top-level heading, not that it should display large and bold. HTML is about the meaning of data, and not so much about how it is presented style-wise.

Although these three table tags are great at specifying how the table should be laid out, they don't tell us much about the data. Sure, we know that anything within a `<td>` tag is data for the table, but that's about as far as it goes. This calls for a few more tags to describe the data more effectively.

| Start Tag | Purpose | End Tag | Closure |
|-----------|---------|---------|---------|
| `<thead>` | Table header | `</thead>` | Optional |
| `<tbody>` | Table body | `</tbody>` | Optional |
| `<tfoot>` | Table footer | `</tfoot>` | Optional |

These three tags are for giving a more logical structure to the data, and are used to group table rows to this effect. Here's a simple table of employee names and email addresses, with no logical grouping:

```
<table>
  <tr>
    <td>First name</td>
    <td>Last name</td>
    <td>Email address</td>
  </tr>
  <tr>
    <td>Bob</td>
    <td>Peterson</td>
    <td>bob.peterson@company.com</td>
  </tr>
  <tr>
    <td>Julia</td>
    <td>Redgrave</td>
    <td>julia.redgrave@company.com</td>
  </tr>
  <tr>
    <td>Mandy</td>
    <td>Appleton</td>
```

```
      <td>mandy.appleton@company.com</td>
    </tr>
    <tr>
      <td>Stephen</td>
      <td>Courtney</td>
      <td>stephen.courtney@company.com</td>
    </tr>
    <tr>
      <td colspan="3">Updated: 28 August 2002</td>
    </tr>
</table>
```

Figure 11.2 shows this table as it appears in Dreamweaver. Notice that
although it has logical meaning to the human brain, it doesn't necessarily
mean anything to a browser. We can understand that the first row is the
heading row because we know how to interpret the data. However, a
browser cannot detect what's a heading row unless we tell it so.

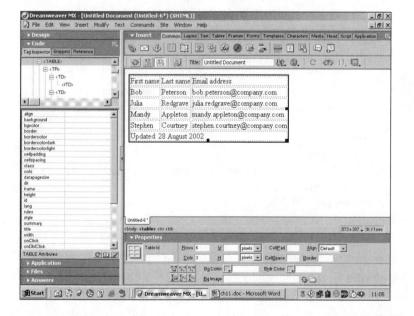

**Figure 11.2**

Although we
can see the
headings, a
browser cannot.

Making use of the table head, body and foot tags, here is how the table
would be more logically laid out:

```
<table>
      <thead>
            <tr>
```

```
                <td>First name</td>
                <td>Last name</td>
                <td>Email address</td>
            </tr>
        </thead>
        <tbody>
            <tr>
                <td>Bob</td>
                <td>Peterson</td>
                <td>bob.peterson@company.com</td>
            </tr>
            <tr>
                <td>Julia</td>
                <td>Redgrave</td>
                <td>julia.redgrave@company.com</td>
            </tr>
            <tr>
                <td>Mandy</td>
                <td>Appleton</td>
                <td>mandy.appleton@company.com</td>
            </tr>
            <tr>
                <td>Stephen</td>
                <td>Courtney</td>
                <td>stephen.courtney@company.com</td>
            </tr>
        </tbody>
        <tfoot>
            <tr>
                <td colspan="3">Updated: 28 March 2001</td>
            </tr>
        </tfoot>
</table>
```

Figure 11.3 shows how this amended table looks in Dreamweaver. As you can see, it renders no differently in Dreamweaver than if I had not used the additional tags; but the difference is that the data is structured logically, helping those with nongraphical browsers, and even search engines.

Unfortunately, Dreamweaver has no graphical method for inserting <thead> and <tfoot> tags, so this must be done from within the Code view.

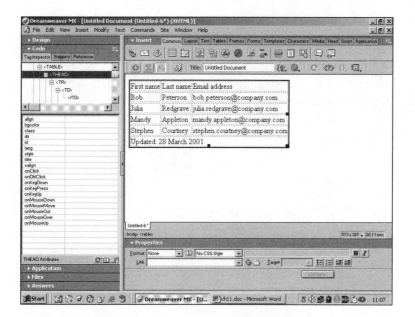

**Figure 11.3**

The amended table in Dreamweaver.

However, it doesn't end there. You must take into consideration another table tag.

| Start Tag | Purpose | End Tag | Closure |
|-----------|---------|---------|---------|
| `<th>` | Table-heading cell | `</th>` | Optional |

The table-heading cell is another device for denoting the structure of the data. Used in place of the `<td>` tag for heading elements, it's another good way to tell the browser that the data forms part of the whole of a heading.

Adding this tag to the table, it now looks like this:

```
<table>
      <thead>
            <tr>
                  <th>First name</th>
                  <th>Last name</th>
                  <th>Email address</th>
            </tr>
      </thead>
      <tbody>
            <tr>
                  <td>Bob</td>
                  <td>Peterson</td>
                  <td>bob.peterson@company.com</td>
```

```
                    </tr>
                    <tr>

                            <td>Julia</td>
                            <td>Redgrave</td>
                            <td>julia.redgrave@company.com</td>
                    </tr>
                    <tr>

                            <td>Mandy</td>
                            <td>Appleton</td>
                            <td>mandy.appleton@company.com</td>
                    </tr>
                    <tr>

                            <td>Stephen</td>
                            <td>Courtney</td>
                            <td>stephen.courtney@company.com</td>
                    </tr>
            </tbody>
            <tfoot>
                    <tr>

                            <td colspan="3">Updated: 28 March 2001</td>
                    </tr>
            </tfoot>
    </table>
```

Figure 11.4 shows this table as it is represented in Dreamweaver. Note how
the table-heading row is now automatically emboldened to indicate its status.

**Figure 11.4**

The headings
are bold.

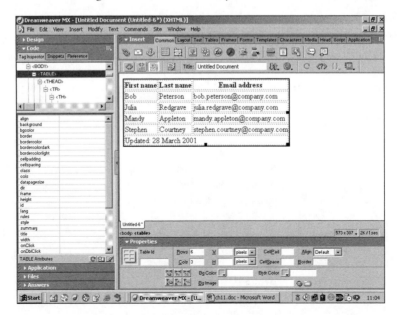

In Dreamweaver, you can tell an existing `<td>` table cell to become a `<th>` table cell by selecting it and checking the Header box in the Property inspector.

What we have done now is taken a table that displays data perfectly well and enhanced it by giving the data a structure. You might ask what the point of this is when the table is only ever read by a human. The answer is simple: The table is read by a browser first, which interprets the data for the user to view. By adding in these extra snippets of information, the web developer gives the browser every possible opportunity to present the data in a way that the user can understand.

## Tables and Nonvisual Browsers

Although most graphical browsers manage to display a table in a way that is immediately and easily processed by the human brain, nongraphical browsers have a tougher job on their hands.

The nongraphical browser has to be able to interpret a page so that it can be understood through the medium in which it has to present it. This might be through speech, through ASCII, or even through Braille.

Take a moment and look at this far simpler table:

```
<table>
  <tr>
    <td>Student</td>
    <td>Score</td>
  </tr>
  <tr>
    <td>A</td>
    <td>34</td>
  </tr>
  <tr>
    <td>B</td>
    <td>23</td>
  </tr>
  <tr>
```

```
      <td>C</td>
      <td>65</td>
    </tr>
    <tr>
      <td>D</td>
      <td>45</td>
    </tr>
</table>
```

Figure 11.5 shows how the table displays in Dreamweaver. Notice how the table is very basic and immediately understandable, but has no logical structure so far as HTML is concerned.

**Figure 11.5**

A basic table in Dreamweaver.

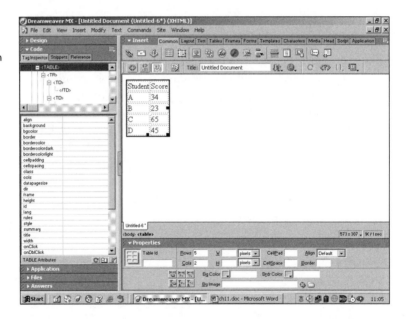

The real mystery about developing web sites is that the developer really has no idea about how the code is going to be viewed or otherwise experienced. If I were given the task of designing a speech browser, I would probably have it speak the lines of the table in turn, top to bottom, left to right. My browser might verbalize the simple table as follows:

```
Student, Score.
A, thirty-four.
B, twenty-three.
C, sixty-five.
D, forty-five.
```

As you can see, it makes a little sense, but not a great deal. It's not an ideal way to present the information, because it's actually coming across as a string of data rather than the information it should appear to be. Imagine what would happen as soon as the table got any more complicated than this one.

Let's modify the table to use table-heading tags to give the table a little more structure. Modified, the table would look like this:

```
<table>
  <tr>
    <th>Student</th>
    <th>Score</th>
  </tr>
  <tr>
    <td>A</td>
    <td>34</td>
  </tr>
  <tr>
    <td>B</td>
    <td>23</td>
  </tr>
  <tr>
    <td>C</td>
    <td>65</td>
  </tr>
  <tr>
    <td>D</td>
    <td>45</td>
  </tr>
</table>
```

We have now given the speech browser a crucial extra nugget of information. The browser can now discern a heading from the rest of the data. This is bound to affect the way the table is verbalized, and it now might sound more like this:

```
Student A, Score thirty-four.
Student B, Score twenty-three.
Student C, Score sixty-five.
Student D, Score forty-five.
```

The table immediately takes on more meaning, and can be more readily understood by the user.

## Note

> Don't misunderstand the point. There is no suggestion that this is precisely how speech browsers work. I am suggesting a way in which a speech browser could work if the author designed it to. In the same way, as a web developer you can never be sure of how your page is being viewed, and so structuring the page logically really helps such browsers to interpret the data correctly. One of the key aspects of marking up a page correctly and to web standards is to make sure that the page can be read by technologies that we haven't even thought of yet.

This is why it is so important to mark up pages not only for presentation, but also in terms of structure. It is especially important that you do so if there's any possibility that users might view your site with unusual browsers. If you are developing a web site for other web developers, this might not be so much of a consideration (because web developers are going to be viewing the site with the latest graphical browsers). If the intended audience is the public at large, however, it should definitely be a consideration.

# Browser Support for Tables

The vast majority of current browsers, and certainly all graphical browsers in use today, support the rendering of tables. So common are tables in HTML, that most nongraphical browsers in use support them as well.

The problem comes not with whether a particular browser supports the rendering of tables—because nearly all do—but with how a particular browser chooses to render it.

Look at the simple table of students and scores again:

```
<table>
  <tr>
    <th>Student</th>
    <th>Score</th>
```

```
    </tr>
    <tr>
      <td>A</td>
      <td>34</td>
    </tr>
    <tr>
      <td>B</td>
      <td>23</td>
    </tr>
    <tr>
      <td>C</td>
      <td>65</td>
    </tr>
    <tr>
      <td>D</td>
      <td>45</td>
    </tr>
</table>
```

In a graphical browser, such as Internet Explorer, the table might look Figure 11.6.

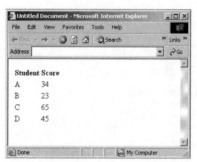

**Figure 11.6**

Our simple table in Internet Explorer.

In a nongraphical browser, such as a *Personal Digital Assistant* (PDA) or a mobile phone, however, the table might be rendered more like this:

```
- - - - - - - - - - - - - - - - -
| Student | Score  |
|---------|--------|
| A       | 34     |
| B       | 23     |
| C       | 65     |
| D       | 45     |
- - - - - - - - - - - - - - - - -
```

As you can see, the way in which the table is rendered by two different types of browser varies tremendously. The real challenge when designing tables is to make them render reasonably in all your target browsers.

If your site is being developed for desktop computer users (as most web sites today are—rightly or wrongly), the task is made easier by fairly good support and rendering consistency between the major browsers in use. Even with so-called safe browsers, a number of known issues will cause your tables to render differently.

## Known Issues

When it comes to rendering differences between the major browsers, a number of known issues exist. The good news is that these are fairly well documented around the web and are not difficult to learn or insurmountable problems in themselves.

### Collapsing Cells

Netscape Navigator 4 as a problem with empty cells. Cells with no content tend to "collapse" and fail to display on the page, although a space for them is reserved. This is particularly noticeable when the cell has a background color or image assigned, in which case the missing cell can stand out like a sore thumb.

Look at this basic table, for example:

```
<table bgcolor="#000000" width="200">
  <tr>
    <td> </td>
    <td> </td>
  </tr>
  <tr>
    <td> </td>
    <td></td>
  </tr>
  <tr>
    <td> </td>
    <td> </td>
  </tr>
  <tr>
```

```
   <td></td>
   <td> </td>
 </tr>
 <tr>
   <td> </td>
   <td> </td>
 </tr>
</table>
```

Notice how most cells have been given a nonbreaking space as content. However, two cells have been left totally empty.

Figure 11.7 shows the table displayed in Internet Explorer 5. Notice how that even though two cells are totally empty, the table renders as expected. Figure 11.8 shows the same table, as viewed in Navigator 4. Notice how the empty cells have been collapsed and the background color no longer displays for those cells. Also table background colors do not display, so any "gutter" between table cells will show through as the page background color.

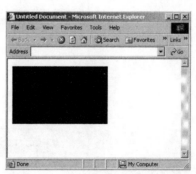

**Figure 11.7**

A table viewed in Internet Explorer 5.

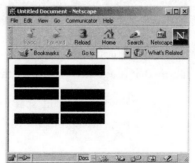

**Figure 11.8**

The same table viewed in Navigator 4.

This can be a real problem, especially when using tables for layout. Dreamweaver will always insert a nonbreaking space on your behalf when creating a table to prevent the collapse, but a nonbreaking space is essentially a textual element. The result of this is that the nonbreaking space is subject to all the same rules as a line of text. This means that any font, size, and line spacing that you may have defined in your style sheet will naturally take effect on the space.

The problem comes when you need to have a very thin row. Perhaps you want to use the row as a horizontal line, or even just a thin spacer between page elements. The height of the row will always expand to be able to contain that nonbreaking space, despite any row height values you have set (see Figure 11.9).

**Figure 11.9**

Notice how even though the row is set to 2 pixels high, it stretched to accommodate the nonbreaking space.

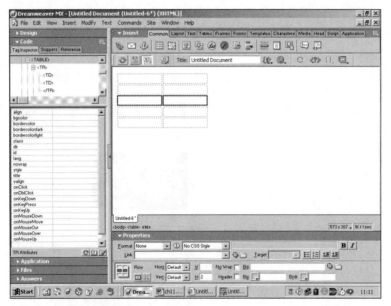

Notice that although the selected row in Figure 11.9 has a height of 2 pixels specified, it is significantly higher than this due to the nonbreaking space.

Removing the nonbreaking space enables you to accurately control the height, but presents a problem when the cell collapses (see Figure 11.10).

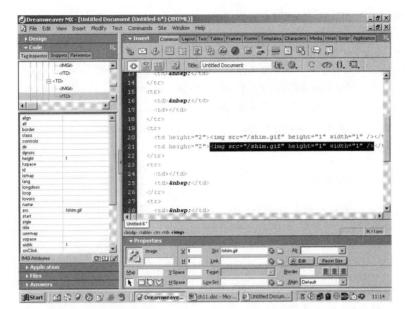

**Figure 11.10**

Replacing the
nonbreaking
space with a
small transparent
GIF gets around
the problem.

Notice that in the row in Figure 11.10, this problem has been rectified, and what's more, the cell hasn't collapsed. This was achieved with the use of a transparent GIF (or *shim*) image. By replacing the nonbreaking space with a shim, it is possible to control the size of the area (the height of a row, or the width of a column) without the cell collapsing, because it now has some content.

This technique is widely used and accepted as a good way to control how a table displays in the browser. You learn how to use spacer images to control table layout later in this chapter.

## *Caution*

If your table has any cell padding or cell spacing values assigned, this could affect your ability to make a table cell very small, because these settings would conflict. When you need absolute control, it is sensible to set your cell padding and cell spacing to zero. Remember that if you give no value at all, both will default to about two pixels. Actively set these values to zero to maintain control.

## Table and Table Cell Background Images

As you know, HTML enables the developer to specify a background image for table cells and even for whole tables. This enables the developer to build more visually appealing tables and also to put images into table cells while still allowing the cell to compact if necessary. Unfortunately, there is inconsistency between the two major browsers, Internet Explorer and Netscape Navigator 4.

Here is a basic table with a background image applied:

```
<table width="100%" border="1" background="abc.gif">
  <tr>
    <td> </td>
    <td> </td>
    <td> </td>
    <td> </td>
    <td> </td>
  </tr>
  <tr >
    <td> </td>
    <td> </td>
    <td> </td>
    <td> </td>
    <td> </td>
  </tr>
  <tr>
    <td> </td>
    <td> </td>
    <td> </td>
    <td> </td>
    <td> </td>
  </tr>
</table>
```

For clarity, I have left the cells empty apart from the obligatory nonbreaking space—to show the effect more clearly. The background image used is a simple GIF showing the letters of the alphabet—to aid easy recognition of repeats (see Figure 11.11).

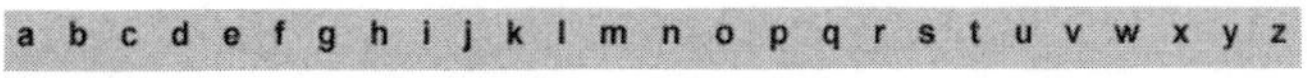

a b c d e f g h i j k l m n o p q r s t u v w x y z

**Figure 11.11**

The simple GIF showing the letters of the alphabet used to test different background tiling behaviors.

Figure 11.12 shows how the table displays in Internet Explorer. Note how the image displays across all cells and repeats vertically when needed. Figure 11.13 shows the table as it displays in Netscape 4. Notice how the image starts again for each and every table cell. As you can see, Navigator 4 is particularly unhelpful when it comes to table backgrounds, making the developer's life a much harder one. However, you'll be pleased to hear that there is a workaround for this problem. It's not a total solution, because it introduces extra code that would otherwise not be needed; but as I say, it serves as a workaround.

**Figure 11.12**

The table displays correctly in IE6.

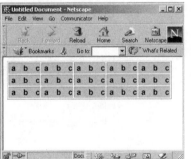

**Figure 11.13**

Navigator 4 makes a mess of the table.

The problem occurs when a new cell begins. It is at this point that the background starts to repeat; so we would be safe to say that if our table had only one cell, the problem would not exist. This leads us to the key to getting around the problem. We create a new, single cell table and move our original table to nest within that one cell. Then by removing the background image from the original table and applying it to the new table, we can

achieve the same effect. It is important, however, that the original table has
no other background colors applied; otherwise, the image will not show
through from beneath. We do, however, need to apply a transparent GIF (or
shim) image to the table as a background, to convince Netscape that we
are in charge.

Our table now looks like this.

```
<table width="100%" border="0" cellspacing="0" cellpadding="0"
➥background="abc.gif">
  <tr>
    <td>
      <table width="100%" border="1" background="shim.gif">
        <tr>
          <td> </td>
          <td> </td>
          <td> </td>
          <td> </td>
          <td> </td>
        </tr>
        <tr >
          <td> </td>
          <td> </td>
          <td> </td>
          <td> </td>
          <td> </td>
        </tr>
        <tr>
          <td> </td>
          <td> </td>
          <td> </td>
          <td> </td>
          <td> </td>
        </tr>
      </table>
    </td>
  </tr>
</table>
```

It is clear to see how the one table is nested within the other, allowing the
background image to shine through.

Figure 11.14 shows how the table now displays in Netscape Navigator 4.

**Figure 11.14**

Our improved
table now
displays
correctly.

As you can see, the fix worked well; and although we have had to introduce some extra code, it is probably worth it because it enables Navigator
4 users to get the most out of the page in question.

## Cascading Style Sheet Effects

I discovered a very strange browser inconsistency once when developing
a business-to-business portal site. Although my table cells and images were
lining up beautifully in Internet Explorer, things were going seriously amiss
with Navigator 4.

It was only when I resorted to moving the suspect table out of my page
and into a test page to work on rebuilding it that I discovered the problem.
Moving the table into a new, blank page had the effect of disconnecting
it from the style sheet. This immediately rectified the problem, although it
took me a little while to connect the two factors in my head.

What I'd done was to redefine the `<td>` tag in the style sheet. Because all
the text in the site was supposed to have a line height of 140 percent, I
thought that the easiest way to do this was to redefine all table cells to give
any text within them 140-percent line height.

This worked as planned with IE, but Navigator 4 chose to give all objects
140-percent line height, be they text or not. The result was that my
images were being given extra spacing around them that threw out the
alignment of the table.

The workaround was to remove the line-height setting from the table cell and create a new custom class that could be applied to all text. As I was working with Templates, this worked equally well because I was able to put the code for this outside of the editable region.

The important thing to remember is this: Netscape Navigator 4 seems to apply CSS attributes that would logically belong to text in any element on the page. This is why my images were being thrown out of alignment. Internet Explorer, on the other hand, does not behave this way, choosing to apply such attributes only to text.

### Style Cascading

There are slight differences in the way in which styles cascade through elements between Navigator 4 and Internet Explorer. In IE, for example, style settings inherit through to table cells, but in NN they do not.

Look at a practical example of this. Consider this basic page:

```
<html>
<head>
<title>Cascading test</title>
<meta http-equiv="Content-Type" content="text/html;
➥charset=iso-8859-1">
<style type="text/css">
<!--
body {
    font-family: Arial, Helvetica, sans-serif;
    font-size: 10px;
    font-weight: bold;
    color: #FF0000;
}
-->
</style>
</head>

<body bgcolor="#FFFFFF" text="#000000">
<p>This is some text within the body of the page.</p>
<table width="300">
  <tr>
    <td>This is some text</td>
    <td> </td>
```

```
    </tr>
    <tr>
      <td> </td>
      <td>within a table cell.</td>
    </tr>
    <tr>
      <td> </td>
      <td> </td>
    </tr>
</table>
</body>
</html>
```

As you can see, I've used some simple CSS to redefine the <body> tag to set text to be Arial, to be 10 pixels in size, to be bold, and to be red.

Figure 11.15 shows how this page displays in Internet Explorer. Notice how IE manages to force the text within the table to inherit the font and color, but fails to implement the size and the weight. Figure 11.16 shows the same page in Netscape Navigator 4; NN fails to allow the table cells to inherit any of the style properties from the body of the document.

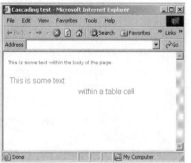

**Figure 11.15**

The page displayed in IE6.

**Figure 11.16**

The same page in NN4.

This problem can be addressed by duplicating the body styles as table cell styles. When done, the page looks like this:

```html
<html>
<head>
<title>Cascading test</title>
<meta http-equiv="Content-Type" content="text/html;
➥charset=iso-8859-1">
<style type="text/css">
<!--
body {
    font-family: Arial, Helvetica, sans-serif;
    font-size: 10px;
    font-weight: bold;
    color: #FF0000;
}
td {
    font-family: Arial, Helvetica, sans-serif;
    font-size: 10px;
    font-weight: bold;
    color: #FF0000;
}
-->
</style>
</head>

<body bgcolor="#FFFFFF" text="#000000">
<p>This is some text within the body of the page.</p>
<table width="300">
  <tr>
    <td>This is some text</td>
    <td> </td>
  </tr>
  <tr>
    <td> </td>
    <td>within a table cell.</td>
  </tr>
  <tr>
    <td> </td>
    <td> </td>
  </tr>
</table>
</body>
</html>
```

With the `<td>` tag now taking on the same properties as the `<body>` tag, the web developer can ensure that the styles will be carried across appropriately.

Figure 11.17 shows how the updated page now displays in Internet Explorer. Notice how all the styles are carried through to the text within the table cells. Figure 11.18 shows the same updated page in Netscape Navigator 4. Notice the massive improvement in how Navigator 4 displays the styles. Now all the attributes are being picked up, whereas before none were.

**Figure 11.17**

The updated page in IE6.

**Figure 11.18**

The updated page in NN4.

# What the W3C Says About Tables

The *World Wide Web Consortium* (W3C) was founded in October 1994, with an aim to "lead the World Wide Web to its full potential by developing common protocols that promote its evolution and ensure its interoperability."

As a body, it is responsible for laying out specifications and guidelines for web technologies, and is generally accepted as the group to listen to when it comes to the web. The W3C (www.w3.org) is responsible for recommending versions and changes to the HTML specification.

As you would expect from a body such as the W3C, its line is to always push for what is "correct" rather than what "works." In the original specification for HTML, tables were designated devices for the laying out of tabular data. Tables were never intended to be used for alignment of page elements, and certainly not in the way they are used today. For this reason, the W3C recommends against using tables for layout and pushes for the sole use of CSS-P for the layout of pages.

This is a rather radical statement when you look at how the world's web pages are constructed at the moment. Virtually all web sites make use of tables for the layout of their pages. For a body such as the W3C to step in and say that this is bad practice is quite a significant move. There are a vast number of considerations when designing pages with CSS-P—including browser support—that are just not an issue when using tables for layout.

## Tables for Layout

The W3C clearly recommends against using tables for layout. Here's what it says in the HTML 4.01 specification:

> "Tables should not be used purely as a means to layout document content as this may present problems when rendering to non-visual media. Additionally, when used with graphics, these tables may force users to scroll horizontally to view a table designed on a system with a larger display. To minimize these problems, authors should use style sheets to control layout rather than tables."

As you saw in Chapter 8, "Advanced CSS Design," providing a modern, flexible page layout in CSS-P takes a little bit of extra effort but is perfectly achievable in the current day. The proviso is that we know what sort of browsers our audience is using to visit our site, and are comfortable enough to decrease the level of support for those using bad browsers such as Navigator 4.

So what can we do? If web developers keep on coding for older browsers, will the web ever move forward? As far as I can see, no one would ever need to upgrade his or her browser, and so we would remain in this position for a very long time to come.

The Web Standards Project (`http://www.webstandards.org/`) has a suggestion for us. Their recommendation is to notify the user if they are using a browser that is not standards-compliant. They suggest two ways to do this:

• Redirect users with noncompliant browsers to a page asking them to upgrade.

• Display a polite message to users with noncompliant browsers, recommending that they use a standards-compliant browser, but allow them to view the site anyway.

Obviously, the first approach is rather harsh, and not something a developer would want to do on a client's professional business site. For most of us, the second method could offer a good solution.

Figure 11.19 shows the home page of A List Apart (`http://www.alistapart.com/`), a site developed by Jeffrey Zeldman of the Web Standards Project. (This is how the page appears in Internet Explorer 6, a standards-compliant browser. As you can see, the page displays well and looks perfectly normal.)

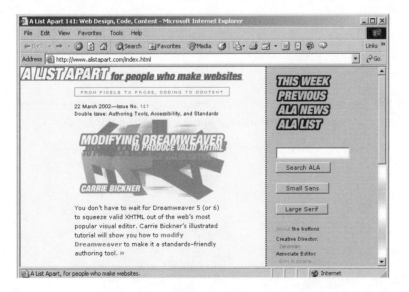

**Figure 11.19**

A List Apart viewed with IE6.

Now compare this to Figure 11.20, the same site as viewed in the noncompliant Netscape Navigator 4.7. Not only does the page display totally differently (because of the design's reliance on CSS-P), but at the very top the user is presented with a polite message recommending that he upgrade his browser.

**Figure 11.20**

A List Apart viewed with NN4.7.

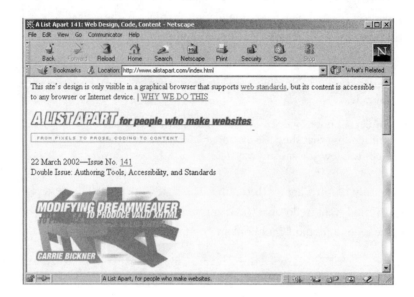

In my opinion, this is a realistic way web developers can start to make a difference to the way the web is viewed and the rate at which it moves forward. Just designing sites that force users with older browsers out isn't so helpful; enabling them to view the site, while recommending that they would do better to upgrade to a standards-compliant browser, is a good move.

*Tip*

You can find out more about the **Web Standards Project** at their web site (http://www.webstandards.org/).

## Accessibility

One of the main points that the W3C brings up about the use of CSS-P in preference to tables is that of accessibility. One of the key points to consider when developing a web site for high levels of accessibility is the use of unusual user agents, such as text to speech browsers.

With such browsers, the page is not rendered in the usual way, but read through (minus the markup) from top to bottom. This causes interesting results when it comes to tables. The previous chapter on layers covered how tables are read when linearized by a nongraphical browser.

### Note

Linearization is the process whereby the source of an HTML page is read through from top to bottom, taking the data as it comes. The process takes no account of how the data would be rendered in a graphical browser.

Notice how the data is arranged in three columns of three items. This is a fairly common layout of data, but look how it is represented in the HTML:

```
<table width="300">
  <tr>
    <td><strong>1</strong> - Cat</td>
    <td><strong>4</strong> - Dog</td>
    <td><strong>7</strong> - Badger</td>
  </tr>
  <tr>
    <td><strong>2</strong> - Mouse</td>
    <td><strong>5 </strong>- Rabbit</td>
    <td><strong>8</strong> - Fox</td>
  </tr>
  <tr>
    <td><strong>3</strong> - Horse</td>
    <td><strong>6</strong> - Elephant</td>
    <td><strong>9</strong> - Penguin</td>
  </tr>
</table>
```

Were this page to be read by a nongraphical browser and therefore be linearized, the data would be presented to the user as follows:

```
1 - Cat
4 - Dog
7 - Badger
2 - Mouse
5 - Rabbit
8 - Fox
3 - Horse
6 - Elephant
9 - Penguin
```

As you can see, the order of the data is a far cry from the original order and could potentially lead to a nasty zoo-keeping mishap. This is a vital consideration when designing tables for a wide audience.

However, it's not all doom and gloom when it comes to using tables and trying to design for accessibility. There are often ways around these problems. Figure 11.21 shows this table again in a browser.

**Figure 11.21**

The animal table in Internet Explorer.

It looks exactly the same as before, but there is a crucial difference. Take a look at the code:

```
<table width="300">
  <tr>
    <td>
      <table width="100%" cellspacing="0" cellpadding="0">
        <tr>
          <td><strong>1</strong> - Cat</td>
        </tr>
        <tr>
          <td><strong>2</strong> - Mouse</td>
```

```
          </tr>
          <tr>
            <td><strong>3</strong> - Horse</td>
          </tr>
        </table>
      </td>
      <td>
        <table width="100%" cellspacing="0" cellpadding="0">
          <tr>
            <td><strong>4</strong> - Dog</td>
          </tr>
          <tr>
            <td><strong>5 </strong>- Rabbit</td>
          </tr>
          <tr>
            <td><strong>6</strong> - Elephant</td>
          </tr>
        </table>
      </td>
      <td>
        <table width="100%" cellspacing="0" cellpadding="0">
          <tr>
            <td><strong>7</strong> - Badger</td>
          </tr>
          <tr>
            <td><strong>8</strong> - Fox</td>
          </tr>
          <tr>
            <td><strong>9</strong> - Penguin</td>
          </tr>
        </table>
      </td>
    </tr>
</table>
```

Those with sharp eyes among you will have noticed the technique I've brought into play here. By creating a master table of three columns but only one row, and then nesting smaller tables inside each of those cells, the data now appears in the correct order in the code. Of course, when linearized the code will be read as follows:

```
1 - Cat
2 - Mouse
3 - Horse
```

```
4 - Dog
5 - Rabbit
6 - Elephant
7 - Badger
8 - Fox
9 - Penguin
```

This accurate reading of the data could prevent that nasty zoo-keeping accident that could have cost the lives of many animals and innocent civilians.

This method works by splitting the data up into a single dimension. That is, the data always resides within one column or one row. By having data going in two directions like our original table did (we were using rows and columns), the possibility for misinterpretation was introduced. By keeping the data in multiple, single-dimension blocks, we have been able keep it readable by all browsers and have removed, or at least vastly reduced, the possibility of error.

## Making Tables Easy to Read

I am of the opinion that web accessibility doesn't solely refer to making sites accessible to those with disabilities. The term can be used to describe how easy a web site is to read and view in general terms.

On this note, I urge you to consider the design of long tables of data. It's not only those with less than 20/20 vision who suffer when trying to read large tables of data, it's all of us, because huge amounts of data can be overwhelming. Here are some points to consider:

- **Text size.** Allow enough space for the text to breathe in its cell, without making the text too small to read.

- **Text weight.** Make key pieces of data bold to make the table easier to scan.

- **Line height.** Don't cram the data together—web page real estate is free, so don't be afraid to let your table run long if it makes it easier to read.

- **Row color.** Use alternate background colors on your table rows so that the eye can easily track a single line as it moves along it.

# Controlling Your Page with Tables

Most web developers are familiar with the fact that an HTML element on a page is difficult to control without something to contain it. This is where tables come into play, as an HTML-based alternative to CSS-P. Web developers have been using tables for years to control the way a web page is laid out.

After you have been working with tables for a little while, it soon becomes possible to build up very complex tables to hold a design together. There are various tips and tricks used to manipulate tables into the shape and space the developer needs them to conform to. This section covers some of those ways to control table layout.

## Using Spacer Images to Control Layout

As far as a browser is concerned, a table holds tabular data, and it is the browser's job to make sure that data displays in the best way possible. Unfortunately, this can tend to mean that browsers can be slightly liberal with the way they space columns and rows, and will sometimes fudge the figures to make data fit instead of following the exact dimensions specified by the developer in the HTML.

When it comes to using tables as a layout device, this attribute of browser behavior can prove to be something of a difficulty. For example, a browser might choose to widen a column rather than lengthen it if there is nothing to prevent adjacent columns from squeezing together. When the design dictates that those neighboring columns should be left as whitespace, this effectively "breaks" the design.

The solution to this problem often comes in the shape of a shim. In this context, a shim is a usually one pixel-by-one pixel transparent GIF image. This image, weighing in at far less than one kilobyte, can be reused throughout each page and the whole site without adding anything noticeable to the download time of the site. The beauty of a shim is that it can be resized using the `width` and `height` attributes of the `<img>` tag to fill any gap in a table and prevent it from resizing or collapsing.

## Liquid Design

*Liquid design* is a term used to describe a web page whose design reflows and adjusts to fit the available space in the browser window. Thankfully, tables make designing a liquid page as easy as pie, provided a few basic rules are followed.

### Use a Master Containing Table

By containing the entire content of a page within a single, master containing table, the web developer can control the layout more precisely than if several tables were used freely on the page.

With some browsers, however, the page will not display until the entire table (and therefore, page) has been downloaded. This results in the page not displaying as it loads. The effect this has will vary from page to page, and should be weighed up as part of the design process.

### Absolute Versus Relative Values

For a web page to be able to stretch and adjust to the user's browser window, the page must be calculating its values from that browser width. The easiest way to do this is to discard the use of absolute width values (such as 600 pixels) and replace them with relative width values, such as 100 percent. That 100 percent is referring to the width of the page, so HTML already has a built-in mechanism for working with liquid designs.

### Define Fixed Values and Leave the Rest Blank

After you have set up your table at 100-percent width, you need to specify the width of those elements that should not stretch in pixels. For the cells that should stretch, the most successful method is to divide the percentage values among the cells so that the total equals 100 percent. This ensures that the correct parts of your page stretch and compress as the window is resized, holding your design together as you had intended.

# Building a Page with Tables

In the Chapter 8, you learned how to design a basic page using CSS-P. As a direct comparison, we are going to design the same page using a table, and then push our page further to include some new elements and look at different ways in which tables are used.

Figure 11.22 shows a diagram of the sort of simple page we are going to build. It has two columns—a Menu column and a Content column—and one header row. A good, basic design like this will help you get to grips with the techniques.

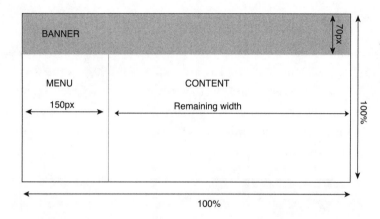

**Figure 11.22**

The plan: a really simple starting point.

## Step 1: The Page

The first thing to do is to set up a basic, empty page. Open a new, blank page in Dreamweaver and save it. Next you need to make sure all page borders and margins are switched off, because this will enable you to truly stretch the page over 100 percent of the browser window. Open the Page Properties window from the Modify menu and set all the margin properties to zero (see Figure 11.23). While in this dialog box, you may want to choose a background color for the page. I'm going to leave mine as white, just because it shows up nicely on the printed pages of this book.

That should be all that needs to be done to set up your page. Next you need to consider the table that you are going to use. As you will have worked out by now, you need two rows and two columns—one for the menu and one for the content.

**Figure 11.23**

The Page
Properties
dialog box used
for setting
options that
govern the
entire page.

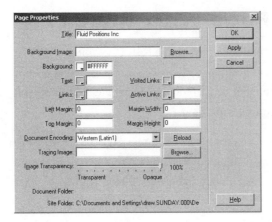

## Step 2: The Table

Using the Insert Table object, you need to insert a table that is two rows
by two columns, and that has no border and 100-percent width. I'm
going to set the cell padding to 10 pixels and the spacing to 0. This is how
the table is represented in Dreamweaver. As can be seen in Figure 11.24,
Dreamweaver automatically shows the two columns of 50-percent width
each and the two rows.

**Figure 11.24**

Dreamweaver
automatically
evens out
columns in new
tables, showing
both at 50% in
this example.

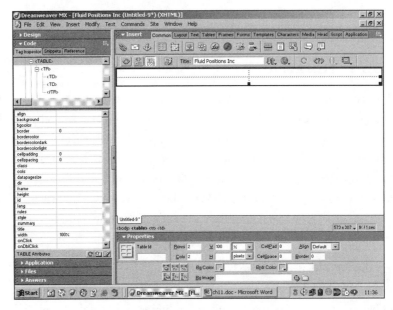

The first thing to do is to merge the cells of the top row to create the banner. Select both cells, right-click, and select Table > Merge Cells. Alternatively, you can use the equals button on the Property inspector. Set the background color for the cell to gray and the height of the row to 70 pixels.

In the next row, you need to have the Menu column (the first column) a lot narrower than the Content column, so using the Property inspector, set the width of the columns to 150 pixels for the menu and leave the final column blank. This should allow the content to stretch to the available width. At the same time, it's a good opportunity to set the vertical alignment of the cells to `"top"`.

As it stands, here is the page now:

```
<html>
<head>
    <title>Fluid Positions Inc</title>
</head>

<body bgcolor="#FFFFFF" text="#000000"
leftmargin="0" topmargin="0" marginwidth="0" marginheight="0">
<table width="100%"  border="0"  cellspacing="0" cell-
padding="10">
  <tr>
    <td colspan="2" bgcolor="gray"> </td>
  </tr>
  <tr>
    <td width="150"> </td>
    <td> </td>
  </tr>
</table>
</body>
</html>
```

If you compare this code to that of the page built with CSS-P in Chapter 8, you see an obvious saving in code by avoiding using a table. When populated with content, the page looks like what's listed here. Notice how I also have had to sacrifice some structure by separating menu items with line breaks. An alternative way to do this with tables is to nest the links with a small table of their own. This would have made the code even more verbose than it already is, however.

```
<html>
<head>
<title>Fluid Positions Inc</title>
</head>
<body bgcolor="#FFFFFF" text="#000000"
leftmargin="0" topmargin="0" marginwidth="0" marginheight="0">
<table width="100%"  border="0"  cellspacing="0"
➥cellpadding="10">
  <tr>
    <td height="70" colspan="2" bgcolor="gray">
        <h1>Fluid Positions Inc</h1>
    </td>
  </tr>
  <tr>
    <td width="150" valign="top"> <p> <a
    ➥href="/index.html">Home</a>
    <a href="/about/"><br />
        About us</a> <a href="/positions/"><br />
        Find a Job</a> <a href="/contact/"><br />
        Contact us</a> </p></td>
    <td valign="top"> <h2>We can find you a better job!</h2>
      <p> The following text consists of a mock Latin which
      ➥has been based upon the average frequency of
      ➥characters and word lengths of the
    English language in order to reproduce a
    <a href="javascript:;">reasonably
    accurate</a> overall visual impression.
    ➥Lorem ipsum dolor sit amet,
    consectetur adipscing elit, sed diam nonnumy
    ➥eiusmod tempor incidunt
    ut labore et dolore magna aliquam erat volupat. </p>
    <p>
    Et harumd dereud facilis est er expedit distinct.
    ➥Nam liber a tempor
    cum soluta nobis eligend optio comque nihil quod a
    ➥impedit anim id
    quod maxim placeat facer <a href="javascript:;">possim
    ➥omnis</a>
    es voluptas assumenda est, omnis dolor repellend. Temporem
    ➥autem
    quinsud et aur office debit aut tum rerum necesit
    ➥atib saepe eveniet
    ut er repudiand sint et molestia non este recusand.
</p></td>
  </tr>
```

```
</table>
</body>
</html>
```

## Step 3: Browser Testing

To be honest, I couldn't find a browser in which this basic table didn't work nicely. The page displays well and resizes as planned in all the browsers on which it was tested. Figure 11.25 shows how the page looks in Internet Explorer 6.

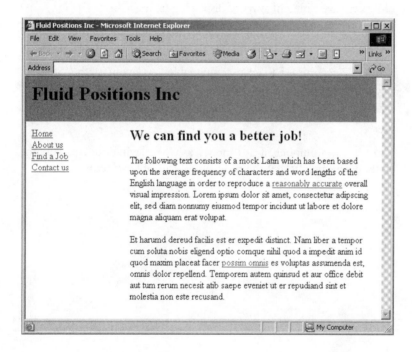

**Figure 11.25**

The page viewed in IE6.

# What to Take Away from This Chapter

- A table is an HTML device for displaying data in an organized way.

- Quite few different tags can be used when marking up a table; each has its own meaning and causes the table to be represented differently in different browsers.

- You can aid browser interpretation of a table by marking the data in terms of structure, not just in terms of style.

- Browsers support tables very well; however, some more unusual browsers have different ways of displaying tables.

- When it comes to designing a table for maximum browser compatibility, a few known issues exist. These are usually easy to deal with.

- The W3C recommends against using tables for layout, with CSS-P suggested as a practical alternative.

- You can design tables in ways that offer maximum accessibility for users.

- You can use a number of tips and tricks when laying out a page with tables. These help to get the most out of the table structure.

# Chapter 12

# Advanced Frame Design

Objectives:

- Gain an understanding of how frames are used.

- Decide when frames are the best solution, based on the relative advantages and disadvantages.

- Build and implement an inline frame solution.

Most web developers I know hate frames; they are seen as an outdated, unfashionable, clumsy solution. Web developers who are willing to recommend a frame-based solution are becoming few and far between. I feel pretty much the same way about frames, but I also believe that in a number of circumstances frames cannot be ignored as the best solution to a problem. It seems that after years of frame abuse on the web, the baby is being thrown out with the bathwater. Sometimes nothing but a frameset will do, and it is important for a web developer to recognize those situations to be able to prescribe the best solution.

This chapter attempts to increase your knowledge and understanding of frames to know when not to dismiss frames as a possible solution, and also when frames should be totally ignored in the name of philanthropy.

# What Are Frames?

Although not introduced into the HTML specification until version 4.0, frames have been in use since the days of Netscape Navigator 2. Originally designed as a convenient method of viewing multiple HTML documents simultaneously, frames tend to be used slightly differently today.

Most web developers use frames not to show multiple documents in one window, but to construct one document from many. Of course, there is zero difference technically; we are still just sectioning the window and pulling different files into different areas, but the end result for the user seems totally different.

Look at an example of this. Figure 12.1 shows a frameset containing two frames. The top frame contains (what we will imagine to be) a complex scientific paper. The bottom frame contains a glossary of terms to aid the user when reading through the paper. This was traditionally a common way to use frames. By offering the two documents in one window, the user has the glossary of terms right at hand whenever it is needed. This means that the user won't lose her place in the paper while having to look up any technical terms. However, it is rare to see an implementation of frames like this on the web today, partly because the way we organize our data has evolved and become more efficient, and partly due to human laziness.

**Figure 12.1**

Two documents within one window.

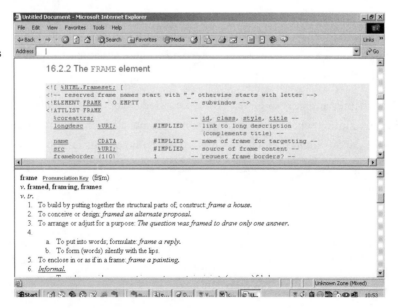

In the days before programs such as Dreamweaver (cast your minds back), maintaining a web site was a real hard slog. If you needed to update a single link, you often had to open every page in your favorite text editor and change the link every time it occurred. I am a firm believer that the core skill needed to be a web developer in those early days was patience.

Pretty soon, web developers cottoned on to the fact that splitting the site navigation off into a separate HTML document, and then piecing it back with the content using frames, would make the whole process of main-taining links much simpler. All that would be required to update a link would be to change it in the one page. What's more, download times would be reduced because the user wouldn't need to keep retrieving that navi-gation HTML with every page of content.

It very quickly became commonplace to see web sites adopting this method of two frames—navigation versus content. Figure 12.2 shows an example of a page that uses this approach. This is pretty much how frames are still used today. The visual impression given to the user is of a single page, but to the developer it is a single page made up of a number of pages.

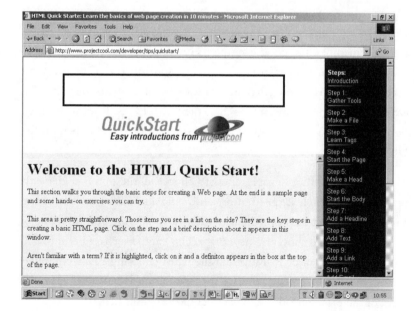

**Figure 12.2**

A frameset with separate navigation and content frames.

Of course, this method is not as transparent to the savvy user as a technology such as *server-side includes* (SSI). The use of a frameset soon becomes apparent by the strange way that fragments of the page scroll and leave the rest behind. This is sometimes read as an advantage of using frames, in that the navigation is always accessible no matter how far the user has scrolled through the content. However, many users find this disconcerting and rather strange, because they have been led to think that what they are viewing is a single document, up until that point.

There are advantages and disadvantages to using frames. It becomes the web developer's job to weigh these and come up with the best solution for the particular task at hand. Nine times out of ten, the developer will come back with an equally good solution that has fewer problematic side effects than frames do. However, there is always that one problem best addressed with frames, and it is for those times when that problem comes along that we take a close look at frames now.

## Using Frames Effectively

You may be struggling to think of a good example of frame use. Such is the overwhelming number of sites that use frames badly that it can be difficult to remember any good examples. However, one particular example stands out in my mind. The Dell Computer Corporation (`http://www.dell.com/`) has an innovative tool on their web site that enables users to configure and purchase their own PC. Sadly now removed from their U.S. web site (a great shame), the tool can still be seen on the UK site (`http://www.dell.co.uk/`).

The configuration tool enables users to choose all the optional elements of their system, such as speed of processor and amount of memory, from a number of select boxes. As the user makes a choice, the bottom frame of the set refreshes to show the new price. This can be seen in Figure 12.3. Recognizing that price is always an issue when choosing a new computer system, the developers at Dell have managed to provide feedback (in the form of the price update) with every choice the user makes.

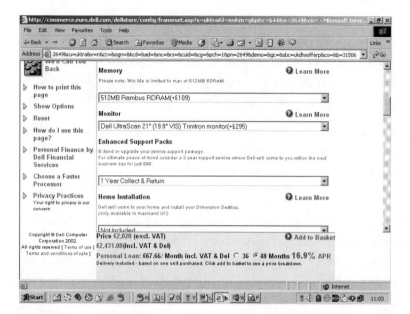

**Figure 12.3**

A great use of frames.

The result is a tool that is extremely easy to use and enables the user to maintain control through the whole process. Of course, this helps put to rest any worries the user might have about buying online. The user knows exactly which components will be included with the computer he purchases and knows exactly how much everything is costing at every step along the way.

Consider how you might re-create this design without the use of frames. You could have a single, static page with the total price at the bottom, but that would mean the page would need to be reloaded every time a choice is made. Not only would this be awkward for the user, but it would also be technically complicated to get each of the previous selections to be reloaded correctly. What's more, the total price would not always be in view, so the user would have to scroll back and forth. On such a long page, this would be a real pain.

I think it's fair to say that a regular, static page won't do the job. How about using layers? DHTML enables the developer to update things dynamically, which would solve the refreshing problem. The select boxes could be inside a layer, which scrolls independently of the rest of the page, so the price would always be visible. Could this be a solution?

I think it could, provided that you know that all your site's visitors are using a browser capable of displaying this page accurately. The last thing you want is for a user to come to the site with the intention to buy, but leave because the interface is not working properly. That user is more likely to go to a competitor than to call up a salesperson on the phone.

If you can be 100-percent sure that those visiting your site will be able to use a layer-driven system, it sounds like a great alternative. If users are hitting your site with browsers such as Netscape Navigator or even AOL's own browser, you might want to think again.

As you will see in the next section, frames are well supported now, because they are quite an old technology. You would be hard pressed to find a user running a browser older than Navigator 2. Although there are still users like that, you must choose whether to exclude those few users running browsers with no frames support or the many more who do not have a browser capable of displaying layers to a reliable level. This is why the developers at Dell opted for a frames solution; it was just the only way to do it.

## Browser Support for Frames

As far as the web goes, frames are an old technology. Having been in place since early versions of Navigator and Internet Explorer, support has been carried through to modern browsers, with the technology being incorporated into the HTML specification at version 4.0. Although support among browsers is good, there are still browsers out there that were either written before frames came about or that are not capable of displaying frames for other reasons.

A *Personal Digital Assistant* (PDA) device might be perfectly capable of browsing regular web sites, for example, but might not be able to display a frameset due to restrictions on screen real estate. Nongraphical browsers (such as ASCII browsers or speech browsers) also may have trouble translating framed pages. Other browsers might work out the frameset correctly, but not support some of the features used and so might display the end product incorrectly.

The following sections discuss the level of support available for frames.

## *<noframes>* Content

Any web developer who has worked with frames is aware of the consequences of a frameset page being visited by a browser that does not include frame support. Users are basically delivered a blank page—in fact, a page that contains no recognizable tags. To get around this, the <noframes> tag was created. The <noframes> area of a page can hold a regular <body> tag and all the content you want to show to users who do not have frames support in their browsers.

Thinking this through, it doesn't seem logical that a browser written before frames were conceived should even know about such a tag. The answer, however, becomes clear with a little understanding of how browsers process tags. A web browser reads through an HTML document and renders any tag it recognizes. Because HTML is fault-tolerant, the browser just ignores tags it does not know how to render. It is for this reason that <frame> and <frameset> tags are ignored.

This brings us to the <noframes> tag. There is no way on earth that a browser can recognize a tag created after it was written, and so this tag is ignored as well. However, the <body> tag within it is understood, and so this portion of the page is rendered as usual. It is only frame-capable browsers that know about the <noframes> tag, and so specifically ignore the <body> tags within it. This is how frame-capable browsers know not to interpret the <noframes> content and how older browsers manage to render a sensible page.

### What Should *<noframes>* Content Contain?

Let's think of a scenario in which a user might be accessing a site with a browser that is not capable of rendering frames: A web developer is on her way to the first meeting with a very big client. While waiting to board her train, the developer hears an announcement that the train has been seriously delayed. Knowing that she can't be late for the meeting, she reaches for her PDA and her mobile phone and brings up a web browser to try and access a directory service to find an alternative means of transport.

Unfortunately, the site that covers her region uses frames, and so she can't access any of the data. Rather distraught at the thought of losing this major client, she decides the best thing to do is to phone up and explain the train delays as soon as possible. Fortune is not on her side (it would spoil the story if it were); she has forgotten to bring the client's phone number with her.

She brings up another web browser on her PDA and goes to the address of the client's current web site. You can see what's coming, can't you? The site uses frames, and again she has no access to the contact details. By the time she finally manages to get to the client's offices, the gentleman she was supposed to meet has already given up on her and called up her close competitor to arrange a meeting.

A tragic story, I'm sure you'll agree. Had those web sites implemented a good set of `<noframes>` tags, much heartbreak could have been avoided. That said, what sort of content would our web developer have been looking for? Three distinct levels of content can be included in the `<noframes>` tags:

- **No content.** Just a message informing users that they need to have a browser capable of displaying frames.

- **Partial content.** The main items from the site that are considered essential. These might include a summary of the information included on the site and some contact details.

- **Full content.** The entire information set from the web site, presented outside the framed environment so as to be viewable by all users.

As you can imagine, the "no content" option would not be much help to our web developer in distress. The only use for this approach is to let users know what the problem is. Without `<noframes>` content, the user is presented with a blank page. Informing the user of the nature of the problem is some help, but not a huge amount.

The "partial content" option is the approach I would expect many web sites to take. You don't want to leave your visitors out in the cold, but to provide and maintain a second version of the site is uneconomical. The "full content" option is the ideal as far as the user is concerned; if you are able to achieve it, you'll have some extremely satisfied customers.

The simplest way to provide full content for your frameless visitors is to provide a comprehensive menu of links to each page in your site, within the <noframes> region of your site's main frameset. Link each menu item to the content document that would normally have gone into the frameset. This way, the user can navigate around the site by using the links and by pressing the back button to return to the menu each time. Although far more primitive than a normal site, this method will enable all users to access the content.

Here's what the <noframes> content might look like:

```
<noframes>
<body bgcolor="#FFFFFF" text="#000000">
<h1>Welcome to the My Company Web site.</h1>
<p>Your browser doesn't support frames, so you'll need to use the
list of links below, and click your 'back' button to
➥return to this page each time.
</p>
<p>Thanks!</p>
<ol>
  <li><b>About </b></li>
  <ul>
    <li><a href="/about/history.htm">Company History</a></li>
    <li><a href="/about/vision.htm">Company Vision</a></li>
    <li><a href="/about/jobs.htm">Vacancies</a></li>
  </ul>
  <li><b>News </b></li>
  <ul>
    <li><a href="/news/news.htm">Latest News</a></li>
    <li><a href="/news/releases.htm">Press Releases</a></li>
  </ul>
  <li><b>Products </b></li>
  <ul>
    <li><a href="/products/whizmotron.htm">Whizmotron
    ➥4000</a></li>
    <li><a href="/products/sloopwiggle.htm">Sloopwiggle-na-na
    ➥80</a>
    </li>
    <li><a href="/products/buy.htm">Where to buy</a></li>
  </ul>
  <li><b>Case Studies </b></li>
  <ul>
    <li><a href="/casestudies/1.htm">Case Study 1</a></li>
```

```
    <li><a href="/casestudies/2.htm">Case Study 2</a></li>
    <li><a href="/casestudies/3.htm">Case Study 3</a></li>
  </ul>
  <li><b>Contact </b>
    <ul>
      <li><a href="/contact/address.htm">Address</a></li>
      <li><a href="/contact/phone.htm">Phone numbers</a></li>
    </ul>
  </li>
</ol>
</body>
</noframes>
```

Figure 12.4 shows how this page would look to a user visiting the web site with a browser that cannot display frames. As you can see, this simple approach offers a great solution if your web site uses frames. It enables all users to gain access to the data, but at the same time doesn't involve too much extra work to keep both versions up-to-date.

**Figure 12.4**

The `<noframes>` content on a web site.

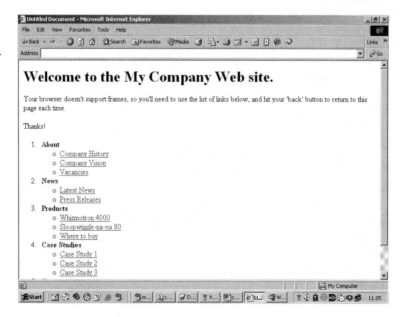

## Rendering Differences

On the whole, frames tend to render well and pretty much the same in most major browsers. After all, all we're talking about is dividing the window and loading different HTML documents; there are no objects, as such, to render. As with any technology, however, there are a few differences across browsers in the way the frames are rendered. Most of these problems exist because of the lack of a standard for frame implementation before HTML 4.0.

For a long time, frames were a lawless entity with no rules to live by. Having been in use since Navigator 2, different browser manufacturers adopted their own interpretation of frames and implemented them in their browsers the way they felt frames should work. Unfortunately, this means that there are a few inconsistencies with the way frame support is implemented in older (pre-HTML 4.0) browsers. As I said earlier, because frames don't render any objects as such, there's not much room for inconsistency. However, one thing is rendered within a frameset: the frame borders.

### Frame Borders

Other than the framed pages themselves, frame borders are the one object drawn by the browser when a frameset is displayed. This is the one opportunity that early browsers have to muck up things, and they rise to the challenge admirably.

The three main differences are as follows:

- **Color capability**. Some browsers manage to display colored borders, whereas others ignore this option totally.

- **Visibility.** Some browsers allow for the visibility of the border to be turned off, whereas others display a border come what may.

- **Width.** Some browsers allow for the adjustment of border width, whereas others don't. Also the standard width of the border varies from browser to browser.

Most of the issues with borders will go unnoticed in this day and age, either because your visitors will not be using browsers old enough to encounter these problems or because you will have the borders turned off anyway. Of course, even if you turn off borders and visitors come to your site with a very old browser, they will still see the borders. This is a minor point of style, however, and I should imagine that the content of the framed pages would suffer far worse problems than the simple frame border does.

The key, as always, is to be aware of the differences and to test with all the platforms and browsers with which you expect your site to be viewed. The differences in frame borders are minor and not likely to affect the modern web developer (but knowledge is power, as they say).

## Measurements

Far more of a concern in browser inconsistencies is the way that different browsers calculate the width and height of frames. Netscape Navigator 4, in particular, can cause enormous problems because of the method it uses to work out exactly where frame divides should fall. Generally speaking, Navigator manages to calculate the dimensions correctly to the nearest three or four pixels. This also is subject to change when the browser window is resized, even if frames are given absolute dimension values. This in itself would not be so much of a problem if all browsers worked this way. The problem arises because browsers such as Opera, Internet Explorer, and Konqueror all manage to calculate pixel-perfect framesets.

What this means in real terms is that after you have calculated the width a column needs to be in IE to fit your content, by the time it gets to Navigator, you could be as much as four pixels shy, causing the last letter of each word to be hidden, or equally badly, causing a scrollbar to appear. Unfortunately, there is no easy workaround for this little problem. The way that Navigator calculates its frame sizes is the eighth wonder of the world and is a problem built deep in to its rendering engine. Fortunately, however, this has been fixed in version 6 of Netscape Navigator.

There is one way to deal with the problems with Navigator 4 and its frame-dimension miscalculations. By using JavaScript to detect the browser being used, it is possible to redirect Navigator users to a different frameset page, with adjusted dimension values. Although not an elegant solution, if your design dictates that the frameset must be laid out just so, this is a possible solution to the problem.

The Dreamweaver Check Browser behavior is a useful tool for the job. When your intention is to redirect Navigator users to a different frameset page, your Check Browser settings might look like what is shown in Figure 12.5.

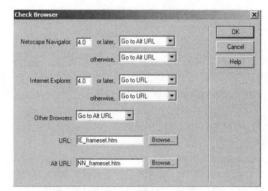

**Figure 12.5**

The Check Browser behavior offers a host of useful options.

Because a frameset document has no `<body>` tag, this behavior cannot be applied `onLoad` to your standard frameset page. Instead, a doorway page needs to be created that will direct the browser to a choice of framesets—those with Navigator to one, and everyone else to the other.

*Note*

Chapter 4, "Advanced Browser and Platform Compatibility," looks more closely at methods for redirecting certain browsers, including a close examination of the Check Browser behavior.

## Advantages of Frames

Frames would never have been invented if they did not have a number of advantages over other available methods. This part of the chapter examines the advantages of using frames over the alternatives available. The object is to give you some insight into when frames can be used and why they might be the appropriate solution for a given job.

## Managing Data

Web pages are *stateless*. That is, each page stands alone and has no concept of what has occurred in previous pages or what may occur after it has been closed. When a page is closed, any data it held or choices the user made are forgotten (unless that data is stored somewhere and made available to other pages).

One way to do this is to use cookies to store the data, and then to retrieve it with another page. Another approach is to use frames. The problem with stateless pages is that they lose their data when the page is closed. Page closure can happen when the browser is shut down or just when a link to a new page is followed. The latter causes the problems as someone is navigating around your web site.

Consider this simple frameset:

```
<frameset rows="*,1">
  <frame name="content" src="contentframe.htm">
  <frame name="data" src="dataframe.htm">
</frameset>
```

Notice the two simple frames. One is extremely small and takes up only the single-pixel row at the bottom of the page. The other fills up the rest of the window.

By loading the content into the `"content"` frame, and enabling users to navigate as they please, you now have one page that is always reloading, but another that does not reload for the duration of the site visit. All of a sudden, you have a basic place where data can be stored without the need for cookies or any server-side scripting.

By using JavaScript, you can send values over to the data frame and store those values in hidden form fields. This may sound complicated, but it is actually quite simple. Our dataframe.htm file would look like this:

```
<html>
<head>
<title>Data Frame</title>
<meta http-equiv="Content-Type" content="text/html;
charset=iso-8859-1">
</head>
```

```
<body bgcolor="#FFFFFF" text="#000000">
<form name="form1" method="post" action="">
  <input type="hidden" name="visitorName">
</form>
</body>
</html>
```

As you can see, this simple page contains only a form (**form1**) with a single hidden input field (**visitorName**). This field is going to be used to store the name of the current web site visitor, so that it can be retrieved later. Next take a look at the contentframe.htm page. First off, Figure 12.6 shows how it appears in a browser.

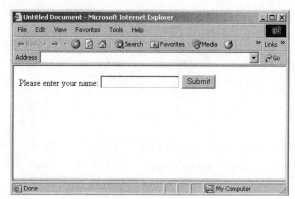

**Figure 12.6**

The user is prompted to enter their name. Little do they know that there's some secret frame trickery in use!

The code for the page looks like this:

```
<html>
<head>
<title>Content Frame</title>
<meta http-equiv="Content-Type" content="text/html;
charset=iso-8859-1">
</head>

<body bgcolor="#FFFFFF" text="#000000">
<form name="form1" method="post" action="">
  Please enter your name:
  <input type="text" name="visitorName">
  <input type="button" name="Button" value="Submit"
 onClick="parent.data.document.form1.visitorName.value =
```

```
document.form1.visitorName.value;document.location='thanks.htm
➥';">
</form>
</body>
</html>
```

As you can see, I've used some JavaScript triggered by an onClick event. Here's a breakdown of what that JavaScript is doing. First of all, this is the address of our hidden field down in the "data" frame:

```
parent.data.document.form1.visitorName.value
```

The parent navigates up and out of the "content" frame and up to the frameset. Then data directs you to the frame named "data" and then to the value of the object in form1 called visitorName. This simple use of the *Document Object Model* (DOM) has enabled us to locate the hidden form field quite easily.

The JavaScript then sets the value of that field to this:

```
document.form1.visitorName.value
```

This is the address of another field. This time it's one within the same document (contentframe.htm), and it's also called visitorName. This is the text field where you capture the data from the user.

So far we have found the hidden field and set its contents to be the same as the text box. All that is left to do is to move the user on to the next page:

```
document.location='thanks.htm'
```

This line of code just changes the location of the document to be the page called thanks.htm.

Take a look at the code behind this new page, thanks.htm:

```
<html>
<head>
<title>Thanks!</title>
<meta http-equiv="Content-Type" content="text/html;
➥charset=iso-8859-1">
</head>
```

```
<body bgcolor="#FFFFFF" text="#000000">
<script language="javascript">
document.write('Thank you, ' +
➥parent.data.document.form1.visitorName.value);
</script>
</body>
</html>
```

This is another simple page that uses the DOM again to retrieve the data from the hidden field. The `document.write` statement tells the browser to write some text to the screen. The text it is to write is `Thank you`, and the value from our hidden field. Figure 12.7 shows what it looks like in the browser after I have entered my name (Drew).

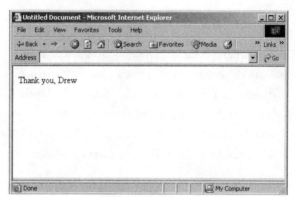

**Figure 12.7**

The page thanks the user by name. Success!

Logically, this is how the five-step process works:

1. Gather data from the user.

2. Write the data to a hidden field in the data frame.

3. Move the user on to the next page.

4. When required, retrieve the data from the hidden frame.

5. Write the data to the screen, or otherwise use it in a way appropriate to your application.

Of course, there are all sorts of different ways in which this data can be used, all of which are probably more useful than displaying a visitor's name. For example, you can use this method to set up a basic shopping cart, by having multiple hidden fields in your data frame and writing to them as items are added to the cart. When the user reaches the checkout, the data can be retrieved. You also can use this method to gather data on a multipage form.

## *Caution*

> **If the user refreshes the page (either by clicking the browser's refresh icon or by pressing F5), the data in the hidden fields will be lost. This could occur in a Netscape browser if the page is resized, because this can cause a reload, and when the page is reloaded it is set back to its original state. The only way to avoid this is to write the data out of the browser with a cookie or a server-side script.**

## Maintenance

Before programs such as Dreamweaver came along, maintaining a web site was an extremely tedious task. One advantage of using frames is that maintenance time for links and such can be vastly reduced. Consider an example of this. You have a corporate web site that consists of two main frames. The first is a navigation frame with your site's main links. The second is the frame into which all the content is loaded.

Imagine that one of the company's products is rebranded, and so you need to make sure that references on the web site are updated. Your first stop would obviously be the main navigation links. Had your site not used frames, you would be looking at going through every page of the site, updating the same link time and time again. Because you used frames, it's just a case of changing the link once.

This is more or less the traditional argument put forward for how frames save development and maintenance time. However, we are Dreamweaver users, and we have tools such as Templates, the Library, and sitewide find and replace to do these tasks for us. The powerful tools built into Dreamweaver as standard almost negate this argument for frames as a time-saver. You may now be starting to doubt my sanity—having just put a point forward as an advantage and then in the next breath dismissed it. This still is an advantage of frames, however, just not one that the Dreamweaver developer would ever need to use.

## Consistency

Another way in which frames can aid web development is in the level of consistency that can be gained from not having to duplicate code throughout many pages of your web site. If your site's logo and title are in a frame at the top of the browser window, and the site's footer displays in a frame at the bottom of the window, for instance, this information does not need to be included in every content page.

This then eliminates the possibility that a developer could forget to include the header and footer on some pages, and also the possibility that this code could be modified in any way and become inconsistent throughout the web site. However, this is yet another advantage of frames that a Dreamweaver developer would not need to make use of. Dreamweaver offers tools such as Templates and the Library, which negate this advantage. A developer using Dreamweaver can re-create this advantage in a much neater and more elegant way than using a frameset.

## Working with Scripts

I was recently involved in a project that a colleague was dealing with, where the client wanted a functioning, problem-free, table-based site converted to use frames. My colleagues and I were a little concerned and bemused by this until it transpired that the client was having some heavy-duty, server-side scripting done on the site.

The programmers appointed to carry out this scripting were concerned that the full-fledged pages would be too difficult for them to work with, and so by using frames, they would be able to work on basic blank pages with no complex tables or images to worry about. For the project at hand, this seemed quite sensible. Although the best solution would have been to get the same company that was designing the site to do the scripting, under the circumstances they probably made the right decision. Having programmers work on complex graphical pages could have resulted in the pages coming back into our studio at the end to be repaired. This would have cost the client a lot more money and would have damaged their tight schedule. A framed solution enabled the client to get their project online in a timely fashion, and the programmers got to work with pages that they couldn't accidentally mess up.

I imagine that if the web site is a success, it will come back in a few months for conversion back to tables, or even CSS-P. However, a framed solution was the best way to move forward under the conditions and the timeframe.

It is not uncommon to find those skilled in writing advanced web functionality struggling to keep an HTML page from falling apart. These two skills are totally separate, and this should be identified if a project is to be successful. It's a bit like a family friend asking you to come over and help him with his computer hardware problems. My response usually is, "I'm a web developer; I have no idea about hardware!" However, it is often assumed that I'm just "good with computers."

The same is true on a web project. A programmer cannot be considered to be a designer, in the same way that a designer is not asked to program. Of course, there are those who can be both; be prepared to give a programmer a little leeway if he upsets a design, however, and be aware that a designer could equally mess up some code without realizing it.

In the particular situation described here, Templates could have been used to good effect, had the programmers implementing the server-side code been using a tool such as Dreamweaver MX. Dreamweaver would prevent the programmers from accidentally throwing out the design while implementing their code.

## Problems with Frames

Where there are benefits, there are problems, and frames are absolutely no exception to this. Quite the opposite, in fact, in that the disadvantages seem to outweigh the advantages for an awful lot of projects. The following sections cover some of the problems associated with using frames and how to get around them.

## Search Engines

A major consideration when developing a web site using frames is how search engines will index the site. Many search engines index sites using a software program known as a *spider*. Spiders are known to have trouble indexing frames, because the main way a spider crawls around the web is via links. With a site based on a frameset, it is vastly more likely that the spider is not going to find many links to follow on a page, if it can find your content at all.

The problem is that the first thing most framed sites do is to split the main navigation off into a frame. As a result, most of the content pages then don't have any links on them at all, so the spider has nothing to follow. A great many spiders can't even find any of the site's content pages, because spiders often don't understand frameset tags. Spiders do, however, interpret `<noframes>` tags in the same way as any browser that has no frames support. This means that the spider can read the data within the tags and will follow any links found there. Now you can see the importance of having good `<noframes>` content. A web developer who has implemented a solution similar to the one described earlier in this chapter will find that search engine spiders have a great deal more success indexing a site with a full navigational menu in the `<noframes>` region.

Another problem to consider when using frames is that of a search engine linking to one of your content pages directly. If a spider discovers a page and decides to index it, it will record the precise URL of that one page and not the URL of your frameset. This means that as soon as your page is brought up in a user's search results, she will visit your site without your frames in place. The user could then be stranded within your site, wanting to find more information but not being able to get to any.

Although some Dreamweaver behaviors use JavaScript to redirect a page that is not within a frameset back to the frameset page, spiders can spot this JavaScript redirect and are likely to treat it with disdain. Spiders shun pages that use JavaScript redirects because many sites try to fool the spider into indexing the site based on one page that immediately refreshes to another. By filling a page with keywords that do not relate to the site in question, devious web developers try to get their site indexed in categories unrelated to the content of their site. When users follow the link from a results page, the JavaScript immediately redirects them to a different page.

Search engines are obviously keen to cut down on this practice, because it dilutes the effectiveness of their search results. If a user is constantly redirected to, typically, pornographic web sites when looking for unrelated content, the user is likely to stop using that search engine and try an alternative one.

The search engine companies take the line that no legitimate page would want to immediately redirect to another, and so they class any page that does this as an attempt to trick the spider. As a result of this, any site that uses this technique for legitimate reasons runs the risk of not being indexed by any search engines. This fact renders the trick of redirecting back to the frameset page absolutely useless, because the chances are that no one will ever see the page anyway because the spider just won't index it.

Of course, web-savvy users can find their way back to your home page by modifying the URL of the page. However, you can't rely on the average web surfer to have the knowledge or patience to do this, so an alternative method has to be found. Call me old-fashioned if you will, but I rather like the idea of a simple link back to the home page or major site section at the bottom of each content page. This basic courtesy enables any stranded visitors to get back to your home page and reenter the site through the frameset as was originally intended. What's more, it enables them to find any other related information your site may contain that is of interest to them.

## Navigation

Frames are often criticized for the effect they have on navigation. The fact that multiple pages are being viewed simultaneously, and that any of those pages can link to any other page in any of the available frames, is bound to have a confusing effect on both the technology and the user. A few specific issues surround the use of navigation with frames; the following sections examine these.

### Browser History

One of the main complaints aired about frames and their navigation is that frames can make a browser's back button behave erratically. In fact, a back button can only behave logically; it is web developers who often use tricks to force a frameset to behave in a strange way. A good example of this is when JavaScript is used to give the effect of changing two frames simultaneously. Of course, what actually happens is that the two frames are changed in quick succession.

The browser records these events in the order in which they occur, so clicking the browser's back button only moves the most recently changed frame back through the history, instead of changing both frames as the non-savvy user might expect.

This is not only confusing for the user, it also can make a site hard to use and difficult to navigate. No web developer wants to make a site that confuses users to the point that they leave; however, many still deploy solutions such as these, which do just that.

### Orientation

With a standard web site built with flat HTML pages, users can easily get a good feeling for their position in the site as they navigate around. They have visual clues such as the location bar in the browser, which often gives a good idea of the hierarchy of the site. In addition to this, one click loads one page, which is a very simple concept and is comforting to the user.

The introduction of frames to a site often removes a number of these securities. The fact that the browser's location bar displays only the address of the frameset can leave users a little unsure as to where they are. In fact, users can't even be sure whether they are still within the same web site, which leads to loss of trust.

By changing only a portion of the screen at once, the user has no concept of the hierarchy of the web site and so can find it difficult to navigate. A traditional single-page approach offers only one location for the information you are viewing, and a frameset confuses this. The user could be viewing different pieces of information from all across the site, on one page. This leads to disorientation, which inevitably will lead to the user leaving the web site.

## Bookmarking

As noted previously, when viewing a framed web site, only the URL of the frameset page appears in the browser's location bar. This poses a problem when it comes to bookmarking pages. When users want to add a page to their Favorites or bookmarks within the browser, the browser picks up and saves the address for the location bar, and thus bookmarks the entire frameset. Now when users subsequently click the bookmark to reopen the web site, they are taken to the frameset's initial page selections rather than to the point in the frameset to which they had previously navigated.

The point of bookmarking is to be able to return to a specific page without having to try and find it again. Framesets remove this useful function and instead force users to renavigate the site to locate the information they require.

For Internet Explorer users (currently a majority of the market), a partial solution to this problem exists. By implementing some browser-specific JavaScript, web developers can add a page to the user's Favorites programmatically. This means that the correct content page can be added to the Favorites (rather than the frameset page) by clicking an "Add this page to your Favorites" link or button.

A behavior exists to help web developers add this functionality easily within Dreamweaver: Favorites Fever! This behavior is available from my own web site (`http://dreamweaverfever.com/`) and can be installed using the Macromedia Extension Manager available from the Exchange for Dreamweaver (`http://www.macromedia.com/exchange/dreamweaver/`).

Figure 12.8 shows the Favorites Fever! behavior. By default, the URL of the page will be saved to the Favorites (`location.href`), but it is also possible to specify the location of a different page. This proves particularly useful for framed pages because the web developer can specify the location of the exact content page.

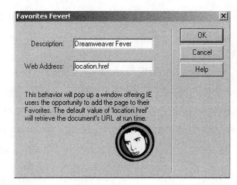

**Figure 12.8**

The Favorites
Fever! behavior.

## Note

It is not currently possible to provide a link for
Navigator users to add a page to their bookmarks. The
programmers at Netscape did not provide this facility,
and so it is possible to offer this functionality only to
those with Internet Explorer. However, the behavior
will fail without error for those visitors not using
Internet Explorer.

## Increased Server Load

When requesting a web page via HTTP, a number of events takes place.
First the browser makes an initial request to find the server on which the
page resides. The server responds to say that it exists and is ready to serve
pages. The browser then makes the request for a specific page, and the server
returns it.

The result of this is that the amount of network traffic generated is more
than the size of the web page on the server. If the page is 4K, there might
be 1K of communication to add to that, making the amount to be moved
5K. This extra communication is vital to the process, but the load it adds
for one page is not generally noticeable. However, it does mean that
retrieving very small files is less economical than retrieving larger ones. A
100K file with 1K of protocol communication has an overhead of only 1
percent, but a 1K file has an overhead of 100 percent. Therefore, downloading a single 4K document is more economical than downloading
four 1K documents. Framesets that use a number of pages rather than a

single, larger page have an increased download overhead and therefore will not display as quickly.

This also has implications for the server. In the same way that retrieving a file incurs a network overhead above the actual size of the file, the web server incurs overheads for each file retrieved. Generally speaking, the server performs better if it is retrieving one larger file than if it has to dash around its disks to retrieve a number of smaller files.

The overhead here is physical. Access to a disk requires the drive head to move to the appropriate place on the disk to retrieve the information. When it is there, it can read as much as it likes quite quickly. If the server has to find four different files, however, that's four outings for the drive head to move the appropriate segment of the disk, which is the slowest part of the process.

A single larger document can be retrieved far more efficiently than a number of documents whose sum is equal to that of the larger. Simply put, framesets are slower.

## Skewing Server Logs

An increasing number of web development teams rely on web server logs to give them a picture of which pages on their web site are being hit more or less than others. Web server logs are good as a general guide to this, especially when comparing one page on your site to another.

However, the use of frames for a web site is known to affect the accuracy of the reporting. It is impossible to gain accurate statistics for the number of visitors hitting any page that is called within a frameset. This is largely due to the inconsistent methods used by browsers to report this occurrence.

## Unusual Scrolling

One of the complaints often voiced by less-experienced web surfers is that framed pages seem to scroll in an unexpected way. For the seasoned, technology-aware web user, the way in which frames scroll does not seem to be anything but logical. If the visitor is not familiar with, or is not able to identify, the technology behind the page, however, the scrolling methodology can easily seem strange.

Logically, when a page within a frame has content that is longer (or wider) than the size of the frame, scrollbars appear. This is the proper way for a browser to behave, because it provides uniform access to data that runs off the bottom (or side) of the viewable area.

When the frameset has been designed to be invisible to the user, with borders and such turned off, however, the fact that a particular area can suddenly have a scrollbar can come as a shock. Normally, a scrollbar will appear only at the rightmost side of the page, and will extend to the full height of the page. When framesets are implemented, however, this rule is turned on its head, and scrollbars can appear within any frame, no matter where it sits on the page.

Users might find this behavior strange, and although the scrollbar is a familiar device, the placement of it can be a surprise. For many sites and their audiences, this won't be much of a problem; for some web sites, however, it is something to take into consideration. Ask yourself whether the choice to use frames is making your visitors feel uncomfortable.

## Printing Problems

Some folks like to print web pages. No, unfortunately I'm not making that up—there are people in this world who think a web page is best viewed on paper. Alarming as this may be, because there seem to be quite a few of them (most of them in management, I assume), they need to be accommodated.

Frames print really badly. There's no getting around the fact that if users insist on printing your page and that page is based on frames, they are going to have major problems. This stems from the fact that a framed page is actually a collection of pages. Most browsers tend to print the frame most recently clicked (the frame that has focus) when the user clicks the Print button. In most cases, this results in the user fetching a hard copy of your navigation links from the printer. The more savvy users will be aware of this fact and will know to give the appropriate frame focus before clicking the Print button, but the majority of users will not.

Of course, a browser cannot print the entire frameset accurately as it is portrayed onscreen. The fact that any one of the frames might have long content (and therefore scrollbars) means that to represent this content on paper would break the layout. Some browsers offer facilities to print each page in the frameset in turn, but this feature is pointless, because the user often requires only the contents of one frame.

This problem can be partially addressed by providing the user with a "print this page" link on each content page. The action of clicking the link gives that frame the focus, so the print action will act on that frame only. This relies on the user clicking the appropriate link rather than the icon in the browser toolbar, of course.

A number of behaviors available on the Macromedia Exchange for Dreamweaver (`http://www.macromedia.com/exchange/dreamweaver/`) offer cross-browser printing facilities. A behavior such as this would enable you to create a "print this page" link with great ease.

# Inline Frames

The standard HTML frame is not the only type of frame in use on the web today. A different sort of frame—the inline frame, or *iframe*—offers an alternative way to implement frames.

Iframe is a technology much more recent than traditional HTML frames. You will read about this technology in the following sections, discover what it is, how it can be used, and how well the different browsers support it.

## What Are Inline Frames?

Microsoft introduced inline frames in their Internet Explorer browser. Currently supported only in versions of IE3+ and in NN6, inline frames have not commonly been used, although support is beginning to pick up.

Just as with a layer, you can place an inline frame anywhere on a page, and it can exist as an object within that page. The difference between an iframe and a layer is that the contents of the iframe come from a different source.

Dreamweaver MX does not include full support for inline frames, although it is still possible to work with them. Massimo Foti (`http://www.massi-mocorner.com/`) has created a Dreamweaver object that enables the web developer to work with inline frames as if they were layers in the Dreamweaver Design view. Later in this chapter, you will use this extension to build an inline frame.

Those who are currently using iframes the most seem to have one objective in mind. It is increasingly common for web companies to sell their services to other web companies for inclusion on their sites. These services are usually information (such as weather reports or news) but also can be service applications (for example, "get a quote for x-related service"). In these circumstances, the company buying the services needs to brand the page to fit with their own web site.

This is where inline frames often come into play. An iframe enables web developers to embed other pages from other sites within their own pages. This can prove extremely useful for cobranding, because it means that your visitors have access to the services offered by the partner company without having to leave your own site.

## Browser Support for Inline Frames

As mentioned, inline frames are currently supported in Internet Explorer from version 3. They also are supported in Netscape Navigator 6, but certainly not in version 4. In the past, this was the main reason iframes were not used. Web developers were not keen to exclude Netscape users or to have to build an alternate page. As use of Netscape browsers drops and drops, however, web developers are becoming increasingly eager to use technologies such as the iframe to achieve the task at hand.

We are going to use Massimo Foti's iframe object to create an inline frame in Dreamweaver. Thankfully, Massimo has been very wise (as he always is) and has included an option to provide a message to visitors who do not have an iframe-compatible browser. This feature enables the web developer to implement an iframe solution, knowing that the few visitors without a compatible browser who might happen to visit the web site will receive a friendly error message, rather than a browser error or a jumbled mess.

## Creating an Inline Frame

Figure 12.9 shows the Main tab of Massimo Foti's iframe object. This object can be downloaded from http://www.massimocorner.com/ and can be installed using the Macromedia Extension Manager. I am using version 1.0.

### *Note*

**A number of useful inline frame extensions are available on the Macromedia Exchange for Dreamweaver (http://www.macromedia.com/exchange/dreamweaver/), including an iframe Property inspector.**

**Figure 12.9**

The Main tab of the iframe object.

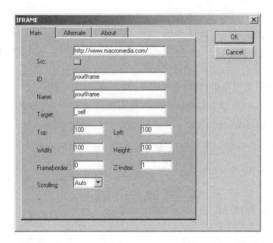

As you can see, there are a host of different options available. The most important one for our purposes is the Src field. Just as with normal HTML frames, Src stands for "Source," and is the page URL that should be loaded into the frame. Enter your URL here. I'm going to enter http://www.macromedia.com/ for mine. You can even use the yellow folder icon to browser for a local file, if you want.

You can set the name and ID for your frame if you like. I recommend doing this if you plan to use more than one iframe on a page. You also have a choice of scrolling options, from the standard Yes, No, and Auto. These work exactly like layer scrolling options.

Figure 12.10 shows the Alternate tab of the iframe object. This tab enables you to enter the message visitors will see if their browser does not support inline frames. After you have set your message, most of the other settings are good at the default, so click OK and add the iframe.

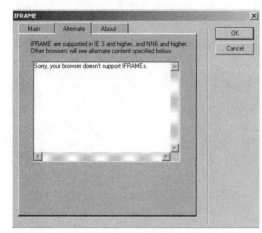

**Figure 12.10**

Specify a message for those who can't view inline frames.

The code for our page looks like this:

```
<html>
<head>
<title>IFRAME Test</title>
<meta http-equiv="Content-Type" content="text/html;
charset=iso-8859-1">
</head>

<body bgcolor="#FFFFFF" text="#000000">

<iframe
 src="http://www.macromedia.com/"
 name="yourIframe"
 id="yourIframe"
 target="_self"
 frameborder="0"
 style="position:absolute;
  width:100;
  height:100;
  top:100;
  left:100;
  z-index:1">
Sorry, your browser doesn't support IFRAMEs.
```

```
</iframe>

</body>
</html>
```

As you can see, the iframe appears just like a layer in the Dreamweaver Design view. You can now size and position the iframe to your needs. Figure 12.11 shows how my page looked in a browser after some repositioning.

**Figure 12.11**

In Dreamweaver, the iframe displays as if it were a CSS layer.

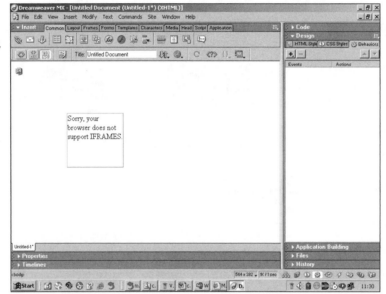

# What to Take Away from This Chapter

- Frames provide a way to split up the screen to display multiple documents simultaneously.

- You can find some really good examples of frame usage on the web, but these tend to be overshadowed by the number of terrible implementations.

- A good many browsers support frames, because they have been on the scene for a long time. However, they were introduced into the HTML specification only at version 4.0—quite late in the life of HTML.

- There are a number of rendering differences between older browsers that implemented their frames support before the HTML specification was published.

- People visiting your web site with a browser that doesn't support frames will be able to see a page only if you have implemented <noframes> tags.

- A good <noframes> region will enable a user to access the entire content of your site through a nonframed interface.

- There are a number of advantages to frames, including the management of data, ease of maintenance, and consistency in design.

- Frames also have their problems. These include problems with search engines, navigation issues, difficulty in bookmarking and printing, increasing load on the server, and skewing the data provided by server logs.

- Standard HTML frames are not the only sort of frame. Inline frames enable a web developer to create a layer-type object that acts as a "window" into another page.

# Chapter 13

# Advanced Browser Windows

Objectives:

- Understand the different ways in which the browser window can be manipulated.

- Learn from real-world case studies how browser windows can be used in new and interesting ways.

- Build a simple online image gallery using pop-up windows.

The browser is a tool through which the web is delivered to the people. To the web developer, a browser is a tool of the trade. It is the canvas on which our sites are painted. Dreamweaver is our paintbrush, and HTML is the paint. The web is like one big worldwide art gallery—a new canvas at every turn.

In fact, the browser is much more of a tool than the painter's canvas, which sits passively while it is painted. The browser forms the basis of the interaction between the site and the user and is the web developer's front line.

As a web developer, it pays to be familiar with each intricacy of the browser. It pays to know what the browser can and cannot do and how it will react under certain circumstances. This is not an easy task. A great number of browsers are available, and they all behave differently. What's more, new versions of these browsers are being released all the time. To keep up with all the changes takes dedication and a lot of research time.

This chapter hopes to serve that research and help you gain a greater understanding of the browser and the way in which it uses windows. This chapter covers what a browser is, how browser windows are used, and how we can implement them within our own work.

This chapter discusses the reasoning behind many choices regarding the way in which browser windows are used, with a hope to providing some good "rules of thumb" for different browser situations.

# Understanding the Role of the Browser

No web developer needs to be told what a browser is. We are all familiar with the software we use to view web sites, to a greater or lesser extent. On the most part, a web developer will have a good knowledge of how to operate a browser to an advanced level just from having to use one all the time.

The browser has the job of requesting web pages, and then deciding how to render them to the best of its ability. Making use of technologies such as HTML, CSS, and JavaScript, the browser follows a set of rules to display the page, as it believes the author intended. Of course, not all browsers render pages in the same way. Fortunately, they are pretty good on the whole, and the discrepancies come with the finer details.

### Note

Chapter 4, "Advanced Browser and Platform Compatibility," looks at the many issues surrounding browser compatibility, including discussion of how pages are rendered differently by different browsers.

In addition to the common technologies such as HTML, CSS, and JavaScript, the browser has its own set of rules for defining the way it behaves and the tasks it can perform. Some browsers add additional scripting languages (Internet Explorer can run client-side VBScript), and most allow for the addition of plug-ins (such as the Flash Player). However, they also govern their own response to valid code and user behavior.

From every aspect from how a page is refreshed, right down to the number and types of options presented for the user to set as preferences, the browser has total control. In addition to this, different browsers offer different additional services and tools to enhance the user's browsing experience. Internet Explorer 6 now includes a built-in Media Player, as well as the ability to check how well your shares are doing from a special toolbar. (To me, this sort of utility seems like a step backward. Surely the web is about access to information. Having a special toolbar to access information from the web is like having a browser within a browser. The difference is that the toolbar narrows your access to information and allows you to view only the information from one source; it is removing user control and choice. I would personally rather use the browser to go to my favorite financial site myself.)

These choices can lead to problems for the web developer. When building a site, the developer can never be sure what sort of features and toolbars the user will have access to. In fact, it's not even necessary for a browser to provide a back button (although I shouldn't imagine many people would use that browser if it didn't).

These are factors that must be considered when dealing with browser windows—and especially when trying to create particular effects with them. It's all good and well wanting to control a browser in a certain way, but the developer needs to understand how each browser reacts, to be able to achieve this.

# Using the Browser in Interesting Ways

Of course, a web site doesn't necessarily have to be built around a single, large browser window. There are other ways of using windows to organize information logically or even just to create an impressive user experience. This section includes two case studies of web sites that use the browser in an interesting and innovative way. Both sites were built by Lateral, and include extremely off-the-wall uses for the browser window, and interaction between those windows.

Lateral (`http://www.lateral.net/`) is a small, independent web consultancy based in the UK. Established in 1997, they focus on providing their clients with creative strategies and executing those strategies using a support network of business partnerships with specialist companies and their own network of companies. Their pioneering expertise and professional approach has attracted recognition both within the new media industry, as well as the consumer market. You can find out more about Lateral by visiting their web site.

### Caution

Both the sites discussed in this section are very experimental in both their design and use of technology. I've heard reports that both sites can occasionally cause the browser to behave unexpectedly, and sometimes crash. For that reason, I recommend saving any work you have open before visiting them!

### Case Study: *Geri-Halliwell.com*

The first official web site for the ex-Spice Girl Geri Halliwell took an interesting approach to the browser window. By using 12 different browser windows to compartmentalize the different site sections and content items, navigating the site takes on a whole new dimension.

The user is no longer dealing with large pages, where a link from one page fills the environment with another. The user is now left navigating an area closer to a framed layout than a flat HTML one. Figure 13.1 shows the site at its open state before any navigational choices are made. See how links to main site sections are compartmentalized into their individual windows.

Note also that the central windows of the set are reused for different content items. Clicking a section heading changes the content of that window to the main index for the section concerned.

Figure 13.2 shows the same site after a few selections have been made. Note how the chosen selections have changed to display the content, as well as a contrasting background image.

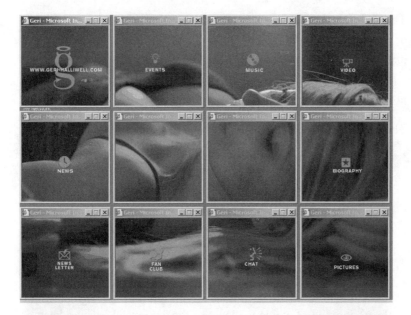

**Figure 13.1**

Geri-
Halliwell.com at
its opening
state.

**Figure 13.2**

Geri-
Halliwell.com
mid-navigation

The sensation of navigating this site is actually quite strange. By clicking a link, part of the window changes to provide the section content. However, the feeling is that you are still on the same page, but with new information revealed.

The use of the browser window is extremely interesting because a series of pop-up windows have been used to formulate a solid structure, which makes up the whole of the site. Under more usual circumstances, pop-up windows are used as a supplementary item to the main page; for this site, however, the pop-up windows form the main page.

This site demonstrates the following key browser window techniques:

- **Opening a browser window.** This is a basic technique that has been taken to the next level. By opening 12 windows simultaneously, the standard approach to popping up a window has been extended.

- **Controlling which items of "window furniture" display.** The controllable features such as toolbars and the status bar have all been disabled to maintain the visual effect and to keep control of the windows.

- **Positioning a window.** Each of the 12 windows is carefully positioned to create the site layout. JavaScript can offer precise control of the positioning of windows, down to the last pixel. However, keeping track of window positions is a task in itself.

- **Targeting links to different windows.** As you will see later in this chapter, there are different ways to target links and other browser windows. This site uses standard HTML targeting.

- **Innovation.** The key to using pop-up windows is to use them appropriately and where necessary. This design uses the previously discussed techniques in an innovative way, providing the sort of edgy design appropriate to this application.

Figure 13.3 shows the site after it has been fully navigated and all the sections have been visited. The background image of each window changes to indicate visited areas, and after all the areas have been viewed, a new background picture is visible.

Many of the objections voiced by visitors to this site centered on the fact that closing the site down is very difficult, because the user has to click the close buttons of 12 pop-up windows and one launching window. As you will see in the next case study, this is a problem that the developers were able to address.

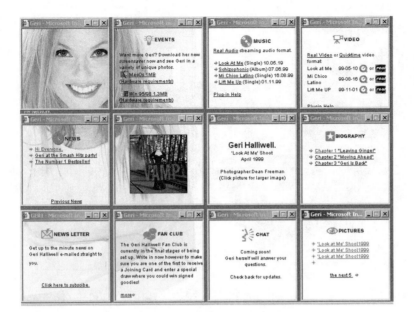

**Figure 13.3**

All site sections have been visited.

## Tip

The live version of Geri-Halliwell.com has been updated since Lateral's multiwindowed site went live. However, the site is archived and accessible from the Lateral archive pages (http://archive.lateral.net/).

## Case Study: Levi's Twisted Engineered Jeans

The Levi's brand is a household and globally recognized name, and when it came to the web site to promote their new line of "Engineered" jeans, Levi's required something a bit special. Stepping in with another multi-window design, the team at Lateral built on the success of the Geri Halliwell web site, taking the concept several stages further.

Figure 13.4 shows the Levi's site at launch state. As you see, it is made up of 25 different browser windows. (One of these is concealed behind the double-width window.)

**Figure 13.4**

The Levi's
Engineered
Jeans site at
launch.

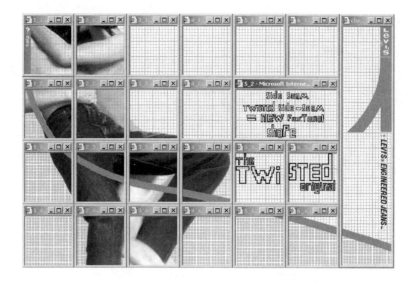

Unlike the Geri Halliwell site, the Levi's site used its windows in many
different configurations. Windows are frequently resized to provide the main
focus for a content item, and then shrink down to take a back seat again
as soon as another link is fired up.

Figure 13.5 shows how the site rescales its windows to provide different
configurations and create visual interest.

**Figure 13.5**

The windows
resize when
needed.

The browsing experience with this site is yet again far removed from that of a normal site, and is even quite some way removed from that of the Geri Halliwell site. Although the site does have structure, this structure is not immediately obvious to visitors to the site. Clicking a link resizes various windows within the site and loads in new content. Clicking another link then sets these windows to new dimensions, loads new content, and proceeds.

The reuse of windows is a great technique that provides an interesting visual effect. Although there is no obvious structure to the site, with the subject matter concerned, this is not a hindrance. Being able to freely explore the site without the constraints of normal structure is actually a liberating experience. Because the aim of the site is to promote a new line of jeans, and the aim of the user is to discover more about this line, it does not matter in the slightest that there is no discernable structure.

Being able to wander around the site freely enables the user to just have fun and discover more about the product instead of worrying where he "should" be navigating and in what order. The very free feel of the site is down to the use of pop-up windows in no small part. The fact that the windows are constantly reused and resized to fit the user's choices gives a feeling of remaining within one safe environment while somehow discovering new ones. This paradox is by no means uncomfortable, just new and refreshing.

Figure 13.6 shows the site in a state in which the normal matrix of windows is apparently discarded and the user is left with just four frames. Radical changes in the environment such as these should feel uncomfortable, but thanks to the excellent implementation, they feel as natural as a single window.

Note how the developers have chosen to use the smallest window size available to them by default. Each of the little windows is 100-by-100 pixels square. This is as small as a browser window can be opened.

*Tip*

Later in this chapter, you will learn the reason why a browser window cannot be opened at or resized to a size smaller than 100 pixels.

**Figure 13.6**

The layout differs for each section.

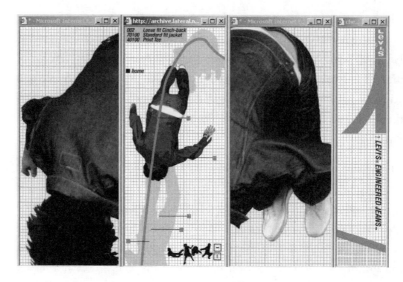

The design is fascinating for the users, because they have no idea where they will end up next. This unusual approach mirrors the radical design of the jeans that the web site is promoting. Levi's Twisted Engineered Jeans totally reevaluate the way a pair of trousers is constructed and cut, and the web site carries that approach forward into an online medium.

Lateral has managed to solve a problem with this site that existed with the original Geri Halliwell multiwindowed site: the user needing to close every single window of the site to exit. Although this wasn't an enormous issue with the Geri Halliwell site, because it used only 12 windows, the Levi's site uses twice that amount, and so would be a real pain to try and close by hand.

Getting around this problem, the developers managed to implement a solution whereby the entire collection of windows is closed as soon as one of their number is exited. By using some clever JavaScript, one of the windows continually checks to make sure the others are open. Should they not be, it switches into an exit procedure that closes all the other windows belonging to the Levi's site.

For the users, this means that as they close one window, the other windows close behind it. This is a particularly useful feature when dealing with a web site that uses in excess of 25 browser windows. Closing the whole lot down by hand would be a tedious task.

This is a great breakthrough and improvement over the Geri Halliwell site, where the user had to close each window in turn to escape from the web site. After all the windows have been closed, users are presented with a short message explaining what has happened, just in case they closed a window by mistake and managed to shut the whole site down. Figure 13.7 shows this message.

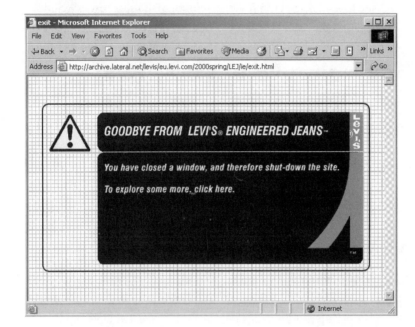

**Figure 13.7**

The user is presented with a message after closing the site.

In addition to those demonstrated by the Geri Halliwell web site, this site demonstrates some key browser window techniques.

- **Resizing windows.** The site manipulates its windows to great affect, opening up new and different working areas for different elements and sections of the web site.

- **Focusing windows.** Windows are given focus to bring them forward in the stacking order. This technique enables the developers to more precisely determine the stacking order of windows to draw the user's attention to the desired area of the site.

- **Advanced interaction between windows.** Going a step further than the HTML targeting method used by the Geri Halliwell site, this web site uses JavaScript to control the contents of each window.

- **Closing windows.** As discussed, some clever scripting used by the web developers enables the user to close down the entire site by just closing one window. This has obvious timesaving advantages for the user and generally increases general user experience and reinforces the brand values of quality and convenience.

Through the implementation of the preceding techniques, the developers of this site have managed to provide a solution that uses browser windows in not only an innovative way, but with a great degree of usability and style.

# Spawning New Windows

It is always a debate whether a web site should spawn new windows with each link or whether they should just load in the same window. It's usually the web team who says links should open in the same window, and the marketing department who thinks that spawning a new window will somehow delight the user as they are now able to browse both the new site and the original one.

## Advantages of New Windows

A number of factors truthfully can be considered advantages of spawning new windows with each link. By default, a link will open up in the same window as the page calling that link, thus unloading the page and replacing it.

This can be a pain, however, if the user wants to retain the original page. If the page being linked to is of less importance than the page linking to it, it may well be advantageous for the link to open up in a new window. Dreamweaver makes it easy to open a link in a new window. After defining your link, just select _blank from the Target menu in the Property inspector (see Figure 13.8).

**Figure 13.8**

Setting a link target is straightforward.

If the user is likely to then return to the linking page, opening the link in a new window saves the user the inconvenience of having to navigate back. Similarly, the subject of the linked page might lead the user to close the window rather than use the back button. An obvious example of this is linking to an image such as a JPG or GIF. Developers commonly link a thumbnail image on a page to a larger graphics file. The instinctive reaction to this always seems to be to close the window rather than click the back button.

I'm sure a psychology expert could explain this behavior; for the web developer, however, it is enough to just recognize it. The reaction to this behavior is to open links to graphics files in new windows. This way, when users click the close button to kill the window, they are presented with the original page of thumbnail images as they expect to be.

New windows are also advantageous when the content of the page to be opened is supplementary to that of the linking page. Web sites commonly use new pop-up browser windows to display such information as help topics, covering usability issues that might arise within the page. It's not too helpful to receive advice about a page you can no longer see, and so a new pop-up window is an excellent way to provide the user with useful information, while still enabling the user to view the page that information applies to.

## Disadvantages of New Windows

Just as with any technology, where there are advantages, there are disadvantages as well. By default, a link will open up in the same window as the page calling that link, thus unloading the page and replacing it.

This is great for keeping the user's desktop neat and tidy. On the whole, the user should be in control of her environment, and she should feel that way too. The mere fact that clicking a link opens the page in the same window offers the user this control. The user can, of course, choose to open the link in a new window should she choose to do so.

As you saw earlier, the two sites in the case study made the decision to open a number of new windows. At the time they were launched, many users expressed extremely adverse reactions. Of course, with the sites in question this didn't matter too much because the sites were mainly marketing exercises, and after all, there's no such thing as bad publicity.

However, such user reaction should not go unnoted for those who are developing less bold sites. Users are often frustrated by so many browser windows opening. Some reasons for this frustration are as follows:

- The user did not ask for all these windows, and so he feels like he is no longer in control. At best, the user doesn't mind too much but would have preferred to have been asked or given the option.

- New windows are an extra burden on computer resources. If the user is already pushing his computer to the max, extra windows are not welcome.

- Closing down lots of windows that you didn't ever want open is a time-consuming pain in the butt.

These are just some of the factors that can influence a user's opinion about links opening in a new window. At the end of the day, the user can always decide to open a link in a new window for himself. This is a feature built in most browsers, and is usually on the context menu. If there is not a clear argument for opening a link in a new window, it's probably best not to do so.

## Letting the User Decide

Although there is a strong case for giving the user the choice to open a link in a new window or not, web developers cannot afford to ignore the fact that many web users do not know how to control their browser properly. If we were to take a poll, more than half of the current online community would probably not know that the option to open a link in a new window even exists. Fewer of those would actually remember to make use of it.

In the interest of good web site interface design, therefore, give the user the feeling of control (even if the user is useless and flapping in the wind). A neat way to do this is to provide a page-wide option for all links opened. JavaScript enables you to govern the target of all links in the page.

This technique is widely used on many web logs (or blogs). These are sites whose content often focuses on documenting interesting and new places to visit on the web. As a result, visitors are always linking out to external sites, and so the ability to open a link in a new window is a common requirement.

Figure 13.9 shows an example of this. Plasticbag.org is a popular UK blog and offers its visitors the choice to open links in new windows (by using a checkbox to indicate their choice).

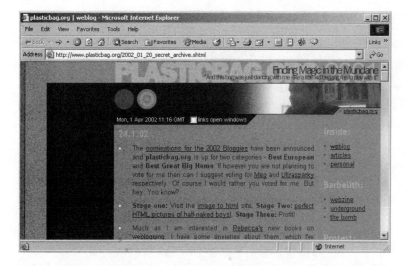

**Figure 13.9**

Plasticbag.org offers the user an easy choice.

As you can see, this offers users a simple and straightforward way to express their preference without the need to know how to use advanced features of their browser. This basic JavaScript takes advantage of the DOM and the ability to set the properties of links in this way. The code falls into two sections: a function that sits in the head of the page (or in an external JavaScript file), and the trigger, which calls the function `onClick` of a checkbox.

```
function targetLinks(isChecked){
  if (isChecked){
    myTarget = "_blank";
  }else{
    myTarget = "_self";
  }
  for (var i=0; i<=(document.links.length-1); i++) {
    document.links[i].target = myTarget;
  }
}
```

The checkbox would use the following code. The `this.checked` statement returns whether the current object (`this`) is checked. The value is true or false.

```
<input type="checkbox" onclick="targetLinks(this.checked)" />
```

If the box is checked, the function loops through all the links in the document and sets their target property to `_blank`. If the box is not checked (or has been unchecked), all the link targets are set back to `_self`.

You can use this logical and practical approach to the problem in a variety of ways. It's not always necessary to use a checkbox for this, although it is an obvious choice of interface device. The code can equally be adapted to run from a link or any other scriptable element. The important factor is the loop through the links on the page to reassign the target. Here's the code snippet that we're really interested in:

```
for (var i=0; i<=(document.links.length-1); i++) {
  document.links[i].target = myTarget;
}
```

The code instigates a basic loop through every link in the page. This is performed using the DOM and its capability to address and set properties of elements of any given nature. The advantage of this approach is that users can make their own choice without the need for knowledge of the more advanced features available in their browser. This is a great boon in terms of usability. This sort of feature adds extra functionality to your pages and adds value.

# Controllable Elements

A computer's operating system dictates that all windows should have certain features. For example, both Microsoft Windows and Apple MacOS do not allow a window to be opened that does not have a button to close it. In addition, all windows should have a title bar and an external border.

There are, however, a number of features of the browser window that the browser itself can set to be visible or not. These include, among others, the browser's toolbars, menu bar, and status bar.

Figure 13.10 shows the Dreamweaver Open Browser Window behavior. This shows some of the more common features that can be controlled when opening a new browser window.

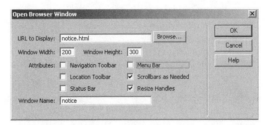

**Figure 13.10**

The Open Browser Window behavior.

As you can see, you have a number of options besides the dimensions and name of the window, including the following:

- **Navigation toolbar.** This browser toolbar houses items such as the forward and back buttons, the print button, and the stop, home, and refresh buttons. Turning this bar off denies the user access to the simple navigational options the browser offers.

- **Location toolbar.** This browser toolbar displays the address (URL) of the current page and enables the user to navigate to different web sites.

- **Status bar.** This bar at the bottom of the browser window indicates document-loading status and shows the destination of links. Turning off this bar leaves the user working blind when it comes to following links from your page.

- **Menu bar.** This is the very top bar that holds the browser's menu options. The File, Edit, View, Tools, and Help menus are held here for speedy access.

- **Scrollbars.** These can be turned off completely, or can be left on so that they appear when the page is longer or wider than the window. Note that turning scrollbars off prevents the user from being able to scroll the length of the page should it spill over the window dimensions.

- **Resize handles.** These enable the user to resize the window. Should these be disabled, the user would not be able to adjust the designated size of the browser window, potentially causing problems for users with unusual browsers, devices, or screen dimensions.

In addition to these options, some browsers offer more options. Massimo Foti's Launch Window behavior offers the two extra following two options (see Figure 13.11).

**Figure 13.11**

Massimo Foti's
Launch Window
behavior.

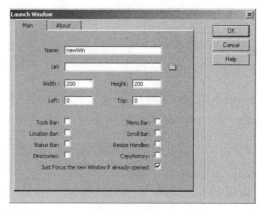

- **Copy history.** This copies the history of the current window into the new window. This means that instead of having no history, the new window will have exactly the same history as the one that launches it.

- **Directory toolbar.** This is the toolbar that some browsers use to store the user's personal links (or even links to special services such as shopping or searches). The browsers that use such a toolbar enable you to turn it off.

Different browsers will, naturally, have different available toolbars and features, and will need to be controlled in their own way. However, many common features are available, as outlined earlier.

To gain a full understanding of browser window control, I think you should look at the code used to open a new browser window. Here's the basic function that the standard Dreamweaver behavior inserts into the document:

```
function MM_openBrWindow(theURL,winName,features) { //v2.0
  window.open(theURL,winName,features);
}
```

As you can see, JavaScript can parse three main parameters to dictate the attributes of a new browser window: the URL of the page that should appear within the window, the name of the window, and any special features that should be turned on or off. These special features are dependent on the browser, but JavaScript defines them as listed in Table 13.1.

| Table 13.1 | Special Window Features Provided via JavaScript | |
|---|---|---|
| Feature | Description | Browser |
| channelmode | The window should appear in Channel mode. | Internet Explorer |
| dependent | Whether the window should be considered a child of the opener. | Navigator |
| directories | The toolbar containing personal links and utilities, such as shopping, searches, or "what's cool" features. | |
| fullscreen | The window should open up in Full-Screen mode. | Internet Explorer |
| height | Specifies the height of the window. | |
| hotkeys | Keyboard shortcuts are disabled for windows with no menu bar. | Navigator |
| innerHeight | The height of the window. | Navigator |
| innerWidth | The width of the window. | Navigator |
| left | The horizontal coordinate of the left edge of the window. | Internet Explorer Navigator |

*Continues*

| Table 13.1 | Continued | |
|---|---|---|
| Feature | Description | Browser |
| location | The bar containing the location (or URL) of the document. | |
| menubar | The bar containing the menu items. | |
| resizable | Whether the user can resize the window. | |
| screenX | The horizontal coordinate of the left edge of the window. | Navigator |
| screenY | The vertical coordinate of the top edge of the window. | Navigator |
| scrollbars | Enable scrollbars where necessary. | |
| status | The status bar at the bottom of the browser window. | |
| toolbar | The browser's navigation bar containing the forward, back, sop, refresh, and print buttons. | |
| top | The vertical coordinate of the top edge of the window. | Internet Explorer Navigator |
| width | The width of the window. | |

These features are available through JavaScript for all browsers. Some are available for the two main browsers, as denoted.

# Pop-up Windows

When the subject of browser windows is brought up, most developers immediately think of pop-up windows. They are by far the most regularly used window device on the web today.

You can use pop-up windows in many different ways, and this section covers some of them.

## Uses for Pop-up Windows

Pop-up windows enable you to do many things, and many developers use them in different ways and with varying levels of effect.

Some common uses for pop-up windows are detailed in the following section, but this is by no means an exhaustive list. You can use pop-up browser windows in a great number of ways to enhance the design and information flow for the users of your web site.

## Advertising

Possibly the most inappropriate and annoying use of pop-up windows is for advertising. Many web sites, even some of the largest, have taken on this approach. The principal is to open a new pop-up window when a user hits the site, to display an advertising message.

Unfortunately, this approach has a very negative effect on users. Opening a new pop-up window is very useful if it contains relevant information or help, but opening a new window that contains nothing but an advertising message is a turn-off more often than not.

Figure 13.12 shows a pop-up advertising window.

**Figure 13.12**

A pop-up advertising window.

Because this approach has been around for some time now, users expect any pop-up window that is opened when launching a site to be an advertising message. Therefore, users tend to close these pop-up windows even before the page loads.

This is bad for a number of reasons. First, the advertiser has not got their message across. Second, users feel bombarded by advertising and are less likely to feel confident about the site. Not only is this approach to advertising ineffective, it also puts the user into the mindset that a pop-up window means an advert, and so they must close it. If you want to include pop-up windows upon load, this can be a real problem.

## Help Systems

Another common use of pop-up windows is for help systems. When working within a web page that requires additional explanation, it is normal to expect the user to take advantage of any help systems present.

Without the use of pop-up windows, clicking a help system for further information would take the user away from the page with which he is dealing. When a user is likely to be confused anyway, this extra change could add to the confusion even more.

This is why it is great to use pop-up windows in these circumstances. The user can open a help page that appears on top of her page, but which doesn't replace it. The user can then retrieve the information that she needs and continue to use the page without ever leaving it. This is a great boon, because the user is then able to keep the help system open, and thus it becomes available for any circumstance within that page where it might be needed.

Consider the example of a complex web form. The form may be part of a registration process that includes some quite specific questions that might easily lead to confusion. By having the help pages open in a pop-up window, the user can continue to fill out the form while referring to the pop-up window when necessary. As soon as another query arises, the user can again navigate the help system without ever leaving the complex form she is filling out.

## Expanded Content

Chapter 12, "Advanced Frame Design," discussed how a split-framed page can provide the user with primary content in one area and secondary, supporting content in another. The effect can be achieved without frames, too. The pop-up window can solve this problem in a different way.

The example I showed originally was of a technical document in one frame with a dictionary or glossary of terms in other. This enables the user to reference the glossary and improve his understanding of the document without having to every leave the page that he is reading.

The situation here is very similar to that of the pop-up help windows. The aim is to enable the user to view supporting content without every having to leave the main document. In this situation, keywords can be highlighted in the technical document, which open up a pop-up window with an explanation of their meaning. When reading the document, a user just has to click a word that requires further explanation. The glossary appears, but the user doesn't lose his place in the original text.

## Pop-up Image Windows

Pop-up windows are often used when a page's content consists of a number of thumbnail images. The developer naturally wants to make a full size version of these pictures available, and so uses a pop-up window to display the larger view. For every image that needs to be displayed, however, a new HTML document must be created to house it. Linking directly to the image is possible, but it is not as elegant because the image will have a default border around it, making it difficult to frame the image correctly. By putting the image into an HTML page, these borders can be turned off so that the pop-up window can "hug" the edges of the image.

The problem with this approach is that the developer then needs to create a large number of small pages to fill the pop-up windows. With an image gallery of hundreds of photographs, this can be an enormously time-consuming task, not to mention a tedious one. What's more, all those pages have to be uploaded and stored on the web server.

You will have noticed that I'm building up to a solution. Yet again a Dreamweaver extension comes to the rescue; this time, however, it's one I wrote myself. The Open Picture Window Fever! behavior enables the developer to specify the larger image that should be opened in the pop-up window. It then uses JavaScript to create a new window that has no page borders and so is able to hug the dimensions of the image.

This means that it's no longer necessary to create a new HTML document for each image, because this document is created on-the-fly using JavaScript.

### Creating a Web Gallery

Using the Open Picture Window Fever! behavior, I am going to construct the beginnings of a online gallery of pictures. To do so, I follow these steps:

1. Insert the thumbnail into the page.

   The principal of a gallery of this nature is that thumbnail images are offered as a quick preview, and the user can then choose to enlarge the pictures of interest.

2. Select the thumbnail and apply the behavior.

   Open Picture Window Fever! can be found under the Fever category in the Behaviors panel. Figure 13.13 shows the Open Picture Window Fever! dialog box.

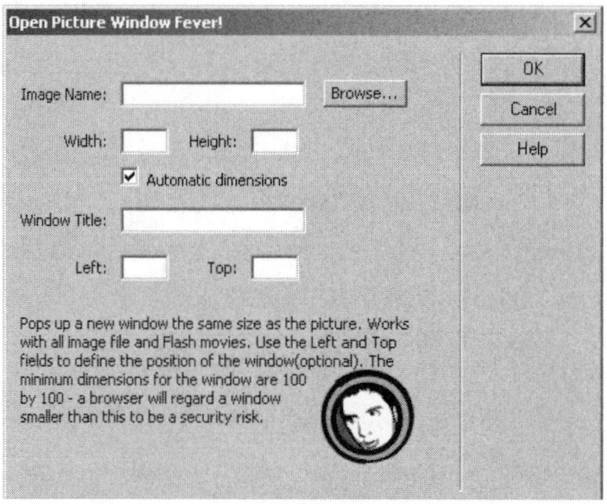

**Figure 13.13**

Open Picture Window Fever! dialog box.

3. Browse for the image.

   It is also possible at this point to set other variables, such as the title for the window and the location at which the pop-up window should appear. The image dimensions are automatically detected, but these can be changed if you want.

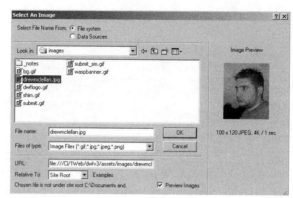

**Figure 13.14**

The image dimensions and a preview are displayed when you select your image. (Look mom, it's me!)

4. Click OK to confirm the details.

The behavior is now applied. All that is left to do is to repeat the process for each image in the gallery.

Open Picture Window Fever! also works with Flash movies (SWF). It also accepts all web images, including GIF, JPG, and PNG.

---

**Tip**

> You can download **Open Picture Window Fever!** from the **Macromedia Exchange for Dreamweaver** (http://www.macromedia.com/exchange/dreamweaver/) or **from my own web site** (http://dreamweaverfever.com/).

## Window Behaviors

A number of Dreamweaver behaviors are available for manipulating browser windows. Some are downloadable from the Macromedia Exchange for Dreamweaver, some from third-party sites, and some are built right in to Dreamweaver from the outset.

### Open Browser Window

Open Browser Window is a standard Dreamweaver behavior that ships with Dreamweaver MX. Figure 13.15 shows the main dialog box and its options.

**Figure 13.15**

The Open
Browser
Window
behavior.

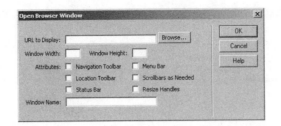

Open Browser Window is used to launch a pop-up window containing a
defined HTML page. As you can see in Figure 13.15, a number of options
are available to control the various aspects of the pop-up window. This is
a particularly useful behavior, one that you can use for most basic pop-up
window requirements.

## Massimo Foti's Window Suite

A step beyond Macromedia's Open Browser Window is Massimo Foti's
Window Suite. It covers many basic and more advanced window-manip-
ulation techniques. You can download the Window Suite from
http://www.massimocorner.com/. The Window Suite includes the
following behaviors:

- **Control Window.** This behavior enables the developer to blur,
  focus, close, or reload a window (see Figure 13.16).

**Tip**

The focus feature can prove very useful if loading a
new page into a window that already exists. Focusing
the window will bring it back to the front, should it
happen to have been moved behind other windows.

**Figure 13.16**

Control Window
behavior.

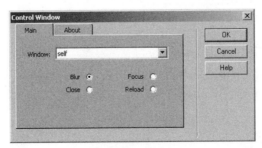

- **Go History Window.** This behavior enables the developer to create an event that will step through the browser's history a set number of steps. This can be useful for creating back and forward buttons.

- **Launch Window.** This behavior is similar to the Macromedia Open Browser Window behavior, but has a host of extra features.

- **Load URL in Window.** This behavior enables the developer to target a given window name with a new URL. Offering one simple option, this behavior can prove very useful when used in conjunction with the other behaviors in the suite.

- **Manage Window.** As you will see later in this chapter, the Manage Window behavior has a great many useful features. Not only can the developer choose to resize the window, he also can move the window or even scroll it (see Figure 13.17).

- **Print Window.** This behavior just uses the browser's printing facilities to print the current window's contents. This functionality does not work with very old browsers.

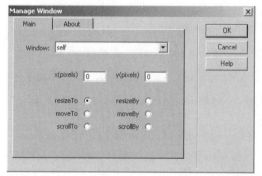

**Figure 13.17**

Manage Window behavior.

- **Set Window BgColor.** This behavior sets the background color of the current window.

- **Set Window BgImage.** This behavior enables the developer to set the background image of the window.

# Communication Between Windows

In both the case studies at the beginning of this chapter, you saw how communication was achieved between browser windows. Although many would be open at a time, clicking a link in one window would update the contents of many of the windows.

This technique is quite common with sites that take advantage of multiple-window setups. To manage multiple windows effectively, the developer needs to be able to control them. There are two elements to this control process. The first is the ability to name a window. The second is being able to target commands and pages at that window.

## Naming Windows

You can name a window in three primary ways. One uses HTML, and the others use JavaScript.

- Targeting a nonexistent window name
- Specifying a window name as the window is opened
- Specifying a window name subsequently

The first method is used when opening a new window when following a standard HTML link. By specifying a target for the link that is not the name of a current browser window, a new window is opened and given that name.

Take a look at an example of this. Suppose that you were to create a link like this:

```
<a href="newpage.htm" target="Fred">open new window</a>
```

So long as no other browser window exists with the name Fred, this link would open up a new window and give it that name. Incidentally, the name of a window can be read and set using JavaScript. This can be useful for proving our work. Consider the preceding example. While developing a web site, I would need to know that my window had in fact been given the name

Fred, otherwise my code wouldn't work. I can test this by using some JavaScript in the newpage.html (that is, the opened) document.

```
<script language="JavaScript" type="text/JavaScript">
    document.write("window name: " + window.name);
</script>
```

This very simple chunk of JavaScript will write the name of the current window to the screen. As per the example, the opened page would appear as shown in Figure 13.18.

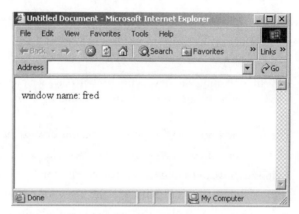

**Figure 13.18**

The JavaScript in the page correctly reports the window name as fred.

This brings us to the second way to name a window. If the window is being opened by JavaScript within a page, it is possible to specify a name for the window, as follows:

```
<a href="javascript:;" onclick="window.open('newpage.html',
➡'Fred')">
open new window</a>
```

The preceding JavaScript opens a new window containing mypage.html and with the name Fred. This approach basically has the same effect as the HTML approach discussed as the first method.

The third way you can open a window uses JavaScript to change the name of a page that is already open, as follows:

```
<script language="JavaScript" type="text/JavaScript">
  window.name = "Fred";
</script>
```

Placed in a page, the preceding JavaScript sets the name of the page's window to Fred. This can be placed in any standard HTML document, and will take effect as soon as it is parsed. This property can be read as well as set, as demonstrated earlier. These three ways to set the name of a window cover just about every scenario a developer is likely to encounter in day-to-day work.

## Targeting Windows

This brings us to the next part of the exercise: targeting the window. You can do this in two basic ways. The first uses HTML, the second JavaScript.

- Use the `target` attribute of the anchor (`<a>`) tag to specify the window name.

- When opening the new window with JavaScript, specify it as an object, which can later be addressed directly by name.

The first method is by far the most straightforward, but does not offer as many options of control—only one in fact. The target for any link is easily set in Dreamweaver using the Property inspector. By just entering the name of the window you want to target, the behavior of the link will be modified as to open the linked page in the specified window.

The resulting code looks like this:

```
<a href="newpage.html" target="Fred">Click here</a>
```

The second method is more complex and requires an understanding of how JavaScript is used. To be able to control a window after it has been created, it is essential that the window be defined as an object at the moment of opening.

The following is some simple JavaScript to open a window:

```
window.open('newpage.html','Fred')
```

However, this would cause the opening page to lose control of the new window. To keep control, you need to say this:

```
Fred = window.open('newpage.html','Fred')
```

This then defines the window as an object called Fred, which is then fully accessible throughout our opening page.

### Note

**It is not possible to take control over a window that your page has not opened itself as a "child" window.**

This opens up a huge number of options for controlling the child window. To get back to the original task of opening a link in a new window, for instance, you can now do this with an extremely simple JavaScript call, as follows:

```
Fred.location = "newpage.html"
```

However, the usefulness of this targeting does not end with changing the document that is loaded into a window. Any element within the new window can be targeted and read or set just as if it were within the master page. For example, we could submit a form (**form1**) in the window as follows:

```
Fred.document.form1.submit()
```

It really is as simple as that. The name of your window replaces the default "window" keyword used in the DOM to specify the current window.

## Positioning Browser Windows

From time to time, a web developer may need to position a browser window in a precise place on the user's screen. Looking at the example of the Levi's Twisted Engineered jeans earlier in this chapter, you can see how this technique was demonstrated to the upper limits. For the Dreamweaver user, a useful extension that helps deal with this is available.

Part of Massimo Foti's Window Suite, the Manage Window behavior can be used to control a number of window aspects, including positioning. Figure 13.19 shows the Manage Window dialog box.

**Figure 13.19**

Massimo Foti's
Manage
Window
behavior.

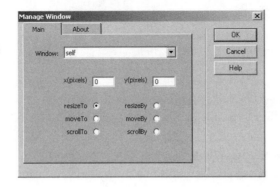

The behavior offers a number of options, but the one we are interested in now is moveTo. This, as the name suggests, moves a browser window to the defined location on any event. In a great many cases, this would be applied to the <body> tag onLoad (so that the window would be moved to the new location straightaway).

## Tip

The Manage Window behavior is part of Massimo Foti's Window Suite, which you can download from his web site (http://www.massimocorner.com/).

## Centering Windows

Developers often ask how to center windows. Although there is no direct way to center a window on the screen (there's no center attribute), it is possible to center a window using a little bit of JavaScript.

Using JavaScript, it is possible to get the dimensions of the user's screen resolution. When you know this and the dimensions of the window you are trying to open, centralizing a window is a breeze. Look at the mathematics:

```
(screen width - window width)/2 = left position for window
(screen height - window height)/2 = top position for window
```

Some typical code might look like this, to open a window 200-by-200 pixels square:

```
<script language="javascript" type="text/javascript">
<!—
var myHeight = screen.availHeight;
var myWidth = screen.availWidth;
var finalHeight = (myHeight - 200)/2;
var finalWidth = (myWidth - 200)/2;
window.open("opener.htm","opener","width=200, height=200,
left="+finalWidth+", top="+finalHeight);
//—>
</script>
```

# Closing Browser Windows

By following a very similar technique to that used for targeting a window and changing its URL, you also can harness this power to close a window. Of course, this works only with windows that have been opened by your controlling page—that is, child windows. If it were possible to close any available window, there would be the potential for abuse, as you will read about later in the "Window Security" section.

## Closing Itself

By far the most straightforward way to close a window is from a link within the window itself. This is the most direct way to close a window because it does not require communication between windows.

JavaScript defines a method for the window object to perform this task. Unsurprisingly, it's called `close`. Because it is the window itself we are closing, we can use the shortcut `self` to denote the current window. As a result, the code to close the window would be this:

```
self.close()
```

Extremely simple, I'm sure you'll agree, but a useful snippet all the same. Integrated into an HTML link, your code might look like this:

```
<a href="javascript:;" onclick="self.close()">Close window</a>
```

*Note*

> If you are closing a window that has not specifically
> been open by your site, a security message will dis-
> play. See the "Window Security" section later in this
> chapter for more information.

### Closing Another Window

When it comes to the matter of closing a window other than the current window, things start to get a little more complicated. That said, it's not too seriously complicated, and basically follows the pattern we used earlier in this chapter.

Earlier, you discovered that by declaring a child window as an object at the time of opening, you could control everything about it via the DOM. We used this code to open our window:

```
Fred = window.open('newpage.html','Fred')
```

This just opens a new window called Fred, which contains the page newpage.html. Because our new window is totally accessible by the name Fred, we can now say this:

```
Fred.close()
```

This will close the window called Fred. Remember that you can close a window only that you have opened. What's more, be sure that your window is open before trying to close it!

## Window Security

Browser windows present a number of security issues. These are not security concerns for the user, however; they are only issues for a developer.

Most browsers have built-in safeguards to protect users from any malicious coding techniques. These safeguards mostly involve warning messages that pop up whenever a suspect action is detected.

## Sending Email

There is a really basic way to send a form via email. By putting `mailto:` and an email address in the `action` of the form, you can use the visitor's default email client to send the data. Chapter 3, "Advanced Forms," covered this technique.

However, the browser views this technique as a security risk. Potentially, a web developer could use JavaScript to send a form without the user knowing. This would result in the owner of the web site being sent every visitors' name and email address without them knowing. As you can appreciate, that's not a good position to be in. To combat this, yet still provide the honest web developer with some useful functionality, the browser displays a warning message whenever this technique is used (see Figure 13.20).

**Figure 13.20**

The browser displays a warning message to alert the user to a possible security issue.

Although it looks unprofessional for the honest site, this warning is vital to prevent abuse of the system. There are no ways to prevent this warning message popping up, other than to avoid the 'mailto' method and use a server-side script. Chapter 3 details many different options for sending email from a web site form.

## Security Issues Surrounding Closing Windows

Earlier in this chapter, we looked at ways to close browser windows. Some of these methods involved closing the window itself, and some involved closing other windows open by the browser. Note that a browser will only allow a page to close a child window—that is, a window that the page itself has spawned.

The reason for this is to prevent unscrupulous coders from closing any of your browser windows that they see fit. This could be very irritating. Imagine visiting a web site that deems itself so important that you shouldn't have any other web sites open. The site could close all of your other open browser windows without you even asking it to.

To battle this problem, the browser will display a warning whenever a page tries to close windows it did not specifically open (see Figure 13.21).

**Figure 13.21**

The browser gives the user a chance to prevent a window closing itself.

Again, there is no way to avoid this message appearing, unless you code your pages carefully so as to never evoke this message.

### Window Size

Another issue crops up from time to time with pop-up windows. Web browsers consider any window less than 100-by-100 pixels to be too small to possibly contain a legitimate web page. This is fairly reasonable; I cannot think of any case where a window would be needed that is smaller than this size, because it would be near impossible to fit any useful content within it.

The danger is that a page could spawn a new window so small as to not be noticeable. If this were possible, a small, unnoticed window could go on running scripts long after the user believes that he has closed a site down.

# What to Take Away from This Chapter

- The browser is a web developer's blank canvas and can be manipulated in a number of ways.

- There are pros and cons for spawning new browser windows with each page link.

- By using some simple JavaScript and by manipulating the DOM, it is possible to give the user the choice of opening a new window.

- A number of elements are controllable by the web developer, and others are not.

- Pop-up windows can be used for a number of different purposes, including advertising, help systems, and to add secondary content to primary.

- Browser windows can be manipulated to close themselves or other windows under their control.

- Browser windows can be named and targeted.

- Browser windows raise some security issues, but these should not be a major stumbling block.

# Part III

## Developing Projects Further

# Chapter 14

# Building Web Applications

Objectives:

- Gain an understanding of what is meant by the term *web application*, and the technologies involved in application development.
- Learn about the process one needs to go through in building a web application.
- Find out how to take your application development to the next level and create robust, scalable applications.

The day will come, you'll be having a meeting with a prospective client, and the meeting is going really well. The client loves your ideas, adores your previous work, you get on like a house on fire, but then the bombshell is dropped.

"We want our users to be able to register on the site and then log in to a members' area where they will be able to search our database of widget-related information; that won't be a problem, will it?"

You say, "No problem." You need this job, and you can always find a subcontractor, right? However, wouldn't it be a fantastic addition to your skill set to be able to do this work yourself? It just happens that the tool you have on your desktop, your familiar environment for web page design, Dreamweaver MX, is also an advanced visual environment for web application development.

This chapter discusses why you might want to look at these features of Dreamweaver MX and how to start expanding your skills into the exciting world of building web applications.

# What Is a Web Application?

Put simply, a *web application* is software that can be used via the web, without users needing to have any other software installed on their machine, other than a web browser. Typically a web application incorporates scripts that are run when a user interacts with a web page, such as submitting a form, and a database.

Traditional web sites are built by creating HTML pages and graphics and uploading them to the server, where visitors can type in the URL and read the contents. If you want to make a change, perhaps to add some latest news to your home page, you have to edit the HTML file and re-upload it to the server.

With a simple web application, the developer would create the pages and graphics and also create a news page that retrieves its contents from a database. The news page can be added to by going to a form with a web browser and adding the content via the form. When the form is submitted, the contents of that form are added to the database. When a visitor comes to read the news page, the application retrieves the content from the database and sends it back to the user's browser, as HTML.

The user needs no special software; and, because all the browser sees is HTML, so long as you ensure that the HTML that the application produces works cross browser, the browser will have no problems displaying it.

### How Does It Work?

Staying with the example of a news page, look at what actually happens when someone wants to add some data via the online form.

### The Web Browser

Our user, armed only with a copy of Internet Explorer, goes to the page, which contains a form. The form will enable her to add a title and a news article to the site. She completes the form and clicks the submit button.

### The Application Server

The page to which the form submits contains some scripting that lets the application server know it needs to pass the data to the database. When the application server is passed this page, it takes the input from the form and passes it to the database.

### The Database

On being passed the information in a way that it can understand, the database inserts the title and news item into the correct place.

### The Application Server

No error message is returned from the database, so the application server runs the rest of the page, which passes a thank you page in HTML back to the browser.

### The Web Browser

The browser displays the Thank You page. The user reads it and knows that the news item is now available on the site.

When a visitor comes to the site, his browser makes a request for the news page; the scripting on that page prompts the application server to retrieve the news item from the database and assemble the news page on-the-fly; and the user sees the new news item as an HTML page in his browser. If visitors are to "view source" on this page, they will see the HTML only as in a static site, because the page is built before it is returned to the browser.

This is what is meant by server-side scripting or code. Unlike client-side code (such as client-side JavaScript) that you can see in the source of the page, code parsed by the application server is not displayed to, and does not have any affect on, the browser. Figure 14.1 demonstrates this flow of data between the browser, web server, and database.

**Figure 14.1**

Diagram to show client/server model.

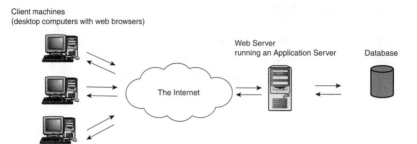

Client machines
(desktop computers with web browsers)

Web Server
running an Application Server          Database

The Internet

## What Can a Web Application Do?

You probably use web applications every day. Examples of web applications include the following:

- Search engines such as Yahoo! and Google
- Online stores such as Amazon.com
- Communities such as Yahoo! Groups
- Web-based email such as Hotmail
- Your online banking service
- A service that enables you to update a "blog," or online diary, without using FTP

These examples are all fairly large-scale. On a smaller scale, you might use a web application to search an existing Access database, or as discussed already, enable addition to site content without needing to alter and upload HTML pages. The following sections discuss common uses of web applications.

### Content Management

*Content management systems* (CMSs) are a current buzzword. A CMS is just a way to enable effective management of site content, including easy ways to keep the content up-to-date, searchable, and easily organized on the site.

A CMS will enable content authors to add, edit, and manage content without needing skills in HTML and will ensure that each content author is adding content consistent with the site's overall look and feel.

Many propriety CMSs are available, and the price for these systems can range into millions of dollars—beyond the price range of most of our clients, and also full of features that are not needed for most clients.

Content management—whether just enabling your client to edit the content of a few key pages or perhaps a more advanced system—is one of the main reasons web applications are necessary. Database-driven content brings with it many advantages. Although these might not seem immediately obvious, or useful during initial development, they will enable future growth and feature building for the site.

### Separation of Content and Markup

After you have the content stored in a database, design changes don't mean having to go through all the content and reformat it. Combine content in a database with CSS and you have an incredibly easy-to-maintain site.

### Reuse Content

If your content is stored in a database without any style information, you can reuse it. Perhaps you have several sites hosted on a server that deal with different areas of a common subject. Even if those sites all look radically different, you can pull some content from one onto the other without needing to duplicate the actual data in both places.

### Archive

By being held within a database, your data is, in effect, archived already. As the amount of content on a site builds up, there is no need to lose older information because the database makes searching easy.

*Serve Personalized Content*

Because the content is held in a database, it is easier to select content based on various metrics. Such metric information may be visitor-provided (via completion of a form on the site) or may just be information that you can deduce. If you set a cookie on a visitor's first visit to the site, you will be able to recognize that user on his subsequent visits to your site and tailor the content to that user.

## Online Shopping and Payment

A common web application example is the online store. An online store web application enables users to browse products and add them to their "basket." At the end of the visit, the web application enables the user to make a secure payment for all the products.

A fully featured online store application would normally allow for updating of products and pricing via a secure site administration area; produce reports for the store owner of purchases made; and allow for the integration other features, such as quicker ordering for return customers, product suggestion, and so on.

## Community Features

Chat rooms, web mail, bulletin boards, and forums are all examples of web applications that allow for online communities to be built up. One example of this type of web application is Yahoo! Groups. You create a Yahoo! Groups account by entering some details into a web form. By submitting the form, you trigger the application to add your details and send you an email. You confirm that the address is actually your email address by replying to the email. All of this is automated. There is no unhappy person sitting in the Yahoo! offices reading all these emails.

After you have an account, you can sign up for groups and choose how you want to read emails from your groups—on the web, or the application can send them to your registered email address. You can add to a collective database of pictures and information, and you can find out about the other users of your group.

### Searchable Databases

Frequently your client will have existing information to which they want to enable users of their site to have access. A database, by its very nature, is searchable. By using the application server, you can utilize this functionality of the database to enable users to enter the terms they want to search for into a form in their web browser. After the form has been submitted, the application sends the database a query that will return a result based on those terms. The application then sends that result back to the web browser as HTML, and the user gets the information that he or she needs.

As discussed in the next chapter, many databases can be connected to via a web application; and in this way, you can easily enable integration of clients' existing systems with their web sites.

### Online Learning

You hear a lot about "e-learning" these days. Whereas learning online used to consist of reading static documents about the subject you were studying, today's e-learning web applications allow for dynamic, interactive environments. Students can assess their skills with online quizzes and tests and communicate with tutors and other students as part of their learning experience.

When a static web site is being used for teaching purposes, students can follow the tutorial, perhaps fill out a test, and then send it to their tutor. In an interactive environment, the test can return results immediately. An interactive learning environment may even suggest areas in which students should study further, and may enable students to continue with their study session at their own pace.

### Intranet and Extranet Applications

An *intranet application* is one that is hosted on an internal network, to be accessed only by those with access to the network. Intranets tend to be hosted behind a firewall within a corporation or organization to keep data away from those without authorization. To a user accessing the application with her web browser, the pages will look much like any other site, except only those within the internal network can view them.

An *extranet* is a private intranet application that can be accessed externally. For instance, many companies have employees who work from home (either full or part time). An extranet application enables those employees to access the company's intranet and get to the information employees on the internal network can access.

Intranet and extranet applications represent a growing use of web-based technology. In many ways, designing for an intranet, extranet, or even the Internet is very similar. The main differences relate to security levels and how you approach them. An in-house network will likely have much more potentially sensitive data on it than you would expect to deal with on most Internet sites. If you were to give access via an extranet to this type of data, you would be wise to seek advice on security practices.

## Web Applications Versus Static Sites

When a user's browser requests a static HTML page, the web server just finds the page and returns it to the browser. No processing of this information occurs on the server. The browser just interprets the HTML when it receives it. HTML is not a programming language. Its purpose is just to mark up text so that an application that can interpret HTML (a web browser) will display the text with that formatting. In practice this means that whatever you have uploaded to your server is what the user sees; there is no way for that to be changed without copying over the file with another HTML file that has the changes in it.

To circumvent HTML limitations, we are used to using client-side scripting, such as JavaScript, to make our pages "interactive." However, JavaScript is run on the client side, in the browser, and is reliant on your user having a browser that will support JavaScript for it to work. Once again, if a request is sent to the web server for a page containing client-side code, the server just returns that page to the browser; the code is not processed on the server at all. JavaScript is also a bad choice for any level of security or private information because all the information has to be stored on the page, where anyone who knows how to View Source can see it.

## Why Develop Web Applications?

Your client sells widgets. Currently they have 100 widgets listed on their site. Next month 50 new widgets are to be added to the catalog, and 30 widgets will be removed. The client sends you a list of the widgets to remove and the widgets to add. You go through all the HTML pages deleting widgets, moving the tables around so that they still display in alphabetic order. Then you add the new widgets. Every month a new file of widgets arrives, and the process continues.

If the widgets were held in a database and displayed dynamically on the page, each month the client could select all the widgets that he would like to remove and delete them from the database. He could then add all the details for the new widgets. The widgets could then be displayed dynamically on the page, so there would be no need to reorder them manually.

Perhaps the client would then like to enable people to download a text file listing all the available widgets. With a static site, this would mean creating the text file every time the widgets list was updated, thus duplicating your work. When the widgets are being displayed dynamically, it is a simple case of writing a script that will write the list to a text file rather than to the browser.

One year down the line, you need to redesign the site. With a static site, this would mean having to recode all those pages of widgets to get them to fit with the new layout. With our dynamic site, we have to change only one page because we create each page of widgets on-the-fly from the database.

The web application in this scenario streamlines the site creation work process, ensures that the products all display in a coherent format, and removes the need to duplicate data to do different tasks. Users of this site would notice no difference in the way the information is presented.

By now you probably have a good idea of what a web application can do. You probably already have some ideas about how you can use this kind of functionality in your sites. The web today is a dynamic and interactive medium. Clients and employers see what is available on other sites and, without understanding the technology behind it, know what they want.

What many clients want today is far removed from the online brochures we built in the past.

By adding application development to your skills, you are going to become more marketable and employable. Even if you decide to stay more in the design world and work with application developers, understanding the technologies involved will enable you to talk confidently about them.

### Getting Started

Macromedia Dreamweaver MX is a great place to start your application development journey. In the familiar, visual environment, you will spend less time learning the software and more time concentrating on your application. Dreamweaver MX enables you to see working results quickly, instead of spending weeks learning syntax. For many simple, small-scale applications, you will probably not have to see the code at all.

Before you dive in and start building, there are various concepts that are worth understanding. The rest of this chapter introduces you to those fundamentals of application development.

## Database Integration

You have already read a bit about databases in this chapter; it would be hard to talk about web applications without mentioning them. Some form of data storage is at the core of nearly all web applications, and most of the time that data storage is by way of a relational database.

If you have ever worked with CGI scripts to add "guest book"-type functionality to a site, you may well have stored data in a text file, one line for every entry. If you wanted to retrieve and edit a single line relating to one user from the text file, you had to write a routine that would look through the text file and find that line.

The advantage of database use is that you remove much of that logic from your scripts and enable the database to handle it, which not only takes less time to write, but also takes less time to execute. The more complex your application becomes, the greater these advantages. You might not immediately see much difference between the speed of a simple guest book application after moving it to a database from a text file. After you have complex logic and multistep operations occurring, however, your database will outperform the text file–based system, simply because it is doing what it is designed to do.

## What Is a Database?

A *database* is a store of information, organized in such a way that it is searchable and editable. When we talk about databases in the context of the web, we are generally discussing a relational database or *relational database management system* (RDBMS).

Relational databases are comprised of tables—in which the data is stored. Each table in the database is made up of records (horizontal rows of data) and fields (vertical columns) as shown in Figure 14.2. When you retrieve, insert, delete, or otherwise manipulate your database, you are using what is termed a *query*.

The records in a database table are unordered; in the actual table itself, they will appear in the order that you insert them. When you query the database, however, you can retrieve these records in any order that you want.

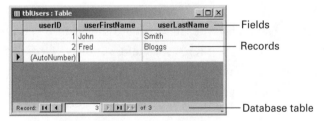

**Figure 14.2**

A database table showing records (rows) and fields (columns).

Data can be retrieved from the database by comparing the value of data held within a field to a search. Suppose that you have the database table here and ask the database to "give me all fields from any record in the table named users where the field userFirstName is John":

| UserID | UserFirstName | UserLastName |
|--------|---------------|--------------|
| 1 | John | Smith |
| 2 | Fred | Bloggs |

The database will return the following:

| 1 | John | Smith |
|---|------|-------|

Tables in the database can be linked to other tables by fields that contain matching data. Suppose that your database contains another table that looks like this:

| FavoritesID | userID | favoritesColor |
|-------------|--------|----------------|
| 1 | 1 | Red |
| 2 | 2 | Pink |
| 3 | 2 | Orange |

You could ask the database for "all fields in all records from the tables favorites and users, where the field UserID equals 1." If you were to do so, the following information would be returned to you:

| 1 | John | Smith | 1 | Red |
|---|------|-------|---|-----|

As you can see, the data being returned by the database is, in effect, another table. When you are working with information from a database in Dreamweaver MX, this returned information is called a *recordset*. You can think of your recordset as being this table of returned data. It might be one row or many, depending on the query that created the recordset.

## Talking to Your Database

The language of your database is *Structured Query Language* (SQL)—not to be confused with SQL Server, which is a RDBMS from Microsoft discussed in the next chapter. When you are building web applications with Dreamweaver MX, you will find that most of your SQL is written for you. However, it will do you well to understand a little of the syntax; it isn't difficult and will help you greatly later on.

Different database products have SQL syntax variations. However, these tend to be fairly minor and well documented. A reasonable knowledge of SQL syntax will stand you in good stead whichever database you happen to be using.

SQL is based on the English language and is easily readable. Consider the earlier example when you wanted "all fields from any record in the table named users where the field userFirstName is John." In SQL, it would look like this:

```
SELECT * FROM users WHERE userFirstName = 'John'
```

In SQL, ★ means all. In this example, ★ means all fields. To retrieve only the fields userFirstName and userID from the database, the SQL looks like this:

```
SELECT userID, userFirstName FROM users WHERE userFirstName =
➥'John'
```

If you want to insert a new user into the Users table, you could use this SQL syntax:

```
INSERT INTO users (userFirstName, userLastName)
➥VALUES ("Mary", "Snow")
```

To delete a row, you could use the following:

```
DELETE FROM users WHERE userID = 1
```

A full SQL reference is beyond the scope of this chapter (and this book). I hope that the preceding examples familiarize you enough with SQL for you to be able to understand what is happening in your code in Dreamweaver MX. If you want to delve further into web application development, you should add a good reference book on SQL to your bookshelf.

## Database Design Principles

Good planning is key to a successful database for your web application. Before you even start to create a table for your new database, sit down with a pen and paper and plan it out. What will be stored where? What do you need to be able to retrieve? How will it all link up?

If your database design is successful, it will enable your application to grow over time without needing you to rewrite the database, it will allow easy transfer of data, and it will make your actual coding of the web application itself much easy.

## Relationships

In a world of perfect database design, there would never be any duplication of data in your database. Each field (apart from the linking primary key and foreign key fields discuss in a moment) should be unique in the database.

We link our tables by way of a primary key and foreign key. The primary key in the first table is userID. A primary key must be a field that is unique among the records in that table. Usually when we create a primary key field, we will let the database automatically put a unique number in there to ensure that we don't accidentally try to duplicate the ID of a record.

The foreign key in the earlier example is in the Favorites table. This foreign key is the primary key of the Users table. However, here we may have duplicates because we want to be able to match duplicate rows in Favorites table to a single row (relating to a user) in the Users table.

This linking of tables creates what is called relationships. Just to confuse matters, there are three types of relationships: one-to-one, one-to-many, and many-to-many.

### One-to-One

A real-life example of a one-to-one relationship is that of the legal status of husbands to wives. One husband can have one wife. If, in your database, you had a table of women and a table of men and wanted to link the husbands to the wives, you would link the primary key in the Women table to a foreign Key in the Men table with a one-to-one relationship. You know that there can be only one matching record returned from this relationship. This relationship is shown as relationship A in Figure 14.3

### One-to-Many

Perhaps in our database we also have a table of children. Each woman could have more than one child in the Children table. By linking the primary key of the Women table to a foreign key in the Children table and using a one-to-many relationship, you could retrieve the woman and all children linked to her. You know there will be only one woman, but the number of children is variable. This type of relationship is shown in Figure 14.3 as relationship B.

### Many-to-Many

Now suppose we have a table of pets, and we want to show which children own which pets. A pet could be owned by many children—in the case of brothers and sisters—and each child could own several different pets. Therefore, to link a variable quantity of children with a variable number of pets, we need to use a many-to-many relationship.

To create the many-to-many relationship, we need to create another table. The purpose of this table is just to show this relationship. The table will contain two foreign keys, the primary keys from both the Children and the Pets table. This type of relationship is shown in Figure 14.3 as relationship C.

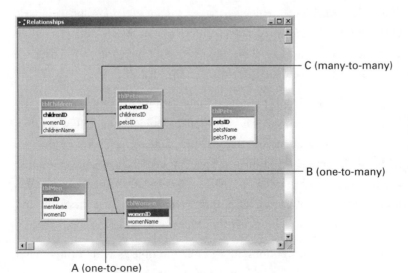

**Figure 14.3**

A relationship diagram from an Access 2000 database demonstrating the one-to-one, one-to-many, and many-to-many relationships.

## Naming Conventions

Using a set method of naming your tables and fields will make it easier for you to work with your database later. If you are working within an organization, you may find that there is already a preferred method of naming database objects, and you'll sound like you know exactly what you are doing if you ask what the company policy of naming database objects is! For most of us, however, we find our own method through what works best for us.

You should always follow some basic rules when naming objects and fields within your database.

1.  No spaces in names

2.  No reserved words

3.  No strange characters in names

"No spaces in names" is easy enough to understand. If you need to use two words to identify an object, you can use the underscore character (_) or just join the words together. "Reserved words" are words that are reserved by the version of SQL you are using. Some common reserved words are *date*, *time*, *first*, and *last*. By following a naming convention, such as the method detailed in this section, you eliminate the problem of accidentally using a reserved word. Using strange characters, as in any non–alpha-numeric characters, in object names is generally a bad idea. Many characters (such as ` @ # *) may have special meaning in SQL, depending on the database that you are using, and are therefore best avoided.

The naming convention I tend to follow is to prefix each table with tbl. For a table that contains user information, I would name it tblUsers. I then prefix each field name in the table with the table name. Therefore, the user ID would become usersID, the user's first name usersFirstName, and so on. Doing this means that each of my tables is consistently named, which makes it easier when I am writing script that interacts with the tables, because I know what I called each field without having to go look it up.

Other common conventions are to prefix all objects with a three-letter code—tbl for table, fld for field, and so on. For the most part, whatever works best for you is just fine.

## Database Terminology Reference

This section briefly explains some of the common terms that you are likely to encounter when working with a database. Knowing some terminology will enable you to ask questions that can be answered. Therefore, it's worth knowing the proper names of things.

### Data Types

Each column in a table has a type. The *type* lets the column know what kind of data is expected there and enables you to insert and retrieve data with ease, because you know what format it will be in. There is some variation in data types among different RDBMS (as discussed in more detail in the next chapter).

### Foreign Key

A *foreign key* is a field that refers to the primary key of another table.

### Normalization

*Normalization* refers to the process of removing repeat information from your tables.

### Primary Key

A *primary key* is a field that uniquely identifies each row in the table.

### Reserved Words

When designing your database, you need to be careful to avoid using reserved words as field names or table names. *Reserved words* are things such as *date*, *time*, *first*, and *last*. By using a naming convention for your objects and fields, as discussed earlier in this chapter, you can avoid accidental use of reserved words that will cause problems when you come to access your database from your web application.

### Stored Procedure

A *stored procedure* is a SQL statement stored inside the database. Stored procedures are complied and will usually be faster than running the same code on the page.

### SQL

*SQL* (Structured Query Language) is a programming language for interacting with a database. SQL (pronounced S-Q-L) is both an ANSI and ISO standard, but different RDBMSs have extensions and limitations within the basic language.

### Trigger

A *trigger* is just a stored procedure executed in response to some other action. For instance, you could write a trigger that updates another table every time an action happens to your Users table.

# User Access and Security

Member-only sections, admin areas, and personalized content are becoming a common feature of many sites today. If you are, as in the earlier example, to enable updating of content via a web form, you need some way to ensure that only the authorized person can add content to the site. The last thing you want is a rival company discovering the location of your admin page and posting a news item that points your visitors to their site! By implementing a system whereby the user logs in with a username and password, you can ensure this area is kept only for those who have access to it.

It is only a small step further to create a members-only area, where multiple users can have access to an area. When you have users logging in, you must have some way to identify who they are. Therefore, you can serve user-appropriate content. Consider, for example, the Amazon.com web site. If you visit the site and purchase a book, and then you log in again, you will find suggestions of books that you might be interested in purchasing (based on your previous purchases). This is an excellent way to increase sales, and it makes users feel that the site is accommodating their needs. It's like walking into your local bookstore and getting suggestions from the owner about the latest web development books (because the owner remembered that last time you were in you purchased a Dreamweaver book).

This technique doesn't have to be confined to e-commerce sites. Perhaps you are designing a site for a school, parents and children can register and log in to an area just for those connected directly with the school. When parents log in, they are presented with the latest information on parents' evening and social events for the PTA. When children log in, they see information about the upcoming auditions for the school play and can read the results of the latest football match.

In this scenario, all users could have access to all areas of this members-only section, but they are given the quickest access to those areas that interest them most. This could be taken a step further by creating a system that showed content only to those who have the correct privileges to view it.

## Logging In

How does a members-only section work in practice? To allow a user access to certain pages only when logged in, we need to do two things:

1.  We need to provide a way for the user to tell us who they are (logging in).

2.  We need to have a way to check who they are after they have logged in so that we don't have to ask them to identify themselves on every page.

### Who Are You?

To identify our users and allow them to log in, we need to have a table in our database of usernames and passwords. This could be held alongside other personal information about the user. In the school site example, this data would probably be entered into the database by the site administrator, because only a set group of people (students registered at the school and their parents) would be allowed access to the site. For a site such as Amazon.com, the information is added to the database when a user signs up.

When users log in, they enter their username and password, which we then compare with the information held in the database. If we find a match, we allow them to proceed into the members-only section. If we find no match, they have either entered the wrong details or have no right to access this area, so we print a message to the screen giving them some information on what they should do next.

## Maintaining State

After we have our users logged in, we need some way to identify them as they move around the site. Otherwise, we would have to ask them for their username and password each time they wanted to access a page within our members-only section. This ability to track a user, so that we can identify them throughout their visit to the site, is called *maintaining state*. Maintaining state becomes vitally important if you have to deal with an online store application or in any other situation in which mixing up user data would lead to grave consequences.

The decision about how you will maintain state is something that you should consider early on. Maintaining state is a big cause of developer headaches and beer overconsumption, due to the inherent stateless nature of the web. When you, the user, make a request for a page from a web server, the server receives your request and sends back the page you want. At that point, it promptly forgets who you are. There could be 100 users all requesting pages from the server, and it has no way to really keep them separate, nor is it interested in doing so.

You can maintain state in three ways:
- Cookie crunching
- Session sniffing
- QueryString reading

The following sections discuss each of these ways to maintain state in turn. Be aware, however, that this is just a general overview of the methods. After you have chosen an application server for your project, read up some more on the methods it supports and the specifics of those methods for that environment.

### Cookie Crunching

After logging in a user, we want to be able to remember who that user is from page to page. A common way to do this is to use cookies. A *cookie* is a text string containing name-value pairs, stored on the user's hard drive. If you search on your computer for "cookies," you will find at least one folder, more if you use different browsers, containing cookies.

For the school web site example, we could write a cookie to the user's hard disk when he logs in. The cookie would contain his userID. By checking for a valid user ID on each page (by looking in the cookie), we know we have a bona-fide user. Cookies can be stored just for this visit to the site (and deleted when the user closes his browser) or they can be persistent— enabling us to let the user come back to the site without logging in again and/or to remember their personal information for another visit.

### Session Sniffing

Similar to cookies, we have *sessions*. Most application servers have some form of session available. A session works in a very similar way to a cookie, and in fact, your user must have cookies enabled to be able to accept sessions. They work by storing the user information in memory on the web server for the duration of that user's visit. They expire when the user has not been active on the site for a set amount of time.

Unlike cookies, sessions cannot be used to remember a user if she returns to the site after a specified period of time; they persist only for the duration of a user's visit.

### QueryString Reading

If for some reason you do not want to maintain state with either of the preceding methods (cookie crunching or session sniffing—for instance, if it is vitally important that even users with cookies disabled have access to the site—you can just pass some information in the QueryString from page to page and then check on each page whether this is a valid user. You may have seen sites doing this. You can see when this method is being used by looking at the URL of the page you are on, which might look something like this:

```
http://thedomain.com/order.asp?sessionid=
➡51C2C1AA-76BC-41D8-AE29-CC070D27FD4C
```

The information after the question mark is called the QueryString, and this part of the URL can be used to pass information from page to page.

Although this method can work very well and avoids problems when users do not want to accept cookies, you need to plan very carefully what information you will use to identify visitors. If I just passed the user ID on the QueryString and then the page checked for a matching user ID, for instance, it would be very tempting just to increment the user ID a few numbers to see whether I could manage to identify as someone else.

Passing state information around on the QueryString can be a developer's nightmare. You need to ensure that each page of your application passes this information to each page it links to, and you have the problem of a user just typing the URL of a page (minus the QueryString) into their browser, at which point state has been lost. In many situations, and with a good deal of thought, however, this method can work very well.

It is, of course, possible to combine methods of maintaining state on one site. You might choose to use cookies for a site's administrators—because you can explain to them that they will need to have cookies enabled to use the administration area (in the interests of security and ease of use). For the site's general users, the number of pages that they will be accessing in a members-only area may be relatively small, and so using the QueryString method will mean you don't need to be concerned with ensuring users have cookies enabled.

## Taking Care of Personal Information

When you begin to take personal information and store it in a database on your site, you need to consider how you will keep that data secure, and also how you will make your users feel happy about giving you their information.

I'm writing from the UK where we have very strict laws governing the storage of personal information, which falls under the Data Protection Act. Although other countries may not have such measures in place, much of the Data Protection Act, in relation to the storage of data on the web, is common sense and, if followed, will enable your users to feel secure with registering on your site.

## A Privacy Policy

What are you going to do with your users' data? Most companies aren't about to sell their mailing lists to the nearest spammer, but it is always a good policy to let your users know this. If they are concerned about junk email, seeing that you have a policy not to sell or otherwise pass on their data might mean the difference between them signing up or purchasing from your site and clicking the back button. The UK Data Protection Act web site (`http://www.dataprotection.gov.uk`) has this to say about a good privacy policy:

> "As a matter of good practice and as an aid to encouraging confidence, a privacy statement should describe not only what a web site operator does with personal data but also what it does not do. It should also tell individuals something about their rights and how to exercise them… The privacy statement must include the physical address of the web site operator unless this is clearly visible on the site."

(Data Protection Act 1998 Compliance Advice document. Although it's quite hard to find, at the time of writing it's available at `http://www.dataprotection.gov.uk/dpr/dpdoc.nsf/ed1e7ff5aa6def30802 566360045bf4d/e2c551e040f8f0a880256a8f0036bf54/$FILE/faqsweb.pdf`.)

Before you write your privacy policy, you (or your client) need to consider the sort of information you want to collect and what you want to do with it in the immediate future, and, whether there is any possibility that you might use it in some other manner further down the line. Additionally, if you have any agreements with third parties, such as a cobranded area of your site, where data relating to individuals could be passed to the third party, these should be made plain as well.

You are likely to be collecting two main groups of information: personally identifiable information and mass anonymous information.

### Personally Identifiable Information

Personally identifiable information refers to information that can identify the individual. This includes things such as email addresses, mailing address, date of birth, credit card details, social security or national insurance numbers.

Personally identifiable information is collected with the knowledge of the user and can be linked directly to that user. It does not include information such as an IP address, browser, or other computer details unless this information is stored in such a way that it can be linked to other information that would be classed as personally identifiable. An example of this is if you check the user's browser and OS version and log it in a database alongside the user's name and email address, or if you track which pages a user visits with a cookie and then log that information against the user's personal details.

### Mass Anonymous Information

Mass anonymous information refers to information that cannot be tied to a user. For instance, releasing statistics of what percentage of your users had visited the site using which browser version would not be seen as releasing personally identifiable information without consent.

Aggregate statistics of your user base—which countries your users come from, the average age of your users, and so on—do not normally fall under the category of anonymous. If you are likely to use information in this way, however, it is good practice to state this in your privacy policy.

## Children and Young People

It is worth mentioning the additional complications that arise when a site with personalization features is aimed at children and young people. The accepted standard is that when taking personally identifiable information from children less than 12 years old, parental consent should be obtained.

This is obviously going to be easier to police if your web site is aimed at a select group of young people who can be identified and checked up on individually (such as a school web site). In all other cases, when the site is aimed at young people, often the only way to obtain satisfactory consent is to implement a policy of obtaining postal consent before enabling young people to interact on the site.

## Keeping Information Secure

After you have collected data from your users, you need to consider its security, both the method of storage on your site and during any transactions. This becomes vitally important if you are dealing with payment details such as credit card numbers.

First, you want to ensure that there is no way your application can easily expose customer details. For example, you don't want to use an ID in the QueryString that enables someone to change the value and see other details. Second, plan—as well as possible—to guard against hackers seeking your data. When a high-profile company is hacked and credit card details exposed, it tends to hit the news. Even if your endeavor is relatively small, your client will probably have read some of these stories and will want to know what you have done to ensure security.

The golden rule is, if in doubt ask someone. If you are required to build a highly secure application, and you are unsure about what you are doing, you may need to take advice from someone who does.

### On Your Server

The next chapter discusses application security and how it relates to the various web and application servers in detail. In general, you need to be confident that where your site is hosted is secure. If you are using shared hosting, you need to ask the hosting company what measures they put in place to ensure security of data on the servers. If you're considering a hosting company, ask around. Check the relevant newsgroup for the application server you are using on news://forums.macromedia.com. This is good place to solicit advice as to the reliability and security of a hosting company. You also should search Google groups at http://groups.google.com; search for the hosting company's name. Remember that every hosting company will have some people complaining about it. Therefore, look for genuine reports of security alerts, preferably backed up by an article in the press, online or offline.

If you are using a database, such as Microsoft Access, your database should not be stored within the publicly visible web site. If you have shared hosting, you should be told where to put your database. If you can type http://www.mydomain.com/mydatabase.mdb into a web browser and download your database, you have problems; anyone who guesses the database name can download the database and have all your information.

If you need to take credit card numbers or very sensitive information (for example, medical information that could be damaging to the individual if allowed into the public domain), you should use Secure Sockets Layer (SSL) and invest in a secure certificate for the site. SSL allows an SSL-enabled server to connect to an SSL-enabled client—the browser. Information sent over an SSL connection is encrypted and so cannot easily be picked up while in transit between the browser and the server. The browser also displays the server's certificate so that users can identify whether they are sending the information to the right company or organization. According to Figure 14.4, it is clear that Amazon.com is to receive any payment made via this secure server.

**Figure 14.4**

The secure certificate from Amazon.com.

Some hosting companies offer shared SSL. Shared SSL means that you share a secure certificate with other clients. This arrangement works out cheaper and works well if you have just a limited need for SSL. Remember that if you use this service, the name on the certificate will be that of the hosting company and not the domain name of the company that owns the web site. Therefore, it is wise to put a notice to this effect on the page that enables users to submit their details.

### While in Electronic Transit

Email is not secure; there is little point in implementing a secure ordering system if your system then emails credit card numbers or other potentially sensitive information to the site administrator.

If you need to transmit sensitive information via email, look at the data encrypting and decrypting options. You should never send any information via email in an unencrypted format if that information could be harmful in the wrong hands. The most common way to encrypt email information is with *Pretty Good Privacy* (PGP).

PGP works by the creation of public and private keys. The private key enables the user to decrypt messages and is protected by a pass phrase that the user chooses when she creates the keys. The public key enables other users to encrypt a message for the holder of the private key of that pair. To be able to encrypt mail using PGP on the server, your server must have PGP installed and the site administrator must have generated a public-private key pair so that that they may decrypt the emails sent to them. You can find out more about PGP at the International PGP home page at `http://www.pgpi.org/`.

## Online Payment Systems

If you are building a site where users need to pay for some goods or services—whether a single subscription to paid members-only information or a large shopping cart application—at some point you will need to actually take and validate that payment. Sooner or later, most developers will face this scenario. Therefore, this section touches on the options that you have. When the time comes, you will know what to advise your client and where to begin to select the best solution for your needs.

## Taking Payments Online

The kind of payment option you will choose will ultimately come down to the status of the person who is taking the payment. One factor to consider is whether the person taking payment has merchant status and can process credit cards already—for instance, a brick-and-mortar store that wants to sell some products online. Another factor is whether you need automatic validation of payment—for example, if you want to enable users to pay for some software and then, if their credit card is approved, download the software. Another factor to consider is what security measures for the storage and collection of information you have, or are willing to put in place.

### Rolling Your Own

Unless the site is a very large operation, it is probably not advisable to take payments on your own server, particularly when these payments need to be automatically validated. Setting up your own online validation system is very costly. If the client wants to validate offline, your option is to store the payment details (under an SSL connection) in a database or email them to the client using encrypted email. If you are storing card details in a database, only store them until the client has retrieved them. The client will need to log in to a secure area, retrieve the card details, and then update the record to show that the payment has been taken. At this point, you should remove the details from the database. A good method and one that many stores use is to delete all but the first or last four characters of the card number so that the card can still be identified if the user makes another payment.

If site owners want to validate card payments offline, they need to have a merchant account that enables them to take "cardholder not present" payments. If they don't have this sort of account in place already, they must confirm with their bank that they can have this type of account before work is started.

## Payment Gateways

The advantage of using a payment gateway is that none of the credit card details are stored or validated on your server, so your security concerns for the application are lessened. In practice, most small to medium web sites that need to take online payments use some type of gateway.

Some payment gateways enable the transaction to take place without the user ever appearing to leave your site. Users fill in their details on an SSL-enabled page with your certificate. When they click submit, the details are sent to the gateway over a secure connection, processed, and, depending on whether the payment is authorized or declined, the user is then directed to the relevant page of your site for an accepted or failed transaction. The site owner then receives the payments via the gateway provider. That payment is often received by logging in to a secure area on their server to retrieve the details; alternatively, because many gateway services are provided by the banks that offer merchant accounts, the funds are transferred directly to the account in question.

Other payment gateways enable you to link to a page on their secure server where the user details are collected. The advantage to this is that you do not need to have your own SSL certificate. If you are linking off to another site for payment, it is wise to alert the user to this with a message on the page that links off to the service (because users may feel uncomfortable about making their payment on an unknown site). Luckily, many of the payment gateways are used on so many sites that they are becoming trusted household names in themselves. Therefore, if you use a known payment gateway, your users may find that payment gateway more trustworthy than your own security! A good gateway enables you to pass variables to it that are then returned back to a script on your server. These scripts enable you to log the payment as accepted or declined in your own database. You can then allow access to a paid-only area and/or enable the download of software automatically.

Gateway costs vary widely. Some charge for setting up an account. Some take a percentage of the payment. Unless you are tied to using a certain provider—for instance, the client's bank or some other existing arrangement—thoroughly research before choosing your recommended provider, taking into account not only what is required in the short term, but also considering any future plans for the site.

### Hosted Stores and Payment Systems

At the lower end of the market, various companies offer fully hosted online stores. These can be a cheap and accessible way to provide online payment services. However, they usually offer few options to customize the store into your brand and can look less than professional.

Some systems offer a method by which payments can be taken by sites where the owner has no merchant status. These systems include big-name operations such as Paypal (`http://www.paypal.com`). The usual process is that the system takes a payment, validates and processes it through its own system, and then pays the money into the owner's account. Although these systems can be very useful to a small site, particularly one where the product is not guaranteed to be successful, they come at a price. Often the user also has to have an account with the provider, the system is not customizable, and the provider takes a large cut of the sale price for providing the services. Once again, different providers vary in their terms and conditions. Investigate before committing yourself to any one service.

# Getting Started with Web Applications

If you have read this far, you should understand how learning to develop web applications can really add to your skill set. Most likely, you can think of some ways to use applications to streamline your workflow; give added value to your web sites; and enable the building of community features, personalized content, and a dynamic, interactive environment for your visitors.

The next chapter discusses some of the tools that you need for web application development and deployment. For now, however, it's important that you learn the techniques common to all platforms and environments.

## Defining the Problem

Application development is about solving problems. Your client or boss is unlikely to say, "We need a web application." She is far more likely to come to you asking how nontechnical users can easily update content without needing to know HTML, how to manage an online store with thousands of products, or how to enable user feedback and discussion or online voting. If your application is successful, your client's problem will be solved. They will think you are a marvel and will recommend you to everyone they meet.

We began this chapter in a fictional meeting, with a request from a client. The client wanted the users to be able to register on the site and then log in to a members-only area where would be able to search a database.

Take this as a starting point. Before you get anywhere near the code, you need to find out what is really required. What you are told you need may differ significantly from what you actually need to solve this problem. The trick is to find out what is actually needed and how all aspects of immediate need will be covered and future need accounted for by your solution.

### Registering on the Site

Does the client want the users to register and then be able to log in immediately, or does the client want to manually validate users before they gain access? What information does the client want to receive from users before giving them an account?

### Members-Only Area

Will members have individual logins? Do they need the ability to change their usernames and passwords? Will this area, or the database, contain another other content?

## Searchable Database

Is there an existing database that the client wants to use as the online version, or are you expected to build the database? If there is an existing database, what format is it in? After it is online, how do they want to add new information to it?

You need to get the answers to these questions before you start work. Otherwise you are going to find it very difficult to plan the project thoroughly, and you run the risk of the client suddenly changing their mind on a key part of the implementation halfway through development. An agreed-upon plan for development is crucially important when building web applications because the implications of changes midway through a project are greater than with traditional static sites.

## Breaking Down the Problem

So, you've defined the problem. After talking to the client and finding out exactly what is needed for this project, you can come back to them with a proposal that looks something like the one discussed in the following section.

### The Proposal

- **Registration**

  *Members sign up.* Required fields on the signup form will be First Name, Last Name, and Email Address. Other fields will be Age, Sex, and Favorite Type of Widget.

  After signup, members will be sent their password in an email to the address they used to sign up. They will then be able to log in with that email address and password. There will be a lost-password function to mail forgotten passwords to the registered email address.

- **Members-Only Area**

  After log in, users will be taken to a page that greets them by name. Users will be able to view their details and change their passwords automatically.

- **Database**

  The database is in Access 2000 format. Once online, the client would like to be able to add new information to it without having to download the database and re-upload it. They would like users to be able to view all entries, sorted by date, and also to perform a simple keyword search on it.

## Looking at the Big Picture

A necessary skill for the application developer is to be able to step back and look at the problem from all aspects, including the following:

- Users moving around the site, entering the wrong things into input boxes, and forgetting their password

- The site administrator trying to update the site among a packed schedule of other important jobs

- The underlying technology that enables the data to end up in the right place at the right time and the application that enables smooth running of the site

A good way to ensure that you are looking at the whole picture, before you even write one line of code, is to sketch out how people will use the site.

After you have your proposal and the client is happy that this covers everything they need, sit down with pen and paper and map out the flow through the site. Make sure to account for every step the user or site administrator may take. You need to think not just about what happens if everything goes smoothly and the user enters all the correct information at the correct time, but also (and perhaps more importantly) what happens when the user enters entirely the wrong information.

By planning for users who are unable to complete required form fields—those who enter weird characters into form fields, those who forget passwords, those who click the submit button 20 times, and all the other things that users are very good at—you will be well on your way to building an application that survives when things go wrong. Because they will go wrong, the trick is to get out of the resultant error as gracefully as possible!

## Defining the Solution

So now you know what you need and when it needs to happen. To find your solution, you just need to understand what your application needs to do to enable the user flow through the site that you have just mapped out.

### Breaking Down the Tasks

When faced with a big application, it is easy to become overawed by the scale and complexity of it all and become unfocused. You can break down most applications into their component parts. After you have broken them down, it is easy to assign time for each task, which makes the project as a whole seem far less scary and enables you to focus on smaller deliverables rather than one enormous task.

Returning to our proposed application, we could break down the tasks as follows:

- Select the database, web server, and application server
- Build the login and security functionality
- Build the members-only section
- Creating the administration section

You can break down these tasks even further. To build the login and security functionality, for instance, you first need to build your database tables. Then you must include a way for users to add their details, which creates a log in for the tables. Then you need to write the code that checks that your users are allowed access to the page they are on.

### Working Through the Tasks Logically

Obviously, some of the preceding tasks impact others. Before you can do anything, you need to decide on your server model and database. (The next chapter discusses why you might go for one option over another.)

Looking at the other tasks, you need to be able to identify your users for both the members-only section and for the administration pages. Therefore, the login and security are good places to start because you need to include the check of whether a user is registered on each page.

You can save a great deal of time by developing the system in a logical and systematic way. By doing so, you also may be able to identify problems as they occur. For instance, you can build and test all the user login pages. If they work well, add the page to which the user is taken upon successful login. If that page causes an error, you can be fairly sure that you have introduced something into the code of that page that is causing the error.

## User Interface Design

No matter how much of a code poet you become, your users are going to be impressed by how easy the site is to use, and not by your coding skills. To users, the interface—how they interact with your application—is all that matters.

Users expect things to work in a certain way; so look around the web, see what everybody else is doing successfully, and implement that same functionality. Visual clues are very important to make users feel that they understand where they are and what they are doing. You might think that the weird and wonderful buttons you designed for an online store application are very cool; if that means that nobody ever purchases anything from the site, however, you have failed.

My four-year-old daughter can't read yet, but I've watched her navigate a web site with ease. What she is doing is remembering familiar user interface concepts. When she comes to a new page and needs to know what to do, she looks for something familiar and clicks it. That familiarity is what is needed for an intuitive user interface, one in which the user feels totally comfortable and knows what to do next without having to think too hard about it. After all, if it is too much like hard work to use your site, there are plenty of others out there.

Response speed of your application is also very important. This obviously has implications on every level of your application. Purely on a user interface level, however, make sure that your users are not left waiting for large images to load when they are trying to perform an interaction that takes them over several pages.

Ease of use is vitally important for web application development because you are asking your user to do things. When a site does not require any more user input than looking at the screen and managing to get from page to page, people are more likely to appreciate your artistic talents. In 99.9 percent of cases, when you are tasked with building an application, usability, speed of response, and creating a good comfort level for the user will be the things that ensure a successful completion of the job.

## Putting It All Together

Working from your plan, and bearing in mind the user's point of view at all times, you should now be in a good place to begin to build your application. If you have thoroughly prepared by this point, you will have done more than many developers out there. Your client will know what to expect, and you will always have your plan to return to if you are feeling a bit lost.

You will probably find, even with good planning and particularly in your first few applications, that something doesn't quite work out as planned. If that happens, and you know that you need to change some aspect of your plan, go back to the plan and think about how this change will impact other aspects. By keeping the application as a whole in mind while you work on each part of it, you will avoid either duplicating code needlessly or accidentally breaking some part of the application by changing things elsewhere.

## When It All Goes Wrong

If this is your first foray into the world of application development, remember that there are going to be days when it all seems to be going horribly wrong. Unlike static sites—where, if a page breaks, it affects only that page—an error in a web application can appear to cause problems everywhere. Learning techniques to quickly understand and isolate bugs will stand you in good stead whichever platform you are developing for.

To make sure that you are getting the full error messages as returned by the server, if you are using Internet Explorer, follow these steps:

1. Go to Tools > Internet Options > Advanced.

2. Uncheck Show Friendly HTTP Error Messages.

The "unfriendly" error messages will quickly become your friend. They provide you far more information and often are all you need to figure out what an error actually means.

### Database Errors

When you are working with a database, many of the errors you will see on a day-to-day basis will come from the database. If your SQL syntax is correct (and that, of course is the first thing to check), you probably are not passing something to your SQL that it needs. Within an application, for instance, you might POST a form to a page that contains the user's identification. On that next page, you want to do a SELECT from the database using that user ID, and then display all the information about that user on the page. However, you get an error on the page that should display the information.

A useful technique when you encounter something like this is to write out the SQL statement on the page to make sure that it is complete. In the preceding scenario, when you get the application to write out the SQL, you might see something like this:

```
SELECT * FROM tblUsers WHERE userID =
```

You will see that there is no user ID displayed in the SQL, so the database doesn't know which record to return. Now that you know what the problem is, you can look for the cause. Perhaps the page that did the POST has the hidden field named differently from how you are trying to pick it up on this page, or the ID isn't being written to that field in the first place.

### Syntax Errors

Whichever application server you choose, you need to find a reference to the errors it returns if it is unhappy with your code. Errors returned by the application server can be cryptic at best, although you will soon learn the common ones.

Errors that don't relate to the database are often the result of misspellings, case sensitivity (on UNIX platforms), general incorrect syntax, and so forth. The error should give you a line number on which the error occurs.

Therefore, if you go through the line carefully, you will often find the problem.

### When It "Just Doesn't Work Right"

Harder to solve than error messages is when your application just isn't doing what you expect. Usually the culprit will be a flaw in your application-build logic. In a complex application for which many steps take place after each operation, however, it can become very difficult to isolate exactly where the application stops behaving as you want.

When this happens, it is vital to step back and try and think about what is happening in a logical manner. Although the problem may seem illogical, I have learned that yelling at it and throwing desk accessories rarely does any good at all (and scares small children and neighbors). Go from a point where things are working and take it step by step. After each step, check that what is supposed to happen has happened. Check in the source to see that hidden fields that should be populated are populated and that the data you expect is in the QueryString. If you perform an operation that should insert some data into the database, check to see that it is all there as expected.

By going through carefully and logically, you will often spot the problem. If you still can't see it, a good technique is to grab a willing volunteer and explain what is happening as you go through the steps. Often the very act of explaining what should happen on each page will trigger the realization of why it isn't working.

## Usability Testing

What happens next? Your web application is built, and you're all ready to go live and see real users enter live data into your system. Before you hit that button, however, take a last chance to do some final testing of the system.

If your application is designed for nontechnical users, you need some nontechnical users if you want to really test it. Grab your mom or the old lady next door or the office junior who can just about manage to send an email without crashing his computer. Sit your nontechnical user down in front of your application and ask the user to use it. Take notes.

Watch carefully and see the user seems unsure of what to do next. Does the user seem to find it easy to complete each section? What happens when the user does something "incorrectly?" Does the system prompt the user for the correct information or is the user left not knowing what he did wrong and how to perform the steps so that the system will accept his input?

Even the most well planned and executed applications will probably exhibit some issues when real users confront them. When you are in the midst of building your application, it is very difficult to put yourself in the place of the user and to think as someone who has never seen this site before. If you can manage to run a few tests with real, nontechnical users, you should end up with a better application for it and less chance of your client phoning you up because people are complaining about cryptic error messages.

# Next Steps with Web Applications

Macromedia Dreamweaver MX is an excellent tool for building web applications, particularly for those who have not ventured into this area before. Working visually usually shortens the learning curve of application development. It enables you to understand the concepts and logic before you have really got to grips with the syntax of your chosen scripting language. At some point, however, you are going to come up against something that needs a little more custom development than Dreamweaver MX can handle.

## Getting into the Code

You can pick up a lot of your chosen language just by keeping one eye on the code that Dreamweaver MX is entering as you build your applications. Try to look at the code that is inserted. Where are the SQL statements? How does it execute them? Where are you writing data back to the page? Just by doing this, the syntax will start to become more familiar to you. When you come up against a problem that does involve some hand coding, you will find it easier to recognize what you need to change and why.

Get a good reference book for the language that you are using, even if you are using Dreamweaver MX to complete most tasks. Use the book to see the logic behind those tasks. You'll find that the code that Dreamweaver MX puts on your page and the code in most books will look different. After all, Dreamweaver MX is written to cover many different platforms and servers; the code needs to be slightly more generic than if you are writing it by hand knowing which database and server you are using. You should be able to see the similarities, however, and this will help you when you need to edit or write a section by hand.

Use the resources on the web. I reference specific resources for the different scripting languages in the next chapter. For any language, database, and server you choose, you can find a wealth of resources available at no cost online. Use them to read up on tricks and techniques, to find out about security alerts that might affect your chosen environment, and to keep abreast of new developments and ideas.

## Building a Robust Application

A robust application is one that will survive whatever is thrown at it, one that will recover or exit from any errors gracefully, and on that is very diffi-cult to be compromised intentionally (by someone attempting to hack into the system) or accidentally (by someone with admin privileges destroying key data, for example).

We have touched on these subjects somewhat during this chapter. One thing to bear in mind, however, is that the more complex your applications become, the more points of failure there will be (making your planning even more important and your thorough testing more crucial).

The biggest risk to your data is not evil people wanting to hack your system. Although they do exist and the risk should not be discounted, the biggest risk is the people with the ability to destroy the data mistakenly. Although you don't want your users to have to jump through hoops to buy some-thing, you do want your administrators to have to confirm their actions when they are administrating the site. If data is to be deleted, for example, make sure they get the chance to check and confirm that action before it happens.

When it comes to security, think about adding the following features:

- Disabling of accounts when an incorrect password has been entered three times in succession.
- Logging of failed authentication requests (in case a pattern is emerging).
- Logging of errors that have occurred.

  You can even go so far as to send an email when an error occurs. When errors occur as users are on a site, it is unusual for someone to contact them and identify the error. Another good reason for logging errors is that they could be occurring because someone is trying to break through your security measures.

All of these methods are about taking things a step further, away from just getting things to work and toward covering all eventualities. You'll sleep better for it and gain a reputation as someone who not only solves existing problems, but also as someone who has planned for when things go wrong.

## Planning for the Future

It is never a good idea to build a web application as if nothing will ever change. Things change very quickly when you are talking about web-based products. By keeping future growth and change in mind, and planning for that possibility, you may add a few hours to the initial project, but you will save countless future hours of rewriting an application that has been written in stone.

### Keeping It Scalable

When talking about scalability in the context of a web application, *scalability* means the ability to serve extra traffic or requirements without totally rebuilding the application.

For instance, you may have chosen to build your site with all the data stored in an Access database. This is the way that many people with small, fairly low-traffic sites start out. If your site is the roaring success you dreamed of, you may find that your choice of database needs some reassessment. A well-planned relational database and application should enable that move relatively simply with only small changes to the code of the application to enable smooth transfer of the database.

## Making It Modular

Designing your application as a modular system has great advantages when you need to add some more functionality. Although a web application needs to work as a whole, each distinct part can and should be relatively self-sufficient. There are exceptions to this, but for the most part you should be able to remove some functionality without rewriting the rest and you should be able to add a new section easily. With good planning, it is possible to map out exactly what part of the application affects each other part so that you will know what you need to edit to enable integration of the new functionality.

## Comments and Documentation

This brings us neatly to comments and documentation. If you are building anything other than a simple application, you will probably need to produce documentation for whoever will be administrating the application. You also should write some documentation for yourself—because if you ever come back to this, you'll find it difficult to remember what you did and why.

Keep a file of any pertinent information about the development, any decisions you made for a specific reason or request, and where the configuration information is stored. Comment your code thoroughly because someone who has never seen the application before may need to understand it. This will be more important if you are working within a company where someone else may have to take the project on after you. Even if you are developing a site for yourself, however, it is amazing how quickly you can forget key elements of the design process after an application goes live and you move on to other things.

## Useful Development Practices

The less code you need to write, the less likely it will be that you introduce bugs into your application. By centralizing your most commonly used functions and scripts, you are not only going to streamline your development so that you spend less time on each application, but you also will reduce the likelihood of introducing problems and make fixing any that do arise far easier.

### Reusable Functionality

As you develop more applications, you will find yourself performing the same actions over and over again. To an extent, Macromedia Dreamweaver MX helps you automate the repetitive tasks of inserting, editing, and deleting data. When you start writing more of your own code, however, you will find that by creating reusable functions or even just code snippets, you will save a lot of time in relocating the code to perform various tasks.

Macromedia Dreamweaver MX has some built-in functionality that assists you to store, reuse, and share your useful code with your development team. The following section discuss these built-in functions.

#### The Snippets Panel

The Snippets panel enables, as its name suggests, the storage of small "snippets" of code that you find useful when developing applications. The Snippets panel was discussed in more detail in Chapter 1, "Expert Web Design."

#### The Server Behavior Builder

You can add to the server behaviors already available in Dreamweaver MX, and those available for download from the Macromedia Exchange, by writing your own server behaviors. As you become more proficient in your chosen scripting language, you will find it relatively easy to use the Server Behavior Builder that is included in Dreamweaver MX to turn your code into behaviors that can be applied quickly and visually and shared with your development team.

## Server-Side Includes

*Server-side includes* (SSIs) do exactly what they say on the tin. They are files that are included on your page when the page is on the server, before the resulting HTML is returned to the browser. This means that you can have a piece of code that you need included on many pages in a single file, and when you need that piece of code, just add a line telling the server to include that code when the page is called. This has obvious advantages when compared to having that code on every page. In a section of your site that is members-only, for instance, you would need to have code, at the top of every page, that would check whether the user is logged in. If you put this code into a separate include file, you can just add the link to the file on each page; the actual code is only in one place. If you decide to change that code, you need to do so only one time and not go through every page of your members-only section to make the changes.

You will sometimes see include files with the file extension .inc. This is a bad idea, particularly when those files contain data such as your database connection string. inc files will not be parsed by the server if they are called by name. Therefore, if you have named your database connection include connection.inc and I type into my browser `http://www.yourwebsite.com/connection.inc`, I will get the exact location of your database and your username and password. Give your include files an externsion like .asp or .cfm so that the server parses the file. Anyone guessing the name and typing it into a browser will not be able to see the actual code because the server will parse it.

## Stored Procedures

I mentioned stored procedures and triggers in the section of this chapter on database design. Stored procedures are not supported by all RDBMSs, but are a useful way to move logic from the page into the database. You can use a stored procedure for most of the interaction with the database that you would otherwise do with SQL on the page.

Stored procedures and triggers are compiled and therefore run faster than code on your page and save making multiple calls on the database to complete a multistep operation. You can just pass variables to the stored procedure and let it do all the necessary interaction with the different tables.

It then returns either a recordset or just a value that lets you know whether the action was completed successfully.

### Server Components

Another way to move logic from the page is to use components, such as COM objects in ASP or JavaBeans when working with JSP. The next chapter discusses this capability in more detail.

# What to Take Away from This Chapter

- There are many differences between the way that a static HTML site works and the way that a web application serves its content to visitors. By understanding these differences, you will feel more comfortable with the logic required for application development.

- Web applications can be used in many different circumstances, large and small, wherever true interaction between the user and the web site is needed.

- An understanding of databases and how they work with your application is necessary.

- Planning of the application is very important. A well-thought-out process will enable easier, faster development.

- Keeping the user in mind through development will ensure that the users of your application understand how to interact with it.

# Chapter 15

# Tooling Up for Application Building

Objectives:

- To understand the choices that you need to make to develop web applications.
- To understand your choice of operating system, web server, application server, and scripting language, and how these selections impact on each other.
- To be able to set up a local development environment for the server model of your choice and understand any implications of running a local web server.
- To understand what is necessary to deploy your applications.

The preceding chapter discussed why you might want to develop a web application and how you go about planning and developing your applications. This chapter looks more closely at the tools you need both locally for development and remotely for hosting your applications, and the choices that you need to make as to the platforms and server models for which you are to develop.

Moving into application development for the first time can seem a little scary because of the new terminology to understand and a whole host of choices that need to be made to do the smallest thing. I hope to introduce you to the tools of the trade so that you are well informed as to your choices and can ask the right questions when you need further help.

To develop and host your web application, you first must make a series of choices as to which operating system, web server, application server, and scripting language you are going to use for your live server and how you will develop and test your application locally.

This discussion concentrates on the server models supported by Macromedia Dreamweaver MX, as follows:

- ASP with JavaScript or VBScript
- ASP.NET with C# or VB.NET
- ColdFusion
- JSP
- PHP

You may already know something of these languages, which perhaps will make your choice easier. You'll find that most application developers specialize in just one or two languages, so don't feel that you are going to need to learn how to develop in all of them! In the following pages, you will read about the pros and cons of each of the languages, the platforms and servers that support them, and why you might choose one over another.

Trying to get nonbiased advice about one platform over another and one language over another is difficult. Whatever your choice, someone will be only too happy to tell you it was the wrong one! Particularly if you are in the position of just starting out with application development, you need to make a choice based on which language is best for you and the types of applications you are likely to end up building. A platform and language that is excellent for building small Content Management Systems may not be appropriate when needing to produce a highly secure system for taking payments, and vice versa. However, many of the concepts of application development are the same across all languages and environments; so, after you have a good understanding of one language, you will find the learning curve considerably shorter if you move to another.

Some questions you might want to ask yourself while researching your choices include the following:

- How large are the applications I am likely to want to build?
- Which languages do I already know? For instance, have I already done quite a lot of Perl? Did I learn any Java in college?
- Am I tied to any platform, or can I choose hosting on a project basis?

Bear in mind your actual needs when you are doing your research. By doing so, you will be able to see whether a criticism or advocacy for a particular platform or language even applies to your situation and enable yourself to make sensible, informed decisions as to the best way forward for you.

# The Operating System

When you upload your site to a remote web server, you are uploading it to another computer. Just as the operating system that you run on your computers at home or in the office enables you to run certain software and not other software, so the operating system of that remote computer implicates on what server software can be run on it. The main players in the server operating system market are without doubt UNIX and Microsoft Windows.

## Linux

*Linux*, http://www.linux.org, was originally developed by Linus Torvalds, a student in Finland, as an open-source version of the UNIX operating system. Version 1.0 of the Linux kernel was released in 1994 and, with the help of developers around the world, the operating system has developed and gained much popularity particularly in the server market. Linux is developed under the GNU General Public License, and anyone may download and use the source code for free. However, particularly in the case of server installations, various companies packages and sell "distributions" of Linux along with the support one would expect when purchasing software from a company.

Linux is a very stable OS; it is rare for a problem with one application to cause the entire system to need a reboot (which is obviously an advantage when running a server on the system). When well configured, it is highly secure, and patches for security flaws tend to be very quick in development because of the huge community of developers working on Linux around the world. Additionally, because Linux is open-source and can be installed as many times on as many machines as you want at no more cost, it enables relatively cheap, good-quality hosting. Also you can have your own Linux development server at home or in the office for the price of a cheap computer system because there are no license fees. Hardware requirements for a basic Linux system tend to be far lower than for a Windows 2000 system, for example. If you have an older machine to spare after upgrading your main, development computer, you could consider installing Linux on it as a test platform. (I have a P133 happily running Linux with Apache, PHP, and MySQL installed.)

The downside for some users may be the lack of support for certain servers or scripting languages (as discussed later). Additionally, setting up and configuring Linux is not going to be as simple as putting a CD in and going through the wizards. This shouldn't be an issue for a hosting company, but may be for your own development environment.

## Microsoft Windows

Computers that are being used to run web servers and have Windows installed are likely to be running either Windows NT4, Windows 2000 Server Family, or the new .NET Server Family.

The advantage of building your web application to run on a Windows plat-form is that, on a balance of probabilities, you are likely to be running Windows on your own machine. Therefore, if you don't have access to a development server of your choice, you can develop your applications on the machine on which you are running Dreamweaver MX, knowing that they will be hosted in a similar environment. As you will see later, however, there are ways to develop on a Windows machine and then move to a Linux or UNIX platform if that is the choice you make. Therefore, you don't need to feel tied to what you have available on the desktop.

## Other Platforms

Despite the Linux and Windows platforms being the most widely used, other operating systems are being used to run web servers. There are various UNIX variants as well as Linux in existence—OpenBSD, FreeBSD, and Solaris to name just three. Some companies host on Mac servers, some-thing that may increase with the release of Mac OS X, which is UNIX-based and able to run Apache and other UNIX web servers.

# The Web Server

Next in the list is your web server. Having decided on the operating system you would like (or are forced) to host on, you need to consider which web server software for which you are going to be building your application.

A *web server* is a computer with web server software installed that allows it to serve pages via *Hypertext Transfer Protocol* (HTTP) over the Internet. Just about any computer can be made into a web server, although live web servers that are available on the Internet tend to be fairly high-specification machines. You can install web server software on your own personal computer to develop and test your applications.

When a web server receives a request for a file, either directly from the browser or via an application server, it retrieves the file from its file system and sends it back to where the request originated. This exchange happens using HTTP. Additionally, most web servers conform to the *Common Gateway Interface* (CGI) standard, which enables them to run external programs.

## Choosing a Web server

If you have already chosen a preferred operating system, you may find your choices more limited at this point. Table 15.1 shows the relationship between your choice of operating system and web servers available.

| Table 15.1   Applications Supported by Operating System and Web Server Combinations | | | |
| --- | --- | --- | --- |
| Server | OS | Price | Application Server Support |
| Apache | Windows, Linux, UNIX (including Mac OS X) | Free. | PHP (as module or CGI). |
| | | | JSP (with Tomcat or other Java server), ASP with third-party application server such as Chili!Soft, ColdFusion. |

*continues*

| Table 15.1 | Continued | | |
|---|---|---|---|
| Server | OS | Price | Application Server Support |
| IIS | Windows | Included in Windows licensing fee. Server licenses are more expensive than workstation. For shared hosting, this may have an implication on monthly/yearly costs. | ASP, ASP.NET, PHP, JSP (with a Java server), ColdFusion.<br><br>It is advised only to run PHP as a CGI with IIS as the ISAPI version is unstable. |
| iPlanet | Windows, Linux, UNIX | $1495 per CPU | JSP, PHP, ASP with third-party application server such as Chili!Soft, ColdFusion. |
| Zeus | Linux, UNIX (including Mac OS X) | $1700 per server machine up to 2 CPUs | JSP (with Tomcat or other Java server), PHP, ASP with third-party application server such as Chili!Soft, ColdFusion. |

As well as the obvious consideration of support by the operating system when choosing a server platform, you need to consider the following:

- Whether you have decided on a scripting language or database that is dependent on one platform or another.

- How you are hosting the eventual application. If you need to host on in-house servers, your decision may be made for you. If you are using shared hosting at a hosting company, you can choose your server and then find your hosting.

- An open-source solution may be cheaper in initial outlay because of no license fees to pay, but there may be other costs involved in support if you are planning to look after your own live web server and are from a Windows rather than UNIX background.

- If security is a big issue for you due to highly sensitive data being stored, you need to do some research to make sure that your chosen solution offers the security that you require.

At present the main contenders for the server market are Microsoft IIS5 and Apache. Apache is by far the most used web server software hosting sites at time of writing this book, with 58.43 percent of web sites surveyed by Netcraft running Apache, 29.13 percent running a Microsoft server, 2.92 percent running iPlanet, and 2.18 percent running Zeus. Refer to the Netcraft Web Server Survey for more information (`http://www.netcraft.com/Survey/`.

## Apache

*Apache* (`http://www.apache.org`) is an open-source HTTP server and is free to use. Like many other open-source projects, it is maintained and developed by a team of volunteers from around the world with input invited from anyone who uses the software. The software can be downloaded from the Apache web site. You also can find documentation on the site to help you install and configure the server.

Apache can be run on most operating systems, including most UNIX variants (Solaris, Linux, FreeBSD), Windows 95/98/NT/2000/XP, Mac OS X, and NetWare 5 and above. As well as serving web pages, Apache also can execute CGI scripts.

As an open-source product, there is no official support for Apache. As with many large, open-source projects, however, many companies offer support for servers running Apache. Therefore, it is not necessary to have vendor support for the product.

## Internet Information Server

*Internet Information Server* (IIS) (`http://www.microsoft.com/iis/`) is a Microsoft product that runs only on Microsoft Windows operating systems. Windows NT4 comes with IIS4, Windows 2000 Professional/Server Family has IIS5 on the CD, and Windows XP (Professional and Server versions) ships with IIS5.1. To run a version of IIS on Windows 98, you can download *Personal Web Server* (PWS). PWS is a cut-down version of IIS. It is not recommended to use PWS as anything other than a development environment, so you are unlikely to see it deployed on live servers.

If you want to run a live web server or even a busy intranet server on Windows, you need a server license rather than a workstation license. The workstation license allows for only 10 concurrent connections, which is fine for testing applications but is obviously unsuitable for any live web site.

IIS offers CGI functionality and also the Internet Server API (ISAPI) to extend the server capabilities. ISAPI is discussed in more detail later in this chapter.

### iPlanet Web Server

*iPlanet Web Server* (`http://www.iplanet.com`) is the third most used server according to Netcraft. It supports various varieties of UNIX and Windows operating systems and is a commercial product (being a division of Sun). With iPlanet coming from Sun, it is often the server of choice for those wanting to run the Solaris (UNIX) operating system and develop applications with Java, because support for Java is tightly integrated with the server. iPlanet is the successor to the Netscape Enterprise web server.

### Zeus Web Server

*Zeus Web Server* (`http://www.zeus.com`) is a commercial product. One of its main selling points is its security features, which include a scalable SSL implementation and ease of security management via an administration server. It is available for most UNIX platforms and Mac OS X and is the main web server used by some very large companies, including eBay, because it really stands out when serving vast amounts of traffic (at which point, it becomes a far better option than Apache). You are less likely to find Zeus on shared hosting, which explains its smaller market share. However it has an increasing share in the higher end of the server market.

### *Web Server Terminology Reference*

Here are fuller descriptions of some of the terms used when discussing web servers:

- **Common Gateway Interface (CGI).** CGI works as a module of the web server. CGI works by allowing a program (such as a Perl or C script) to be run on the server that accepts input (such as data submitted via a form) and returns output to the browser. The CGI program is called with a new process for each request that is made and is therefore inefficient and slow insofar as server performance goes.

- **The Internet Server Application Programming Interface (ISAPI).** ISAPI is an API that enables developers to extend the functionality of the web server by creating an application that can be called from a web page.

- **Open source.** Open-source software is software that has the full source code of the program available, with no constraints on its use. This means that, unlike conventional software, developers are free to improve, adapt, and fix bugs in the software as they see fit. You can find a full definition of open source on The Open Source Initiative web site at `http://www.opensource.org/docs/definition.html`.

- **Operating system.** An operating system is a program that is loaded into the computer at boot and manages all other applications that run on the computer. The most common operating systems in use at the time of writing this book are versions of Microsoft Windows, MacOS, and flavors of Linux.

- **Virtual server.** On one web server, you can host many independent web sites. These are known as *virtual servers*. Virtual servers allow the mapping of different IP addresses to different directories, which each act as a separate web server.

# The Application Server

The next choice you will need to make will be which application server you want to use. The application servers this chapter focuses on are those that support the server models that you can use in Dreamweaver MX; these being ASP, ASP.NET, ColdFusion, JSP, and PHP.

As discussed in the preceding chapter, the application server is the software that parses your scripts and returns HTML to the browser, acting as an interface between client input and the actual web server. Instead of the web server taking requests directly from the browser, the request is first passed to the application server, which then requests the data from the web server and processes its before returning the output to the browser as HTML, XML, or binary data.

Some application servers are more tightly integrated into the web server than others; an example of a very integrated server and application server is IIS and ASP or ASP.NET.

## Choosing an Application Server

Your choice of application server will depend on your choices of operating system and web server and also the technology that you want to use to build your application. For some technologies, such as ColdFusion, you have only one choice of application server. Other technologies are supported by several different servers; these application servers are discussed in conjunction with the technologies they support.

## Active Server Pages

*Active Server Pages* (ASP) is based on the ISAPI architecture. In fact, ASP is implemented as a system ISAPI *dynamic link library* (DLL) called asp.dll. Asp.dll is frequently referred to as the *ASP runtime*. When the server receives a request for an ASP page, the ASP runtime processes the page. ASP is a Microsoft technology and, as already mentioned, is tightly integrated with IIS. Therefore, it a good choice if you want to work on a Windows server running IIS.

ASP is not a language; it is a technology. ASP pages can contain both HTML and script from any scripting language that supports ActiveX scripting. These include VBScript, JScript, PerlScript, and Python. Dreamweaver MX however, supports only the most common languages of VBScript and JScript.

Although ASP is a Microsoft technology, and most ASP developers go on to host their applications on IIS, there are other choices as well as IIS running on the Windows operating system.

### IIS with the ASP Runtime

If you intend to build applications with ASP, more likely than not you will be hosting on Windows servers with IIS and the ASP runtime. An obvious advantage of this environment is that it is what ASP was developed to run on and what most tutorials and help files will presume that you are developing on the Windows/IIS platform. IIS4 (shipped with NT4) supports ASP2, whereas IIS5, which is shipped with Windows 2000, supports ASP3.

### Chili!Soft ASP

*Sun Chili!Soft ASP* (`http://www.chilisoft.com`) is a product of Sun Microsystems and allows the running of ASP on web servers other than IIS. Support at present is for Apache, iPlanet, and Zeus with support for the Solaris, Windows, Linux, HP-UX, AIX, and Sun cobalt operating systems. The latest version (3.6.2 at the time of writing) offers ASP2 support, *Open Database Connectivity* (ODBC) drivers, an excellent management console, and the "spice pack" (which contains components similar to those COM objects you would use if your application were running on IIS). Sun Chili!Soft ASP is an impressive product and worth considering if you prefer developing in ASP but would rather not be tied to the Windows operating system.

Sun Chili!Soft ASP is a commercial product and therefore is going to involve a financial outlay. If you consider the cost of Windows licensing, however, that may not be too much of an issue. Parts of ASP are not supported in the current version, although the code that you will be developing with Dreamweaver MX is supported and the Sun Chili!Soft ASP web site even mentions support for Macromedia products as a selling point.

### Instant ASP

*Instant ASP* (iASP), `http://www.halcyonsoft.com`, is Java-based and promises to provide ASP support on any Java-enabled server. Instant ASP 2 supports the ASP3 specification and the scripting languages VBScript and JavaScript. It also boasts an impressive collection of components available with the default installation. These enable easy porting of applications from the IIS environment—one reason many people feel tied to that environment is because they use COM objects that would not be available on a different platform.

As with Chili!Soft, iASP is a commercial product and comes at a price. Based on the specifications listed on the site, if your chosen hosting company offers ASP support via iASP, you should have no problems developing for it.

## ASP.NET

*ASP.NET* (`http://www.asp.net`) is one of the technologies that makes up the Microsoft .NET framework. Whereas classic ASP allows only the use of scripting languages, ASP.NET means that you can develop with full programming languages, including VB.NET and C# (the two languages available in Dreamweaver MX for the ASP.NET server model).

ASP.NET, like ASP, relies on a module of the web server but also utilizes the .NET framework to leverage more powerful functionality. The .NET framework is available to download from Microsoft for those running IIS5 but is integrated into .NET server and IIS6.

ASP.NET applications are compiled. However, you do not need to manually compile your code because the .NET framework automatically detects the changes and dynamically compiles the files so that they are served faster for subsequent requests. ASP.NET is a very new technology, and fewer resources are available for developers (as compared to for classic ASP). If you like to keep ahead of the crowd, however, you might enjoy working with ASP.NET; Dreamweaver MX enables you to do so visually.

ASP.NET is obviously a Microsoft technology. However, Halcyon Software (developers of iASP) are developing a new product called iNET (`http://www.halcyonsoft.com/products/iNET.asp`), which claims to be a complete Java-based implementation of the Microsoft .NET framework. This is obviously a very new implementation, but such developments are worth watching out for if you are interested in working with .NET but would rather stay away from Microsoft web servers.

## ColdFusion

*ColdFusion* is a tag-based server scripting language (*ColdFusion Markup Language*, CFML). To run your ColdFusion applications, you need to be running ColdFusion Server, which is a Macromedia product. With ColdFusion being developed by Macromedia, there is, as you would expect, excellent support for the language through the product line. The Macromedia web site, `http://www.macromedia.com/software/coldfusion/resources/flash_coldfusion/`, offers a host of resources for working with Macromedia Flash MX and ColdFusion.

Being a tag-based language, ColdFusion is a natural choice for many designers and developers who have a good knowledge of HTML. The language can be extended with custom tags as well as user-defined functions, which can be created using CFScript. ColdFusion applications can integrate with the major component standards, such as COM, CORBA, and Enterprise JavaBeans (EJB).

ColdFusion is available for Windows, Solaris, HP-UX, and Linux operating systems; and for any web server that supports ISAPI, NSAPI, Apache API, or CGI, which includes all the web servers discussed earlier in this chapter. Most ColdFusion applications can be moved from one platform to another without any problems. However, it is wise to consult the latest documentation if you are likely to need to move your application between platforms.

ColdFusion is a commercial application and therefore are going to involve a financial outlay for your own servers should you be hosting yourself. However, ColdFusion shared hosting can usually be obtained at a similar cost to ASP shared hosting.

## JavaServer Pages

*JavaServer Pages* (JSP), `http://java.sun.com/products/jsp/`, are part of the Java family as developed by Sun and are an extension of the Java servlet technology. *Java servlets* are platform-independent modules that can extend the capabilities of the web server. JSP uses tags and scriptlets written in Java and is comparable to ASP when used in this way.

A huge advantage with using Java technology is its cross-platform nature and its support, as you will see, by many application servers. Pages created with JSP should be able to run on any server on any platform. If you want to create platform-independent applications, JSP is a good technology to use.

You can run your JavaServer Pages on many application servers. I have provided details of the most common options. Many of these are commercial options. However, you could develop your applications locally using an open-source solution, such as Tomcat. If you do so, your application should run on any host that is running any other Java application server. During development, however, bear in mind the platform that it will eventually end up on so that you don't introduce something that is platform-specific.

### JRun

*JRun Server*, `http://www.macromedia.com/software/jrun/`, is billed by Macromedia as follows:

> "...the easy-to-use J2EE compatible application server for deploying and managing server-side Java applications."

JRun Server is available for Windows, Solaris, HP-UX, Compaq Tru64, SGI IRIX, and Linux; and can work with any web server that supports ISAPI, NSAPI, Apache API, or CGI, which includes all the web servers discussed so far in this chapter.

Although, as a commercial application server, JRun obviously entails paying for licenses; however, it is considerably less expensive than the other commercial JSP application servers on the market.

### Tomcat

*Tomcat*, `http://jakarta.apache.org/tomcat/`, is an open-source implementation of Java servlet and JSP technologies, and is developed under the Jakarta Project at the Apache Software Foundation. You can download Tomcat from the Apache web site.

Tomcat is not just for Apache, although that is a common combination. You can use Tomcat with any web server that supports JSP and servlets, such as iPlanet web server, IBM WebSphere, and others.

### IBM WebSphere

*WebSphere*, `http://www.ibm.com/websphere`, is a Java application server from IBM. It provides support for Java servlets, JSP, and Enterprise JavaBeans.

IBM WebSphere application server runs on AIX, HP-UX, Linux, NetWare, Solaris, Windows 2000, and Windows NT4.

### BEA WebLogic

*BEA WebLogic Server*, `http://www.bea.com/products/weblogic/` `server/index.shtml`, is a commercial Java application server with support for JSP, servlets, Enterprise JavaBeans, and the full J2EE specification.

The server is available for Windows 2000/NT4, HP-UX, Solaris, and Linux; and you can download a trial version if you want to try out the server locally.

### PHP

PHP, `http://www.php.net`, which stands for PHP: Hypertext Preprocessor, is an open-source scripting language especially suited for web development and can be embedded into HTML. Its syntax is similar to C, Java, JavaScript, and Perl.

One of the great advantages of PHP is that it runs on most platforms and web servers. The most common combination for a production server is Apache with PHP. However, it is supported by Linux, HP-UX, Solaris, Mac OS X, OpenBSD, and Windows (for the operating system); and by many web servers, including Apache, IIS, and Zeus. It can run as a CGI or, for servers that support this, as a module compiled into the server.

Other advantages of developing with PHP are that it is free to download and install for testing purposes and has excellent cross-platform support. There is built-in support in PHP for much functionality that you would have to purchase a third-party component for when using ASP.

Disadvantages for some developers will be the lack of commercial support with an open-source product, when compared to developing with a commercial technology. A friendly and helpful community has built up around PHP development, and you will find people happy to help you get started with PHP.

### *Application Server Terminology Reference*

**You are likely to encounter some of the following terms that relate to application servers:**

• **Component Object Model (COM) objects**

*COM objects* are components that can be called from an ASP page to perform some functionality. They are a Microsoft technology, written to the Microsoft Component Specification. One common use of COM objects is for sending mail—using CDONTS or using third-party COM objects to upload files or resize images on-the-fly. Many COM objects are available for use. Good hosting companies offer a selection of the most useful ones or will install those that you create or purchase.

• **JavaBeans**

*JavaBeans* are components written in Java and part of the Java 2 specification. JavaBeans make applications easier to maintain by separating out the programming logic from the pages. One way in which you might use a JavaBean is to connect information to your database from a JSP page.

Like the rest of the Java specification, JavaBeans can be moved between different servers and platforms.

# The Database

The database in which you choose to store your application data is the final piece of the puzzle. As with web and application servers, the choice of operating system will influence which database you may use. Because a database does not have to on the same physical server as your site, however, it is perfectly possible to be using a Microsoft database hosted on a Windows 2000 server, while the rest of your application is hosted on the Linux platform.

## Choosing the Right Database

This discussion focuses on two kinds of databases: file-based and database servers.

## File-Based (Desktop) Databases

A *file-based database* is a database such as Microsoft Access 2000. When you create an Access database, a file is created with an .mdb extension. If you want to use this database on a web site, you upload the file, usually to a directory that is not accessible from the Web.

An advantage of using a file-based database is that many people have one already available to them with Microsoft Access. In addition, they are often a simpler way to start designing databases because the environment is familiar if you have used Office applications in the past. However, the file-based model does have some major disadvantages that you would do well to consider, including the following:

- **Security**

  Security is of greater concern when working with a file-based database. After all, it is very easy for someone who manages to gain access to the server to just download the entire file, at which point they have all of your data. If you have a file-based database on a server used to store any kind of personal information, ensure that you have secured it in as many ways as possible. You should be able to password-protect the database and, as mentioned earlier, store it somewhere on the server where it cannot be downloaded from a web browser.

- **Inability to work on the live database when the file-based database is on the server**

  After you have uploaded your file-based database, what happens if you then need to add another table to it? You have to download the database, make your changes, and then re-upload it. And consider what happens if the database is added to while you are making those changes: When you re-upload, you will lose that information. Additionally, the pages that are using the database will be offline while the transfer is occurring—not a good situation if you are on a slow dialup connection!

  This may not be too much of a problem for you, depending on the type of application that you are building, but it is worthwhile bearing in mind.

- **Performance**

  File-based databases are not designed for large, high-traffic applications. Most of the databases were designed to be desktop databases. Although it is useful to be able to use them on the web, you may start to have problems with speed and even with data corruption if an application is getting a large amount of traffic.

Having looked at the problems with file-based databases, you might be wondering why anyone uses them at all. For some applications, they make perfect sense. A file-based database might work well for a small intranet for your workplace on which there will never be a lot of users at any one time, for instance. Consider that in this scenario, the existing information that you want to utilize is in Access. It makes good sense to remain with Access, particularly because it makes your application inexpensive to build (because you already have the Access license).

Small content management solutions, such as an updateable news page for a web site, can manage fine on a file-based database. In fact, any application not likely to have a large number of people trying to add simultaneously to the information will more than likely be fine. There are also ways to convert databases to more robust models should that be needed. Access has a wizard to convert a database to SQL Server. (I have converted Access databases to MySQL in the past without any problems.) Therefore, although your choice of database is an important one, if you are just starting small with an application that may grow with time, do not think that you must invest in an enterprise-level database server immediately.

The basic concepts of creating a relational database do not change when you move between databases. If you are just beginning your exploration of database-driven application development, the ease of use of a file-based database such as Access can mean that you can get to grips with database design without having to deal with a complex interface.

Some file-based or desktop databases that you may consider using for your applications include the following:

- Microsoft Access
- FoxPro
- FileMaker Pro

### Microsoft Access

Access is a popular *relational database management system* (RDBMS) that is developed by Microsoft and ships with Microsoft Office Professional or Developer or can be bought as a separate product.

The benefits of choosing Access as your database include the fact that it is relatively easy to use, and if you are used to other Microsoft products, the interface is familiar. For many people, the software is already installed on their system because the Office software is commonplace. Even if you need to buy a copy, however, it is cheap compared to many other RDBMSs. Hosting for Microsoft Access databases is easy to come by and not too expensive, although you will need a Windows NT4 or 2000 server to host your application if you decide to use Access as your database. A carefully designed Access database also can be easily upsized to SQL Server should the need change at a later date.

You would be best to decide against Access if you could have more than 15 people using the database at any one time, if there are likely to be many people adding to the database simultaneously, or if you need a very secure database. If you need portability across platforms, Access is not for you. If you are developing in a Mac environment without access to a Windows development server, you likewise would probably not consider Access as your database.

### FoxPro

FoxPro, `http://msdn.microsoft.com/vfoxpro/`, is a Microsoft product that is available only for the Microsoft Windows operating system. The FoxPro database is part of Visual FoxPro, which you also can use to create COM objects that can be called from ASP pages.

Microsoft positions FoxPro as a developer-level database in comparison to Access. If you already have skills in Visual FoxPro, this might be a sensible choice for you; you would have a head start on many people in your ability to create components. FoxPro is not a popular web database. If you have existing skills with FoxPro, it may be worth looking at for you. However, you will probably find more help, tutorials, and advice available if you develop with Access (if you want to use a file-based database).

### FileMaker Pro

FileMaker Pro, `http://www.filemaker.com/`, supports Windows, Mac Classic, and Mac OS X environments and is used as a desktop database by many Mac users. It is possible to access a FileMaker database via ODBC, but this solution does not work well in practice. Therefore, it is not recommended to use a FileMaker database as a web database with Dreamweaver MX. However, you will find your FileMaker database-creating skills transfer easily to others.

## Database Servers

A variety of database servers is on the market. A database server will offer a higher level of security than a file-based database. Typically you will be able to set up tables of users and groups who have access rights to the database.

Database servers also tend to offer a higher level of functionality than the file-based databases. Remember, however, that there is a huge difference between database servers both in functionality and cost. (The differences between the databases are discussed later in this chapter.)

### IBM DB2

*DB2* is IBM's offering to the enterprise database market. Although it is not used as frequently as some of the other databases we are looking at in shared hosting situations, DB2 is the database of choice in some organizations. If that happens to be the company you work for, you may find that you need to work with it for your web applications.

DB2 runs on must operating system platforms, including Linux, Windows, and Solaris, but not Macintosh platforms at the present time. If you are working with other IBM products, such as WebSphere, you may choose to use DB2 because of the tight integration between the products.

You would be unlikely to be using DB2 in a shared hosting environment because it is not the database of choice for web hosting companies, which are more likely to offer MySQL or SQL Server.

## MySQL

*MySQL*, `http://www.mysql.com`, is the only database supported by Dreamweaver MX for the PHP server model. Because web hosting on Apache with PHP and MySQL is a very common combination, however, it is probably your most likely choice if PHP is your application server of choice.

MySQL is an open-source database; for most users, there is no license fee. You may just go to the site, download the version for your operating system, and install it. There is wide support for many operating systems. At present you can get a version of MySQL for Linux, Windows, Mac OS X, Solaris, FreeBSD, HP-UX, AIX, SCO, SGI Irix, Dec OSF, and BSDi.

MySQL doesn't come with a nice visual environment in the manner of Access. However, you can download a few excellent front ends for MySQL (as discussed later in this chapter).

You also can export an Access database to MySQL, which is helpful if you have developed a site with an Access database and then want to host it on a server running the Linux operating system, for example.

MySQL is a good choice if you need to store a large amount of data, are likely to go over the user limits for Access, are working with PHP, or are developing on Mac OS X. MySQL is a very robust, fast database. It is particularly suited to content management systems and systems on which a lot of data needs to be stored and selected.

You may find MySQL lacking if you need a very complex RDBM. MySQL has no support for subselects, foreign keys, or cascading deletes. Additionally, no stored procedures or triggers are available in MySQL. Because many people never use this functionality, however, that may not be an issue for you. A recommended book that will help you get up to speed with MySQL is Paul Dubois's *MySQL* (New Riders Publishing).

### Microsoft SQL Server

*SQL Server* is a Microsoft RDBMS that is tightly integrated into the Microsoft Windows operating system. It can be installed only on the Windows operating system (a disadvantage for those who want to work in a UNIX or Linux environment).

It is relatively easy to get inexpensive shared hosting with a SQL Server database, and this makes SQL Server a common choice for ASP developers who need something more robust than Access but are hosting with a hosting company on shared servers. It is also possible to upsize an Access database to SQL Server relatively easily. Therefore, moving from Access to SQL Server is an obvious upgrade path for the developer whose web site has become more popular than first imagined and is finding that Access is not coping well.

SQL Server supports stored procedures, triggers, and user-defined functions written in Transact SQL. If you are moving on to SQL Server after working with Access, you would be well advised to start to understand these advanced database features. They can speed up your application considerably and allow for more robust, manageable code.

### Oracle

Oracle, `http://www.oracle.com`, was the first commercially available database to use the SQL language and to be ported to a wide range of platforms. It runs on various UNIX, Linux, and Windows platforms. Oracle has the largest market share of the enterprise-level RDBMSs, and is the most likely choice for large companies and organizations, making it likely that you will encounter Oracle at some stage in your application development career.

You will probably know if you need Oracle. It is a high-end solution; for the majority of web applications that the solo developer or small web shop builds, it will not be an obvious choice. It is not a database that you are likely to find on shared web hosting. If you are building a solution for a larger company, however—such as an intranet—you might find that you have to work with Oracle because of the sheer amount of data that needs to be manipulated.

Oracle has its own extension to SQL called PL/SQL. As with most databases, however, the basics of SQL are the same. Only after you get into stored procedures and other extensions to SQL do you begin to see differences in the implementation and language.

### PostgreSQL

*PostgreSQL*, `http://www.us.postgresql.org/`, is an open-source database. It runs on most UNIX and UNIX-variant operating systems, such as Linux, Solaris, SCO, HP-UX, and Mac OS X. Binaries also are available for the Windows platform. Although it is generally not advised to run the database server in a live environment on Windows, you may want to install it for development purposes.

PostgreSQL supports stored procedures and triggers written in PL/pgSQL, which is an extension of SQL similar to Oracle's PL/SQL.

For more information, refer to Korry Douglas's *PostgreSQL* (New Riders Publishing).

## Database Differences

We have already touched on some of the differences between databases as we discussed each model. The main considerations when choosing a database are how robust the database is, how many users it can support, and which features it has to support more advanced database programming. Table 15.2 offers a quick reference for these differences.

| Table 15.2    Table Showing Differences Between Database Features | | |
| --- | --- | --- |
| Feature | Database | Support? |
| *Triggers* | MySQL | No |
| | PostgreSQL | Yes |
| | SQL Server | Yes |
| | Oracle | Yes |
| | IBM DB2 | Yes |
| | Access | No |

*continues*

| Table 15.2 Continued | | |
| --- | --- | --- |
| Feature | Database | Support? |
| | FoxPro | Yes |
| | FileMaker Pro | No |
| *User-defined functions* | MySQL | No |
| | PostgreSQL | Yes |
| | SQL Server | Yes |
| | Oracle | Yes |
| | IBM DB2 | Yes |
| | Access | No |
| | FoxPro | Yes |
| | FileMaker Pro | No |
| *Foreign key support* | MySQL | No |
| | PostgreSQL | Yes |
| | SQL Server | Yes |
| | Oracle | Yes |
| | IBM DB2 | Yes |
| | Access | Yes |
| | FoxPro | Yes |
| | FileMaker Pro | No |
| *Subselects* | MySQL | No |
| | PostgreSQL | Yes |
| | SQL Server | Yes |
| | Oracle | Yes |
| | IBM DB2 | Yes |
| | Access | Yes |
| | FoxPro | Yes |
| | FileMaker Pro | No |
| *Transactions* | MySQL | No |
| | PostgreSQL | Yes |
| | SQL Server | Yes |
| | Oracle | Yes |
| | IBM DB2 | Yes |

| Feature | Database | Support? |
|---------|----------|----------|
| | Access | Yes (with Microsoft Transaction Server) |
| | FoxPro | Yes |
| | FileMaker Pro | No |
| *Views* | MySQL | No |
| | PostgreSQL | Yes |
| | SQL Server | Yes |
| | Oracle | Yes |
| | IBM DB2 | Yes |
| | Access | Yes (called queries) |
| | FoxPro | Yes |
| | FileMaker Pro | No |

## Data Types

*Data types* enable you to set what type of data is to be inserted into each field of your database. In all the databases covered in this discussion, there are data types for various different text, numeric, date, time, and currency fields. These data types vary from database to database, and you will need to know these differences particularly if you decide to upgrade an application from one database to another.

The documentation, or any good reference, for the database that you have chosen should give you an in-depth explanation of the data types that you can use and in which situations you should use them.

The differences between databases—that is, the features that they offer— were covered in the descriptions of each database. Remember that although a database may not appear feature rich, sometimes many features are unnecessary, and such databases are often much faster than their more featured counterparts.

## Connecting Your Application to the Database

For your application to retrieve data from your database, you need to make a connection to it. The manner in which you make that connection will depend on your choice of application server and database. Often you have several connection options for each choice. You will need to make your database connection before you start working with Dreamweaver MX and dynamic data because Dreamweaver MX needs to be able to read your data to work with it.

### Open Database Connectivity Connections

If you are developing and hosting on Windows using ASP, ASP.NET, or ColdFusion, you can connect to the database using ODBC. ODBC is a standard protocol for accessing information in SQL database servers.

### ODBC Data Source Name

*Data Source Name* (DSN) connections can be created in Windows in the ODBC Data Source Administrator. Just follow these steps:

1. Go to Start > Settings > Control Panel.

2. Open Administrative Tools.

3. Open Data Sources (ODBC).

4. Click the System DSN tab, and then click Add. A list of database drivers will display. Select the driver for your database.

5. Depending on the database you are using, a dialog box will display enabling you to locate your database. For file-based databases such as Access, you need to browse to the location of your file. For database servers, you need to enter the location and connection information for the server, and the database to which the DSN points.

The advantage of using a DSN is that, if your hosting company or live server allows this, you can set up a DSN of the same name there; your application should transfer seamlessly from your development server to the live server.

It is possible to use a DSN with a MySQL database on Windows. You must download the MyODBC software (`http://www.mysql.com/downloads/api-myodbc-3.51.html`). After you have downloaded and installed MyODBC, you will see the driver for MySQL when you set up a DSN.

After you have set up your DSN on the machine, you can connect to it from your application. In Dreamweaver MX, you can specify that you want to connect using a DSN; Dreamweaver MX will write the necessary code for you.

Note that if you are developing for ColdFusion MX, you first must define your DSN from the ColdFusion Administrator.

### ODBC DSN-Less

For an ODBC DSN-less connection, you do not need to create a system DSN. Instead, you just include the driver and connection information within the connection string itself. You need to have the correct drivers for your database on your system. These will be installed when you install the database; for MySQL, however, you do need to install the MyODBC drivers.

### OLE DB

*OLE DB* stands for object linking and embedding database. It is the best way to connect to a database when using ASP on a Windows server. OLE DB connections are made by way of a connection string that specifies the provider for the database that you are using and the location of the database.

### JDBC

*Java database connectivity* (JDBC) is the standard for connecting Java-based applications to a database. JDBC works cross platform and therefore enables the exceptional portability of Java applications. The best type of JDBC driver to use is one that is specific to the database to which you are trying to connect. Many databases, particularly those that come from companies that offer support for Java—such as IBM, DB2, and Oracle, ship with JDBC drivers. For other databases, you must locate third-party JDBC drivers for your database. You can search for drivers for your database of choice on the Sun web site at `http://industry.java.sun.com/products/jdbc/drivers`.

# Your Development Environment

To get the best out of Dreamweaver MX, you must set up your application server and database of choice locally. This section briefly covers some of the issues involved in installing and running your own web, application, and database servers for testing purposes. The focus here is on software that is cheap or free to install locally for development purposes. Each of the setups could easily cover a chapter of a book such as this. However, this discussion should provide enough information to get you started—while still explaining how complex the setup is for each option. After you have chosen the environment you want to work with, you would do well to do further research into the installation and configuration of your development environment.

## Running a Local Web Server

If you are running Windows as a desktop machine and want to develop in ASP on IIS, you have the simplest setup. With Mac OS X, however, Mac users now have options. If you have access to a Linux machine for development purposes, you can remotely connect to that with Dreamweaver MX.

### Installing IIS

If you are running Windows 2000 or XP Professional, you will find IIS on your Windows CD. To install it, follow these steps:

1.  Go to Start > Settings > Control Panel > Add/Remove Programs.

2.  Select Add/Remove Windows Components.

3.  Check the Internet Information Services checkbox.

You must put the Windows CD in the drive. Then IIS should install without any problems.

To check that your web server is installed, open a web browser and type `http://localhost`. You should get the default IIS home page. You are all set to use IIS as your web server and application server for ASP pages.

### Note

**There is no way to install IIS on Windows XP Home version or Windows ME.**

If you want to use Dreamweaver MX just for ASP pages, the preceding installation steps are all that you need. To use IIS5/5.1 for your ASP.NET applications, however, you need to follow some additional steps.

For ASP.NET, you must ensure that you have the latest version of the Microsoft Data Access Components (MDAC) from Microsoft. You can download these from the Microsoft web site at `http://www.microsoft.com/data/`.

After downloading and installed the MDAC, you are ready to install the ASP.NET framework. You can get ASP.NET version 1.0 as a download from `http://www.asp.net/download.aspx`.

At the time of writing, two versions are available to download: .NET Framework Redistributable and .NET Framework Software Development Kit. Either download enables you to run ASP.NET applications. So unless you are on a very fast connection, you will most likely go for the first option because it is a much smaller download.

After downloading your preferred version, you will be walked through the installation process by way of a familiar "wizard." After installation, you will still be able to run classic ASP pages as well as ASP.NET applications.

### Installing PWS on Windows 98

If you are working on Windows 98, you can install PWS to test ASP pages. There is no way to test ASP.NET applications on a 98 installation. PWS comes on the CD with Windows 98. Run the PWS setup.exe program that can be found in the addons/pws folder of your Windows 98 CD. Otherwise, you must visit the Microsoft web site and download PWS. PWS is a cut-down version of IIS. If you are serious about application development with ASP, you should definitely upgrade to either Windows 2000 or XP Professional.

### Installing Apache

You can download Apache for free from `http://httpd.apache.org`. At this web site, you should be able to find a version for your operating system. When downloading and installing Apache, consider the application server that you are going to use with it. For many developers, installing Apache and PHP or Apache and Tomcat (for JSP) on Windows enables them to create applications in a familiar, Windows environment and then transfer them to a server running the Linux operating system.

- **Windows.** Instructions for downloading and installing Apache on Windows are available at http://httpd.apache.org/docs/windows.html. If you follow these instructions, you should have little problem installing Apache.

- **Linux.** You may well find that Apache has been installed with your Linux installation. If it has not been, you can check to see whether there is a package (RPM or DEB) available for your Linux distribution or download the source from the Apache web site and compile it yourself.

- **Mac OS X.** Apache is installed by default with Mac OS X. To install PHP support, you must download and configure PHP (a very simple process on OS X).

### PHP

If you want to use PHP with MySQL on either Windows or Linux, you should install MySQL first so that PHP will see that it is running.

### *Windows*

To install PHP on Windows, first download PHP from `http://www.php.net`. You should find the Win32 binaries versions there. Download the CGI Plus Server API version. Unzip the file you download into a directory. Find the file php4ts.dll, which you need to copy to the System32 folder of Windows. Copy the file php.ini-dist to the Windows folder and rename it php.ini. You need to open **php.ini** in WordPad or a similar text editor and find the line that starts with "extension_dir." This line needs to point to the extensions subfolder of the folder into which you unzipped PHP. Then find the line that starts with "session.save_path" and point that to your Windows TEMP folder.

You can use PHP with either IIS or Apache. If you want to use PHP with IIS, run it as a CGI rather an ISAPI; the ISAPI installation is problematic for many users. To install PHP as a CGI to run with IIS, follow these steps:

1.  Go to Start > Settings > Control Panel > Administrative Tools > Internet Information Services.

2.  Right-click your web site in the tree view and select Properties.

3.  Now select the Home Directory tab and the Configuration button. Go to the Mappings tag and click Add. Select the Add Mappings tab. Browse to the PHP executable on your system and enter **.php** in the Extension field.

4.  Restart IIS. You should be ready to serve PHP pages as CGI from IIS.

If you want to use PHP with Apache on Windows, after you have installed PHP you need to follow these steps:

1.  Open up the httpd.conf file in WordPad or another text editor.

2.  Add the following three lines to the bottom of the httpd.conf file:

    ```
    LoadModule php4_module c:/php/sapi/php4apache.dll
    AddType application/x-httpd-php .php .php3 .phtml
    AddType application/x-httpd-php-source .phps
    ```

3.  Check that the `LoadModule` line points to the php4apache.dll file.

4.  Save changes and restart Apache.

PHPTriad, `http://www.phpgeek.com/`, is a product that will install a PHP web server environment on Windows. This includes Apache, PHP, MySQL, Perl, and PHPMyAdmin (an admin interface for MySQL built in PHP). If you want to get up and running quickly for PHP, this is worth looking at.

### Linux

Depending on your choice Linux distribution, you may be able to install PHP and MySQL via your package management system. PHP.net does not have Linux binaries available for download on the site and suggests that you check out the versions available on the web site for your particular Linux distribution. If you installed from the CD, PHP and MySQL are likely to be on the CD. Otherwise you can download the source from `http://www.php.net/downloads.php`.

### Mac OS X

The Apple web site includes detailed instructions for setting up Mac OS X for PHP. You can find these at `http://developer.apple.com/internet/macosx/php.html`.

## A JSP Development Environment

When considering your development environment for JSP, you have many options (both commercial and open source). This section considers two options: a development environment with Macromedia JRun and one with Tomcat.

Setting up an open-source JSP development environment on your computer can be relatively complex in comparison to some of the commercial offerings (such as JRun). However, it is perfectly possible. Although a full tutorial is beyond the scope of this discussion, this section should point you in the right direction. To set up a local web server for JSP, you need the software discussed in the following subsections for either Windows, Mac OS X, or on a Linux system on your network. (I am presuming that you already have a working Apache install for these steps—although Tomcat can work with other web servers.)

### The Java Development Kit

You download the *Java Development Kit* (JDK) from Sun (`http://java.sun.com/`). If you are on Mac OS X, you can download it directly from Apple (`http://developer.apple.com/java/`).

### Mod_Jserv

*Jserv* is an apache module that you need to get Tomcat working with Apache. You can download it at `http://java.apache.org/jserv/`. You need to ensure that Apache is configured to allow loadable modules.

### Tomcat

You can download Tomcat from `http://jakarta.apache.org/`. There is no installation program. It comes as a single compressed file, and you just need to unzip/decompress it into a directory and check the installation instructions to ensure that you have set the environment variables correctly for your system. On Windows, you must open the Command Prompt DOS window and type the following:

```
SET JAVA_HOME=C:\the_path_to_the_JDK
SET TOMCAT_HOME=C:\the_tomcat_directory
SET PATH=%PATH%; C:\the_path_to_the_JDK\BIN
```

On Linux, you will need to do something like this:

```
JAVA_HOME=/the_path_to_the_jdk; export JAVA_HOME
TOMCAT_HOME=/the_Tomcat_directory; export TOMCAT_HOME
PATH=$PATH:/the_path_to_the_jdk/bin; export PATH
```

Check the documentation that comes with Tomcat for more detailed instructions. You can test that your Tomcat installation is working correctly by starting Tomcat and then typing the following into a web browser:

```
http://localhost:8080/examples/jsp/
```

Tomcat also operates as a standalone server. If it is running, it will display an Examples page with some working examples of JSP code. If you can run these examples, Tomcat is working as it should.

To get Tomcat working fully with Apache, you must get Apache to load the Jserv module when it starts. On both Windows and Linux, open up httpd.conf file and look for the section where the modules are loaded. You need to add the following line to that section:

```
LoadModule jserv_module modules/ApacheModuleJServ.dll
```

For Linux, replace ApacheModuleJServ.dll with **mod_jserv.so**.

At the end of the file for Windows, add the following:

```
Include "c:/tomcat_directory/conf/tomcat-apache.conf
```

For Linux, add the following:

```
Include /path_to_tomcat/conf/tomcat-apache.conf
```

You then need to restart Apache. You should now be able to view the Tomcat examples directly on the web server at `http://localhost/examples/jsp/`.

### Macromedia JRun

If you think setting up Tomcat looks horrendously complex, you can set up a development environment for JSP using Macromedia JRun. You can download the developer edition of JRun from the Macromedia web site at `http://www.macromedia.com/software/jrun/trial/`.

This developer edition is limited to three connections, and so is no use for a live web server; however, it is fine for local development or learning. If you need to buy a full copy of JRun web server, you can find all the details on the Macromedia web site. As with Tomcat, you must download and install the JDK from Sun (`http://java.sun.com/`).

After you have run the installer and installed JRun, you must ensure that it is communicating with your web server. To do so, configure the JRun Management Console (JMC). Upon launch, the JMC will run an easy-to-use wizard to walk you through the steps needed. JRun, like Tomcat, can be run as a standalone web server. If you are just using it for development purposes, you do not have to install a web server and test your applications directly in JRun.

## ColdFusion

ColdFusion MX Developers Edition for Windows is supplied with the Windows version of Dreamweaver MX. Therefore, if you want to dive into ColdFusion development, you should find yourself with an easy setup.

The Developer Edition of ColdFusion is a nonexpiring and fully featured version of ColdFusion Server and allows use on a single computer to develop ColdFusion applications. This Developer Edition is available only for Windows at the time of writing. However, applications developed on Windows for ColdFusion should transfer without problems to Linux or other UNIX hosting running ColdFusion server. ColdFusion 5 needs to have a web server installed to function. With ColdFusion MX, you have the option to run it as a standalone server, in which case you can test your applications with only ColdFusion MX Server running.

## More Than One Web Server on Your Computer

If you are running Windows as your local, development server and want to be able to develop with two different web servers—for instance, to work with ASP on IIS and PHP on Apache—you can do that. You just need to give one of the servers a different port on which to listen for requests.

It's easier to change Apache's port than IIS's. So after you have your servers installed, go to the Apache httpd.conf file (which is the configuration file for the web server) and find where it says "Port 80." Change that to a different port number, such as 800. Restart the Apache web server. Now when you want to look at a page on IIS, use the following:

```
http://localhost/
```

To use Apache, just put the port number on the end, as follows:

```
http://localhost:800
```

## Installing and Administering Databases

File-based, desktop databases have their own GUI that will shield you from the raw SQL used to create, edit, and delete tables. If you have a good knowledge of SQL, it is perfectly possible (and often quickest) to create your databases at the command line. For most people (and particularly those moving from a desktop database to a database server), however, a nice GUI will shorten the learning curve by giving an easy-to-understand interface in which to perform the tasks. Often the available GUIs have other functionality, such as importing data from other RDBMSs, which can make them useful even if you are a command-line type of person.

### Enterprise Manager

Enterprise Manager is available on the SQL Server CD or by downloading the 120-day trial of SQL Server from the Microsoft web site. The client tools are still active after the trial ends (so you may administer a remote SQL Server database). Unfortunately, the download for the SQL Server trial is more than 300MB. If you are on a slow Internet connection, purchasing the SQL Server 2000 Evaluation Kit (currently $7.95) might be a better option! You can find this at `http://www.microsoft.com/sql/downloads/default.asp`.

Enterprise Manager enables you to administer your SQL Server databases via a GUI that should be familiar to anyone who has used another Microsoft database, such as Access or FoxPro. It allows connection to remote databases and also transfer of data between remote databases.

### GUIs for MySQL

MySQL does not come with any *graphical user interfaces* (GUIs) in the same way that databases such as Access do. However, you can download several excellent tools to administer your database, including the following:

- **DBTools.** DBTools (http://www.dbtools.com.br) is a GUI for Microsoft Windows to manage MySQL databases. It is not strictly open-source software, but presently is free to download and use. The team is working on support for other databases.

- **MySQL-Front.** MySQL-Front (`http://anse.de/mysqlfront/`) is a GUI for Microsoft Windows connecting to local or remote MySQL databases. The interface will seem familiar to anyone who is used to working with Access or FoxPro and will help to bridge the gap for those moving to MySQL from a desktop database.
- **phpMyAdmin.** PHPmyAdmin (`http://www.phpwizard.net/projects/phpMyAdmin/`) is a web-based MySQL administration tool commonly used by hosting companies to allow administration of MySQL databases by their users. You also can install it locally if you have a local web server with PHP installed.

### GUIs for PostgreSQL

The most popular Windows GUI for PostgreSQL is pgAdmin (`http://www.pgadmin.org/`), which can connect to a PostgreSQL database running locally on Windows or to a database running on a development server (which can be Windows, Linux, or Mac OS X).

The software uses the PostgreSQL ODBC driver, which you can download from psglODBC at `http://odbc.postgresql.org/psqlodbc.php?DocID=index`.

### GUIs for Use on Mac OS X

Many of the options mentioned earlier are for Windows. There are, however, several excellent options for Mac OS X. SQLGrinder (`http://www.advenio.com/sqlgrinder/`) enables working with any database that can make a JDBC connection and ships with support for MySQL and PostgreSQL. Adding support for new databases is just a case of adding the new drivers to a folder and restarting SQLGrinder.

## Security Implications

After you have installed and started to run a local web server and/or database server, you need to consider the same security aspects that anyone running a live web server must consider.

The terms and conditions of many ISP providers prohibit the use of your connection to run a live web server. However, development servers should not cause problems provided that your server is not wide open to any attacks that might be launched on an unprotected server. To a port-scanning device, a local development web server looks exactly the same as an unprotected live server; you are asking for trouble if you do not take basic measures to protect your server. The easiest way to do so is to install some kind of hardware router or firewall that will make it look to the outside world as if you are not running any servers.

If you have no choice but to have the machine that is directly connected to the Internet running a web server, take precautions to ensure that you do not become a target. Installing firewall software on your computer will alert you to possible attacks. Zone Alarm is a popular choice; a free version is available for personal use at `http://www.zonealarm.com`. If you are running IIS on Microsoft Windows, visit the Windows Update site regularly to ensure that any security patches are installed. Microsoft release patches stop people exploiting security flaws.

If you are running local, development database servers, read the manuals and ensure that the security features are utilized, instead of leaving everything at the default settings. By doing all these things, you minimize the chance of someone picking on you to have their dubious fun!

## Hosting Your Site

The last thing you might want to consider when choosing which platform, web server, and application server to develop for is where you will host your completed application. You should consider this before beginning development; where shared hosting is concerned, not all hosting companies are equal! For instance, you may want to use DSN connections to connect your application to the database. However, not all hosting companies allow this, or they may allow only a limited numbers of DSNs to be set up. Knowing at the outset what your hosting company will provide for you could save a lot of time and expense later on.

## Finding Hosting for Your Chosen Environment

If you are relatively new to application development, you are likely to be exploring shared web hosting for your first applications. The ease with which you will find the hosting and the expense of that hosting will depend on which combination of operating system-web server and application server you have chosen.

PHP and MySQL/PostgreSQL hosting is generally fairly low-cost and easy to find. These days, ASP hosting that allows connections to an Access database is also relatively low-cost. Databases such as SQL Server and Oracle will incur a higher charge because they have license fees that your hosting company will need to pass on to you. Java hosting is often significantly more expensive; however, you can find lower cost hosts using the open-source option of Tomcat with MySQL. It does pay to ask around. The Macromedia newsgroups for Dreamweaver MX are a good place to start; a recommendation from someone who has experience with a company is better than just comparing marketing blurbs on hosting company web sites.

Note that you do get what you pay for in terms of hosting. You can find very cheap hosting out there; and, if you just want somewhere to try out your new skills, cheap hosting may be good for you. For important, database-driven web applications, however, you need to have reliable hosting. There is no point to building a great application if no one can get to use it, or if it is unusable because an overloaded shared server makes it too slow. You need to work more closely with your hosting company when deploying a web application than you do with a static site. In addition, it is worth paying a little extra to know that they will be able to assist you if necessary.

## Uploading Everything to the Site

When you create a static HTML-based web site, making your site live is as simple as ensuring that you upload all the pages and graphics. Deploying your web application is slightly more complicated; if you have chosen your web hosting carefully, however, you should have all you need available— it's just a matter of linking it all up.

When you come to actually uploading your pages to the server, you can use Dreamweaver MX's built-in FTP and site-management capabilities. Alternatively, you can use your favorite FTP client. Uploading of the actual pages that make up the application will not be any different to uploading static HTML pages as long as you have ensured that anything that points to something on the server is changed for the live server (such as your connection string).

## Server Setup

If you are setting up your own live server (for instance, if you have built an intranet), you just need to ensure that the live server is set up in the same way as your development server. You need to ensure that the application server is running and will serve pages in the folder into which you plan to put your application. You might need to create a virtual directory for the content.

## The Live Database

If you are hosting your application on shared hosting, you will be told where to upload your pages. If you are using a file-based database, such as Access, you should have been given a directory outside of the main site files directory to which to upload your database.

If you are using a database server, you should have some information about how to connect to the server and transfer your database by using web-based tools such as phpMyAdmin, connecting directly to the server via a command-line utility, or by using software such as Enterprise Manager. Your hosting company should be able to advise you as to the best ways to connect and transfer data to your live database.

If you decide to re-create your database from scratch on the live server, instead of transferring the table structure, make sure that you name each object exactly in the same way as in your development database. If you use a different database on the live web server from the database you have developed with (a common path is to develop in Access and deploy with SQL Server), you must test extensively to ensure that the application still functions correctly with a different RDBMS holding the data.

## Database Connections

If you have used a DSN to connect your database to your application, you need to create this DSN on the live server or ask your hosting company to do so for you. If you have used any type of connection string, ensure that it is pointing to the database and uses the correct login information—it will most likely be different from that used on your local database server. On shared hosting, your hosting company should be able to advise or may have help pages on its web site explaining where and how you can connect to your database.

## Testing Servers

When working on complex, live applications, it is always a good idea to implement some kind of testing server in between your development server and the live site. This staging server can use the same database as the live application to ensure that nothing in there is likely to cause any problems. Your testing server doesn't need to be an entirely new virtual directory. If you are on shared hosting, you can just create a folder for testing and check out new additions to the site in there before deployment.

This is particularly important when you cannot mirror the live environment exactly on your local development setup. Those developing in PHP on a Windows operating system for deployment to PHP on a UNIX server, or developing with ASP on IIS and then using Linux/Apache and Chili!Soft ASP as the live application server, need to ensure that they haven't introduced any platform-specific functionality into their application. The best way to do this is to run tests on the new pages on the live server before deployment.

## Creating Backups for the Site

When you build a static web site, you ordinarily have your live copy on the server and a local copy. You might burn a copy to CD or store it on a Zip file to make sure that you have a backup if the worst happens and your machine and the hosting company's server blows up on the same day. With a site that stores most of its information in a database, things are not so simple.

You need to ensure that the data in your database is backed up regularly. On a very busy site, that may need to happen once a day or more. Other sites may need the data backed up only once a week or month. It depends on how often data is added to the database. If you are on shared hosting, check with your hosting company to see what kind of backup service they offer, and how quickly your data can be restored if the worst happens. If the hosting company cannot help, you must make sure that you download your database or export your data regularly so that you can restore it to a reasonable state. Even if your hosting company takes responsibility for this, it is never a bad idea to make a copy of the data regularly… just in case!

## What to Take Away from This Chapter

- Application development requires the making of some fairly involved choices right from the outset. Because the choices impact each other, research the options together before making final decisions for any application.
- Each different option has its pros and cons. Whether these apply to you depends on the sort of application that you want to develop.
- You can set up a full development and testing environment locally, often at no cost. The setting up of this environment does need to be done carefully to avoid the opening up of security problems with your internal network.

# Chapter 16

# Controlling Your Environment

Objectives:

- Gain a full understanding of the available preference options in Dreamweaver.
- Learn how to edit the Dreamweaver File Extensions list.
- Learn how to define or redefine the file transfer method used when FTP'ing files in Dreamweaver.

User control has always been one of the strongest selling points for Dreamweaver. The way that it's possible to configure almost every last detail is a testament to the value Macromedia places on users and their ability to control their own environment. Software that works the way users want it to, or enables them to change it to work that way, will ultimately provide the best user experience. Web developers will not continue to use a piece of software that doesn't work the way they like or produce the standard of code they want. This is one of the reasons Dreamweaver is so widely used within the web design and development industry.

This chapter examines closely the many options available for customizing Dreamweaver. Besides the ability to extend Dreamweaver through JavaScript, there are a lot of options to control the working environment and the code Dreamweaver produces. These range from the most basic of user preferences to the more complex options—from the color of the code in the Dreamweaver editing environment, to the formatting and indentation of that code in the final page uploaded to your web server.

# Setting Preferences

Dreamweaver offers a huge amount of choice when it comes to setting preferences for the day-to-day operation of your environment. This is always in your interest, and it is well worth taking the time to become familiar with the wide range of options available. Even if a particular option isn't relevant right now, it may be for the next project. Having a good knowledge of the options available will enable you to make the most of your working environment and the pages you produce using Dreamweaver. The following sections cover all the different options available for you to set as preferences.

## General Category

The General category of the Preferences window offers a number of configuration options, as shown in Figure 16.1. This tab houses some general file and editing options that are used throughout the program when Dreamweaver is reading, writing, and saving HTML.

**Figure 16.1**

General category of the Preferences window.

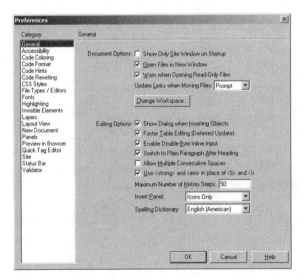

## Document Options

Let's start by examining the different document options available.

### Show Only Site Window on Startup

When launching Dreamweaver, a new blank web page opens by default. This can be very useful, especially if you want to get right down to work and try an idea out. It also can be harmful, however, in that it's entirely possible to forget to save the file before starting work. This can lead to bad paths and links within the document.

Some people prefer not to have a new, blank web page opened when they start Dreamweaver. If you tend to work on sites where you are not authoring new pages regularly, but instead are modifying existing pages, you might want to select this option. When selected, it prevents this blank page from being opened, and instead presents you with the Site window to use as a launching pad into your work.

### Open Files in New Window

By default, double-clicking a page in the site window, or browsing to File > Open, opens the selected file in a new Dreamweaver Document window. This is useful if you need to work on multiple files at one time—maybe even copying and pasting information or developing interaction between the pages.

On the other hand, this can sometimes lead many windows being open simultaneously, which can slow down the computer by using a slice of memory for every open document. Besides, the classic Dreamweaver workspace uses a lot of windows as it is; so unless you're using the MX workspace, all those windows get become a pain to deal with. The Open Files in New Window feature is there for just this circumstance. Unchecking the box results in Dreamweaver reusing the current document window to load new pages.

## Warn When Opening Read-Only Files

Under a number of circumstances, a Dreamweaver document may become read-only. A prime example of this is when using the Check In/Check Out tools. Another case is when a client has supplied files on a CD-ROM that have been copied to the developer's hard disk, but have not been set back to being read/write.

Dreamweaver, like other modern software programs, gives you a way to deal with read-only files. If you attempt to open a read-only file, Dreamweaver displays a warning that the file cannot be written to and suggests that you might like to save the file under a different name.

Of course, the experienced web developer does not need to be told how to deal with a read-only file, but it is always useful to be alerted to the fact before you start making any changes. Dreamweaver includes the Warn When Opening Read-Only Files option for this purpose. Commonly, this should be left checked.

## Update Links When Moving Files

Dreamweaver has very powerful site-management capabilities. Part of the functionality is the capability to update all the links to one particular file if that file is renamed or moved elsewhere in the site. This is an extremely useful feature, but also one that can be dangerous if not used with due consideration. If you allow Dreamweaver to update a link in error, the resulting mistake will be strewn throughout the web site. The Update Links When Moving Files option offers some safeguards against mistakes.

The super-confident user may select the Always option, resulting in links being updated whenever a file is moved or renamed. This is all well and good, but I often encounter circumstances in which I specifically do not want Dreamweaver to update my links. A prime example of this is if I swap in a different version of a page for testing purposes. To do this, I typically rename the original file to something else and give the new file the name of the original. In this situation, I need Dreamweaver to keep track of the filename rather than the file itself. If all the links were to change, I wouldn't be able to test my new page.

Another available choice is the Never option, resulting in links never being updated when files are moved or renamed. This has the effect of turning this feature off, unless manually invoked by using the Change Link Sitewide tool from the Site menu. Although this limits a really useful function, it offers a good amount of protection from the situation described earlier. Dreamweaver will not update any links, and so there is no chance of any mistakes occurring that might damage your site.

The default option is Prompt. Using this option, you are asked in each and every case whether the links to a particular file should be updated. As you've seen, sometimes it is useful for Dreamweaver to update links, and sometimes it might be inappropriate. This makes the Prompt option the perfect compromise because every case can be considered on its own merits.

## Changing the Workspace

As you will be aware if you have used any previous version of Dreamweaver, this version brings with it a new interface option. The Dreamweaver MX workspace builds on some of the successful features in the Macromedia ColdFusion Studio and HomeSite, combined with the classic Dreamweaver interface elements with which you are already familiar.

The Dreamweaver MX workspace is available in two different configurations for Windows users. The first has the main selection of panels on the right (familiar to Dreamweaver 4 users), and the second configuration HomeSite/Coder style keeps its panels on the left like HomeSite and ColdFusion Studio. For those who still favor the old-style Dreamweaver interface, this option is available as well.

Macintosh users do not have the option to use the new workspaces, unfortunately, although many of the new features have been integrated into the old multiwindow interface.

### Note

Unlike most of the other Dreamweaver preferences, changing the workspace takes effect only when you restart Dreamweaver.

## Editing Options

Next we'll take a look at the different editing options available in the General category.

### Show Dialog When Inserting Objects

A number of the Dreamweaver objects available from the Objects panel display a dialog box, offering some options, before the object is inserted. Two prime examples of this are the Insert Image object, which enables you to browse for the image to insert, and the Insert Table object, which enables you to set the dimensions and the layout of the table. Unchecking the Show Dialog When Inserting Objects option suppresses these dialog boxes and instead assumes either default properties or the settings last used.

In the case of the Insert Image object, an empty image tag is inserted, with no source or size attributes. The user is then able to set these via the Property inspector. The Insert Table object adopts the settings from the previous use of the object. Again, you can adjust these settings via the Property inspector.

This feature could prove useful if you need to insert many objects into a page or group of pages and can accept the default or previous setting offered. This is an obvious time-saver because it eliminates a step from the processes.

### Faster Table Editing (Deferred Update)

Not everyone runs Dreamweaver on a super-fast computer. Smaller companies are not always able to update their hardware as often as they would like, and so Macromedia has again kept the user in mind by creating this option.

When selected, this option defers the update of the table until you have finished making your edits, or finished typing text into the table, and click away from the table.

This offers a distinct benefit to users of slower machines, because modifying large tables full of data can take a toll on the computer. The last thing a developer wants to do in that circumstance is have to wait for an age between each tweak. It's far better to enable the developer to make some changes and then update the table after all the changes are done.

By default, the Faster Table Editing option is checked. Users with speedy computers may want to uncheck it for a while and see how it works for them.

### Enable Double-Byte Inline Input

Some languages with complex sets of characters need twice the amount of memory space for each character. These languages are known as *double-byte languages* and require slightly different treatment by computer software to function correctly. Dreamweaver supports double-byte character input, and this option can be used to enable it.

### Switch to Plain Paragraph After Heading

Because of their very nature, most headings use up only one line on a page. This useful option instructs Dreamweaver to switch from the heading style to a plain paragraph style after the user presses the Enter key. That is, if you press Enter, while writing heading text into an <h$n$> tag, Dreamweaver closes the <h$n$> tag and opens a new <p> tag for you.

### Allow Multiple Consecutive Spaces

By default, Dreamweaver behaves just like a web browser in its treatment of spaces. A browser will treat any number of blank spaces in your HTML as a single space to be displayed onscreen. This is why pressing the Spacebar multiple times in the Dreamweaver Design view will insert only one space.

Although this is an extremely good feature that encourages accurate and lean code, on occasion you might want Dreamweaver to behave more like a word processor in its treatment of spaces. The Allow Multiple Consecutive Spaces option causes Dreamweaver to insert a nonbreaking space ( ) for each press of the Spacebar. Use this option with caution; those nonbreaking spaces are not normally necessary and will increase the weight of your page and also will cause lines to break unnaturally.

### Use *<strong>* and *<em>* in place of *<b>* and *<i>*

Anyone familiar with using HTML to structurally mark up a page will tell you that tags such as bold and italic are not particularly useful—because they do not describe the nature of their contents, just how they should be displayed. Because CSS is the tool of choice for stating how things should display, HTML should be used to describe the text. For this reason, using strong and emphasis tags are a better choice for structural markup.

In nearly all browsers, the default styling of `<strong>` and `<em>` is just the same as `<b>` and `<i>`, so there's really no need to stick with these older, less-descriptive tags.

### Maximum Number of History Steps

An extremely useful Dreamweaver feature is the ability to step back through your edit history a large number of steps. Using the History panel, it is possible to undo back to a defined point in the history of the document, since it was last saved.

The Maximum Number of History Steps option enables you to set the number of edits kept by Dreamweaver in its undo memory. The default is 50, and you can increase or decrease it as appropriate to your own working preferences.

### *Caution*

It may be tempting to set a very high number in the history steps to give yourself maximum undo protection when working. Be warned, however, that Dreamweaver keeps the history steps in working memory, and so the larger the number of steps, the more memory used. Users of low-powered computers will find that reducing the figure to 5 or 10 steps will increase Dreamweaver performance.

### Insert Panel

The Insert panel houses many of the features that are the absolute workhorses of document production in Dreamweaver. To make access to them easier, a few options defining how the objects display are available.

By default, the Insert panel displays only the icons for each item. This default setting reflects the Icons Only option. In addition to the icons, the textual names of each object can be displayed, using the Icons and Text option. Finally, if you prefer to turn the icons off altogether and just have the text names, you can select a Text Only option.

In truth, these options were really more suited to the old-style, vertical Objects panel that was part of the Dreamweaver interface from versions 1 through 4. In the modern Dreamweaver MX workspace, only the Icons Only option seems to be useful, because the text labels are not handled well in the horizontal format.

### Spelling Dictionary

The Dreamweaver Spell Check tool checks all words against a dictionary file. By default, you can use 14 different dictionaries when spell-checking your work. English (American) is selected initially, you can easily change this to the language of your choice. It affects only the spell-checking of visible words in your web pages.

## Accessibility Category

Dreamweaver MX has a lot of new accessibility features for both the pages you create and for using the software itself. You can enable these from the Accessibility category in the preferences (see Figure 16.2).

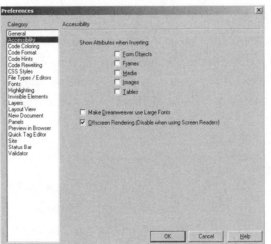

**Figure 16.2**

The Accessibility category.

### Showing Accessibility Attributes

Dreamweaver MX has a new feature for developers who need to make sure their sites are accessible to all. (That's nearly every developer—and probably you.) The method Dreamweaver takes is to prompt the user to enter all the appropriate attributes when inserting code via the built-in objects.

This can be extremely useful, because it doesn't allow the developer the opportunity to forget to add all the little things that go into making a site more accessible. Groups of objects can be switched on individually when required. I suggest that it is safer to turn these options on rather than forget to add the attributes yourself and run the risk of having to add them later.

### Accessibility Settings for Dreamweaver

Dreamweaver has a couple of options for users with less-than-perfect vision. The option to use large fonts within the application can prove helpful if your eyesight isn't so good. I find this option useful until about 10 a.m. when the caffeine sinks in.

The second option is to disable Offscreen Rendering. Dreamweaver uses this technique to reduce the visible flicker an application can create as it refreshes its display. Because this can make things difficult for users with screen readers, there is an option to disable it. If you don't use a screen reader, leave Offscreen Rendering switched on.

### Code Coloring Category

The Code Coloring category of the Preferences window houses some options that dictate the color of the code when viewed in Code view (see Figure 16.3). Code-coloring options have vastly increased in Dreamweaver MX with the helpful addition of color schemes.

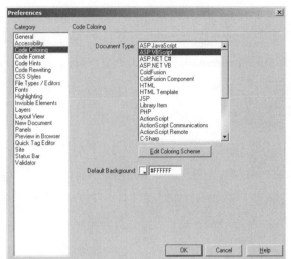

**Figure 16.3**

Code Coloring category of the Preferences window.

## Setting Code Color Preferences

You have a number of options available that govern the way code is colored in the Code view. These options include background color, default text color, the color used for tags, comments, and the like.

### Document Type

You can set the color scheme for any particular document type. Dreamweaver works with a wide range of different documents, and each one can be selected in turn and various attributes set. For each attribute with a color scheme, both the foreground and the background color can be set, along with whether the text should be regular, bold, italic or underlined.

### Background

The Background Color setting relates purely to the color used for the background of the Code view, and not to any document settings that affect the way a page is viewed in a browser. The default setting for this is #FFFFFF (white), making the Code view very pleasant to use.

## General Notes on Code Coloring

Dreamweaver describes each aspect of the code and enables the user to set his own preferences. The following sections list some of the more common options.

### Text

The Text Color setting refers to the color of any plain text in the document that will appear on the page. Anything that is not a tag or a script element, but just regular text, will appear in this color.

### Comments

HTML and JavaScript comments will be shown in the color selected here. HTML comments are denoted like this:

```
<!-- Your comments go here -->
```

JavaScript comments are denoted in two different ways. For a single-line comment, comments are denoted as follows:

```
// This is my comment
```

For a multiline comment, comments are denoted as follows:

```
/*
These are my comments
They span more than one line.
*/
```

### Reserved Keywords

Any scripting or programming language has its own reserved keywords. *Keywords* are words that take on a special meaning within the language and that cannot be used legitimately outside of their context.

Examples of reserved keywords in JavaScript are `function`, `document`, `for`, and `if`.

## Other Keywords

Aside from reserved keywords, a scripting language can make use of other keywords. These are usually keywords that can be redefined under some circumstances. For example, the keyword `eval` could be defined as a regular variable, whereas a reserved keyword such as `for` could not. By default, Dreamweaver colors these keywords brown. Examples of keywords in JavaScript are `eval`, `open`, `close`, `write`, and `writeln`.

### *Tip*

**I sometimes work on an LCD notebook screen and find it hard to distinguish between the black of the default text color and the dark brown of the keywords. I usually change this setting to a much lighter brown to increase the contrast between the two.**

## Strings

A *string* in a scripting language such as JavaScript is considered to be any text between single or double quotation marks. The outermost quotation marks are taken to be the delimiter for the string. For example, the single quotation mark in the following line would not break the string, because the double quotation marks are taken as the delimiters:

```
"William Shakespeare's plays are excellent"
```

In the next example, the single quotation marks are the delimiters, and the double quotation marks don't break the string:

```
'I saw a performance of "Romeo and Juliet" - it was marvelous'
```

Similarly, because the preceding is denoted as a string, the hyphen is correctly interpreted as a hyphen and not a minus. By default, Dreamweaver colors strings in green.

## Code Format Category

The Code Format category of the Preferences window houses some options that dictate the presentation of the code produced by Dreamweaver (see Figure 16.4). These include options to set indenting, to set the way lines break, and to set the case options for tags and their attributes.

**Figure 16.4**

Code Format
category of the
Preferences
window.

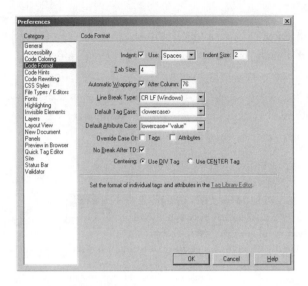

## Indentation Options

Indentation helps to make code more legible. By properly indenting each line of the page, it is possible for the developer to get an idea of the structure of the code and clearly see the relationships between any two elements. Quite simply, the farther indented an item is, the less structural importance it holds. It is particularly helpful to indent code because it makes the page easier to understand if you have to come back to it after some time, or if it has to be worked on my a different team member.

### Indent

The first option offered to affect the indentation of your source code is the option to use tabs or spaces to offset each line. This is a matter of personal preference, but I tend to use the Spaces option rather than the Tabs option because I sometimes like to edit pages directly on the web server, using a very basic command-driven text editor. In such editors, it is not always possible to set the indentation value for tabs, and so your code can end up being overly spaced, to a point where it becomes difficult to work with. However, a tab character takes up fewer bytes than multiple space characters in your file, and so you might want to select the Tabs option if file size is a priority.

Dreamweaver also has the option to use extra indentation to display tables and frames with greater clarity. By default, the option to indent these items is set, but you can remove this if you prefer them not to be indented. It's a good idea to leave tables and frames to be indented, because they can become quite complex, and the indentation helps to make the code for complex structures more understandable.

The final indentation options available dictate the size of the indentation. You can set both the number of spaces used for indentation and the size of a tab. You can't go wrong with the default values, unless you have a specific purpose in mind.

## Wrapping and Line-Break Options

Whereas in theory an HTML document could be written all on a single line, this is far from a practical solution when it comes to working within the code. No one likes to have to scroll horizontally when viewing a web page, and for the same reason developers don't like to have to keep scrolling left to right when working in Code view.

### Automatic Wrapping

To make working within the source code easier, Dreamweaver offers an option to wrap the lines of code at a certain number of characters. Without this set, the line will continue until a line break. This means that some lines can be very long, and you will need to scroll horizontally back and forth to see your code.

This is slightly different from the Word Wrap function in the Code view. That function reflows the page to make it easier to read when editing, but does not change the format of the code itself after it has been saved and uploaded.

The Automatic Wrapping setting actually breaks the line after a number of characters. That is, Dreamweaver inserts a line break, forcing the code onto a new line within the file, and not just for display purposes.

By default, Dreamweaver wraps code after column 76. (That's after 76 characters to you and me.) This seems to be a useful width if you don't work with your Code view maximized to full width. If you do, you can afford to increase this width to something greater than column 76, depending on your screen resolution.

### Line Breaks

Different computing platforms use different code characters for breaking a line. The three main platforms—PC, Macintosh, and UNIX variants—all have different line-break characters, meaning that you must take care to select the right line break for the systems your web site uses.

If you've ever opened a file from a UNIX or Linux system in a Windows text editor such as Notepad, you'll be familiar with what happens. Line breaks are replaced by strange black block characters, making it very difficult to understand the contents of the file. What you are seeing is the UNIX line breaks represented in the equivalent character from the Windows character set.

You have three options from which to choose: Carriage Return Line Feed (CR LF) for Windows systems, Carriage Return (CR) for the Macintosh, and Line Feed (LF) for UNIX and Linux systems.

## Case and Centering Options

As a web developer, you have an obligation to not only look after what's happening on the page visually, but also to be aware and in control of the method being used in the code to achieve that visual effect. When in the past it was inconsequential if your tags were upper- or lowercase, or whether you used a division or a center tag to center your code. With the web standards currently emerging, it is becoming more and more important to pay careful attention to such things.

### Case for Tags and Attributes

Back in the good old days of early HTML, all the specifications gave tags with uppercase names and attributes. This wasn't strictly necessary, but was the convention at the time. Many developers who learned to hand code HTML way back then will be familiar with using uppercase tags, and some still do so.

HTML 4 isn't sensitive to the case of tags or their attributes, but emerging standards such as XHTML and XML most certainly are case-sensitive. If you are coding for these new technologies, you will want to set the tag and attribute case settings both to lowercase. If you still prefer to use uppercase tags and attributes, you can choose this as well.

If you are unsure of your preference, it's best to go with lowercase, because this is the more future-proof of the two and is also easier to read if you are working in the Code view at all.

### Override Case Of

Dreamweaver has an option to allow it to overwrite the case of tags and attributes that already exist in the page (rather than just the ones it is creating from scratch). It makes sense to reinforce that here if you have already set a preference for uppercase or lowercase tags and attributes.

### Tag Selection

Dreamweaver allows for the two different methods available in HTML for centering an object. The first method uses a division tag, which has its alignment attribute set to center. This tag would look like this:

```
<div align="center">This is central text</div>
```

The second method uses a dedicated center tag, and looks like this:

```
<center>This is central text</center>
```

Although in a good many (if not the majority) of browsers, both methods are equally well supported, the division tag method is the most up-to-date and will provide the most ease of integration with CSS styling and layout. The `<center>` tag has been deprecated since HTML 3.2, so best to use the `<div>` tag if you can.

## Code Hints Category

Code hints should be familiar to those who have used tools such Macromedia HomeSite or even Bradbury Software's excellent TopStyle CSS editor. *Code hints* are the useful little menus that pop up as you enter code into the code editor. They offer insight and completion options to increase efficiency.

As well as turning code hints on and off, you can set the time delay before they appear and specify which particular menus should pop up. Although they're a really great tool—if they suit your way of working— some users don't like them too much; you can turn them off here. (I love code hints, but I know those who hate them.)

## Code Rewriting Category

The Code Rewriting category of the Preferences window houses some options that set the rules for how, if at all, Dreamweaver rewrites your code (see Figure 16.5).

**Figure 16.5**

Code Rewriting category of the Preferences window.

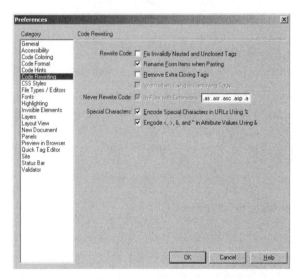

## Rewriting Code Options

One of the strong points of Dreamweaver ever since the first version was that it does not rewrite your code without your say so first. This is still true today, and you can control the code rewriting from this section of the preferences.

### Fix Invalidly Nested and Unclosed Tags

HTML lays down some specific rules as to how tags should be nested. Under regular circumstances, tags should be closed in the reverse order that they were opened. The following example shows correct tag nesting:

```
<div align="right">
  <font color="#0000CC">
    <b>This is some sample text.</b>
  </font>
</div>
```

If tags are not nested correctly, Dreamweaver will optionally correct them for you. The following example shows badly nested code:

```
<div align="right">
  <font color="#0000CC">
    <b>This is some sample text.</font>
  </div>
</b>
```

This is an overly obvious example to demonstrate the point, but it's not that uncommon to see the odd tag or two incorrectly nested, especially if the document has been through some major drag-and-drop restructuring.

### Rename Form Items When Pasting

According to the rules of HTML, it is not permissible to have more than one form element with any one name within the page. For example, it is illegal to have two form fields called myField. If this occurs, the value will always come from the element that appears lowest within the form (except, of course, for checkboxes and radio buttons which need to share a name to be part of a logical question group).

For this reason, Dreamweaver will rename any form elements being copied and pasted within the page. That is, if you were to copy a text field called myField and then paste it within the same page, Dreamweaver would automatically rename the field myField2.

On one hand, this feature can be a lifesaver. Absentmindedly copying and pasting a form element without changing its name could cause all sorts of problems when processing the results from the form. On the other hand, having Dreamweaver rename your form elements could be a pain as well, because there could be a legitimate reason for having more than one form element sharing a name. Under this circumstance, Dreamweaver would effectively invalidate the code by updating the field names.

The Rename Form Items When Pasting option is available to enable you to make your own choice, depending on your own circumstances.

### Remove Extra Closing Tags

Occasionally when working directly in the Code view or performing a lot of drag-and-drop editing, closing tags may become disjointed from their opening tags. The option to remove extra closing tags proves very useful in this circumstance.

### Warn When Fixing or Removing Tags

Dreamweaver gives users ultimate control over their own work, while also trying to automate some of the more tedious tasks. The option to give a warning before fixing or removing tags offers the user this control, while still letting Dreamweaver do all the hard work. Selecting to be warned gives users the chance to opt out, should they be working in unusual circumstances and want to keep code that may not be strictly valid.

### Never Rewrite Code in Files with Extensions

You might not want Dreamweaver to attempt to fix some files types under any circumstances. These often include files with special server-side scripting with which Dreamweaver might not be familiar. When dealing with anything similar to HTML, Dreamweaver might misunderstand the code and "break" otherwise valid syntax.

This option enables you to make a list of file extensions that should never undergo code rewriting in Dreamweaver. If I were using an application server that interprets .drew files and their server tags in a special way, for example, I would add .drew to the list, to prevent Dreamweaver from checking my coding.

## Special Character Options

The Web is a technical medium, and as a developer you are writing pages that must be read and interpreted by computers. As such, like any full-scale programming language, some characters hold special meanings. These have to be considered and dealt with appropriately so that these characters can always be interpreted in the intended way.

### Encode Special Characters in URLs Using %

A number of special characters besides spaces cannot be safely used in URLs. To automatically convert special characters into URL-friendly encoded equivalents, make sure this option is checked.

At times, you may not want to use this (almost every project is an "unusual case" in the web industry), so the option is always there to turn off the encoding.

### Encode <, >, &, and " in Attribute Values Using &

HTML is a text-based language. The most basic element is the written word on the page. This is then interrupted with tags to mark up structure and so on, and the tags are denoted by the markers < and >. Of course, these are also regular characters that can legitimately be used in the body of your text. Therefore, to not confuse the browser and have an innocent text character be interpreted as the start of an HTML tag, you have to encode these characters.

The ampersand (&) is used in HTML to denote an encoded character. A less-than symbol (<) is represented as &lt;, and a greater-than symbol (>) is represented as &gt;. This has the knock-on effect of needing to encode the ampersand itself as &amp;.

This option enables you to switch encoding on and off. For the most part, you'll need to leave it on, unless you know of a particular circumstance in which it would be better to switch it off.

## CSS Styles Category

The CSS Styles category of the Preferences window houses some options for how Dreamweaver writes its CSS code (see Figure 16.6).

**Figure 16.6**

CSS Styles category of the Preferences window.

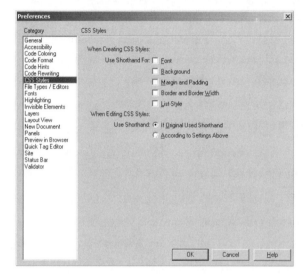

## Shorthand Options When Creating CSS

Dreamweaver offers a number of options relating to the way CSS shorthand is used when writing your CSS code. Some properties are shorthand rules that enable developers to specify the values of several properties with a single property. For instance, the font property is a shorthand property for setting `font-style`, `font-variant`, `font-weight`, `font-size`, `line-height`, and `font-family` all at once. When values are omitted from a shorthand form, each "missing" property is assigned its initial value. Without using shorthand, an example for redefining an <h1> tag might look like this:

```
h1 {
  font-weight: bold;
  font-size: 12pt;
  line-height: 14pt;
  font-family: Helvetica;
  font-variant: normal;
  font-style: normal;
  font-stretch: normal;
  font-size-adjust: none
}
```

Using CSS shorthand, the preceding example can be rewritten like this:

```
h1 { font: bold 12pt/14pt Helvetica }
```

As I'm sure you'll agree, this is an efficient way to express simple CSS definitions. The Use Shorthand For option enables you to specify the elements (if any) for which to use CSS shorthand.

### Note

Although the use of shorthand code makes the document much quicker to type, it can slow down your understanding of the style sheet later on, because it's more difficult to read shorthand selectors.

## Shorthand Options When Editing CSS

When editing an existing page, it makes sense to keep a consistent style of coding throughout. Dreamweaver gives the option to use CSS shorthand if the document already makes use of it. If you do not want to use shorthand at all, it is best not to add new shorthand to the document, and to reformat the existing shorthand into longhand. It never pays to mix coding styles within one document, and it will be a nightmare to work with in the future.

## File Types / Editors Category

The File Types / Editors tab of the Preferences window houses a host of options for defining your favorite editors for given file types (see Figure 16.7).

**Figure 16.7**

File Types /
Editors category
of the
Preferences
window.

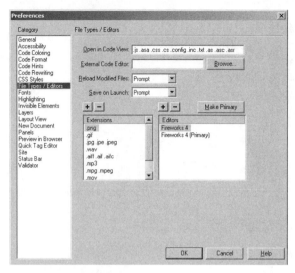

## Editing Options

Dreamweaver works happily alongside all your favorite editors. To specify which files should be loaded in a specific editor, and which should be kept within Dreamweaver, you need to set a few options.

### Open in Code View

It doesn't make sense for Dreamweaver to try and display a number of file types visually. These include JavaScript files, text files, and ASA files as used by Windows servers.

There may be file types that you work with that should be opened by default into Code view. You can list these here, separating each one with a space.

### External Code Editor

If you require more functionality than the Dreamweaver code editor can offer, it is possible to define an external editor here. Personally, I like to use Macromedia HomeSite as my external editor because it offers good integration with Dreamweaver.

## Reload Modified Files

Should a member of your development team edit a file that you already have open in Dreamweaver, you can set this option three ways: always reload the page you have open when a change is made (erasing any changes you have made without saving), never to do so, or to prompt you and let you decide. This also applies if you have made any edits to a file outside Dreamweaver in your external editor. On returning to Dreamweaver, the change will be noticed, and whichever option you have selected will come into play.

The default setting is Prompt because this is usually a decision that needs to be made on a case-by-case basis.

## Save on Launch

Optionally, Dreamweaver can save your current document before launching an external editor. This is usually a good idea because an external editor will often refuse to edit an unsaved file anyway. The Prompt option is again useful because it gives you the opportunity to save the file under a different name should you want.

## Defining Editors for Common Files

Dreamweaver offers the opportunity to define a different external editor for every single file type, should you so want. In reality, however, you will probably be dealing with three or four editors at most (because there is so much similarity among the different types of files we work with on the Web).

As Figure 16.6 shows, available file extensions are listed. Selecting one enables the right-side pane for defining an external editor for that file type. The standard Dreamweaver plus (+) and minus (–) buttons are available for adding and removing items from either list.

## Fonts Category

The Fonts category of the Preferences window houses a host of options for defining the default font settings used by Dreamweaver throughout your working environment (see Figure 16.8).

**Figure 16.8**

Fonts category of the Preferences window.

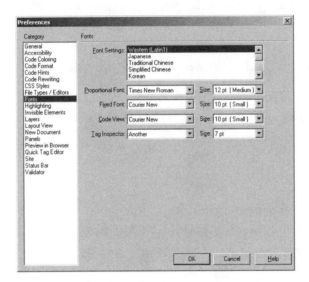

A range of settings dictates how text displays within Dreamweaver. These include a proportional font and size, a fixed-width font and size, and a font and size used in the Code view and Tag inspector.

## Highlighting Category

The Highlighting category of the Preferences window houses a number of options for setting the highlighting color (see Figure 16.9).

The highlighting options are straightforward. Choosing color options for editable regions, locked regions, library items, and third-party tags is just a case of typing in a hexadecimal RGB value or clicking and choosing a color from the palette. The same routine applies for specifying the colors for both live data and translated code blocks. These are used particularly if you are using Dreamweaver MX to work with web applications.

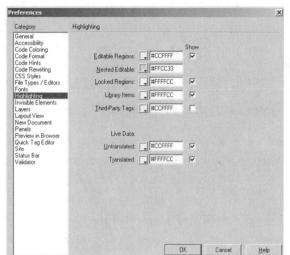

**Figure 16.9**

Highlighting category of the Preferences window.

## Invisible Elements Category

The Invisible Elements category of the Preferences window houses options for choosing which invisible elements are shown in Design view (see Figure 16.10).

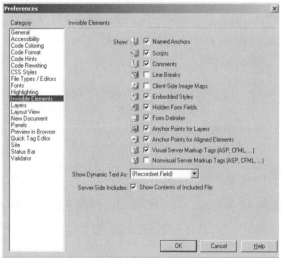

**Figure 16.10**

Invisible Elements category of the Preferences window.

Dreamweaver offers the option to select which invisible elements should be represented in Design view and which should just be ignored. Some are more useful to see than others, and the choice will largely be down to personal preferences (which is what we are setting here after all). The choices can been seen in Figure 16.10, along with the icon used to represent those elements in Design view.

In its visual environment, Dreamweaver needs a method for displaying parts of the page that can be edited, but are not naturally items that would have a visual appearance on the page. Dreamweaver uses small yellow shield icons to represent these "invisible elements." Turning off invisible elements can help give a much better visual impression of how the page will look when edited in a browser. In fact, with all the invisible elements and design aids hidden, the page in Design view looks almost identical to the page when viewed in a browser. However, the invisible elements are much easier to edit and work with if they are displayed.

### Dynamic Elements

The category allows for the configuration of how a couple of dynamic elements display in Design view. The first of these is dynamic text. *Dynamic text* is text being called from a data source such as a database or some other application-level variable. Typically, these are viewed as placeholders until Live Data View is used to bring in the actual data from your data source.

Within the Invisible Elements category, you have the option to specify how the dynamic text placeholders should display. Alongside this is the option to turn off the automatic translation of server-side includes.

### Layers Category

The Layers category of the Preferences window houses a number of options for setting how layers are treated and authored within the page (see Figure 16.11).

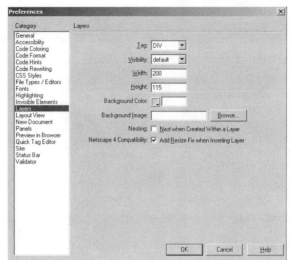

**Figure 16.11**

Layers category
of the
Preferences
window.

## Working with Layers

You must consider many options when designing with layers. Not least of these is one of target audience and browser compatibility. You can use a number of different tags to create your layers, not to mention the nesting issues and the visibility issues. Thankfully, Dreamweaver comes to the rescue and puts you back in control.

### Tag

You can use a number of different tags when implementing layers. These include `<span>` and `<div>`. The safest tag to use in terms of browser compatibility is the `<div>` (or division) tag. This is also the default setting.

### Visibility

You also can set the default visibility of a layer. Options of Default, Inherit, Visible, and Hidden are available and define how the layer displays in the browser. The default setting is Default; no explicit setting is given, and so the layer will adopt the default setting of the browser. A setting of Inherit allows the layer to inherit the visibility settings of its parent object.

### Width and Height

Dreamweaver enables you to set the default width and height of a layer created without using drag and drop. This proves useful if you frequently insert layers of a particular dimension into your pages.

### Background Color and Image

Dreamweaver allows for the setting of a default background image and color so that all your layers come ready with predefined background settings.

### Nesting and Compatibility

The option is given to allow or disallow nesting of layers. Although it is perfectly legal to nest Dreamweaver layers, it is not always desirable to do so because this can cause compatibility problems with some web browsers.

In addition to nesting, the option is available to insert the resizing fix for the Netscape layer, which forces the page to reload each time it is resized in order to prompt Netscape Navigator to redraw the page. Without this, Navigator users will find that the layout of the page is distorted when they resize the window.

## Layout View Category

The Layout View category of the Preferences window houses a number of options for setting how the Dreamweaver Layout view operates and the colors used to display elements within that view (see Figure 16.12).

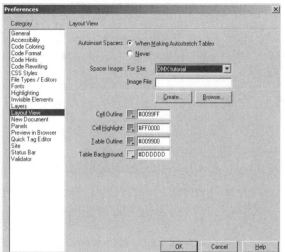

**Figure 16.12**

Layout View
category of the
Preferences
window.

## Working with Spacer Images

An old trick when laying out tables is to force column widths (and sometimes heights) to remain at a given size using transparent spacer or *shim*
images. The Dreamweaver Layout view is designed for those who like to
work with tables in a very visual drag-and-drop way, and so you need to
set your preferences for placing spacer images.

The first choice is whether to use spacer images at all, or to forget the whole
idea and rely on the browser to display the table correctly. You might turn
this off if you want to place spacers yourself or if don't want to use them
at all.

The next option pertains to the actual image file used as the spacer image
for any given site. Dreamweaver enables you to browse for a file that
already exists or will create one for you. Use the Create button to do this.
The image created will be a 1-pixel square transparent GIF—ideal for
stretching around to pad empty cells.

## Defining Color Preferences

Four different color settings are available for the Layout view. These colors
aid ease of use when working in a visual click-and-drag environment.

### Cell Outline

The *cell outline* color borders each layout cell within the Layout view. This does not denote every cell in the logical table, but just those designated layout cells. The outline is solid for the selected cell and dashed for those not currently selected.

### Cell Highlight

Mousing over a layout cell border highlights the cell to indicate it can be selected. This option enables you to set the color used for the highlight. Ideally, it should contrast with the standard cell outline color.

### Table Outline

The edge of a layout table also has a thin border. This option enables you to set the color. The default is dark green. You will probably want to change this if your page has a similar dark color.

### Table Background

The table background color enables you to see the extent of the table at a glance. This color displays in a checkerboard pattern with transparent pixels so that the page background is also visible through it. A color at the lighter end of the spectrum is often a good choice here.

## New Document Category

Dreamweaver MX brings with it a new method for opening new documents. To accompany this method, a new set of preferences is required. Figure 16.13 shows this category.

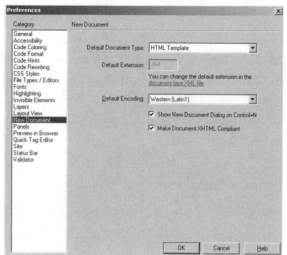

**Figure 16.13**

The New
Document
category.

## Document Type

Dreamweaver knows how to work with a whole host of different document types, but normally you'll be working with one particular sort as a
starting point. This is for the document that is opened by default when
Dreamweaver starts up. Select your option for a default document from the
list of available document types.

## Encoding Settings

You have a number of different encodings available for use with
Dreamweaver. The Default Encoding option enables you to set the
encoding for any new pages. For most people in the Western world, this
setting will be Western (Latin1), but many other choices are available.

## Using Shortcuts

The accepted standard shortcut for opening a new document is Ctrl+N.
However, two different types of behavior are available for this shortcut. The
first is to open the New Document dialog box and make some choices. The
second option is to open up a new document straightaway, using your
default document preferences. The Show New Document dialog box on
Ctrl+N option enables you to choose which method you prefer.

## XHTML

Dreamweaver MX enables you to write pages in both HTML and XHTML, but it needs to know which you prefer. The Make Document XHTML Compliant option enables you to set the default behavior for a new document. Because XHTML is fully backward-compatible with older browsers and is based on the XML standard, choosing this option is usually a good move.

## Panels Category

The Panels category of the Preferences window houses options for enabling and disabling panels within the Dreamweaver launcher and for dictating which panels are always on top (see Figure 16.14).

**Figure 16.14**

Panels category
of the
Preferences
window.

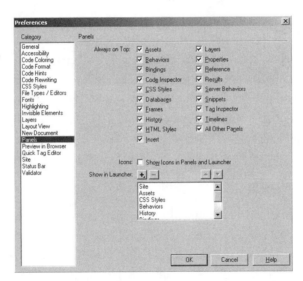

## Stacking Orders

Dreamweaver uses several panels to make up its user interface. Depending on how you like to work, some of these panels will be more important to you than others. To prevent important panels from getting lost behind not-so-important ones, the option is available to keep named panels on top at all times.

## Launcher Options

The Launcher exists in the lower-right corner of the Document window. The options available here enable you to choose not only which panels are available in the Launcher, but also which order they are placed in. Use the familiar plus (+) and minus (–) buttons to add and remove items, and the up and down arrows to change the order of items.

## Preview in Browser Category

The Preview in Browser category of the Preferences window enables you to assign browsers and set other browser options (see Figure 16.15).

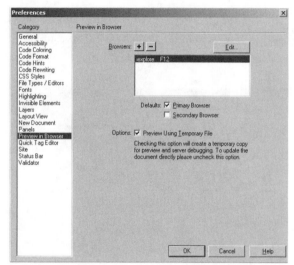

**Figure 16.15**

Preview in Browser category of the Preferences window.

When working on a web page, it is essential to keep checking your work in your target browsers to make sure that everything is displaying correctly. Dreamweaver facilitates this with the Preview in Browser function, which enables you to quickly launch the current page in a browser of your choice to see how it looks. This tab is where you set those choices.

You can define up to 20 different browsers for previewing. Of course, it's fairly unlikely that you'll be testing every edit in 20 browsers, but more likely that you'll want to test often with 2, and only occasionally with the rest. This is where the Primary and Secondary options come in. These enable you to designate a primary and secondary browser for previewing and assign handy keyboard shortcuts to them to make previewing even easier. Setting a primary or secondary browser is as simple as selecting a browser from the list and checking the corresponding box.

The final option allows for pages to be previewed using the local web server. If your page uses technologies such as ASP or Macromedia ColdFusion, which need a server to parse the content before the page displays correctly, you'll need to use this option. Otherwise, any dynamic content on the page will not display.

## Quick Tag Editor Category

The *Quick Tag Editor* (QTE) is a great little tool for making small code changes from within the Design view. There are only two options available, as you can see in Figure 16.16.

**Figure 16.16**

Quick Tag Editor category of the Preferences window.

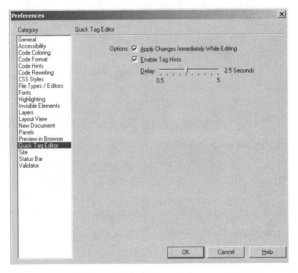

## Using Quick Tag Editor

Although the Quick Tag Editor is by its very nature quick, this doesn't mean that there are no settings to be configured. You can set a number of options to control the way the QTE behaves.

### Apply Changes Immediately While Editing

It's often useful to get immediate feedback when making changes with the QTE, but this can sometimes be slow on complex pages or less-capable computer systems. For the most part, you'll want to leave this switched on, unless you find that Dreamweaver is running slow during QTE use.

### Enable Tag Hints

Another great feature of the QTE is the tag hints feature. Dreamweaver suggests context-appropriate tags and attributes as you type. This can prove very handy because it saves having to type out a good many things. A delay occurs before the hints appear, and you can set this with the slider (refer back to Figure 16.15). I like to have it set at the shortest delay so that the hints appear almost immediately.

## Site Category

The Site category of the Preferences window houses options for the way the Site window is laid out and some general FTP settings that are the same from site to site (see Figure 16.17).

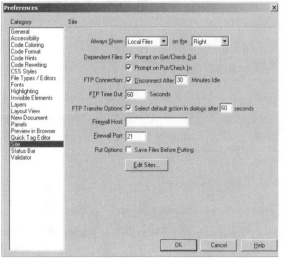

**Figure 16.17**

Site category of the Preferences window.

## Site Map Display and Dependency Settings

The Site Manager is the hub of your web site during development. You can configure it in a number of ways to help your workflow.

### Always Show

This option enables you to set up how the Site window displays. By default, local files display on the right, with the files from the remote server on the left. This really depends on your personal preferences. I know many people like to reverse this so that the order is the same as that of a normal FTP program, with the local files on the left.

I've gotten used to the way Dreamweaver displays it after all this time, and so I think I would find it confusing to change. The option is there to account for everyone's tastes.

### Dependent Files

When using the FTP features, Dreamweaver offers the opportunity to put or get dependent files alongside the file you are currently handling. *Dependent files* are files such as the images that are placed in the document being transferred. You can have Dreamweaver prompt you under both Get/Check Out and Put/Check In circumstances.

## FTP Settings

*FTP* is a vital tool through the site-development process for uploading files to the server for testing and so on. There are a number of ways the FTP utility can be configured globally, rather than on a site-by-site basis.

### FTP Connection

The option is available to have Dreamweaver break an inactive connection after a set amount of time. This is a good idea if you pay for your Internet connection on a timed basis and you don't want any software keeping connections up unnecessarily.

### FTP Time Out

When transferring files over the public Internet, holdups often occur, and the file transfer might not go as smoothly as hoped. The Time Out option enables you to set the period of time that Dreamweaver should try to transfer the file or connect to the server before an appropriate response is received from the remote server.

### Firewall Host

If you do not connect to the Internet directly, but through a firewall as many of us do these days, you need to tell Dreamweaver the address of the firewall host on your local network. This can be an IP address or a host name.

### Firewall Port

As you may be aware, different Internet services operate on a range of common port numbers on any given server. FTP operates on port 21 under normal circumstances, but this may differ if your system administrator decides to move it to something new. This Dreamweaver option enables you to set the port used to connect to your FTP server. If you're not sure, or have not been given a different number by your system administrator, leave this on port 21.

### Save Files Before Putting

If you have a file open in Dreamweaver when you try to upload it via FTP, this option will prompt you to save the file first.

## Status Bar Category

The Status Bar category of the Preferences window offers the configuration options shown in Figure 16.18.

**Figure 16.18**

Status Bar
category of the
Preferences
window.

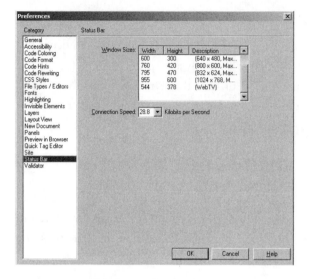

## Using the Status Bar

The status bar is a great utility when developing your site, but is useful only if it contains the information you need. By setting some options here, it is possible to make sure that the status bar contains the information you need to work effectively on your projects.

### Window Sizes

The Dreamweaver status bar holds a useful tool for resizing the Document window to a range of different sizes so that you can see how your page will look in different sizes of browser window. You can administer the list of sizes here by simply clicking any of the values to change them or by adding new values to the bottom of the list. The changes will be reflected as soon as the Preferences window is finalized.

### Connection Speed

The status bar also offers an indication of how long your page might take to download after all the HTML and assets have been taken into consideration. This is measured against a given connection speed, which you can set here.

The default value is 28.8 kilobits per second, but most web users are running on at least 56 kilobits per second these days. You also can type your own value in here if you want.

## Launcher

The status bar is home to the mini-Launcher. Although it's a handy little tool, the option is here to switch it off should you choose to do so. However, it might make more sense to cut it down to just a few items that you use a lot (should you find it is taking up too much space).

## Validator Category

The Validator category of the Preferences window houses options for how the HTML validators should parse your pages (see Figure 16.19).

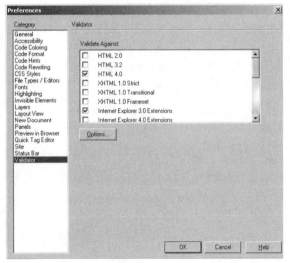

**Figure 16.19**

The Validator category.

Dreamweaver MX introduces a set of validators for different levels of HTML and different flavors of HTML for various browsers. The options mostly consist of the type of validation you want run, but there are a number of global validation options also.

Opening the Options dialog box from this category makes this further set of options available. The user can choose to display errors, warnings, custom messages, and nesting errors, and whether to check for high ASCII errors, quotes in text, quotes that span lines, and entities in your text.

## Defining FTP File Types

As anyone who's ever had to FTP a CGI script to a server knows, there are different ways to transfer files within the FTP protocol. Transfer a file using the wrong method, and the file will not work on the remote server. The two methods are known as *ASCII* and *binary*. ASCII is for text-based files—those that are human-readable. These include HTML, ASP, TXT, CFML, and CSS files. The binary method is for those files that are encrypted or compiled in some way—files that are not human-readable. These include image files, executables, folders, and multimedia elements such as video, Flash and Shockwave movies, and audio files.

Dreamweaver holds a list of the FTP methods that should be used for each file type. Like the Extensions.txt file, this file is totally user-editable and can be found in the Configuration folder. It is called FTPExtensionsMap.txt. Here's how my file looks:

```
AIF     BINARY
AIFF    BINARY
AIFC    BINARY
ASP     ASCII
BIN     BINARY
BMP     BINARY
CFM     ASCII
CFML    ASCII
CGI     ASCII
CSS     ASCII
DCR     BINARY
DIR     BINARY
DOC     BINARY
DXR     BINARY
EXE     BINARY
FLA     BINARY
GIF     BINARY
HTM     ASCII
HTML    ASCII
```

```
JPG      BINARY
JPEG     BINARY
JS       BINARY
LBI      BINARY
MNO      BINARY
MOV      BINARY
MPEG     BINARY
MPG      BINARY
PDF      BINARY
PIC      BINARY
PICT     BINARY
PNG      BINARY
QT       BINARY
RA       BINARY
RAM      BINARY
README   BINARY
RM       BINARY
RTF      BINARY
SEA      BINARY
SHTM     BINARY
SHTML    BINARY
SIT      BINARY
SND      BINARY
SWF      BINARY
TEXT     ASCII
TIF      BINARY
TIFF     BINARY
TPL      BINARY
TXT      ASCII
WAV      BINARY
ZIP      BINARY
```

As you can see, each file type is listed on a new line and presented as the file extension followed by the method: binary or ASCII. A tab separates the two values.

Should I need to add a new file type to the list, it is fairly straightforward to do so. If I want all files with a .drew extension to be uploaded as ASCII, I just add the following line to the file:

```
DREW     ASCII
```

It really is as easy as that. It doesn't matter whether the entry is not in alphabetic order, but it would make life easier when it comes to editing the file if it were. With this in mind, I would insert my new line after the entry for the DOC file type.

For the changes to take effect, YOU need to save the file and restart Dreamweaver.

## What to Take Away from This Chapter

- Dreamweaver offers developers a huge amount of control by enabling them to set many different preferences.
- Dreamweaver preferences can be quickly and easily set via the Preferences window in the Edit menu.
- You can customize almost every aspect of the way Dreamweaver displays elements, from the color settings right through to the time delay before tag hints display.
- There are two different methods for FTPing files: binary and ASCII.
- Each file type can have its FTP method set by editing the `FTPExtensions`.txt file in the Dreamweaver Configuration folder.

# Chapter 17

# Installing Extensions

Objectives:

- Find extensions for Dreamweaver on the web.
- Learn how to install extensions by hand.
- Learn how to install extensions with the Macromedia Extension Manager.

Presuming that you are not reading this book from the back, you will already be familiar with just how useful and powerful Dreamweaver extensions can be. From basic objects that enable you to insert small tags or items of code into your page, right through to powerful commands and behaviors, a whole host of different options and chunks of functionality are available for you to download and install.

Dreamweaver extensions support the whole ethos of the program. Dreamweaver is a visual editing tool to enable you to produce web sites quickly and with greater ease. Dreamweaver doesn't ever claim to be a tool to do all the coding for you so that you don't need to learn HTML or JavaScript, it just enables you to do what you might have done by hand but an awful lot quicker.

Extensions follow this principal through. Although a good many extensions don't ever insert any groundbreaking code (although there are some that do), they enable you to work much faster and will point you in the right direction on those days that your mind is a bit fuzzy. What's more, they help by standardizing the code that you are using. Where I might be tempted to code a slightly different JavaScript routine to open a new browser window on several pages of my site, using the Open Browser Window behavior helps to standardize that code and make things uniform across the site. This helps significantly if you decide to later move all your JavaScript out to an external file, because you need only one copy of the function to run all your open window scripts.

This chapter covers locating and installing Dreamweaver extensions. The discussion covers the use of the Macromedia Extension Manager for the installation of extensions; so if you don't have a copy installed, or think that you might not have the latest copy, you can download it for free from the Macromedia Exchange for Dreamweaver at `http://www.macromedia.com/exchange/dreamweaver/`.

# Sources of Extensions

You can download Dreamweaver extensions from many different places. Some are commercial products, but many are free of charge. Generally, the more complex and specialized extensions have a fee, and as such it should be possible to build their price into the cost of a specific project. Most extension writers, however, are professional developers who work out of hours for their own enjoyment or are companies that supply free extensions as a supporting item to accompany their main software product.

In the days before Dreamweaver 3, there was no such thing as the Macromedia Extension Manager. In fact, the Extension Manager was created only part way through the life of Dreamweaver 3. Most users didn't even know that Dreamweaver extensions existed; and if they happened to find and download one, they would not have a clue how to install it. It was hell. Not only was there no Extension Manager, there was also no Macromedia Exchange.

To distribute their extensions, developers would set up their own web sites containing links to Zip files that held their bare extension files. You might be familiar with the idea that extensions are made from a collection of web files. These would be collected together in a Zip file, and it was left to the user of the extension to unzip the files and work out where in the Dreamweaver file structure they should go. This wasn't too difficult, but did slow the installation process down and was very intimidating for novice users.

A whole wealth of extensions is still available as Zip files, although some extension developers have found the time to convert their old work to modern MXP files to work with the Extension Manager. Later in this chapter, you will learn how to install extensions by hand (without the

Extension Manager) so that you can be confident in taking advantage of some of the wonderful extensions still available as Zip files.

Places where extensions can be downloaded fall into two categories. The first is the Macromedia Exchange for Dreamweaver, and the second is all those third-party sites belonging to enthusiastic developers and companies that support Dreamweaver as part of their business model.

## The Macromedia Exchange for Dreamweaver

If you've been working through this book from the beginning, you will have already been to the Macromedia Exchange for Dreamweaver (the *Exchange*). Don't feel bad if you haven't read the first two parts of this book, however; feel free to read in the order you like—I'm happy with that. In case you need a quick memory prompt, I'll take a look at a bit of the background behind the Exchange.

The Exchange is Macromedia's own solution to the problems that were arising within the Dreamweaver community. Although scores of new and useful extensions were being written, the average Dreamweaver users did not know where to find them and had no real way to search all the available extensions for the item they were looking for. Although some users were grouping together and trying to centralize their extensions (Joseph Lowery started an extensions database, and Massimo Foti welcomed contributions from other developers onto his popular extensions site), there was still the need for a more orchestrated approach.

This is where Macromedia decided to step in and set up a web site that would not only help extension writers get their work out to the public, but also would enhance and add value to their product. Macromedia is, after all, a business. The Exchange was born, bringing not only ease of use but also an increased enthusiasm for extensions into the market.

### The Application

The Exchange is a large web application. Those who are familiar with the more data-driven aspects of Dreamweaver MX will be used to building web applications that consist of a collection of pages that, when put together, create a functional site that performs a task through the web. As with any web application, the Exchange offers a number of key features, including the following:

- **Browse extensions.** The user is of course able to browse through all the extensions on the site and see what is available. Each extension has a description that enables the user to see what it does before it is downloaded. You also can browse extensions by category.

- **Search extensions.** A search facility enables the user to enter keywords and conduct a search of all the available extensions. This proves extremely useful if you are looking for an extension for a particular task, because likely keywords are easy to guess.

- **Download extensions.** There would be little use in having the Exchange if you weren't able to download extensions. This is the primary purpose of the site.

- **Upload extensions.** For users to be able to download extensions, extension writers must be able to upload them.

- **Comment on extensions.** Not only can you download any extension, you also can provide feedback and opinions via the Exchange. The author of each extension might check back and offer advice or response to your comments.

- **Rate extensions.** Some extensions are great, some are less so, and the Exchange's rating system enables you to rate any extension you have downloaded from one to five, with five being the highest.

- **Preview examples.** For some extensions, you can go to a page on the extensions author's site and view an example of the extension in action on a page. This isn't always available for every extension, because it places a time requirement on the developer (who is already giving his time to build a complex extension).

- **Get support.** Many extension writers offer informal support for their work. This may be via a help page on their site, by email support, or by some other method. If the extension is commercial, support will be in greater evidence. If it's a free extension, you're relying on the good will of the author.

## Using the Exchange

As you would expect from Macromedia, the Exchange is pretty comprehensive and feature-packed. Unfortunately, this can sometimes have the effect of making it a little tricky to use until you've found your way around. The first thing you need to do before downloading any extensions is to visit the Exchange and create a username and password for yourself. If you have visited Macromedia's site before and created a Macromedia ID for yourself, you can use this as your login for the Exchange. You probably will have done this if, for example, you have signed up to Macromedia's The Edge newsletter. Otherwise, you need to click the `Get a Macromedia ID` link and follow through the signup process (see Figure 17.1). If you've signed up before but can't remember your password, there's an option for that too.

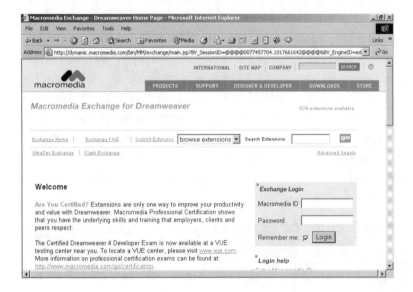

**Figure 17.1**

Sign in or get a Macromedia ID.

After you have signed in, you can begin to find extensions to download. The obvious place to start is the home page. Featured on the home page are two different collections of extensions. The first of these is the 5 Newest Extensions list. This names the five extensions most recently put onto the Exchange after having undergone testing by Macromedia's Exchange team. The second collection is of a small number (usually four or five) of featured extensions.

These extensions have been spotted as being particularly useful or interesting, and so have been brought forward to raise attention to them. In a way, they are the Exchange's "cover story"—the day's top headlines to draw you inside. The list is revised as and when the Exchange team discovers extensions of particular merit. Clicking any of the extension on the home page will take you to the detail page for that extension. As well as enabling you to download the extensions in either PC or Mac format, the detail pages list a full description of the extension, which versions of Dreamweaver and browsers the extension is compatible with, and a small discussion board to voice opinions and to solicit the feedback of other users.

The next thing you'll want to do is to search for an extension to solve a particular problem. On the top of each page on the Exchange is a Search Extensions box. Entering keywords into this box brings up a results page listing possible matches (see Figure 17.2). Searching on the term "fever" brings up a number of extensions I have written myself. (If extensions by other people appear on that list, they're treading on my brand, and I'm sending the boys round.) Just as before, clicking the name of an extension brings up the extension detail page, giving access to all those features discussed earlier, and enables you to download the extension. As you use the Exchange more, you will become familiar with the way the application works. Soon you will be quickly and easily downloading extensions as and when your project requires them.

**Figure 17.2**

A search result.

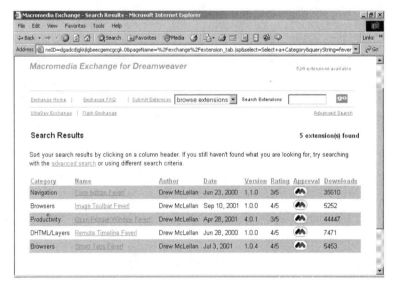

## Third-Party Web Sites

As discussed previously, the Exchange and the Extension Manager are relatively recent inventions, and before their existence most if not all extensions were downloaded directly from the extensions authors' sites. These extensions were just a collection of the bare extension files wrapped up in a Zip file.

Many of these sites are still online and offer the same excellent Dreamweaver extensions that they always did. Although some extension authors have found the time to go back and update their early extensions to MXP files, many prefer to spend their available time writing new extensions instead of updating the old ones. This would seem perfectly reasonable because most extension authors give of their time freely, and so are entitled to spend that time as they see fit.

Of course, anyone can write a Dreamweaver extension and host it on his site. It would be an endless task to try and list them all here. However, a number of popular sites hold large numbers of extensions, including the following:

- **Dreamweaver Fever** (`http://dreamweaverfever.com/`). My own site, holding a number of extensions, particularly those featured in this book.

- **Massimo's Corner** (`http://www.massimocorner.com/`). Massimo Foti is one of the great masters of Dreamweaver extension writing (and is also a Technical Editor for this book). His site contains a great many extensions, many of which are packaged as MXP files.

- **Yaromat** (`http://www.yaromat.com/dw/`). Jaro von Floken has a collection of sophisticated extensions. Like Massimo, Jaro is one of the all-time masters of extension writing.

- **Project VII** (`http://www.projectseven.com/`). Al Sparber and Gerry Jacobsen are true Dreamweaver professionals. Their company, Project VII, specializes in the development of Dreamweaver extensions, tutorials, and publications. As you might expect, their work is of an exceptionally high standard and is exceptionally well supported.

- **DWFile.com** (`http://www.dwfile.com/`). Paul R. Boon and friends host a fantastic resource site offering extensions for download, but also resources for those interested in building their own extensions.

- **Deva Tools** (`http://www.devahelp.com/`). Joseph Lowery and company have developed Dreamweaver extensions for a family of products that will help you create easy-to-use navigation systems for web sites, intranets, and HTML-based help.
- **Dreamweaver Depot** (`http://www.andrewwooldridge.com/ dreamweaver/`). Andrew Wooldridge is another veteran extension developer. His site contains a great many extensions for Dreamweaver. Although not updated as frequently as it once was, there are lots of real gems lurking on this site.
- **Dreamweaver Extensions Database** (`http://www.idest.com/ cgi-bin/database.cgi`). Before there was the Exchange, there was the Extensions Database! Joseph Lowery's collection of extension links is organized helpfully into an easily searchable database.

# Installing Extensions by Hand

Dreamweaver extensions are just a collection of HTML, JavaScript, and graphics files. The difference being that opening these files in your browser won't do you any good. To use an extension within Dreamweaver, you must first place it in the appropriate folder inside the Dreamweaver directory structure.

All extensions live under each user's Dreamweaver Configuration folder. You can find this folder in your operating system's user data store. On a typical Windows 2000 installation, this folder would reside in a location similar this:

```
C:\Documents and Settings\username\Application Data\
Macromedia\Dreamweaver MX\Configuration
```

For Windows 98 users, the Configuration folder is inside your Dreamweaver folder in Program Files. This could be something like this:

```
C:\Program Files\Macromedia\Dreamweaver MX\Configuration
```

Macintosh users will find the Configuration folder alongside all the other Dreamweaver files on their hard disk if they are using System 9 or below. For OS X users, you can find the Configuration folder somewhere similar to this:

```
Macintosh HD\Users\username\Library\Application Support\
Macromedia\Dreamweaver MX\Configuration
```

In both the preceding path examples, `username` should be replaced with the username you use to log on to your computer.

## Tip

If you have trouble locating your Configuration folder, you can always try a search. On Windows computers, go to Start > Search > For Files or Folders. On the Macintosh, use Sherlock.

## Installing Objects

Inside the Configuration folder is a folder called Objects. Not surprisingly, this folder contains all the Dreamweaver objects. The folder is further subdivided into the sections seen in the panes of the Objects panel: Characters, Common, Forms, Frames, Head, Invisible, Frames, and Tools. These folders store the objects that appear in the panes of the object panel of the same name.

An object will usually consist of at least two files (an HTML document and a GIF icon) and sometimes a third file—a JavaScript document. Place these files in the folder of your choice and you're done. The next time you reload your extensions, the new object will be there.

## Note

It is possible to create an object without the GIF icon. If this file is missing, Dreamweaver will automatically substitute a default icon for you. However, it is strongly recommended that you create your own icon.

If you decide that a particular object does not logically fall within one of the predefined folders, you can create your own. Just create a new folder and copy in the files. Dreamweaver will handle the rest.

## Installing Behaviors

If you are familiar with using behaviors, you'll understand the concept of actions and events. It is reasonably uncommon to have to add any new events to Dreamweaver; this usually happens only with the advent of a new browser, and so it's especially rare that you would have to install a new event by hand. However, should you need to do so, you can just drop the HTML file right into the Events folder.

More commonly, you will want to install an action. In a similar way to the Objects folder, you can split the Actions folder into subfolders. Any subfolder of the Actions folder appears as a submenu on the Behaviors list.

Actions will normally consist of an HTML file and a JavaScript file. Just copy them into the Actions folder, and a new entry will appear on the Behaviors list the next time your extensions are reloaded.

## Installing Commands and Other Extension Types

Aside from behaviors and objects, the other likely candidate for manual install has to be commands. Commands are very straightforward to install, and form the same pattern for all the other sorts of extensions available in Dreamweaver.

Installation is literally a case of copying the HTML, JavaScript, and any GIF files into the appropriate folder. Commands go in the Commands folder, inspectors go in the Inspectors folder, and so on.

The important bit is to remember to reload your extensions to make the new items available.

# Installing Extensions with the Extension Manager

The Macromedia Extension Manager takes away the need to know which files should be put where, and in fact distances the user from even knowing that there are particular files being copied.

Extensions that are packaged ready for installation with the Extension Manager have an MXP file extension. It is not possible to install non-MXP extensions with the Extension Manager; you need to install those by hand. On most installations, the MXP file format should be associated with the Extension Manager, so that it is possible to install an extension just by opening the MXP file. If this doesn't work on your system, you need to open the Extension Manager first.

Figure 17.3 shows the Install Extension option in the Extension Manager. Installation is just a case of browsing for the MXP file and then following the onscreen prompts.

During installation of any extension, you are asked to accept a disclaimer. This may sound sinister, but it just says that by installing the extension you are agreeing that neither Macromedia nor the developer of the extension are responsible for supporting the extension or for any damages that may arise from using it (see Figure 17.4). The next time you reload your extensions, the newly installed item will be available. You can learn more about reloading your extensions later in this chapter.

**Figure 17.3**

Installing an
extension with
the Extension
Manager.

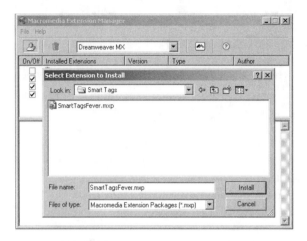

**Figure 17.4**

The Macromedia
Extensions
disclaimer.

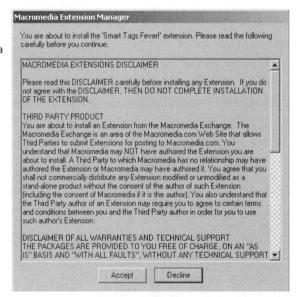

## Managing Extensions

Not only does the Extension Manager enable you to install extensions, it
also enables you to uninstall them. Not groundbreaking news, you may
think. However, this is quite an important feature.

Each time Dreamweaver is started up, all the extensions are read, interpreted,
and loaded into place. This can take a little while with a few extensions
installed. After you've installed a great many extensions (which is tempting

because there are loads of great tools out there), Dreamweaver can start to take a long time to open. Not only is this irritating, it also will gradually start to affect the performance of the software.

Realistically, I don't find myself using all the extensions I've ever downloaded on every single project I undertake. If I did, I would soon have a reputation for building irritatingly bloated sites! More often, I will download an extension for a particular purpose on a particular project, and then not use it again for a good while. For this reason, I always uninstall extensions that I am not going to be using again for a while.

The Extension Manager uses an analogy of turning extensions "on and off." As developers, we know that it is actually uninstalling them, but it doesn't delete the files from your system. The Extension Manager keeps a copy of the extensions that you turn off, so when you need to use them again it is just a case of reinstalling from its backups. This system really does make installing and uninstalling extensions on a project-by-project basis a viable option.

Figure 17.5 shows the Extension Manage and its On/Off column. Turning an extension off and on is just a case of clicking the checkbox.

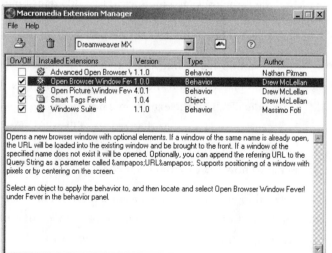

**Figure 17.5**

You can turn extensions off and on at will.

# Reloading Your Extensions

After you have installed a new extension, be that with the Extension Manager or by hand, you need to reload your extensions before the item becomes available in Dreamweaver. With Dreamweaver MX, the only way to do this is to restart Dreamweaver.

When Dreamweaver starts up, it looks through all the extensions in your Configuration folder and loads them as required. This means that any new extensions added to the folders will be picked up as well. Restarting Dreamweaver is the only sure-fire way to get every different type of extension reloaded.

# Packaging Extensions with the Extension Manager

As you are aware, anyone with some HTML and JavaScript knowledge and a willingness to learn can create a Dreamweaver extension. In the same way, anyone who writes an extension can package it as an MXP file and distribute it. The Extension Manager can package MXP files as well as extract them.

An MXP file is the packaged product to two different things:

1.  The collected files that make up the extension itself.

2.  An instruction file telling the Extension Manager where the files should be placed within the Configuration folder, as well as some general details about the extension. These details include the name of the extension and its author, the versions of Dreamweaver it is compatible with, what type of extension it is, and some instructions for the user as to how the extension is used.

This instruction file is called an *Macromedia eXtension Installation* (MXI) file and is in XML format. When it comes to packaging your extension, it is just a case of pointing the Extension Manager to your MXI file; the rest is taken care of by the instructions already coded within it.

## Collecting Your Files

Whereas it would be possible to package your extensions right from within the Configuration folder, I recommend that you copy your extension files to a different location first. Not only does this make writing your MXI file easier, it also helps with versioning issues.

I have a folder called Packaging Bay on my hard disk. It's a cute name and makes the whole process sound rather grand. Within this folder, I create a subfolder with the same name as my extension, and within that another subfolder with the name of the particular version I'm working on. (This proves particularly helpful if you discover problems later on and need to revert to an older version of the extension.) This would mean that I would copy the files for the first version of a new extension called EatMyHat into a folder like this:

```
C:\Packaging Bay\EatMyHat\1-0-0\
```

Of course, this is only a suggested working method based on my own experience; it's not a hard-and-fast rule by any means. After you have collected your files together in the same folder, you can begin to write your MXI file.

## Writing an Extension Installation File

Having collected your extension files together, you can start work on constructing an MXI file. There's no reason you couldn't use Dreamweaver to code your MXI file in, but personally I prefer a dedicated text editor such as Macromedia HomeSite.

The MXI file is written in XML. If you've never used XML before, don't worry. For the purpose of writing an MXI file, it's not much different from HTML with some unusual tags. Open a blank file in your text editor, and you're ready to begin.

### Caution

XML is a much stricter language than HTML. Be careful to follow the syntax closely; otherwise, you may get errors when packaging your file.

### The *<macromedia-extension>* Tag

All XML files have an outer "main" tag. In an HTML document, this is like the <html> tag that tells the browser to interpret the contents as an HTML page. In an MXI file, the main tag is called <macromedia-extension>. The syntax is as follows:

```
<macromedia-extension> </macromedia-extension>
```

This tag must be on the very first line of your file (line 1). The rest of your content falls within this tag. It has a number of important attributes, as discussed in the following sections.

### *name*

This name attribute is the name of your extension. If you have called your extension My Extension, this is the value you should enter.

### *version*

Each extension must be given a version number. This is in the format of 1.2.3, where the first number indicates the major version of the extension, the second number is the minor version, and the third number is the build. You should increment the major version for large changes (new features), the minor version for smaller changes (enhancements to existing features), and the build number each time the extension is repackaged.

### *type*

The type attribute indicates the type of extension. Valid values for Dreamweaver are "object", "command", "behavior"(or "action"), "browserProfile", "translator", "dictionary", "encoding", "floater", "propertyInspector", "jsExtension", "query", "template", "thirdPartyTags", "plugin", "report", "flashbuttonstyle", "suite", "dataSource", "serverFormat", "serverBehavior", and "serverModel".

### *requires-restart*

This indicates whether Dreamweaver needs to be restarted after installing the extension. Possible values are "true" and "false".

An example of the <macromedia-extension> tag is this:

```
<macromedia-extension
    name = "My Extension"
    version = "1.0.0"
    type = "behavior"
    requires-restart = "true">
    <!-- the rest of your tags go here -->
</macromedia-extension>
```

## Extension Description

The <description> tag enables you to give the user a plain-English description of what the extension does. The description itself must be within a CDATA section. This is so that special characters are taken "as is" instead of being interpreted as part of the XML. A typical <description> tag looks like this:

```
<description>
    <![CDATA[This behavior will make you rich beyond your
    ➥wildest dreams.<br>Use it whenever you can, and twice on
    ➥each page!]]>
</description>
```

You can use both <br> and   to format your description, so that it displays well in the Extension Manager.

## User Interface Access

The <ui-access> tag is a description for the user telling her how to access the extension from within Dreamweaver. In exactly the same way as the <description> tag, the <ui-access> tag needs to use a CDATA section, as follows:

```
<ui-access>
    <![CDATA[You can use this behavior by selecting
    ➥My Extension from the behavior panel.]]>
</ui-access>
```

You can use both <br> and   to format your description, so that it displays well in the Extension Manager.

## The Products Container and the Product Tags

It is necessary to specify with which Macromedia products and versions your extension is compatible. A separate <product> tag is used for each compatible product. The <product> tags are then placed within a pair of <products> tags.

The <products> tag has no attributes.

```
<products>
     <!--product tags go here -->
</products>
```

The <product> tag has a number of different attributes, and is an empty tag. This means that it must be self-closing, ending with a />, as follows:

```
<product />
```

### name

This is the name of the supported Macromedia product. Typically this will be "Dreamweaver", but it also could be "Flash" or even "Fireworks".

### version

To specify a version of the product, use this attribute. The version should be a single number; so for Dreamweaver MX, you would say version="6". (Dreamweaver MX is actually version 6). The extension will be installed on any version the same or greater than the number you specify here.

### primary

This value indicates that the product is one with which the extension is primarily intended to be used. Possible values are "true" and "false". A value of "true" implies that the required attribute should also be "true" (as discussed in the following section). For example, a Dreamweaver 4-

compatible extension will work in Dreamweaver UltraDev 4 as well. It would be possible to specify both Dreamweaver and UltraDev in `<product>` tags, but with Dreamweaver as the primary product.

### required

This attribute indicates that the named product is required for the extension to function as intended. The possible values are `"true"` and `"false"`. An example of this is a Dreamweaver extension that hooks into some of the functionality of Fireworks to perform its task. Dreamweaver would be the primary product, but Fireworks would be required as well.

The following code shows an example of the `<products>` and `<product>` tags in use:

```
<products>
    <product name="Dreamweaver" version="6" primary="true"
    required="true" />
    <product name="Fireworks" version="6" primary="false"
    required="true" />
</products>
```

## Author Name

After putting in all the hard work required building a high-quality extension, you'll want to identify it as your own. The tag enabling you to do this is the `<author>` tag. The tag has only one attribute, `name`.

### name

This is just your name. For one of my own extensions, I would state that `name="Drew McLellan"`.

Put together with the `<author>` tag—and remember this is an empty tag—an example is as follows:

```
<author name="Drew McLellan" />
```

## The Files Container and File Tags

All these descriptions of the extension are useless without the extension files themselves. Much like the `<products>` container tags, the `<files>` container tags surround the `<file>` tags that define each extension file to be included.

The `<files>` tag has no attributes.

```
<files>
    <!--file tags go here -->
</files>
```

The `<file>` tag has a number of different attributes, and is an empty tag. This means that it must be self-closing, ending with a `/>`, as follows:

```
<file />
```

### source

This is the name of the file itself. The path should be relative to the location of the MXI file. If you have collected all your files together in one folder, this should be a piece of cake. The filename needs to be a valid name for Windows and Mac. You can separate the folder names using a colon, slash, or a backslash.

### Caution

Some operating systems use case-sensitive filenames. Make sure to use the same capitalization in the MXI file as is used in the filename on your disk. To accommodate Mac users, filenames should fewer than 30 characters long.

### destination

This is the name of the folder into which the specified file will be copied. If the folder doesn't exist, the Extension Manager will create it for you. You can use `$dreamweaver` to refer to the Dreamweaver installation folder. You also can use `$system` to refer to the System or System32 folder and `$fonts` to refer to the Font folder on the user's hard disk.

## *platform*

The `platform` attribute indicates the platform for which the file is intended. If you specify a platform, the file is installed only on that platform; you can, for instance, provide two versions of a file, one for Windows and one for Macintosh, and specify a platform value for each. Valid values are `"win"` and `"mac"`. If you don't specify this attribute, the file is installed on both platforms.

## *shared*

The `shared` attribute indicates whether the file is used by more than one extension. When you use the Extension Manager to remove an extension, a shared file associated with that extension is not deleted as long as other installed extensions refer to that file. Valid values are `"true"` and `"false"`. If you don't specify this attribute, its default value is `"false"`.

The following code shows an example of the `<files>` and `<file>` tags in use:

```
<files>
    <file source="myExtension.htm"
    destination="$dreamweaver/configuration/behaviors/
    ➥actions/"
    platform="win"
    shared="false" />

    <file source="myExtension.js"
    destination="$dreamweaver/configuration/behaviors/actions/"
    platform="win"
    shared="false" />

    <file source="saveButton.gif"
    destination="$dreamweaver/configuration/shared/dwdevguide/"
    platform="win"
    shared="true" />
</files>
```

## An Example MXI File

When collected together and saved with an MXI file extension, you have a working instruction file ready for packaging. Your file should look something like this:

```
<macromedia-extension
    name = "My Extension"
    version = "1.0.0"
    type = "behavior"
    requires-restart = "true">

<description>
    <![CDATA[This behavior will make you rich beyond your
    ➥wildest dreams.<br>Use it whenever you can, and twice
    ➥on each page!]]>
</description>

<ui-access>
    <![CDATA[You can use this behavior by selecting
    ➥My Extension from the behavior panel.]]>
</ui-access>

<author name="Drew McLellan" />

<products>
    <product name="Dreamweaver" version="6" primary="true"
    required="true" />
    <product name="Fireworks" version="6" primary="false"
    required="true" />
</products>
```

```
<files>
    <file source="myExtension.htm"
    destination="$dreamweaver/configuration/behaviors/actions/"
    platform="win"
    shared="false" />

    <file source="myExtension.js"
    destination="$dreamweaver/configuration/behaviors/actions/"
    platform="win"
    shared="false" />

    <file source="saveButton.gif"
    destination="$dreamweaver/configuration/shared/dwdevguide/"
    platform="win"
    shared="true" />
</files>

</macromedia-extension>
```

## Packaging the Extension

After your MXI file has been created, you are ready to package the extension. Open the Extension Manager and choose Package Extension from the File menu. A Browse box will display prompting you to select your MXI file.

After you have selected an MXI file, the Extension Manager will immediately prompt you to choose a location to save the MXP. Save this alongside the MXI in your extension folder.

### Note

If your MXI file contains any errors, you will be alerted to this as you try to package the extension. Don't worry too much; XML is quite strict, and even the smallest typo can prevent the extension from packaging. Check over your code and try to package it again.

After you have packaged your extension and have tested it a few times, you're ready to submit it to the Macromedia Exchange for Dreamweaver. You can discover more about this process and how you can get your extension tested by Macromedia Quality Assurance engineers at http://www.macromedia.com/exchange/.

# What to Take Away from This Chapter

- Extensions are available in many different places on the web, including Macromedia's own Exchange for Dreamweaver.

- Some extensions are packaged for use with the Exchange Manager, but older ones tend to be extension files wrapped in a Zip file.

- These Zipped extensions have to be installed by hand; you must copy the right files into the right folders within your Dreamweaver Configuration folder.

- MXP extensions can be installed directly from the Extension Manager.

- You can use the Extension Manager to turn off unneeded extensions, and then on again when required.

- You can easily package extensions so that other users can install them into their copies of Dreamweaver using the Extension Manager.

- The Extension Manager is used to package extensions into MXP files as well as to install them.

- The MXI file is an XML file used to instruct the Extension Manager and the Exchange how the extension should be installed and used.

# Index

## X-Z

# HOW TO CONTACT US

## VISIT OUR WEB SITE

WWW.NEWRIDERS.COM

On our web site, you'll find information about our other books, authors, tables of contents, and book errata. You will also find information about book registration and how to purchase our books, both domestically and internationally.

## EMAIL US

Contact us at: **nrfeedback@newriders.com**

- If you have comments or questions about this book
- To report errors that you have found in this book
- If you have a book proposal to submit or are interested in writing for New Riders
- If you are an expert in a computer topic or technology and are interested in being a technical editor who reviews manuscripts for technical accuracy

Contact us at: **nreducation@newriders.com**

- If you are an instructor from an educational institution who wants to preview New Riders books for classroom use. Email should include your name, title, school, department, address, phone number, office days/hours, text in use, and enrollment, along with your request for desk/examination copies and/or additional information.

Contact us at: **nrmedia@newriders.com**

- If you are a member of the media who is interested in reviewing copies of New Riders books. Send your name, mailing address, and email address, along with the name of the publication or web site you work for.

## BULK PURCHASES/CORPORATE SALES

The publisher offers discounts on this book when ordered in quantity for bulk purchases and special sales. For sales within the U.S., please contact: Corporate and Government Sales (800) 382-3419 or **corpsales@pearsontechgroup.com**. Outside of the U.S., please contact: International Sales (317) 581-3793 or **international@pearsontechgroup.com**.

## WRITE TO US

New Riders Publishing
201 W. 103rd St.
Indianapolis, IN 46290-1097

## CALL/FAX US

Toll-free (800) 571-5840
If outside U.S. (317) 581-3500
Ask for New Riders
FAX: (317) 581-4663

**VOICES THAT MATTER**

New Riders

WWW.NEWRIDERS.COM

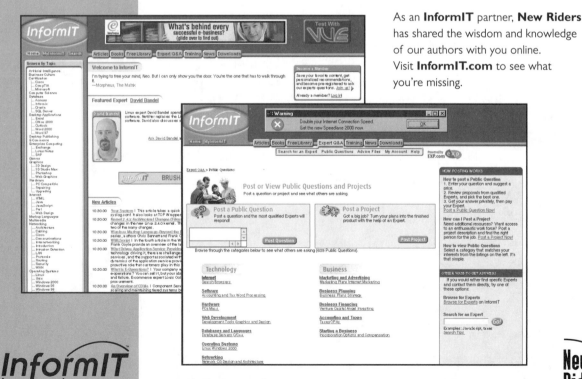

# DREAMWEAVER MX

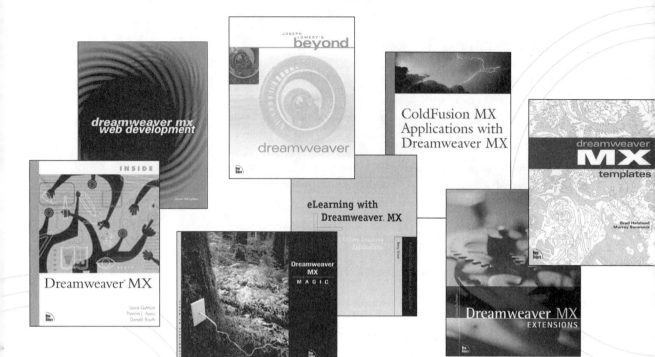

**Inside Dreamweaver MX**
073571181X
Laura Gutman,
Patty Ayers,
Donald S. Booth
US$44.99

**Dreamweaver MX
Web Development**
0735713081
Drew McLellan
US$45.00

**Dreamweaver MX Magic**
0735711798
Brad Halstead,
Josh Cavalier, et al.
US$39.99

**Joseph Lowery's Beyond
Dreamweaver**
0735712778
Joseph Lowery
US$45.00

**eLearning with
Dreamweaver MX:
Building Online
Learning Applications**
0735712743
Betsy Bruce
US$45.00

**ColdFusion MX
Applications
with Dreamweaver MX**
0735712719
David Golden
US$49.99

**Dreamweaver MX
Extensions**
0735711828
Laura Gutman
US$39.99

**Dreamweaver MX Templates**
0735713197
Brad Halstead
Murray Summers
US$29.99
Available October 2002

**Dreamweaver MX Killer Tips**
0735713022
Joseph Lowery
US$39.99
Available January 2003

New Riders

VOICES
THAT MATTER